Brigadier-General H. A. GODDARD, C.M.G., D.S.O., V.D.,
Commanding Officer 1915-1916.

THE STORY OF
THE SEVENTEENTH BATTALION A.I.F.

IN THE GREAT WAR
1914-1918

By
Lieutenant-Colonel K. W. MACKENZIE, M.C.

The Naval & Military Press Ltd

Published by
The Naval & Military Press Ltd
5 Riverside, Brambleside, Bellbrook
Industrial Estate, Uckfield, East Sussex,
TN22 1QQ England
Tel: +44 (0) 1825 749494
Fax: +44 (0) 1825 765701
www.naval-military-press.com
www.military-genealogy.com
www.militarymaproom.com

In reprinting in facsimile from the original, any imperfections are inevitably reproduced and the quality may fall short of modern type and cartographic standards.

BATTLE HONOURS
OF THE
SEVENTEENTH BATTALION.

Incorporated with those of the 17th Battalion
(The North Sydney Regiment)
Australian Military Forces

SUAKIN 1885

SOUTH AFRICA 1899-1902   SOMME 1914-1918

POZIERES   BAPAUME 1917

BULLECOURT   YPRES 1917

MENIN ROAD   AMIENS

HINDENBURG LINE   MONT ST. QUENTIN

GALLIPOLI 1915

DEDICATION.

To the Officers, Non-Commissioned Officers and Men

of the Seventeenth Battalion A.I.F.

who served in

the Great War, 1914-1918.

FOREWORD.

Always there remains with me the memory of the Seventeenth Battalion as I saw it marching along the Abbassia Road at the completion of its training in Egypt. Some twelve-hundred strong, they were a demonstration of physical perfection of Australian youth. In their ranks could be found almost every profession, trade or calling. A gallant sight, those marching men, gay with all the buoyancy of youth, yet withal a most formidable fighting force. No soldier could have seen them as I saw them without being confident that they would, as indeed they did, achieve a glorious record in face of the enemy.

In the intervening years since the Seventeenth brought back to their beloved Australia the laurels they had so well earned, I have seen with admiration the gallant manner in which so many of them fought to gain a footing in civilian life; many, too, with war disabilities, which were ever met with fine courage and without complaint. It has been good to see the fine comradeship, born in the war days, developed and continued up to the present moment. The Battalion Association has done much to weld together the links of the chain of comradeship which grows stronger as the years pass.

I am proud of my own association with the Seventeenth, and, like many old comrades, find happiness in still being in close touch.

H. A. GODDARD.

Sydney, 27th February, 1945.

PREFACE.

THE proposal to write a history of the Seventeenth Battalion A.I.F. was first mooted in 1930, in which year the Battalion Association was formed.

The Official War Historian, Dr. C. E. W. Bean, very kindly made available the War Diary of the Seventeenth, which is the basis of this work. This was supplemented by numerous private diaries of officers and men of the Battalion.

However, circumstances arose which caused the project to lapse. Then came the Second Great World War, and with it the formation of the 2/17th Battalion, whose newly-appointed commander, Lieutenant-Colonel J. W. Crawford, expressed a desire to be furnished with a short account of the doings of the parent unit, for the benefit of the men under his command.

A brochure was prepared. It was so favourably received that the Committee of the Association agreed to my collating the considerable quantity of data already to hand, in order to produce a full history. In due course this was completed, and the Committee, with a true missionary zeal, launched an appeal to members to help in the matter of finance. Within the brief period of five months the requisite amount, and more, had been subscribed.

The history is an endeavour to not only produce a true record of the deeds of the Seventeenth, but also, in a measure, to bring into perspective the factor of human interest — gay humour, which cushioned stark tragedy; high courage, unquenchable morale, and staunch comradeship, which have earned for the Australian soldier a place for all time in the front rank of the world's best fighting men.

And now, thirty years on, the same spirit animates the surviving wearers of the black and green diamond-shaped colour patch, as indeed their colours animate every man of the A.I.F. This spirit has manifested itself in a worthy citizenship, as befits men who have lived through a Great Experience.

ACKNOWLEDGEMENTS.

To Dr. C. E. W. Bean, M.A., D.C.L., Litt. D., Official War Historian; Mr. A. W. Bazley and Captain J. Balfour of the staff of the War Memorial, Canberra, for their invaluable advice and generous assistance in making available the War Diary of the Seventeenth, as well as precis of various operations; and to Mr. A. J. Bowman, A.I.F. Base Records, Canberra, for the Nominal Rolls which he was at such pains to supply.

A full meed of praise is due to my comrades, Messrs. A. J. Baldwin, W. J. Barrie, T. A. H. Breaden, M.S.M., W. H. J. Brown and Major J. P. Taylor, for their whole-hearted co-operation in the work of recording extracts from the War Diary.

I wish to record my warm appreciation of the work of the late Mr. W. Hands, who undertook the task of editing this book, and whose untimely death occurred after he had completed the first seven chapters.

My special thanks are due to Mr. Norman Ellison, of the 103 Howitzer Battery A.F.A., who generously offered to complete the task of shaping into presentable literary form an amateur's effort. Once again the artillery was to be found in close support of the P.B.I. when the signal rockets flared.

To the ladies who kindly typed the script and drew the marginal sketch maps is due a warm tribute for their valued assistance.

And last, but not least, to Mr. J. N. Rogers, late 2nd Battalion, A.I.F., for his kindly advice and helpful criticism; as well as to those of my comrades who encouraged and assisted me in the compilation of the history, I tender my grateful thanks.

K.W.M.

CONTENTS

Chapter		Page
I	Formation and Embarkation	17
II	Training in Egypt	30
III	Gallipoli—Hill 60	48
IV	Quinn's Post—Evacuation	63
V	Egypt, Sinai, France	86
VI	The Somme, Pozieres	105
VII	Ypres and Somme	128
VIII	Winter in Trenches	143
IX	Layton Alley—Lagnicourt	154
X	Bullecourt	174
XI	Menin Road	187
XII	Broodseinde	206
XIII	The German Offensive	217
XIV	Morlancourt	233
XV	August 8th	250
XVI	Framerville Captured	265
XVII	Mont St. Quentin	273
XVIII	Beaurevoir Line—Armistice	288
The 17th Battn. (The North Sydney Regt.)		300
Nominal Roll		309
Honour Roll of the Dead		344
Awards and Decorations		359
Appendices		368

THE BAND. Sergeant H. Rockcliff, Bandmaster.

LIST OF ILLUSTRATIONS

	Page
Brigadier-General H. A. Goddard	Frontispiece
The Band	10
Going ashore at Colombo	38
Disembarking at Suez	39
Lieut. L. G. Fussell and N.C.O's First Reinforcements	43
Machine-gun instruction	43
Number 8 Platoon	44
Private J. W. Cutting	52
Private A. H. Hamilton	52
Bathing at Anzac	62
Waiting for the Mail	62
Colonel Goddard and Capt. Smith on Quinn's Post	66
Steps cut in sap leading to Quinn's Post	69
The Garland gun, Quinn's Post	69
Private W. V. Anderson with sniper's rifle, Quinn's Post	70
Ocean Beach, Anzac	72
Brigadier-General E. F. Martin	99
Private Wm. Jackson	99
Hushi Farm after the shelling, April 25th, 1916	99
Behind the breastworks, Bois Grenier	100
Battalion cooks	100
Major R. J. A. Travers	107
Major J. M. Maughan	107
Drawing rations	107
Major B. Holmes	108
C.Q.M.S. R. C. Austin	108
Private W. L. Flood	108
Sergeants J. P. Taylor and J. M. Lyons	108
The Memorial Cross, Pozieres	155
Sergeant T. A. H. Breaden	155
Group of A Company sergeants	155
R.S.M. V. J. Sullivan, R.Q.M.S. A. J. R. Davison, and Sergeant A. J. R. Baldwin	155

LIST OF ILLUSTRATIONS (Continued).

	Page
C.S.M. A. F. Gilbert, Lance-Corporal W. Davis and group	156
Lieutenant E. F. Edwards	156
The Battalion Transport Section	156
Group of old identities	183
Billets at Clairmarais	184
The Battalion swimming team	184
Captain J. L. Wright	197
Private A. E. Doling	197
Private W. H. T. Burrell	197
Private C. J. Burton	197
A scene on the Menin Road, September 1917	198
Lieutenant J. M. Lyons	209
R.S.M. J. W. Raitt	209
Hell Fire Corner, Ypres, in 1920	209
Despierre Farm, 1917	210
The Battalion football team	210
Lieutenant-Colonel R. M. Sadler	253
Group of Sergeants	253
The Officers, July 1918	254
Major L. G. Fussell	279
Private W. L. Anderson	279
Sergeant M. J. McKay	279
Chaplain F. W. Tugwell	279
Lieutenant F. W. Tindale	280
Captain A. L. McLean	280
Group of officers	280
A German field-gun captured August 8th	291
Captain A. J. R. Davison	291
Trophy presented to 17th Battalion A.M.F.	305
2nd Division Memorial, Mont St. Quentin	306

MAPS

The Gallipoli Peninsula	51
Trenches and mining system, Quinn's Post	65

CHRONOLOGY FROM MARCH 30th, 1915 TO APRIL 24th, 1919.

1915.
March —17th Battalion raised.
,, 30—First ceremonial parade by 5th Brigade.
Apr. 24—5th Brigade marches through Sydney.
May 12—17th Battalion embarks on S.S. "Themistocles" (A 32).
,, 30—Arrives at Colombo.
June 1—First death in the Battalion.
,, 10—Passes hospital ship "Grantala," which signals Italy has declared war.
,, 12—Arrives at Suez en route to Cairo.
,, 13—Training begins at Aerodrome Camp, Heliopolis.
Aug. 10—Marches to Citadel Barracks; returns to Heliopolis the same day.
,, 14—Ordered to join M.E. Force.
,, 15—Entrains for Alexandria.
,, 16—Embarks on S.S. "Alaunia."
,, 18—Lemnos Island.
,, 19—Tranships to S.S. "Elkahira" for Anzac.
,, 20—Disembarks at Anzac; moves to Reserve Gully, thence Bauchop's Hill.
,, 21—Moves to Australia Valley.
,, 24—5th Brigade attached to 4th Brigade.
,, 27—Attack on Hill 60.
Sept. 1—Detached from 4th Brigade; moves into Otago Gully.
,, 4—Relieves 1st Light Horse Brigade at Pope's and Quinn's Posts.
,, 18—Pope's Post handed over to 19th Battalion.

1915.
Oct. 19—Unofficial armistice in front of Quinn's.
Nov. 24—The "Silent Stunt."
,, 25—Lone Turk enters Quinn's and is killed.
Dec. 18—First phase of evacuation of Anzac area.
,, 20—Evacuation completed.
,, 21—Mudros.

1916.
Jan. 4—Embarks on S.S. "Simla" for Alexandria.
,, 8—Alexandria; entrains for Tel el Kebir.
,, 22—Two companies move into Sinai Desert via Ismailia.
Feb. 2—Remaining two companies leave for Sinai Desert.
,, 3—Battalion mans outpost line.
Mar. 6—Relieved by Auckland Mounted Rifles.
,, 7—Moves to Moascar.
,, 16—Entrains for Alexandria.
,, 17—Embarks on S.S. "Arcadian" for Marseilles.
,, 23—Arrives at Marseilles.
,, 24—Billeted in Thiennes, Northern France.
Apr. 7—Leaves Thiennes for Armentieres sector.
,, 10—Relieves Northumberland Fusiliers at Bois Grenier.
,, 25—C Company's billet destroyed by shell-fire.
June 25—5th Brigade raid.
,, 29—Relieved by 16th Battalion. Moves to L'Hallobeau.
July 1—Battle of Somme begins.
,, 9—Seventeenth moves to St. Omer, via Rouge Croix and Eblinghem.

1916.
July 11—Entrains at St. Omer.
 „   12—Arrives Amiens, marches to Argoeuves.
 „   16—Leaves Argoeuves for Cardonette.
 „   18—Rubempre.
 „   20—Warloy.
 „   22—Moves to Brickfield near Albert.
 „   24—Bivouacs in Sausage Valley.
 „   25—Relieves 9th Battalion near Pozieres.
 „   26—Bombing affair in Munster Alley.
 „   28—First assault on O.G. Lines.
 „   30—Battalion still in the trenches.
Aug. 4—O.G. Lines and Windmill captured.
 „   5—Bivouacs on Tara Hill.
 „   6—Inspected by General Birdwood.
 „   7—Moves to Halloy, via Warloy and La Vicogne.
 „   9—Halloy.
 „   16—Leaves Halloy en route to Pozieres.
 „   23—Relieves 19th Battalion, Pozieres.
 „   25—Moves back to Tara Hill.
 „   29—Warloy.
Sept. 1—Beauval.
 „   5—Departs for Poperinghe.
 „   8—Moves to Ypres.
 „   9—Relieves Rifle Brigade in reserve.
 „   27—Rampart Barracks. Ypres.
Oct. 6—Relieved by 25th Battalion, entrains for Godewaervelde.
 „   7—Billeted at Winezeele.
 „   12—Moves to St. Laurence Camp, Poperinghe.
 „   15—Alberta Camp, Reninghelst.
 „   17—Winezeele.
 „   18—Arneke.
 „   19—Bayenghem.
 „   23—Recques.
 „   24—Audruicq.

1916.
Oct. 26—Pont Remy.
 „   28—Embuses for Ribemont.
Nov. 4—Montauban.
 „   6—Moves into front line at Flers.
 „   9—Carlton Camp.
 „   12—Mametz Camp.
 „   15—Montauban.
 „   18—Relieves 27th Battalion in front line.
 „   21—Relieved by Royal Sussex Regiment.
 „   22—Entrains at Quarry Siding for Ribemont.
 „   30—Cardonette.
Dec. 16—Moves to Franzvillers.
 „   17—Dernancourt.
 „   19—Sydney Camp, Fricourt.
 „   20—Montauban.
 „   21—'E' Camp, Trones Wood.
 „   25—Delville Wood.
 „   28—In support Switch and Needle Trenches.
 „   30—Relieves 19th Battalion in front line.

1917.
Jan. 2—Relieved by 20th Battalion.
 „   4—'E' Camp, Trones Wood.
 „   7—Delville Wood Camp.
 „   8—Montauban.
 „   16—Dernancourt.
 „   30—Albert.
 „   31—Shelter Camp.
Feb. 1—Relieves Gordon Highlanders at Le Sars.
 „   5—Relieved by 24th Battalion.
 „   6—Scots Redoubt Camp.
 „   9—Acid Drop Camp.
 „   13—Relieves 18th Battalion in front line.
 „   17—Relieved by 24th Battalion.
 „   18—Fricourt Camp.
 „   23—Sussex Camp.
 „   26—Relieves 18th Battalion at the Butte.
 „   28—Occupies Malt and Malt Support Trenches.
Mar. 2—The Layton Alley bombing attack.

1917.
Mar. 3—Relieved by 24th Battalion. Moves to Shelter Wood Camp.
„ 7—Bazentin Camp.
„ 11—Relieved 27th Battalion at Le Sars.
„ 12—Relieves 28th Battalion at Warlencourt.
„ 13—Moves up to Grevillers.
„ 16—Relieved by 19th Battalion. Moves to Martinpuich.
„ 20—Biefvillers.
„ 27—Bazentin Camp.
„ 28—Fricourt Camp.
Apr. 12—Favrieul.
„ 13—Vaulx-Vraucourt.
„ 14—Relieves 52nd Battalion at Noreuil.
„ 15—German attack on Lagnicourt.
„ 18—Vaulx-Vraucourt.
„ 24—Beunatre.
„ 25—Biefvillers.
May 1—Vaulx-Vraucourt.
„ 3—Second Bullecourt.
„ 8—Entrains at Albert for Fricourt.
„ 6—Biefvillers.
„ 11—Crucifix Camp.
„ 16—Senlis.
„ 18—Rubempre.
June 14—Bapaume.
July 28—Entrains for St. Omer.
Aug. 7—Arques.
„ 10—Clairmarais.
„ 29—Sir D. Haig reviews 2nd Division.
Sept. 12—Steenvoorde.
„ 13—Dickebusch.
„ 20—Battle of the Menin Road.
„ 22—Ypres.
„ 23—Halifax Camp.
„ 24—Wippenhoek.
„ 28—Halifax Camp.
„ 29—Bivouacs east of Ypres.
Oct. 2—Ypres.
„ 6—Relieves 27th and 28th Battalions at Zonnebeke.
„ 7—St. Joseph's Institute, near Zonnebeke.

1917.
Oct. 8—Relieves 27th Battalion on Broodseinde.
„ 9—First Passchendaele.
„ 10—Ypres.
„ 12—Steenvoorde.
„ 26—Dickebusch.
Nov. 4—Takes over front line at Moorslede.
„ 11—Staples.
„ 18—Moolenaere.
„ 19—Steenwerck.
Dec. 15—Pont de Nieppe.
„ 18—Westhoek Ridge.
„ 23—Relieves 25th Battalion at Frelinghien.
„ 31—Relieved by 20th Battalion. Moves to Pont de Nieppe.
1918.
Jan. 4—Le Rossignol Camp.
„ 8—Relieves 20th Battalion in front line.
Feb. 1—Moves to Colomby rest area.
Mar. 8—Le Rossignol Camp.
„ 13—Relieves 20th Battalion in front line.
„ 21—Relieved by 27th Battalion.
„ 22—Kortepyp Camp.
„ 24—Relieves 30th Battalion at Warneton.
„ 31—Relieved by 10th Gloucesters.
April 1—Embuses for Meteron.
„ 2—Entrains at Caestre for Somme.
„ 3—Allonville and Bussy-Les-Daours.
„ 4—Bois l'Abbe, Villers-Bretonneux.
„ 5—Relieves 33rd Battalion in front line.
„ 8—Relieved by 12th London Regt.
„ 9—Gentelles.
„ 12—Relieves 34th Battalion in front line.
„ 15—Relieved by 19th Battalion.
„ 18—Blangy-Tronville.

1918.
Apr. 19—Querrieu.
" 20—Bazieu.
May 1—Warloy.
" 2—Behencourt.
" 5—Allonville.
" 9—La Hussoye.
" 11—Relieves 34th Battalion at Morlancourt.
" 14—The combat at Morlancourt.
" 16—Relieved by 20th Battalion.
" 17—Vaux-sur-Somme.
June 2—Frechencourt area.
" 16—Glisy area.
" 29—Villers-Bretonneux.
July 2—Relieved by 22nd Battalion.
" 3—Tronville Wood.
" 6—Moves into front line.
" 13—Relieves 18th Battalion.
" 15—"Peaceful penetration" raid.
" 18—Relieved by 18th Battalion.
" 23—Relieves 18th Battalion.
" 30—Relieved by 18th Battalion.
Aug. 1—In support at Hill 104.
" 3—Relieved by 24th Battalion.
" 4—Blangy-Tronville.
" 5—Vaulx - en - Amienois, practising with tanks in attack formations.
" 6—Aubigny Switch.
" 8—Fourth Army attacks east of Villers-Bretonneux.

1918.
Aug. 9—Framerville captured.
" 11—Old Amiens Line.
" 17—Embuses for Fouilloy.
" 26—Embuses for Morcourt via La Motte.
" 27—Advances on Peronne.
" 29—Arrives at west bank of the Somme.
" 30—Clery captured.
" 31—Assault and capture of Mt. St. Quentin.
Sept. 4—Moves to Frise for rest and refit.
" 27—Moves forward to Bussy area.
" 28—Hargicourt.
Oct. 1—Relieves 30th and 32nd Battalions at Joncourt.
" 3—The Battle of the Beaurevoir Line.
" 6—Etricourt.
" 7—Tincourt.
" 8—Vignacourt.
" 10—Receives its draft of the disembodied 19th Battalion.
Nov. 11—The Armistice.
" 20—Entrains for Bohain.
" 30—Sivry.
Dec. 1—Silenrieux.
" 25—Christmas at Silenrieux.
1919.
Jan. —Moves to Montigny-le-Tilleul in preparation for return to Australia.
Apr. 24—Final draft entrains at Montignies-le-Tilleul for England.

CORRIGENDA.

Page 16, second column, line 32, for MONTIGNY-LE-TILLUEL read MONTIGNIES-LE-TILLUEL.

Page 35, line 33, for NO read ON.

Page 55, sketch map, for KIAIJIK DERE read KAIAJIK DERE.

Page 63, line 5, for FOREBODNG read FOREBODING.

Page 103, line 8, for CRUMPLED read CRUMPED.

Page 113, line 36, delete.

Page 154, line 25, delete.

Page 175, line 14, for MONO read THE MOON.

Page 181, line 33, for EXCERISED read EXERCISED.

Page 251, line 35, for ASSAULTING read ASSEMBLING.

Page 365, beginning with STARR, B. G., read one line down.

CHAPTER I.

Origin of the A.I.F.—The Australian soldier—Stalemate in Europe at the end of 1914—Recruits flock to the Colours—Liverpool Camp—Decision to raise 5th and 6th Brigades—Colonel W. Holmes appointed to command 5th Brigade—The Seventeenth Battalion is formed—Lieutenant-Colonel J. Paton in command—Initial training period—Lieutenant J. Costello, Chief Instructor—A good Band—Officers gazetted—March through Sydney—A change in the command—Lieutenant-Colonel H. A. Goddard, the new Commanding Officer—The Seventeenth embarks.

IT was not until the Great War of 1914-1918 was in its sixth month that the Seventeenth Battalion was raised and embodied as a unit of the Australian Imperial Force, better known as the A.I.F.

Immediately following the outbreak of hostilities in August, 1914, Great Britain had accepted the offer of the Australian Government to raise and equip an expeditionary force of one complete division, comprising light horse, artillery, infantry and ancillary troops, about 20,000 strong. In the early days of November, 1914, this Division together with one from New Zealand left Australia, via Albany, its destination being England. But so numerous were the applications for enlistment that the authorities decided to raise two additional brigades—one light horse and one infantry, and these were despatched overseas later in the year, to Egypt. To this country the original force, the 1st Division, had been diverted, partly for climatic reasons and partly because Turkey had entered the war on the side of the Central Powers—Germany and Austria—in October.

It was this magnificent body of men, which, by the valour it displayed on the frowning ridges of Gallipoli, in Palestine, and upon the rolling plains of France and Flanders, won for itself lasting renown in the annals of war.

An important factor in the welding of this force into a fighting machine of the first rank was the average Australian soldier's conception of military discipline. To his way of thinking the system existing in European Continental armies was, perhaps, well enough for conscripts; but to one accustomed to having full scope for the development of his strongly individualistic tendencies, it did not appeal. His view of discipline lay in the direction of a willing acceptance of the principle of the team spirit, which his experience in the field of sport had taught him was a vital adjunct to successful combination, and the attainment of the desired objective. His sound intelligence and unbounded confidence developed an aptitude for mastering in a minimum of time the technicalities of the weapons of war, as well as the tactics governing their application. He could also appreciate the necessity for a certain amount of drill, and when occasion called for ceremonial flourish, he could match any regular soldier. Outside this sphere, however, the monotonous repetition of purely parade ground movements, was, to his mind, largely a waste of both time and effort. His somewhat casual regard for the question of saluting every officer he encountered, other than those of his own unit, and for maintaining a consistently military deportment off the parade ground, was frequently interpreted by some persons in authority as a sign of an inferior standard of discipline. But even the majority of these critics, matured in a school, where the concept of discipline was rooted in the degree of smartness with which a salute was given and a clock-work precision in drill movements, after they had experienced closer contact with this unconventional fellow from "Down-under," and when they had seen him in action, they generously conceded that whatever his shortcomings were off the field, his battle discipline left nothing to be desired.

Moreover, the A.I.F. man possessed in full measure the worthiest traits of character inherent in the British breed. He possessed a resolute courage, based on a calm confidence and a firm belief in the cause for which he was fighting, though no outward indication of this sentiment would be forthcoming. He exhibited staunch loyalty to a comrade and a ready acceptance of responsibility—"giving it a go"—as he called it. He was broadly tolerant, but nevertheless was a fierce contender against injustice. He showed more than a sneaking regard for the "under-dog," and his sound commonsense and ready initiative, coupled with the capacity for enduring hardship and extracting humour from any situation, however grim, stamped him as a stout friend and a tough opponent. He was also intensely loyal to his unit, and to be regarded as a representative of Australia in the greatest test of all, was, in itself, a lively gratification. Even this took second place in his estimation, when his regiment, battery or battalion came into the picture. To his way of thinking there was only one "mob"—the one whose distinguishing colour patch he wore on the shoulders of his tunic. Anyone presuming to contest this claim ran the risk of "buying a fight."

In Europe, the first onrush of the German armies sweeping through Belgium and northern France, had been stayed at the very gates of Paris, where the enemy's hopes of a speedy decision collapsed like a house of cards, when the apparently beaten French and British Armies struck back with fury at his victory-flushed legions at the Marne, early in September, 1914, and drove them back in disorder to the Aisne, sixty-five miles from Paris, where he had previously dug positions on the heights along that river. But though the Germans had lost heavily in men, guns and material, they still possessed an overwhelming weight of artillery, and all attempts to dislodge them from these positions proved futile. On their side the hopes of the Allies for an early victory proved equally illusory.

The fall of Antwerp in October, and the subsequent attempt by the Germans to capture the Channel Ports, in which they were foiled by the gallant defence put up by the British Army standing before Ypres—the first battle of that name—when the flower of the Kaiser's Prussian Guard bit the dust, saw the end of major operations in France in that year. The opposing armies had fought each other to a standstill, for the time being at any rate, and this temporary exhaustion coinciding with the onset of winter opened up the possibilities of trench warfare under modern conditions for both sides. The close of 1914 saw the contending armies facing each other in a continuous system of fortified lines, separated in many cases by only a few yards, and extending from the sea to the Swiss frontier.

In the eastern theatre a similar stalemate had developed. Our powerful ally, Russia, invaded East Prussia late in August, 1914, and her "steam-roller" advance for a time constituted a grave threat to Berlin itself. However, by the skilful use of their network of strategic railways, the Germans were able to stop this thrust and, in turn, to destroy two powerful Russian armies at the Masurian Lakes and at Tannenburg. After a series of major battles, with fortune swaying to either side, and culminating in a fierce attempt on their part, the Germans' drive to capture Warsaw was defeated. The enemy had failed, just as he had failed to capture the Channel Ports on the Western Front. At the close of the year he was still thirty-five miles from the Polish capital.

With the advent of 1915, to both the Government and people of Australia came the full realization that ahead there lay a long and hard struggle. The glib utterances commonly employed that the war could not possibly last more than three months had been proved by events to be false, and the reaction thus produced provided a tremendous fillip to the already heavy recruitments, which comprised men from all walks of life crowding the depots, firmly resolved to set no limits to their determination to defend the free democratic institutions of the British race, directly menaced by the system which military-ridden Germany and her Kaiser sought to impose in pursuit of their dream of world domination.

Liverpool Camp, New South Wales, the main training centre, was a veritable city of canvas. Stretching along the flat eastern bank of the George's River were lines of bell-tents, first those of the supply units, then those of the light horse and further along were camped infantry reinforcement contingents and finally the recruits training depot itself. Artillery personnel were quartered at Holdsworthy, a few miles away.

As the daily draft of recruits from Sydney marched into the camp, they were greeted with derisive shouts of "Marmalade," a word synonymous with disillusionment, by the assembled occupants. Marmalade appeared on the mess tables with such monotonous regularity that the troops soon got sick of the sight of it; hence the term.

Then there were the hot, rainless months that followed, and the unchanging routine of elementary drill; the food, often unpalatable, and the hard earth for bed; the relaxation of a dip in the nearby river, at the end of a strenuous day's drilling and the amenities offered by visiting concert parties, or in the form of luxuries purchasable at the dry canteen; the spirit of comradeship engendered by the strange conditions and bound by a common ideal; and lastly, and most abiding, the individual friendships formed that endured even unto death.

Uniforms, rifle and equipment were not yet available, but there was a limited supply of blue dungaree fabric suits and white cloth hats useful for fatigue work. The ranks of the soldiery assembled daily for training presented an assortment of civilian attire that placed them, visually, at complete variance with their military setting. But abounding health and a keen desire to master the elementary details of their new trade, quickly offset these inconveniences. Meanwhile, training, perforce, had to be limited to drill without arms, and to physical "jerks," interspersed by lecturettes on organization, tactics, hygiene and the theory of musketry.

An interesting sidelight on the conditions prevailing at this period is revealed in the diary of a young Scotsman, Alfred McDonald, not then long in Australia, who, like thousands of others living in remote parts, had answered the call to arms. He wrote: "Reported to Victoria Barracks and from there to Liverpool Camp, where our soldiering commenced. We were issued with a blue dungaree suit and white hat, tin plate, mug, spoon, knife and fork; also two blankets and a ground sheet, which was very hard for a few nights. I spent four weeks in the depot learning to form fours and salute. That was all the training we had time for, then. The living was rather rough; no hot water was supplied to clean eating and cooking utensils, and the grease had to be rubbed off with sand."

This was the general position, when, early in February, 1915, it was announced from Headquarters in Melbourne that two additional infantry brigades, the 5th and 6th, together with an additional brigade of light horse, were to be raised. The

5th Brigade would comprise the Seventeenth, Eighteenth, Nineteenth, and Twentieth Battalions.*

The commander of the new brigade was Colonel W. Holmes, a Citizen Force Officer, who had only recently returned from German New Guinea, to which place he had been despatched in command of an Expeditionary Force, upon the declaration of war. The four battalion commanders were Lieutenant-Colonels J. Paton, A. E. Chapman, W. W. R. Watson and H. A. Goddard.

Immediately, steps were taken to establish a separate camp for the new brigade, and the site finally selected was situated at the far southern end of the Liverpool camping area. Selection of personnel and their organization into companies occupied a day or two, and soon each of the four units began to take shape as a separate entity and to lay the foundation of a reputation for discipline and efficiency that marked the work of the brigade throughout the war. As yet no uniforms were to be had, and the bare ground, with only a waterproof sheet for protection from damp, was the couch provided for each man. This was poor recompense after a hard day's training, but healthy youth and abounding enthusiasm disregarded all such minor inconveniences and for extra sleeping comfort, hip-holes were scooped out, after the fashion of bushmen.

Initial training was commenced, forthwith, but as only a limited number of old and very rusty rifles was on hand the syllabus was restricted to much the same work as had been carried out during recruit training. However, the Commonwealth Small Arms Factory was busily turning out rifles.

No regimental officers had been gazetted, the responsibility for training devolving, for the time being, on young militia officers specially called up for such duties. To these officers the men of the original battalions owe much for the ability and zeal they applied to the task of making soldiers out of recruits, who, in the main, had only the remotest acquaintance with military requirements. The work of the officers who ultimately took over from these earnest young subalterns was thereby made much easier.

The story of this period, would not be complete without mention of the man who was primarily responsible for the training of the new brigade, and who never failed to impress his personality and inspire enthusiasm in those with whom his work as officer-in-charge of training brought him into contact. He was Lieutenant John Costello, Chief Instructor at Liverpool Camp. An old soldier of the British regular army, he had fought in many campaigns and had won the Distinguished Conduct

---

*The original intention was to recruit the Twentieth in the 1st Military District, which included part of N.S.W. Subsequently, however, when the 7th Brigade was raised on April 1, it was renumbered Twenty-fifth and a new Twentieth raised in N.S.W.

Medal. Some years before the war he had joined the Australian Instructional Corps as a warrant-officer.

In physique and stature he did not conform to the customary conception as to what the ideal sergeant-major was like, for he was short and slim and lacked the stiff back and squared shoulders of the regular soldier. Nor did he possess the resonance of voice usually associated with the drill instructor; but what it lacked in robustness it was amply compensated for by a penetrating staccato note; while his ability to handle, solo, large bodies of men, was amazing. He could take a partly trained battalion and, after a brief detail, supervise its movement as easily as that of a drill squad. His methods were at times unorthodox, but always designed to capture and retain the interest of his pupils.

To be drilled by "Old Cossy" was more in the nature of a pastime, while the wise counsel imparted to aspiring non-commissioned officers how to handle men, was to prove of immeasurable value to them in the course of time. He, and those like him, responsible for the building of the foundations of a fighting organization, had wonderful material with which to work. And much the best of this material was that group of old soldiers of the British regular services, as well as those who had served recently in New Guinea. Their training and experience fitted them admirably to fill the more important non-commissioned ranks, and their generally sound personal example and sterling soldierly qualities did much to build as fine a brigade as ever left the shores of Australia.

In such circumstances the Seventeenth became part of the A.I.F. on March 30th, when, together with its sister battalions, the Eighteenth and Nineteenth, it was handed over to the brigade commander by Colonel Humphris, the camp commandant. After inspecting the brigade, Colonel Holmes introduced Colonels Paton, Chapman and Watson to their new commands, and complimented all ranks on their steadiness and appearance.

Colonel Paton was another citizen soldier who had given long and efficient service, including that under Holmes in New Guinea. However, his sojourn with the Seventeenth was destined to be short, as owing to a re-arrangement in senior commands in April, 1915, he was replaced by Colonel Goddard of the renumbered Twenty-fifth.

On March 30th all ranks were subjected to a foretaste of the varying weather conditions that subsequently were to be encountered in half a dozen other countries. Just after the brigade parade a violent cyclone struck the camp, laying tents flat and tearing marquees to ribbons. Individually the troops suffered. They had no reserve dry clothing or blankets, and this deficiency, coupled with the havoc caused by the storm, was responsible for a brigade order granting general leave to all ranks until noon the following day. Here the railway authorities did splendid work in co-operation with the military. In a short space of time they provided trains to carry 4,000 men to Sydney. Throughout this uncomfortable experience all ranks remained cheerful and made light of the conditions.

The month of April was half gone when the new rifles and equipment were issued, and their advent was welcomed as being a step nearer the desired goal.

The rifle was the Short Magazine Lee-Enfield Mark III pattern, 303 calibre, and the equipment was made of a strong canvas fabric, comprising a series of detachable parts, such as waist belt, shoulder straps, bayonet-frog, cartridge pouches, knapsack, haversack, water-bottle and entrenching spade carriers, all readily assembled into full marching kit, or any modification thereof, as occasion demanded.

Hard upon this came the issue of uniforms, which consisted of a khaki woollen tunic of a slightly "blousy" cut, with two upper and two lower pockets; corded knee breeches, puttees, and stout tan coloured boots. The hat was of brown felt with a broad brim, the left side turned up and clasped to the crown. A metal badge in the design of a rising sun also adorned the turned up brim side, and on the double collar of the tunic were two similar badges, smaller in size, while on each shoulder strap was fastened a metal "Australia."

The dress of the commissioned officers varied to the extent that they wore close fitting tunics with open collars over shirts and neckties. They also wore leather "Sam Browne" belts, and were equipped with the .45 Webley pistol. When in action, however, the officers dressed exactly like the lower ranks.

One of Colonel Paton's first acts on taking over the command was to organize a band. The only one in the camp at that period was the Depot band, and the Colonel conceived the idea that its members might be induced to come over to him in a body.

Accordingly, he approached Sergeant H. Rockliff, the leader, with the result that the men unanimously agreed to transfer. But unexpected repercussions followed, for, when the Adjutant of the Depot heard of the decision he recalled all the instruments on charge to the band, and without these they would be a band only in name. However, some of the men had their own instruments with them and the deficiency was quickly repaired through collections and subscriptions from all ranks of the Battalion, as well as their friends. From time to time the players received additions to their numbers, and after being known as the band with only one tune, quickly attained a good standard of musicianship under the able leadership of Rockliff, an experienced and capable conductor, who hailed from the

Orange district. The band subsequently received several private engagements, one of the earliest being for the Liverpool Show.

There remained the question of the choice of a regimental march, and after hearing several popular march tunes, Colonel Paton selected an arrangement of "Boys of the Old Brigade," which incorporated the "British Grenadiers."

The names of the original members and the instruments they played are:—

Sergeant H. Rockliff (euphonium), Corporal P. E. Hines (tenor horn), Lance-Corporal W. H. Masters, Privates W. C. Tremain and K. T. Cowans (trombone), Privates K. B. Wilson, G. F. Cook, S. Abbott, S. Talbot, T. N. Cullen, W. J. Glenn, M. Costello, W. Barrie and G. High (cornets); Privates A. C. Harper and J. Irwin (flugal horn); Privates D. H. White and C. Pearce (tenor horn); Privates W. A. Roberts and H. Ferris (baritone); Private A. Seaegg (B.B. flat bass); Privates A. Grix and H. C. V. Thompson (E. flat bass); Private J. F. Arnold (bass drum), Privates J. Dolan and J. Pryke (side drum); Private C. Nimmo (cymbals).

With the completion of the stage of arming and equipping, advanced training was taken in hand; close order drill with arms; musketry, theoretical, as well as practical application; open order work and elementary field tactics, up to platoon standard, was gradually developed, and as the Battalion was now with its own non-commissioned officers as instructors, soon there was evidence of marked progress in general efficiency, accompanied by the growth of a sound team-spirit, which reflected itself in an equally sound standard of discipline.

In due course the newly gazetted officers began to arrive and the Battalion was well upon the road to establishing itself as qualified to take its place as an effective unit of that great fighting force which soon was to show the world the worth of Australia's citizen soldiers.

The authorised establishment of an infantry battalion at this period was thirty-two officers and 944 other ranks, made up of head-quarters, which included signal and transport sections, and a machine-gun section.

The tactical employment of the machine-gun was then regarded as of secondary importance, in consequence of which this highly valuable part of a battalion's organization not infrequently was looked upon as a Cinderella, an object of mixed feelings of contempt and pity. Later their grouping into companies, and then separately as battalions, together with the development of tactics designed to give the fullest support, both in the attack and defence, elevated this hitherto despised arm of the service to its rightful place.

The infantry battalion itself was to be affected by the introduction of the Lewis gun as part of the establishment, but in 1914 dependence for fire power rested exclusively upon the rifle.

The officers gazetted were:—Lt.-Col. J. Paton, C.O.; Major E. F. Martin, 2nd I.C.; Capt. A. B. D. Brown, Adj.; Major G. R. Short, Q.M.; 2nd Lt. E. H. McCulloch, Sig. Off.; 2nd Lt. C. G. Johnston, Tpt. Off.;

A. Company:—Capt. C. R. A. Pye, Capt. H. M. Beiers, Lt. C. R. Lucas, 2nd Lt. R. A. Pye, 2nd Lt. F. Gombert, 2nd Lt. R. C. Anderson.

B. Company:—Capt. L. Griffiths, Capt. E. W. Kirke, Lt. H. L. Bruce, Lt. E. T. Harnett, Lt. J. R. Nunn, 2nd Lt. D. F. Doull.

C. Company:—Capt. R. J. A. Travers, Capt. J. Murphy, Lt. C. A. McBride, 2nd Lt. E. T. Manefield, 2nd Lt. R. V. Spier, 2nd Lt. H. E. Shaw.

D. Company:—Capt. J. M. Maughan, Capt. F. L. Lonsdale, Lt. H. W. Johnson, Lt. W. H. S. Sheppard, Lt. L. K. Chambers, Lt. F. G. Barnett.

Lieutenant S. R. Richardson, Machine Gun Officer.

Captain C. N. Smith, Medical Officer.

Chaplain R. Colwell, attached.

The authorities had decided to give the citizens of Sydney an opportunity of seeing the men of the 2nd Division. Since the previous October, when similar units of the 1st Division had marched, Sydney had not witnessed a parade of troops down its streets. The railway authorities announced that special trains would run from Newcastle and the South Coast, and from Orange and Bathurst. So great was the enthusiasm aroused, that complaints were made by residents further west of the failure of the Railway Department to run special trains for their convenience.

The parade was ordered for April 24th, and a light horse regiment, the 5th Brigade and other details were to participate. Special sites were reserved for children. Bands were stationed at intervals along the route.

In Liverpool Camp there was great activity. After an early lunch, the troops entrained for Sydney. At 2.30 the march commenced, the route being along Elizabeth, Park, College, Macquarie, Bridge, Pitt Streets, Martin Place and George Street, all gaily decorated with flags and bunting. The day was fine, though cold, and a crowd estimated at 200,000 lined the pavements and adjacent vantage view points.

The order of march was: One officer and fifty ratings of the French Navy; the Twelfth Light Horse; the 5th Brigade; the 5th Field Ambulance and a detachment of Artillery reinforcements. The parade state of the Seventeenth showed that 32 officers and 905 other ranks were present. The marching troops were greeted with thunderous applause.

Macquarie Street, where the Governor-General, Sir Ronald Ferguson took the salute, held a vast concourse of people. Behind his Excellency and the civil and military dignitaries in attendance, was drawn up a guard of honour comprising a detachment of an English Territorial regiment, which had recently arrived in charge of prisoners from the East. The Englishmen presented a smart and soldierlike appearance as they stood rigidly with sloped arms throughout the march, on the conclusion of which the Governor-General directed the State Military Commandant to express to all ranks his Excellency's approval of the smart appearance and good marching of the troops.

During the days following the march the troops underwent further and extensive training. It was similar to that meted out to their predecessors, the men of the 1st Division, who were then eagerly awaiting orders to attack on to that narrow Beach, which was destined to bear the name, as it does to-day, of one of the most glorious epics in the records of military history, and which still thrills the world, and gave birth to the shining traditions of Anzac, and firmly placed Australia among the nations of the universe.

The new officers, several of whom had served with the New Guinea force, were keen, and their experience and example were soon reflected in the zealous application of all ranks to the serious tasks that lay before them. The occasion afforded an opportunity to concentrate individually on the organization and training of their respective commands.

Late in April Colonel Paton left the Battalion, and pending the arrival of his successor, Colonel Goddard, the command was taken over by Major Martin. Colonel Goddard did not officially assume his new post until May 12th, when he joined the Battalion on the troopship "Themistocles" just before she sailed; but on Sunday, May 9th, he was the guest of his officers at lunch.

Lieutenant-Colonel Henry Arthur Goddard was then forty-eight years of age and had behind him a long and varied military experience, both in Australia and England. He was born in England and from early manhood he displayed an active interest in military matters as a volunteer. In 1899, shortly after his arrival in Australia, he was granted a commission in the 9th Infantry Regiment, Queensland, and by 1913 had risen to the rank of Lieutenant-Colonel commanding the Seventh Regiment.

In civilian life he was a successful merchant, with European connections, and his periodical visits overseas afforded him the opportunity of keeping up-to-date his military experience, by attending manoeuvres in England. For one not a professional soldier he was, therefore, singularly well fitted for command of a battalion on active service. Tall and slightly built, in appearance he was more the type of officer who had spent years campaigning in India, than the city business man. With his intellectual and military qualifications he combined the attributes of sincerity, courtesy, a dry humour and natural dignity in his relations with superiors and subordinates alike; nevertheless, he was a strict disciplinarian, and almost invariably punished to the limit of his authority the man who wilfully strayed from the path of duty. But he was also just, his attitude being tempered by a wide understanding of human nature, and the officer or man who showed that he was a trier had nothing to fear from the "Old Man," as he was affectionately known to all ranks. In 1919 he was promoted Brigadier-General.

Colonel Goddard's right hand man, Major Edward Fowell Martin, then forty years of age, was not an infantryman, having been commissioned in 1903 as a 2nd-Lieutenant in the Army Service Corps, and by 1913 had attained the rank of Major. On the outbreak of war he was appointed to the New Guinea Expeditionary Force as an infantry major, and upon his return to Australia, in 1915, was gazetted to the Seventeenth. Possessed of a reserved manner and a retiring disposition he was accustomed to weighing carefully every problem, a trait doubtless developed in the prosecution of his profession of accountant. But once he had decided upon a course of action he held to that course with characteristic stubbornness. One night, at the battle of Pozieres, he received an instruction to carry out what was thought to be a minor operation, but after thoroughly reconnoitering the position and satisfying himself that its execution that night would result in a disproportionate number of casualties, he, with great moral courage, told the Brigadier his views. Subsequently, when the Brigade Commander himself reconnoitered the position in daylight he upheld Martin's contention.

Throughout his command, from February, 1916 to May, 1918, he zealously maintained the welfare of the men under his command, never committing them to tasks, without adequate preparation and support. Like Colonel Goddard he became a Brigadier-General and subsequently commanded the 5th Brigade during the eventful closing phases of the war.

The important post of Adjutant was filled by Captain A. B. D. Brown, who, like Colonel Goddard, had served in a Queensland unit of the Australian Military Forces, with the rank of Lieutenant in the 8th Infantry Regiment. In private life he held an administrative post in the Public Service which fitted him for the appointment to Adjutant. At 31 years of age, he possessed a keen sense of duty, and if his insistence on formalities was at times over-stressed, he was both sincere and consistent in the execution of his responsible office. He, however, did not remain very long with the Battalion, and later in the year, after being invalided from Gallipoli, he accepted an appointment in the Provost Corps. Subsequently he was awarded the Distinguished Service Order.

Major G. R. Short, Quartermaster, was well above the average age; he was fifty-four and had served with the Australian Garrison Artillery, in which he attained the rank of major. The unwisdom of appointments of officers of similar age manifested itself in his case, for not long after landing at Gallipoli, he became ill and was invalided home to Australia.

The day of the Battalion's departure was now at hand. Issues of every kind of gear had been completed and black kit-bags were packed with items of clothing not required on the voyage, each bag having its owner's name, regimental number and unit painted thereon. For items required on the voyage a white "sea" kit-bag was issued to each man. On May 10th, an advanced party under Captain Griffiths proceeded to Sydney and boarded H.M. Transport A 32, in normal times the good ship "Themistocles," 13,000 tons, of the Aberdeen White Star Line. Its job was to prepare her for the Battalion's reception, loading stores and allotting berths and messes. In the selection of Captain Griffiths for this duty, the Battalion was fortunate in having the services of an officer thoroughly competent by training, for he had been a naval officer. Included in his party were several ex-naval ratings and marines of long experience.

The main body was under orders to embark on May 12th, and was to include the 1st Reinforcements. It so happened that this latter contingent was far short of its requirements in clothing and equipment. For instance, many of the men had no hats, as there were none available for issue. By the afternoon of the 11th, Lieutenant L. G. Fussell, the commander, was faced with the prospect of having half of his men marching hatless through Sydney the following day.

Seriously perturbed, the young officer sought counsel of Sergeant H. D. Stone, an old regular British soldier, who had fought in the Boer War. After a little deliberation he ventured the opinion that the situation was not past redemption. When darkness fell he paraded a file of men and marched them to the hospital situated at the northern end of Liverpool camp. There he intimated that he had come with a requisition from the commanding officer of the Seventeenth Battalion for the hospital authorities to hand over as many hats as could be procured. He returned, his mission completely successful, in fact he had a considerable number of hats surplus to requirements. For this fine display of soldierly initiative he earned the undying gratitude of that zealous young officer, Lieutenant Fussell.

The following morning at 5 o'clock, the notes of an unfamiliar bugle-call aroused the sleeping troops. It was the "old" Reveille which Sergeant-Bugler G. L. Gravenor had selected specially for this momentous occasion, in preference to the short and terse current call.

The long-looked for day had arrived—the day that crowned the hope and resolve of every officer and man; the day, alas, on which many were to see the last of their beloved Australia, some to lie in the man-forsaken valleys of Gallipoli, or in the pleasant fields of France and Flanders. But, on this memorable morning, no such melancholy thoughts even lightly touched the minds of the thousand-odd happy warriors, whose only thought was a firm resolve to put the disturbers of the peace of nations "where they belonged."

At 9.15 a.m. the Seventeenth paraded for the last time on its old training ground, and shortly afterwards, to the rousing strains of "Boys of the Old Brigade" thirty-three officers and 1091 other ranks swung through the camp gates on the Moorebank road, en route to Liverpool railway station. No time was lost in entraining and a little before eleven o'clock the Battalion mustered at Central Station, Sydney, whence it proceeded along Elizabeth, Park, Boomerang and Cathedral Streets to Woolloomooloo Wharf, where the troopship lay. The marching column quickly attracted large numbers of sightseers, and many of the bystanders endeavoured (not entirely without success) to hand out bottles of beer, packets of cigarettes and sweets, and even offered to carry the equipment of the marching men.

By 11.30 the column had arrived at its destination, and the troops began to embark, each man, "sea" kit-bag in hand filing up the gang-way to his allotted place in the company mess deck. By 12.10 p.m. the operation was completed and ten minutes later the ship drew away from the wharf, which was densely packed with men, women and children assembled there to farewell loved ones and friends. There was much hurrahing and kiss-blowing, mingled with tears and smiles, and not a little advice as to how to deal with the enemy. The band played cheery tunes and there was a profusion of flags and paper streamers.

As the ship moved into the stream she was escorted by tugs, motor launches and ferry boats, the harbour reverberating to the "cock-a-doodle-doos" of their sirens, to Neutral Bay, where she dropped anchor to await sailing orders. Just before dusk her commander, Captain Collins, received his clearance and at 4.40 p.m. the majestic bulk of H.M. Transport A.32 moved down the harbour and out through the Heads.

CHAPTER II.

Organized training begins—The four company commanders—Sport and recreation—Colombo the first port of call—Seventeenth sightseeing in organized parties—First death—Arrival at Suez—Seventeenth entrains for Cairo—Aerodrome Camp, Heliopolis—Training for war—2nd Division constituted—Leave to Cairo—Non-commissioned officers of a high standard—General Spens praises Seventeenth—Battalion embarks for Gallipoli.

THE troops lost no time in settling down under the new conditions. Fine weather and a moderate sea assisted to a considerable extent. Probably the majority of them had never previously passed the three-mile limit, and to these the experience of being afloat on an ocean-going steamship held both novelty and imaginative appeal. It was, indeed, a strange adventure upon which they had embarked; nevertheless few, if any of them had any illusions as to the outcome. The heavy casualties sustained during the recent landing on Gallipoli already had told its own story. Thus, every man realised that to match his courage and wits successfully against that tough and brave foe—the Turk, efficiency must be the key-note. Organized training commenced within a day or two, the syllabus varying from physical drill, platoon inspection, musketry exercises and theory; indication of targets and practice in fire-control, with the aid of large paper scenic targets, to lecturettes on tactics, and other subjects of a general military character. Boat drill was also a regular feature.

As yet no tropical kit had been issued, but all ranks were supplied with canvas shoes, which added to their comfort.

The following syllabus, typical of the daily routine, is taken from the diary of Corporal C.C. Brindley. It was copied by him from an order:—

6.0 a.m.—Reveille; 6.30—Mess Orderlies Draw Bread; 6.30-7.30 — Physical Training; 7.30 — Breakfast; 8.0 — Cleaning Fatigues—Police Clear Decks; 9.0—Sick Parade; 9.10-12—Parade—C.O.'s Inspection; 12 Noon—Dinner; 2-4 p.m.—Parade—Mess Orderlies Draw Dry Stores; 5.0—Tea; 5.30—Sick Parade; 6.0—Sling Hammocks; 8.0—First Post; 8.30—Last Post; 9.0—Lights Out; 9.15—Rounds.

Tuesday and Friday afternoons were devoted to "make and mend" purposes.

A 32, prior to her conversion into a troop-ship, had been employed as a one-class passenger-cum-cargo vessel between Australia and England, and was well suited to her new role, being both spacious and comfortable. The officers were accommodated in cabins, and amidships the sergeants had roomy quarters set aside for their use; the lower ranks were distributed over the remainder of the ship. They, as well as the sergeants, slept in hammocks slung on hooks fastened to the beams of the mess-decks.

At the outset of the voyage, effect was given to a wise and very necessary measure, designed to acquaint all ranks with the various crimes and punishments contained in the Army Act. Thus, it was ordered that company commanders should personally recite the entire category of these edicts in the presence of their companies, after the daily inspection parade. This precaution was taken in the interests of all ranks, the majority of whom, perhaps, were ignorant of the existence of any such provisions in the military code. To men suddenly cast in the role of soldiers, and lacking previous experience of such things, the extent and variety of offences and their attendant penalties must have proved a formidable and somewhat bewildering array.

Especially impressive on this occasion was Captain Griffiths's recital of the group of crimes for which the extreme penalty was provided. After putting emphasis on the word death—he would pause. Then, deliberately fixing his monocle to his eye, would focus it on the close, ordered ranks, and a penetrating glare ensured the almost fascinated attention of his audience.

Of the leaders, upon whose shoulders rested the responsibility for training, Captain Cecil Robert Arthur Pye, A Company, was short and slightly built, and like many other professional men in civilian life, had taken up military training as a patriotic duty, prior to the outbreak of war. In 1909 he received a commission in the 3rd Infantry, and later his captaincy in the 16th Infantry Regiment. Pye was a shrewd judge of human nature, also possessing a kindly disposition, which, however, was coupled with an unobtrusive forcefulness of character that would not countenance inefficiency. He was quick to size up a situation and give the necessary instructions to cope with it. During an action he would greet officers and messengers reporting to his head-quarters with the smiling invitation to "tell us the worst." He was killed by a shell at Ypres, in 1917, whilst in command of the Nineteenth Battalion to which he had been earlier transferred. He was twenty-five years of age when gazetted to the Seventeenth.

Captain Llewellyn Griffiths, B Company, had served in the Royal Navy, from which he had retired a few years before the war with the rank of commander, and had come to Australia, where he took up the profession of surveyor. He was a nephew of, and had served under Admiral Sir Harry Rawson (at one time Governor of New South Wales), when the latter was Commander-in-Chief of the South African station. He took part in punitive expeditions on the East and West coasts of that continent for which he held the General Service Medal. He and Lieutenant C. A. McBride, who had fought in the South African War, were the only officers who had seen active service prior to 1914. His insistence on a rigid code of discipline was in accord with the Naval tradition, and he invariably penalised even first offenders without leniency. But he was also scrupulously just, and at all times ready to encourage the genuine trier. Griffiths, who was a big man, in the mid-forties, went through the Gallipoli campaign; but the strain undermined his health, and shortly after the Battalion returned to Egypt, in January, 1916, he was invalided to Australia.

Captain Reginald John Albert Travers, C Company, was also big, possessing an athletic figure. He was one of many public servants who had associated themselves with military training activities in pre-war days. Commissioned in 1908 in the 1st Infantry Regiment, he later transferred to the Intelligence Corps with rank of Captain. At the time of his appointment to the Seventeenth, Travers was twenty-seven. He had taken part in the New Guinea expedition, in the previous August, and this experience served as a useful background in the new sphere of operations. Like Pye and Griffiths, he was a stickler for discipline, although in some minor matters his method of obtaining the required results differed from those of his colleagues. Nevertheless, he was a capable officer. He had devoted much of his spare time to military studies. In 1917, after a period as second-in-command of the Seventeenth, he was appointed to the command of the Twenty-sixth Battalion. He did not accompany the Battalion on the voyage. He reported for duty on July 19th, in Egypt.

Captain John Malbon Maughan, D Company, was another of that band of earnest men who, in pre-war days voluntarily devoted much of their leisure time to military training. First commissioned in 1913 in the 34th, he transferred the following year to the 35th Infantry. Short and sturdy of build, Maughan was thirty-eight when he joined the Seventeenth. Although Australian born he had completed his education in an English University and subsequently entered the legal profession. He served in New Guinea as a subaltern under General Holmes. By education, experience, and temperament he was well equipped for his new post, and under a placid exterior possessed the attributes of quick discernment and sound judgment. He was not the martinet type, overemphasis on ceremony was repugnant to him; but in all practical matters he insisted, with strict impartiality, on smart and efficient performance, which earned the confidence both of his superiors and subordinates. Maughan subsequently temporarily commanded the Twentieth Battalion.

The "make and mend" afternoons were devoted to sporting activities and amusements suited to ship-board conditions. Avenues leading to the discovery of artistic talent within the Battalion were thoroughly explored, and culminated in a grand concert being held on the after well-deck on May 19th. The programme, a copy of which has been preserved by Private A. Earnshaw was:—

Selection:	Seventeenth Battalion Band
Song: "Egypt"	Corporal Bolton
Song: "When the Fields are White with Daisies"	Private Griffiths
Monologue: "The Shop-Walker"	Private McConnochie
Song: "Go To Sea"	Capt. B. Douglas Brown
Song: Selected	Private Lorimer
Humorous Song Selected	Private Clarke
Song: "The Englishman"	Chaplain Colwell
Song: Selected	Private Hopkins
Cornet Solo: Selected	Private K. Wilson
Song: "The Deathless Army"	Rev. R. Finnigan, Y.M.C.A.
Duet: "The Larboard Watch"	Pts. J. Middlemiss & McConnochie
Song: "My Little Grey Home in the West"	Corporal Hodgetts
Selection	Battalion Band
Recitation: "The Progress of Madness"	Private Walker
Song: Selected	Private Tindall
Song: Selected	Private Coleman

God Save the King.

The organizers of the concert were Chaplain Colwell, Rev. R. Finnigan and Chaplain G. T. Walden, Eighteenth Battalion.

Organized competitions in Tugs-of-War and deck games also were features of these free afternoons, which provided scope for the exercise of the prevailing high spirits, and for occasional mild forms of practical joking. This exuberance of spirits was not confined to the men in the ranks. The officers themselves were always eager to give play to their inventive talents in devising "leg pulls."

On one such occasion the victim, an ardent, but very unsophisticated young man, was induced by Captain Griffiths to believe that it was a regular custom to stop the ship at midnight, in order that the ensuing day's supply of fresh fish could be obtained from the watery deep by means of hooks and lines; moreover, that a suitable vantage point from which to view this operation would be the bridge of A 32. Of course, the time selected for the event coincided with the commander's trick on watch at midnight. What Captain Collins said when a solitary, pyjamas-clad figure confronted him on the ship's Holy of Holies, uninvited, cannot be included in this narrative.

Then there was the conspiracy, originated by that "hard case," Private W. ("Spud") Murphy and a bosom friend, with the self-same innocent as the victim. The two had caused it to be known amongst the troops that there was bad blood between them, and, according to custom, would be settled in the boxing ring. The whole Battalion turned out to witness the serio-comic turn and to vociferously encourage the rivals. Suddenly, with a foul blow, Murphy dropped his opponent, and while the latter was writhing in mock agony on the deck proceeded to "put the boot in," to the indignant protests of the onlookers, every one of whom was in the joke. Then the denouement, as "Mr. Verdant Green" pushed his way into the ring and implored the seemingly infuriated Murphy to desist in the name of British fair play.

On the 20th, eight days out, A 32 passed Cape Leeuwin, and canvas awnings were raised in preparation for tropical conditions, while training was reduced to two and a quarter hours in the morning and one and a half hours in the afternoon.

Seven days later the French transport "Sontag," with troops from New Caledonia on board, was sighted ahead proceeding in the same direction as A 32. The troops were paraded, and as the speedier A 32 drew abreast of the Frenchman, the bands on both ships played the "Marseillaise" and "God Save the King" after which rousing cheers were exchanged.

Three days after this event, A 32 steamed into Colombo, after a voyage of eighteen days. All ranks eagerly canvassed the prospects of their being given permission to go ashore, in order to explore the new strange place and to see something of the dusky inhabitants of the land "where every prospect pleases and only man is vile." But as the morning wore on and no orders to that effect had been promulgated, hopes began to fade.

Colonel Goddard had gone ashore to report to the General Officer Commanding the troops in Ceylon, so there was nothing else to do but abide in patience. Towards noon, the Colonel returned to the ship and ordered the officers to parade before him. He informed them that, after some difficulty, he had obtained permission for the men to land in organized parties. It appeared that the behaviour of some troops passing through, previously, had caused the authorities some anxiety, in consequence of which the General had expressed his reluctance to risk a repetition of such conduct.

Colonel Goddard told the officers that he had decided to put the position to the men and leave it to their honour not to abuse the privilege they had been granted. Immediately the conference ended the Battalion was ordered to parade without arms, and, while the barges that were to take them ashore were pulled alongside the ship, every platoon commander put it squarely to his men that any breach on their part not only would be letting down the Battalion, but a reflection as well on the good name of Australia.

The troops were landed and in three parties paraded through the main streets, viewing scenic portions of the city en route. After the march they were supplied with refreshments at the canteen of an English Territorial Battalion. By 6.0 p.m. the last party had returned aboard, not one man being missing.

Years afterwards, Colonel Goddard told how he had succeeded in obtaining leave for his men to land. As a last resort he resolved to appeal to the sporting instincts of the General, whom he offered to bet an even £10 that the men of the Seventeenth would not cause the authorities any trouble. Colonel Goddard's shrewd estimate of the reaction of the Australian soldier to any worthy appeal had secured the desired result, and, incidentally, netted him £10.

At 9 p.m. the same day, A 32 drew out of Colombo, and the next morning the troops observed that she was steering on a course parallel to the west coast of India, the land being in sight throughout the hours of daylight. Fleets of catamarans, the frail looking sailing craft used by fishermen in that part of the world, were encountered, but to their occupants the sight of the giant ship ploughing her way a few cables length distant was evidently not novel, for they appeared to display little interest, even at the sight of the soldiers on board. The following day the land had disappeared from view, the ship having been turned on a nor'westerly course.

Three days out from Colombo occurred the first death in the Battalion, that of Private William John Manning, D Company, no June 2nd. The Battalion paraded for the funeral service, which, in the absence of a Roman Catholic Chaplain was conducted by Captain Murphy. The bier, covered with the Union Jack, was placed near the ship's rail on the starboard side of the after well-deck.

The hush that followed the stopping of A 32's engines was broken by the opening sentences of the solemn office for the dead, on the conclusion of which the band played Chopin's "Funeral March." Then the Union Jack was removed from the bier and Manning's body committed to the sea. A pause, then the staccato words of command: "Firing Party, Volleys—Load!" Three volleys were then fired, after which there rang out the half-triumphant, half-wailing notes of the Last Post, the soldier's call to rest. A few moments silence then the ship's telegraph clanged "full speed ahead," and as A 32 gathered way the troops were dismissed from parade to the tune of a rousing quickstep.

Manning's untimely death occasioned one of those striking displays of spontaneous generosity which is such an outstanding attribute of the Australian character, and resulted in the raising of £123 for the benefit of his widow. His personal effects realised some fancy prices at auction: a razor, £6; shaving brush, £8; two singlets, £9; pipe, £8; tennis shoes, £18; cardigan jacket, £3; toothbrush, £5/15/6 and half a tin of tobacco, £3/12/6. Manning had been married only the day before the Battalion embarked.

June 3rd being the birthday of His Majesty King George, the troops paraded with arms, and after a brief ceremony in honour of the Sovereign, all ranks were granted a holiday.

The weather was now becoming increasingly hot, and by the time the Red Sea had been entered, conditions were almost unbearable. It was the hottest period of the year in that part of the world and the scorching winds and red sandstone land formation, clearly visible to the naked eye, made the passage of those narrow waters like a voyage through Hell.

On June 9th, the second death occurred. Private Rea, 1st Reinforcements, Nineteenth Battalion, passed away suddenly. He was also given a military funeral.

At 10 p.m. the same day a passing ship sent a wireless message that Italy had declared war, and on the following day the hospital ship Grantala, bound for Australia, passed with her complement of wounded.

It was to everybody a great relief when, at 5 a.m. on June 12th — exactly one month after leaving Sydney — A 32 dropped anchor at Port Suez. Disembarkation soon began, and at 1.40 p.m. the Battalion entrained for Cairo. The bright green pastures of the irrigated country, through which the railway ran, and the cries of vendors of "orangees" and "eggs-a-cook" at the stations, provided sensations refreshing, if slightly bewildering, to the troops, after the trying last days of the voyage. At 8.30 p.m. the Battalion detrained at Zeitoun station, a few miles from Cairo, and in the darkness marched to Aerodrome Camp, Heliopolis, on the eastern side of the city.

Aerodrome Camp was virtually a suburb of a vast canvas city tenanted by thousands of Australians belonging to the newly formed units, and reinforcements for the 1st Division, the 4th Infantry Brigade and Light Horse, totalling many thousands. The camps themselves were all within a comparatively short distance of the city, the Seventeenth's quarter-guard tent being situated at the Heliopolis end of the main road leading from Cairo, where it petered out in the desert sand.

The next morning was Sunday, and except for the customary church parade, the day was devoted to sight-seeing, locally, and generally sizing up of the new surroundings. Pending the arrival of tents, the troops were quartered in large wooden mess-huts, but by the following Thursday, the whole Battalion was under canvas.

On the eastern side of the camp lay the officers' lines, regimental office and mess, and opposite, across a broad avenue, the men's lines. At the southern end of this avenue, was a roomy wooden structure for the sergeants' mess. Behind the company lines lay the men's mess huts, and beyond these again the cookhouses, canteens and shower baths, every reasonable comfort having been thus provided.

After church parade Colonel Goddard went round each company in turn, and spoke to the men about pitfalls and temptations in that strange country. He stressed the point that casualties resulting from reckless and unwise actions were as serious as those caused by enemy action.

The following day training for war began in earnest, along with the daily provision of guard and other routine duties. The camp was an open one and there were nine posts on its perimeter for security against prowling natives. The weather, however, was too hot to permit of outdoor training between the hours of nine in the morning and five in the afternoon, and was, therefore, confined to rifle exercises, lecturettes and theory of musketry, in the mess huts during the hottest hours. Platoon and company field training was held on the desert adjacent to the camp in the early part of the morning or late in the afternoon. Subsequently more advanced training, including night operations, was undertaken, and the Battalion carried out its musketry course at Abbassia rifle range.

At 5.30, with the first streak of the cool dawn, the admonitary notes of Reveille would rouse the slumbering troops, and as the last note had died, the band would strike up a lilting quickstep, such as "Wairoa" or "Invercargill," as it marched and counter-marched through the lines. Half an hour later, with ablutions completed and hot coffee consumed, companies, clad in cotton shirts, khaki shorts and pith helmets, would swing out of camp to begin the day's work. Three hours intensive training, after which back to camp for breakfast and a respite of a few hours, with only routine duties to perform, until the declining sun permitted of further outdoor work.

The regulation ration of the troops in Egypt was supplemented by such extras as preserved fruits, condensed milk, sardines, salmon and tomato sauce, purchased from a subsidy by the Egyptian Government of eightpence half-penny per man, per diem.

A sample syllabus taken from Regimental Order No. 7 of June 23rd shows it was designed to obviate working during the

GOING ASHORE AT COLOMBO.

DISEMBARKING AT SUEZ.

hottest period of the day when the temperature often exceeded one hundred degrees. It was:—

    6.0 a.m. to 7.30 a.m.:—Digging trenches.
    7.30 a.m. to 8.0 a.m.:—Bayonet fighting.
    8.0 a.m. to 9.0 a.m.:—Company drill.
    11.15 a.m. to 12.30 p.m.:—Lecture: March discipline, with special reference to night marches.
    5.0 p.m. to 6.30 p.m.:—Extended order; fire control and mutual support; platoons to work in pairs, one platoon standing-by watching the other platoon, the instructors pointing out mistakes. Then change over.
    6.30 p.m. to 7.30 p.m.:—Company drill.

The site of the great encampment was level. During training periods the movement of units, scattered over this area raised pillars of dust, that from a distance resembled smoke. The men and their arms were covered with fine powder. To add to the discomfort of all ranks, the shorts they wore afforded no protection to the knees. Many suffered abrasions as the result of contact with the sand whilst practicing short rushes by sections during attack exercises. But, gradually the troops became hardened, and, in consequence, such incidents were regarded as minor inconveniences.

Sound training. that went hand-in-hand with a healthy spirit permeating all ranks, produced the desired result, and soon every man, so to speak, "was on his toes." No serious cases of indiscipline occurred, and, although there was a comparatively small section of "hard-heads," who appeared before Colonel Goddard, after pay days, the records disclosed few offences that were of a major character.

An example of the uniformly good standard of discipline then prevailing was illustrated during a disturbance which originated in a notorious Cairo street known as "The Wozzir," one Saturday afternoon in July. The incident caused the authorities to become concerned at the prospect of the repetition of a previous outbreak, in which Australian soldiers had been involved and which had culminated in a riot. Thereupon, urgent orders were transmitted to the 2nd Division to furnish picquets to be sent to the city to restore order.

The Seventeenth was the only unit that could muster its allotted quota, the remaining battalions evidently having taken advantage of the Saturday afternoon's respite from training to proceed on unofficial leave for the rest of the day. Order was eventually restored and little damage was done to property; nevertheless, the affair was considered by General Maxwell, General Officer Commanding in Egypt, to be of a sufficiently serious character to warrant the issue of a special order to be promulgated to every unit. In his order General Maxwell censured the conduct of those who took part in the disturbance, and at the same time he singled out the Seventeenth for its good showing on that occasion. Naturally all ranks were elated at this tribute and, figuratively speaking, held their chins several degrees higher, until they learned the nickname that had been conferred upon them by the rest of the 2nd Division. It was "Maxwell's Pink-eyed Bastards."

Early in July, the three new brigades, the 5th, 6th and 7th had been organized as the 2nd Division, with Major-General J. G. Legge as its commander. General Legge was originally given the command of the 1st Division, after General Bridges was mortally wounded, shortly after the landing on Gallipoli, but, following a reshuffle of commands, he came to the 2nd Division.

Solid training of the whole of its twelve battalions became the order of the day. But it was not all work and no play. Within the precincts of the camp there existed facilities for recreation at the end of the day. Marquees, erected by welfare organizations, contained writing materials, games and pianos which became the centres of many impromptu concerts. There was also the wet canteen, where a good glass of English ale could be had. Then there were occasional picture shows and visits by concert parties organized by kindly residents of Cairo. A regular side-attraction was the ubiquitous native dwarf, "Sergeant McKenzie," with uniform and dummy rifle complete, who plied a lucrative trade demonstrating his skill in the detail and execution of rifle exercises.

The officers' and sergeants' messes also were equipped with facilities affording indulgence in such social amenities as circumstances permitted, mainly in the form of invitations to their opposite numbers in other units to dinner and cards, or, perhaps, a sing-song to while away the leisure hours. At week-ends the officers frequently were entertained by Captain Griffiths's sister, who was resident in Cairo. This kind lady and her women friends were responsible for planning and carrying through several very enjoyable parties and trips up the Nile.

For all ranks proceeding on leave, Cairo, with its teeming cosmopolitan population, manners, customs, institutions and the country's ancient monuments and relics, provided a variety of attractions that held an unabated interest. Sight seeing in the direction of the Pyramids, or the zoo, or else in the city itself, a visit to the cool Esbekiah Gardens, reserved for British troops as a pleasure resort, where, on Sunday and Wednesday afternoons, a military band discoursed music, and, nightly, picture shows were given. The museum, which housed many ancient memorials, was also a popular resort, the mummies of long departed Pharaohs being objects of special interest. Reacting in facetious vein to the spectacle, Corporal C. C. Brindley, only a lad, recorded his impressions thus: "We then explored the

Museum. The old beggar that annoyed the Israelites, one Rameses, is now in a case. He looks a hard old case himself, who took a delight in scratching out peoples' names and substituting his own. I bet he did not do so on duty day."

There were also the open air cafes, the lemonade sellers, monkey-boys, guides, white uniformed policemen; the blind beggars and the eternal cry of "baksheesh;" the frequent funeral processions—the better classes having hired mourners and occasionally brass bands playing quicksteps*—a serio-comic linking of East and West; the domed mosques, and the priests calling the faithful to prayer, forming a continuous and variegated picture, which never failed to arrest the interest of the lean brown men from the distant south land.

Turning again to the serious purpose of training for war, it will be recalled that the Battalion's earlier training programmes were more or less restricted to platoon work, but the scope was gradually widened as time went on, to include battalion drill, night operations and route marches. The result of this carefully designed syllabus was early shown by the marked improvement, not only in the standard of discipline, but in the physique of all ranks as well, especially that of the younger soldiers, men about the twenty-year mark.

The Australian soldier, on an average, was, perhaps, a bigger man than the Tommy. An estimate may be made of our men's stature by reference to the size of a guard mounted on one occasion by B Company, comprising twenty-nine other ranks, whose average height was five feet eleven inches. The tallest man was Private L. Rout, who stood six feet four and a half inches.

Much of the credit for the attainment of an efficient standard must be given to the non-commissioned officers, as fine a body as any commanding officer could wish to have. Like the officers, the greater proportion had previous military training and several wore medal ribbons. Throughout their ranks there existed a spirit of comradeship, which made their tasks easier. Therein could be detected the influence of Regimental Sergeant-Major F. B. Cheadle, a shrewd, kindly man, firm on parade, but delightfully informal in moments of relaxation in the mess. He was, indeed, one of that rare species—a popular Sergeant-Major. He held a high reputation as an international footballer, which fact contributed in no small degree to the esteem in which he was held by all ranks.

The four Company Sergeant-Majors, J. J. Fay, W. J. S. O'Grady, F. G. Rae and H. Ronald, were all experienced men. Ronald had served in New Guinea and Rae in the citizen forces.

---

* Lieut. Doull, in his book "With the Anzacs in Egypt" describes such a funeral at which the band comprising three brass instruments and three drums played "Men of Harlech."

N.C.O'S FIRST REINFORCEMENTS.
Lieutenant L. G. Fussell, O.C.

MACHINE-GUN INSTRUCTION.
(Back)—Lieutenants L. K. Chambers, S. R. Richardson, H. L. Bruce.
(Front)—Lieutenant H. W. Johnson, 2nd-Lieutenant H. E. Shaw,
Lieutenant E. T. Harnett.

No. 8 PLATOON.

2nd-Lieut. D. F. Doull, O.C. Sergeant (afterward Capt., M.C.) K. W. Mackenzie. Sergeant (afterward Lieut., M.C.) A. E. Clifton.

Amongst the ranks of Sergeants there was a strong salting of old regulars, such as J. A. Millar, H. Lane, R. Dodd, J. T. Robertson, E. F. Edwards, H. Hodgson, A. G. Davis, F. May, H. E. Rentell, H. D. Stone, J. H. Cornwall, G. W. Norris and G. L. Gravenor. And by way of a contrast to these seasoned soldiers, there were several who, though only in their early twenties, had already acquired a sound experience in leadership in the citizen forces after the inception of the universal training scheme a few years before the outbreak of the war. There was young Eric Lowther, who had resigned his commission to enlist as a private, when refused permission to transfer into the A.I.F. with a commission; G. S. Black, who was for some time a cadet at the Royal Military College, Duntroon; J. P. O'Toole, W. H. Palmer, G. Small, who had also served in New Guinea, and V. J. Sullivan, together with others of more mature age, the majority of whom had served as volunteers in some part of the Empire.

The ranks of the corporals were similarly well balanced. Included in these were J. M. Lyons and C. R. Hannaford, two splendid physical specimens; T. L. Adam, F. W. Smith, E. R. Raine, C. C. Finlay, A. S. Gilbert and J. P. Taylor, all young men who subsequently won commissions. With them were associated other and more mature of the junior leaders, the whole forming a solid core around which, gradually, a disciplined unit was moulded.

It is fitting to give a brief mention to the sixteen boys, of the average age of sixteen years, who had been enlisted as buglers. Several of these lads went through every campaign with the Seventeenth as private soldiers, being absorbed into the platoons when the use of buglers was discontinued about the time the Battalion embarked for Gallipoli.

In the matter of training, the Seventeenth possessed an advantage over its sister battalions in the 5th Brigade. The latter did not arrive in Egypt until about six weeks later, and, consequently, had considerable leeway to make up. Indeed, the standard of efficiency, discipline and training was so consistently good, that when at the end of July, the Battalion was inspected by Major-General Spens, General Officer for Training in Egypt, he told Colonel Goddard, after the parade, that the Seventeenth stood alone of any battalion he had seen, either British or Australian. The General's remarks were in due course promulgated to all ranks on parade and were received with much gratification.

On August 10th, two months after its arrival, the Battalion received orders to proceed to Cairo and garrison the Citadel, situated on a dominating feature in the heart of the city. All ranks were elated at the prospect of even a brief sojourn in comfortable quarters that would bring them within ready reach of the social amenities of the metropolis. The following morning, after an eary breakfast, the camp was struck and the column, headed by Major Martin, temporarily in command, vice Colonel Goddard, who was ill in hospital, moved off, the route leading through a part of old Cairo known as the Dead City.

Arriving at the Citadel Barracks, the men were dismissed. They immediately set out to explore their new quarters and to fraternise with the English Yeomanry Regiment they had come to relieve. However, their stay was to be short-lived, for, during the afternoon, fresh orders were issued to march back to Heliopolis. Late the same afternoon, the Battalion paraded in mass formation on the barrack square ready to move off. It was here that an opportunity was provided to display its smartness and precision at drill. Just as Major Martin was about to give orders to move off, he was joined by the commanding officer of the Yeomanry Regiment. Major Martin, keen to show that the Battalion could drill like any regular unit gave the order "Right Wheel." With the precision of a gate swinging on its hinges, the whole mass wheeled, while the band played "Boys of the Old Brigade." On completion of the movement the Colonel, turning towards Major Martin, ejaculated: "By God, Sir, they drill like regulars!"

Back once again in camp at Heliopolis, the troops resumed the routine training, and any disappointment that may have existed, quickly disappeared on receipt of a rumour that the Battalion would soon receive orders to proceed to Gallipoli. The rumour in this instance, proved to have a solid foundation. Four days later, that is, on the 12th, and nine weeks after its arrival in Egypt, the Seventeenth received orders to entrain for Alexandria with the other Battalions of the Brigade. The following day the 1st Reinforcements marched in from the Reinforcement Camp at Helmiah and was absorbed into the four companies.

The 14th and 15th were spent putting on the finishing touches. Sun helmets were withdrawn and slouch hats re-issued, as were also jack-knives, mess-tins and field-dressings; while the medical officer, Captain Smith, gave each platoon in turn a demonstration of simple bandaging and first-aid to the wounded. Lastly, the unit indication cloth patches worn on the tunic sleeves, just below the shoulders, were distributed. The shape for the 2nd Division was that of a diamond and the two halves into which it was divided were coloured, upper half, black (in the case of Seventeenth), and the lower half, green, representing the 5th Brigade.

Provision had to be made for guarding the men's kit-bags and surplus baggage, which were to be left behind, a detail from each company comprising the guard. As there were no facilities for the operation of the normal type of transport on Gallipoli, 2nd Lieutenant C. G. Johnston, Transport Officer, and his section were ordered to remain at the base.

Excitement and an exaltation arising from the knowledge that soon they were to participate in the "dinkum thing," were sustained by accounts of their experiences narrated by wounded and convalescent men who had recently returned from Gallipoli.

During the period the Battalion was in training, one man actually committed an act of technical desertion by attaching himself to reinforcements of another unit proceeding to Gallipoli. His identity being discovered, he was returned under escort, and subsequently awarded 21 days Field Punishment No. 2, for his misguided zeal.

Stories of heavy casualties, and in not a few instances, highly coloured descriptions of hand-to hand combats with Turks; the machinations of spies and the nests of deadly snipers, some, it was said had proved to be women dressed in military uniform, had contributed, in an effective manner, to bring about excitement. In addition, news had come through that a great new push had been launched the week previously by British, Australian, New Zealand and Indian troops in order to grip the waist of the peninsula, and that all available troops would be required to support this new attack.

On August 15th the Battalion entrained at Helouan station in two trains, arriving at Alexandria at 4.20 a.m. on the 16th, and at 4.15 p.m., embarked on s.s. "Alaunia" with a complement of 32 officers and 941 other ranks.

CHAPTER III.

Seventeenth arrives at Mudros—Tranships to s.s. "El Kahira"—Disembarks at Anzac Cove—Ordered to left sector—Private J. W. Raitt meets General Birdwood—First man killed—Battalion reinforces 4th Brigade—Baptism of fire and Hill 60—Moves to Quinn's and Pope's Posts.

ON the afternoon of August 18th, the "Alaunia" entered Mudros harbour, Lemnos Island, which was situated a few miles opposite the entrance to the Dardanelles, and sixty miles distant from Anzac.

Lemnos was the main base of operations, and the harbour was thronged with British and Ally warships, transports, minesweepers and other craft. The Russian cruiser "Askold," nicknamed "Woodbine"* by the troops, with her five thin perpendicular funnels, lay conspicuously at her anchorage near the entrance to the harbour. The Battalion was paraded and as the "Alaunia" drew abreast of the cruiser, both ships dipped their ensigns in salute.

At 1.30 p.m. on the 19th, orders were received for the Battalion to tranship to a smaller vessel and proceed to Anzac. This ship, the "El Kahira," presently drew alongside and the movement was concluded without a hitch. At 5.40 p.m. "El Kahira" cast off and steamed out into the Aegean Sea.

Towards two o'clock on the morning of the 20th, the stout little craft dropped anchor off Anzac Cove. It was pitch dark. Ahead, stabbing flashes and the rattle of small arms indicated the direction of the trenches. Away on the right, a warship, with the aid of its powerful searchlights, was shelling the Turkish trenches south of Anzac. The new arrivals could plainly see the bursting shells, followed several seconds later by the sound of the explosions. On the left were anchored three hospital ships, their hulls picked out in white and green lights and their large Geneva crosses framed in blazing red, forming a fascinating contrast to the grim setting of the main scene. Presently, in the pale dawn, the outlines of the high ridge, which formed the backbone of the peninsula, could be faintly discerned; and as the ship nosed her way inshore to her allotted anchorage, the deep, narrow gullies and

---

* A brand of cigarettes, five in each packet, which was popular with the British troops.

knife-edge ridges leading from the main mass, were more clearly revealed.

Each man had been issued with 200 rounds of ammunition, 150 of which was held in the cartridge-carriers, and 50 rounds in the haversack. Stores and ammunition were transferred to lighters, which also took the troops ashore. This unavoidably slow process took well into daylight hours to complete, the last tows being shelled by Turkish shore batteries. There were, however, no casualties, although Sergeant B. E. Luffman, of D Company, fell several feet from the ship into the hold of a lighter, fortunately without injuring himself.

By 9.0 a.m. disembarkation of personnel and stores had been completed and the Battalion bivouacked in Reserve Gully —off the northern end of Anzac Cove. Reserve Gully was so narrow that, in order to find sufficient room, the Battalion had to be dispersed on its two almost perpendicular faces in various degrees of insecurity. To add to their discomfort several men were compelled to sit on ledges where lay in shallow graves the bodies of men killed in the earlier fighting. Above them on the northern side towered the famous Sphinx, the reputed nest of a brood of snipers in the early days of the campaign. A mule-track along the cliff-face linked the troops entrenched on Russell's Top, which ran across the head of the gully, with the supply base at Anzac Cove.

Excepting for the uncanny reverberating crack of bullets flying overhead, no signs were evident either of our troops or the enemy. However, it did not take long for the men of the Seventeenth to complete a mental inventory of their unaccustomed surroundings and, their curiosity aroused, they proceeded individually and in groups to explore the front line in the immediate vicinity of the bivouac.

At 3.0 p.m. instructions were received to proceed to Beauchop's Hill (also known as Little Pope's) towards the left, in the direction of Suvla Bay and with the Eighteenth Battalion to place itself under the command of General Godley. Shortly afterwards the move began in full marching order, each man's equipment weighing about 80 lbs.

Platoons advanced in single file at fifty yards distance, as part of the route, immediately to the left of Anzac Cove, ran for about one hundred yards over a small rise, which was exposed to enemy machine-gun fire at extreme range. This rise was crossed by one platoon at a time at the double into a broad sap on the far side, and as each one came into view from the Turkish positions it was fired on. But they got through without a single casualty.

As the men of the rearmost platoon reached the shelter of the sap, they observed that they were objects of admiration by a group of soldiers belonging to an English Territorial Regiment bivouacked in the vicinity. One of the Tommies said to the platoon sergeant: "Be you sportsmen's battalion—choom?" Apparently these fresh complexioned lads from the Eastern countries regarded our men as the possessors of exceptional physical stamina to be able to double such a distance with full packs up.

It was dusk when the Battalion arrived at its appointed position in reserve behind Beauchop's Hill. It was here that the first casualty occurred. Curiously, it was not the result of enemy action. The weather was extremely hot, and this factor, combined with a certain degree of strain due to their unaccustomed experience, had proved an irresistible temptation to several of the men, who had already drunk the contents of their water bottles. There was no supply at hand to replenish them, although in a nearby gully exposed to the enemy, was a well; but the track leading to it had been picqueted by a detail from A Company. One man, however, was so overcome by thirst, that, in defiance of orders, he attempted to force his way past the sentry and persisted, even when ordered to halt by Corporal A. R. Wolfe, who was in charge of the picquet. Thereupon, the Corporal gave the man the point of his bayonet in the left arm, which effectively stopped him. The first casualty through enemy action was Private W. Booth, D Company, who was wounded on the 20th.†

The concern of the troops over the water problem led to a humorous incident in which one of D Company's men figured. He was Private J. W. Raitt, a young Scotsman, who subsequently rose to be regimental sergeant-major of the Seventeenth. The story is best told in his own words: "A night or two after we arrived on Gallipoli, I was one of a party detailed to try to find water. After wandering about half the night we found an old well somewhere on our left, and got as much water as we could drink.

"Struggling back up the hill, in the morning, we passed a soldier sitting down enjoying a great feed of rissoles. He looked just as grimy as any one of us, and being hungry and tired I sang out: 'Half your luck, mate.' I had passed on a little way, when he got up and hailed me. When I got back to him he asked me where I came from. We talked for a while and then he handed me one of his rissoles and said: 'Off you go and tell your mates you have shared Birdwood's breakfast.'"

It was the corps commander, who habitually wore a shirt, breeches and leggings with a helmet, displaying no badges of rank that would identify him as an officer.

---

† A possible rival for this honour was Cpl. S. H. Hodgetts, B Company, who was severely wounded the same night; Hodgetts, however, was at the time attached to 5th Bde. H.Q He later received a commission in the British Army, from which, subsequently, he was invalided and returned to Australia in 1917.

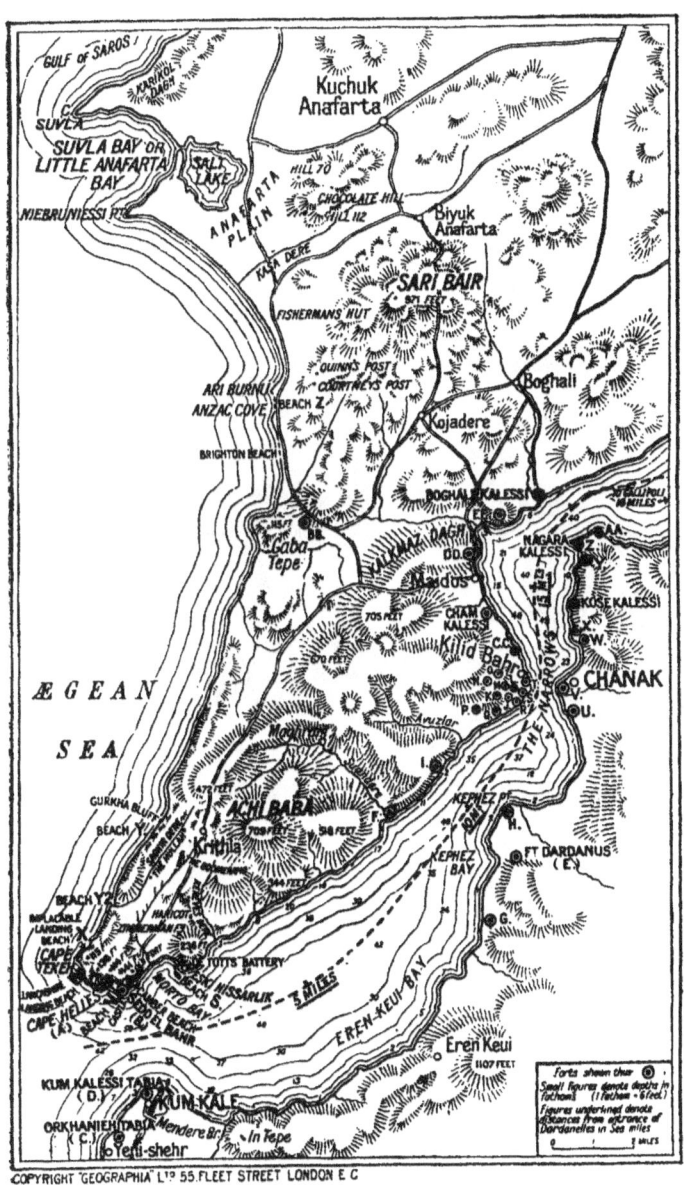

THE GALLIPOLI PENINSULA.

Pte. J. W. Cutting.   Pte. A. H. Hamilton, M.M.

That night the Battalion bivouacked in the open. At 9.25 a.m. the following day, 21st, it received orders to move into Australia Valley, in readiness to support an attack which was to be launched by units of the Anzac Corps as a minor part of an operation that was to be carried out by the IX Corps, the same afternoon, with the object of seizing the hills directly opposite Suvla Bay. At 2.30 p.m. the Battalion moved into position.

Hill 60, the southernmost point of these hills, was the objective set for the Anzac Corps. At 3.30 the attack was launched, but by nightfall only a foothold had been obtained on the hill. It was then realised that the task was too much for troops already worn-out by sickness and hard fighting. The only fresh troops available were units of the 5th Brigade, which were inexperienced. However, General Russell, a New Zealand officer, commanding in that sector of the attack, decided that the hill would have to be captured before daylight, so the Eighteenth Battalion was called on for this purpose.

Without previous reconnaisance the Battalion was launched on the assault. Caught up in machine-gun fire, it suffered the loss of 383 officers and men.

During the previous afternoon, the 21st, the Fourteenth Battalion had assaulted Hill 60 from the south, across the dry bed of a water-course known as the Kaiajik Dere. Troops, numerically inadequate and weakened by hardship and sickness, had been set a task which was beyond their power to accomplish. The advance was brought to a standstill on the farther slope of the dere about 100 yards below the Turkish trenches, where the Fourteenth dug in and held on. Subsequently a sap was cut across the dere, thus linking the new position with the main trench line in the form of a T head. At 8.20 p.m. on the 21st two platoons of the Seventeenth had been detached to reinforce the Thirteenth Battalion, but they were not used and rejoined the main body the following day.

It was while the Battalion was in this sector that it lost its first member killed as the result of enemy action. He was Private G. Tomlinson, of D Company, who was shot dead by a Turkish sniper on the 22nd. Two other men of this company also fell to snipers' bullets. They were Sergeant Luffman and Private A. J. Furless. It will be recalled that Luffman had fallen from the ship into a lighter during the disembarkation at Anzac. Later the same day, he had had another narrow escape while the Battalion was resting in Reserve Gully. A large boulder was dislodged from the ridge above and hurtled down, missing him by inches. Poor Luffman, the third occasion, was not so lucky for him.

On August 23rd, Major Martin received orders that the Seventeenth was to be attached to the 4th Brigade under the command of Colonel Monash, who three years later was to lead the Australian Corps in a series of brilliant victories in France. The task allotted the Seventeenth was to reinforce Monash's depleted battalions in the following order:—A Company to the Thirteenth, B to the Fourteenth, C to the Fifteenth and D Company to the Sixteenth Battalion.

On the 24th, three other ranks were wounded and again on the 25th, Lieutenant B. Holmes, who had recently transferred from the Eighteenth Battalion, and five other ranks were also wounded. Holmes was hit in the head by a piece of shrapnel. On the 27th, Major Travers was wounded and subsequently evacuated.

It was now the turn of the Seventeenth to undergo its baptismal part in the operations. The unsuccessful attacks of the 21st and 22nd had convinced General Birdwood that, as surprise was no longer capable of being employed with effect, it would be a useless waste of lives to launch troops at an enemy ready to reinforce all sides at the point attacked. Moreover, he had not a sufficient number of troops to carry the offensive further, and of those that were available, casualties, sickness, and overstrain had affected the morale of the majority. He, therefore, sought and obtained permission to break-off the offensive.

At the same time, he felt that in order to make his left flank more secure it would be imperative to take the summit of Hill 60. Accordingly, an assaulting force, 1,000 strong, was detailed for this task. It was divided into three groups, right, centre and left. The right group consisted of the following detachments of the 4th Australian Brigade under Colonel Adams:—

Fourteenth Battalion	100 (1st line)
Fifteenth Battalion	50 (1st line)
Sixteenth Battalion	100 (2nd line)
Seventeenth Battalion	100 (3rd line)
Total	350

The centre group comprised 300 New Zealand Mounted Rifles and 100 Eighteenth Battalion, under Major Whyte, a New Zealand officer. Like the right group, it was to be formed up in three lines.

The left flank was made up of 250 Connaught Rangers, under Major Money. A reserve of 50 men of the Seventeenth was provided for the right, and a detachment of another 100 men of the Eighteenth for the centre.

General Russell and Colonel Monash had submitted their joint view to General Cox, who was in control of the operation. They favoured a night attack without bombardment, but General Cox decided that the hill must be assaulted during daylight. Birdwood's plan was to attack the hill simultaneously from three sides, on the 27th, after an hour's bombardment by forty-five land artillery guns and howitzers, assisted by the fire from two cruisers and two destroyers, designed to blot out opposition by the enemy.

The task of the 4th Australian Brigade was to attack across the intervening stretch of open ground sloping upwards, seizing the trench running parallel to and about 100 yards distant, and linking with the centre attack at the point where the trench formed a junction with the maze of trenches interlaced on the western slopes of the hill. The objectives of the centre and left attack groups were these selfsame trenches. The starting lines were those positions finally held as the result of the battle on the 22nd, that of the right attacking group being the line previously mentioned, into which the Fourteenth Battalion had dug itself following that abortive attempt.

During the early afternoon the two platoons of the Seventeenth, numbers 3 and 4, under 2nd-Lieutenants R. C. Anderson and F. Gombert, with Lieutenant R. A. Pye in command, which had been allotted to the third line, together with No. 8 Platoon, Lieutenant D. F. Doull, as reserve platoon, moved out from their respective positions and reported to 4th Brigade Headquarters.

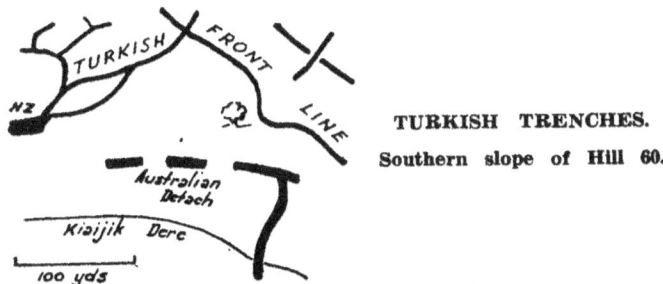

TURKISH TRENCHES.
Southern slope of Hill 60.

The two attack platoons then proceeded up the sap across the Kaiajik Dere, to the advanced trench held by the Fourteenth from which the attack was to be launched. The men of these platoons had been given only a brief description of their part and their officers little opportunity to reconnoitre the positions beforehand. No. 8 Platoon was ordered to take up a position on the south side of the Dere and await further orders.

Each man had been issued with two sand-bags and shovel, as well as bags of "cricket-ball" bombs (in the use of which they had had no previous experience) were distributed. Each man also carried 200 rounds of ammunition and 48 hours rations, consisting of bully beef and biscuits.

At 4.0 p.m. the bombardment opened with a concerted roar from the naval and land guns, and their shells threw clouds of dust skywards as they burst on the crest of the hill, but, unfortunately, none was seen to fall on the trench, which was the objective of the right group of attackers.

One 6-inch shell from a warship burst about 100 yards from No. 8 platoon's position. The noise of the explosion, the thick black cloud of smoke and dust, together with the acrid smell of the fumes, was a distinctly alarming experience for troops as yet unaccustomed to shell-fire. The Turkish reply was not long coming. His shrapnel from guns firing from the direction of Hill 971 enfiladed the jumping-off trench and soon the wounded started to file out through the connecting sap across the dere. The enemy's rifle and machine-gun fire was also terrific. As one man in the attacking party said: "All hearts were throbbing wildly with the excitement of what was to follow."

At 4.30 p.m. the order was given to fix bayonets, and at 5.0 p.m. for the first wave to go over the top. But the trench was both deep and narrow, and no provision had been made to get the assaulting troops out quickly. The consequence was that men fell back shot as they attempted to climb on to the parapet, the few who got out unscathed, lying flat behind any handy clump of bush or feature offering cover from view or from fire and waiting for some sort of line to be formed for the charge.

The first second and third lines suffered heavy casualties from the cruel fire scourging the trench; and then came the Seventeenth's turn. Eagerly the men of A Company scrambled, or were "legged" up on to the parapet, and mingling with the surviving elements of the preceding lines. Gombert, a promising young officer, was killed almost immediately. Pye, another fine subaltern, was severely wounded. For a moment the mixture of several units appeared to be leaderless. Suddenly, from somewhere on the right, a 4th Brigade sergeant jumped up and cried: "Come on, boys," but the gallant fellow was almost immediately hit. However, his example had started the line, which dashed forward.

Men began to fall quickly under the storm of lead, but, possibly because they were fresh and in good condition, eight or nine of the Seventeenth on the left of the charging Australians reached the Turkish trench. The party found that the trench had been evacuated by the enemy, but there were many dead and wounded Turks in it.

Lance-Corporal J. E. Bennett, a red headed, vigorous, athletic and capable leader, immediately assumed command, and proceeded to reconnoitre the position. He found that on the right, about fifty feet, the trench ran to a dead-end, or block, from which a communication sap ran back to a second line, still occupied by the enemy. From his position it was not possible for Bennett to see how much, if any, of the trench to the left was held by the Turks, so he decided to hang on until it was dark. The only ammunition his party had was that carried by each man, in addition to a box of fusee matches and a bag of cricket-ball bombs, which none of the men knew how to use. Their luck held, for the Turks, probably unaware of the weakness of Bennett's party, did not molest them.

At dusk an officer of the 4th Brigade, who, in the meantime had joined Bennett's party, called for volunteers to reconnoitre the left of the position. Private A. H. Hamilton, a mere lad, immediately came forward, and, making his way warily over the bodies of dead Turks which choked the trench, eventually got in touch with the New Zealanders, of the centre party who had gained their objective. The officer to whom Hamilton reported, told him that he would endeavour to reinforce Bennett at the earliest opportunity. Hamilton then returned to Bennett. He found that the officer, who earlier had joined them, had been severely wounded, but the plucky Bennett decided to hold on as long as possible.

At about 9 p.m. the party was reinforced by a detachment of the Ninth Light Horse, which was fortunate, for in the meantime the Turks, having reorganized, launched a solid bombing counter-attack from the right of Bennett's position. But the light horsemen and Bennett's trusty band repulsed them, three of the latter being wounded. When day broke the position was still in our hands.

This episode had its humorous side. Hamilton tells that when the charging detachment was about to jump into the Turkish trench, Private L. H. Dixon slipped and fell backwards on to the corpse of a Turk lying at the bottom. Evidently Adbul had been dead some days. The Turk's viscera was exposed and part of it adhered to the seat of Dixon's breeches. But, critical though the situation, it did not prevent his comrades enjoying the unfortunate Dixon's discomfiture. Soon, however, they were debating in their minds which was worse—fighting the Turks, or being obliged to suffer Dixon's enforced company.

Eventually the plucky band, which had hung on with such tenacity, parched with thirst, and affected by dust and the fumes of bursting shells, was ordered to make its way back and rejoin the main body.

At the same time as Bennett's men were charging across the bullet-swept slope, a dozen others under 2nd-Lieutenant Anderson, with Lance-Sergeant A. F. Gilbert on Bennett's right, made for the trench immediately in front. Several were hit and the remainder went to ground near the parapet from behind which the Turks kept up a hot fire. Gilbert had the skirt of his tunic riddled with bullet-holes, but was himself unharmed. He and a Turk exchanged three shots each, at point blank range, before Gilbert got his man.

Anderson's party had between them a bag of bombs, but no fusee matches. Nothing daunted, the men bowled them at the enemy in the nearby trench. Anderson himself had been wounded, and, as there was no sign of reinforcements arriving, he gave the party, now reduced to six in number, the order to withdraw. This they did successfully, during a brief lull in the firing, and under cover of the haze and smoke.

The extreme left of the Seventeenth's line had better fortune. As each man climbed out of the fire-trench he moved to the flank and lay down in a shallow ditch offering some cover. In charging, they swerved a further slight degree to the left, several, including Privates J. W. Cutting and T. M. Threlfall, reaching that portion of the Turkish trench, which the New Zealanders had succeeded in capturing.

The support platoon, No. 8, was not called on to attack. Twice, in anticipation of such a move, it had been ordered up to the trench from which the attack had been launched, only to find that on each occasion these orders had been countermanded. Subsequently, the platoon was withdrawn, and at dusk was instructed to move across the dere to dig a trench to connect our line with the one just captured by the New Zealanders. Later, they were reinforced by additional details from B Company.

Thus ended the first combat the Seventeenth had entered upon. Actually, the attack itself in this sector was over in a few minutes. It never got properly going; nevertheless, all ranks acquitted themselves bravely in a venture ill-prepared, and launched in the face of point-blank fire, which made the task almost hopeless from the start.

A courageous act was that of Private J. H. Green. Seeing a badly wounded comrade lying out in No Man's Land, he crawled out under a hail of bullets and brought him in. The man was Private C. U. Fuller, who, later, died.

The attacks by the New Zealanders, with the Connaughts on their left were only partly successful, and so that night, and on the following day, the 28th, made every effort to consolidate the position they had won. Meanwhile the sweating, digging party of the Seventeenth toiled desperately to cut a trench in ground almost iron-hard after a hot, rainless summer. They were spurred on to still greater efforts by the shouts and curses of the New Zealanders mingling with the bursting bombs, as the gallant soldiers of the Dominion repelled a succession of counter-attacks delivered by the Turks throughout the night.

To the men of the Seventeenth the whole scene was awe

inspiring. It was something they had not previously visualised. And this effect was scarcely modified by the presence of the corpses of several long-dead Turks, the stench causing men to become violently sick. To remedy this a party was detailed to bury the bodies. Private W. Deonck, a powerfully built young Russian, who had taken part in the charge, was the first to volunteer for the task. Before long he was the sole remaining digger of graves, his mates having become too nauseated to be able to carry on. However, a solution of the problem was soon found. A bargain was made by Deonck and his comrades, whereby the small ration of rum that had been received during the night would be pooled, and issued periodically in doses to Deonck to ensure continuance of the work. It was a complete success. The young Russian's comrades voted him the most cheerful grave-digger they had ever met.

The linking of the positions was continued on the night of the 28th and at one o'clock on the morning of the 29th, the Ninth and Tenth Light Horse, assisted by the Eighteenth Battalion, attacked with bomb and bayonet, and although they succeeded in capturing only portion of the hill the ground gained sufficiently commanded the position to the north, thereby securing the left flank of the Anzac Corps.

The Seventeenth's first action was costly in relation to the numbers engaged, the total casualties being one officer and three other ranks killed and two officers and twenty-three other ranks wounded. Those killed were 2nd-Lieutenant F. Gombert and Privates B. W. Yeomans, M. Chapman, and S. G. Schweitzer. Of the number wounded Sergeant J. T. Robertson and Privates C. U. Fuller, J. Laing, T. Bowmaker and F. Groome, subsequently died. In addition thirty-seven other ranks were reported missing, but the majority of these were eventually accounted for. They had become involved with units of the centre attacking force, those who were wounded having been evacuated through other regimental aid posts. The total casualties of the right attacking force totalled 230.

The Battle of Hill 60 had ended. It also marked the close of the operations which began on August 6th, and as events proved, it was the last major operation of the Gallipoli campaign until the evacuation. From the Australian Official History it is learned that General Hamilton's plan to seize the waist of the peninsula when he had sufficient reinforcements had to be discarded. The War Office told him that none could be spared for this purpose, as the French and British governments were engaged in mounting a large scale offensive on the Western Front. Hamilton, therefore, decided to wait a more favourable opportunity to strike, meanwhile reorganizing his front and resting his tired troops. In the process of this adjustment the 2nd Division was given the honour of holding the right-centre of the thirteen-mile front held by the British armies.

The dispositions of the battalions of the 5th Brigade in the new sector were as follows: The Seventeenth to hold Quinn's; the Nineteenth Pope's and the Twentieth Battalion (which had held it since the 26th) Russell's Top. The Eighteenth Battalion, now only 363 strong as the result of the heavy casualties it had suffered in the attacks on Hill 60, was to be held in reserve.

The plan was not given immediate effect. Upon the arrival of the Seventeenth at the rendezvous in Monash Valley (at the rear of Quinn's Post), on September 4th, fresh orders were received for half of the Battalion to take over Pope's Post to the left and slightly in rear of Quinn's. These two posts were at the time held by the 1st Light Horse Brigade, which had made such a gallant charge during the August operations, and had suffered heavy casualties. Many of their dead were still lying in the narrow No Man's Land, where they had fallen, it being found impossible to bring in their bodies, even at night.

Pope's was named after Colonel Pope of the Sixteenth Battalion, under whose command the Seventeenth was during the recent operations. Pope had barely escaped capture on this selfsame spot on the night of April 25th, by rolling down the hill, just as a party of Turks, pretending to be British officers of an Indian regiment, tried to seize him.‡

The change-over with the light horse units holding Quinn's and Pope's was effected without loss, and all ranks proceeded to settle down to their first real experience of trench warfare. The new position, for the next four months, was held by the Seventeenth without respite and the Battalion suffered all the rigours attendant upon disease, climate, hard diet and a chronic shortage of water.

On September 7th. Colonel Goddard rejoined the unit, after the illness, which, at the end of July, had compelled him to temporarily relinquish the command. From this date, until the evacuation in the following December, upon the "Old Man's" shoulders rested the responsibility of organizing and maintaining an ever watchful defence of Quinn's, a key-position. This, situated precariously on the rear edge of a ridge, afforded no opportunity for the siting, locally, of effective support and reserve trenches, thus rendering it vulnerable to a sudden and swift attack. Faithfully and well this trust was executed by Colonel Goddard and his men.

September 8th marked the date upon which the 5th Brigade reverted to the 2nd Division, after the brief period of its attachment to the 4th Brigade. On the 10th, the Divisional Com-

---

‡In 1917 Colonel Pope gave the writer the full details of this ruse by which the Turks succeeded in capturing two officers and a private of the 16th. Undoubtedly it was Pope's sagacity that saved him from a similar fate.

mander, General Legge, paid a visit of inspection to the positions held by the Seventeenth, as well as the bivouacks and shelters in which they were quartered. Commenting on the "dug-out" which had been constructed for the Regimental Medical Officer, Captain Smith, General Legge remarked "that it was the most comfortably furnished one that he had seen on Gallipoli."**

Smith was a big man, weighing about seventeen stone, and had been a champion oarsman. His casual manner and the apparent indifference he displayed when conducting the daily sick-parade, had earned for him the soubriquet of "White Ghurka," but it was only the malingerers who had any real reason to regard him in this light. In his relations with this obnoxious minority, his attitude was unequivocally callous, leaving not the least room for doubt on that score. When Sergeant Luffman fell wounded by a sniper's bullet, the previous month, and the stretcher-bearers could not get their stretchers into the narrow trench, it was Smith who went up and hoisted the stricken man on to his own shoulders and carried him down to the Regimental Aid Post. It was a fine feat of strength, for Luffman himself was a heavy man.

Between Sept. 3rd and 13th, the casualty list, though not heavy, showed that a steady toll was beginning to be taken of the defenders, mainly as the result of bomb splinters, one other rank being killed and twenty wounded during this period. As the days passed, sickness also helped to swell the quota of casualties. One of the first cases was Major Martin, who was evacuated to hospital on the 15th. He had successfully guided the Battalion through its initial trials and had remained long enough to hand over the reins to Colonel Goddard. He was not away very long, and rejoined the unit at Quinn's.

The following day, Lieutenant Sheppard, D. Company, was severely wounded and the 2nd Reinforcement contingent for the Battalion arrived in charge of two new officers, Lieutenants B. Mendelsohn and C. Doone.

All ranks were rapidly becoming accustomed to the unusual conditions, as well as to a type of warfare, of which they had little conception. Their training had been concentrated on methods of attack; nevertheless, the present situation was regarded merely as a prelude to wider operations. Their high spirits remained unaffected, despite the casualties suffered in their first encounter with the Turks. They performed their tasks cheerfully, regardless of the drudgery of fatigues and the lack of opportunity for any kind of recreation, while their innate good humour and willingness to share the good with the bad, helped to minimise the unavoidable discomforts of their surroundings.

** Diary of Pte. J. C. Black, A.A.M.C. details attached 17th Battalion.

A typical instance of this cheerful attitude is revealed in the following incident, which occurred during this period. A number of Indian muleteers had just been landed and the authorities desired to find men who could speak Hindustani, to act as guides for the mule-trains bringing rations from the beach. In No. 6 Platoon, were two typical "hard-doers," a cockney lad, F. C. ("Tony") Mines and his bosom friend, a Welshman R. ("Bill") Morgan, a stutterer. Relating the incident, Lieutenant Hárnett, commander of the platoon, tells that he entered a bay of the trench in which was a group of his men, including these two worthies, and said: "Are there any men here who can speak Hindustani?" Like a shot, Mines replied: "No, sir, but there's a bloke here who speaks 'hindistinctly.'"

Further re-adjustments were about to be made in the dispositions of units in the sector, and on September 17th orders were received for the half-battalion of the Seventeenth to hand over Pope's to the Nineteenth Battalion on the following day.

(TOP)—BATHING AT ANZAC.
(BOTTOM)—WAITING FOR THE MAIL.

CHAPTER IV.

Quinn's Post a key position—Defended by bombing and mining—Inspection by General Birdwood—Disease causes many casualties—First commissions in the field—An unofficial armistice—Lord Kitchener arrives at Anzac—Decision to evacuate peninsula—Private "Tiger" Meahan has a grim forebodng—Troops suffer privations—"The Silent Stunt"—Lance-Corporal J. Aitken meets a brave Turk—Blizzard causes havoc—Evacuation.

QUINN'S POST was the furthermost position held after the sustained operations extending from April 25th to the early part of June, had died down. Perhaps, on no other part of the front had there been such fierce hand-to-hand fighting, with its attendant heavy casualties. Several times during the month following the landing, the post had been all but lost. The courage and tenacity of its defenders defied every attempt on the part of the Turks to shake their hold; and, between periods of bloody combat, they worked like Trojans to consolidate their hard-won gains.

Quinn's was named after Major H. Quinn of the Fifteenth Battalion. He was killed on May 29th whilst leading a charge to push the Turkish line back from the rear lip, or edge, of the narrow ridge on which the post was precariously situated. Its right flank linked with Courtney's Post and its left rested on a steep and narrow re-entrant called the "Bloody Angle." It was, therefore, in the air, so to speak. The post situated next on the left of Quinn's was named Pope's Post. It was on a ridge somewhat to the rear of, and divided from Quinn's, by the "Bloody Angle," and the right, or eastern branch of Monash Valley, between the Y-shaped arms of which the post lay.

Quinn's Post was about 250 yards in length, and, there was no ground in the immediate rear on which could be sited fire-support trenches. It was divided into six sub-sections numbered one to six, and at the time the Seventeenth took it over there existed a maze of saps, surface tunnels, and mine-shafts, tributes to the assiduous labours of earlier occupants. The three right-hand sub-sections consisted of open trenches, with here and there saps pushed forward to serve as observation posts in No Man's Land, which, at that point was too wide to permit of throwing hand-bombs. Numbers four, five and six, being very close to the Turkish front-line trench, were partly covered by heavy beams topped by soil as a protection from bombs. The uncovered portions were called bombing-pits. It was from these positions our bombers hurled their missiles over six-feet high strips of wire netting, erected on the parapet as a measure of protection from enemy bombs.

The nature of the soil permitted of the digging to a depth of seven feet, without the necessity of revetting the trenches. Fire-steps were cut at intervals and at a height convenient for the average sized man.

In the rear of the three left sub-sections, the ground fell somewhat steeply into Monash Valley, 130 feet below at the point where its Y-shaped arms forked. In order to maintain communications with Quinn's, a broad sap leading from the valley had been cut along a buttress-like feature that rose to a point overlooking the crest of the ridge on which was situated the opposing trenches. The grade, however, was so steep that steps had to be cut in the sap, which forked at a point about fifty yards from the front line trench.

A short distance from the left arm of the fork, headquarters was located. A little to the left were terraces upon which shelters had been erected for the troops detailed as immediate supports. There was also a tin-roofed cook-house, and sand-bagged shelters designed for the use of the regimental aid-post and other offices. Below these terraces and about halfway down the steep slope of the hill, more terraces had been cut to house the troops detailed as local reserves; the general reserve being bivouacked in Wellington Gully leading from Monash Valley to Russell's Top.

Because of the peculiar tactical position, the defence scheme for Quinn's depended mainly upon covering fire from the neighbouring posts—Courtney's and Steel's, which enfiladed it from the right, and Pope's and Russell's semi-enfilading, as well as overhead covering positions from the left rear. From the top of the buttress-like feature machine-gun positions commanded a wide arc, and from there also our snipers and observers carried out their allotted tasks.

In order to counteract the effect of this tactical disability, resort was made to the bomb and the mine from the very inception of the defence. Thereafter, throughout their eight months tenure of Quinn's, the Australians, realising there existed only one safe method of holding such a position, maintained a continuous offensive with these weapons. The Turks were never permitted to snatch the initiative, good bombers and persistent diggers though they were.

An inspection of the map, which shows details of the mining scheme, will convey an idea of the vast amount of effort and skill applied to the construction of the maze of tunnels and galleries.

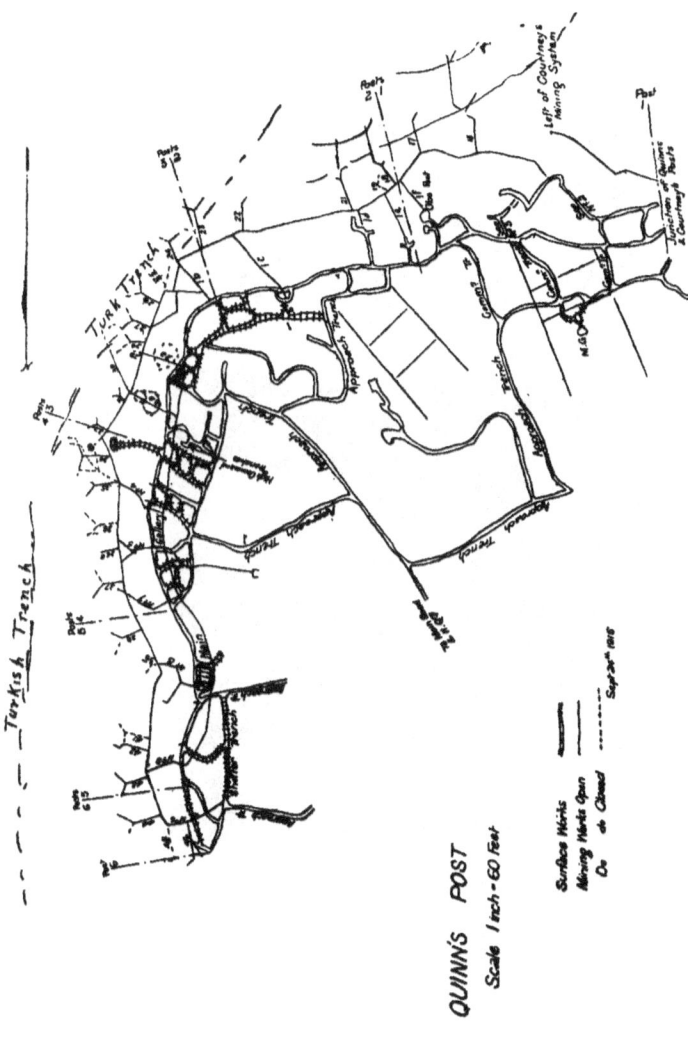

TRENCHES AND MINING SYSTEM, QUINN'S POST.

COLONEL GODDARD ON QUINN'S POST.

Capt. C. N. Smith, R.M.O., in background.

The Battalion intelligence reports, with their daily record of progress, literally by feet and inches, in the direction of vital spots under the enemy trenches, together with the counter-measures employed to defeat his attempts in the opposite direction, disclose a striking testimony to the hardihood and tenacity of the devoted band of men employed on the work. They carried on with their tasks in the face of conditions calculated to test both the physical and moral fibre of the strongest and bravest.

That other offensive weapon, the bomb, which was the product of the close-up trench warfare that had developed, had never figured in the training for war of the infantryman. In consequence, when the necessity for its employment was fully realised, both the manufacture and the training in its use had to be hastily improvised. The first bombs used on the peninsula were made from jam tins filled with explosive and pieces of metal, with a time-fuse. They were known as "jam-tins," but later were replaced by a cast-iron missile, about the size and shape of a cricket-ball, from which it derived its name, and weighing about two pounds. The Australians soon became expert in handling and throwing them, which was effected by a bowling motion of the arm.

Subsidiary to the hand-bomb was the mortar, of which there were two in use at Quinn's, the Japanese‡ and the Garland. The first-named was a well-constructed weapon, although neither accurate nor reliable. Its weight and explosive charge were calculated to do damage to both material and morale. On the other hand, the Garland mortar, or gun, as it was better known, though primitive in both design and construction, was an accurate and effective weapon when served by men skilled in estimating angles and distances. Its barrel was made of a short piece of iron piping, attached to a base-plate and threw a jam-tin bomb, its effective range being about 100 yards.

The method employed in manning Quinn's is set out in the Appendix. The garrisons of the six sub-sections were divided into two shifts, each of six hours. The off-duty shifts were accommodated in the support trenches, so called, situated a few yards in rear of the fire-trench, while to the rear of these, in the vicinity of Battalion Headquarters, the command-post, in charge of an officer of company-commander's rank, was located. Periodically the garrison troops were withdrawn, either to the

---

*The existence of this bomb was responsible for a whimsical story that went the rounds of the trenches. An Australian soldier is supposed to encounter a gigantic Turk, who has wandered into Monash Valley. The Turk is carrying a Japanese bomb in a sack thrown over his shoulder. To the astonished Australian's question: "What the hell are you doing here?" the Turk replies: "I am the champion bomb-thrower of the Turkish Army, and I should like to shake hands with the bloke who threw this one!"

local reserve, or to Wellington Gully, for a rest. This, however, comprised regular fatigues, and the "benefit" derived from the change was often the subject of humorous questioning by the troops. From the reserve was furnished a nightly picquet, which pushed out under cover of darkness to the junction of the eastern arm of Monash Valley and the "Bloody Angle" re-entrant. This picquet was known as the "Bloody Angle Picquet."

Returning to the front line, a study of the map will reveal that numbers 4, 5 and 6 sub-sections formed the key-point of the defence of Quinn's. It was from this sector that a regular bombing was maintained, both day and night, by hefty men who could throw accurately upon targets situated twenty to thirty yards distant. For the protection of these bombers, six-foot strips of wire-netting had been erected on the parapets of the bombing-pits, thereby reducing the target area for enemy bombs. At intervals, leading to the rear, safety-saps had been dug as protection from any bombs that might fall into the trench.

The task of the bomber was a dangerous one and required the utmost degree of coolness, judgment and the ability to think and act quickly. There was never any dearth of applicants to fill vacancies caused by casualties. To men accustomed to making snap-decisions during a surging forward rush on the football field, or countering instantaneously with eye, wrist and foot, the wiles of an opposing bowler, the handling and throwing of bombs came as second nature. But it was not always the enemy's bombs that were the menace. Occasionally, faulty manufacture, or maladjustment of a fuse would result in a premature explosion, at times with fatal results to the thrower.

At one period there was a succession of similar incidents that caused grave concern, owing to the casualties thus caused. At first, the cause of these premature bursts was attributed to carelessness, born of familiarity on the part of bombers holding the missiles too long after the fuses had been lit.

A detailed investigation revealed that the accidents were not due to faulty manufacture or fusing, but to the custom, adopted by bombers on duty in the pits, of fraying the fuses in order to facilitate their ignition. Some of the bombs so treated might not be thrown before the bomber went off duty and the relief man would probably quite unwittingly repeat the fraying process, thereby shortening the length of the fuse by an additional second or two. Steps were, thereupon, taken to remedy this faulty system, with correspondingly fewer accidents resulting from premature bursts.

There was another type of hand-bomb, which was called the

STEPS CUT IN SAP LEADING TO QUINN'S POST.

THE GARLAND GUN, QUINN'S POST.

PTE. W. V. ANDERSON WITH SNIPER'S RIFLE, QUINN'S POST.

Lotbiniere. It consisted of dynamite affixed to a slab of wood, with a handle attached. This bomb was designed mainly for use in the demolition of heavy timbered overhead trench cover. Its value was somewhat limited.

Quinn's was so close to the Turkish trenches, that it was courting certain death to expose one's head above the parapet, even for a moment or two. Periscopes were introduced to facilitate observation; but even this method was fraught with danger. The upper mirror of the periscope provided an easy target for enemy snipers, whose shooting was most accurate. Several casualties were caused through fragments of the shattered mirror inflicting jagged wounds on the head of the observer. There was also a periscope attachment which could be fitted on a rifle, intended for close-range sniping. These were, at best, clumsy arrangements, and employable only under specially favourable conditions.

Such was Quinn's Post, which, for the next three months was destined to be held at the price of many stout-hearted fellows. These, in the bombing-pits, the observation posts, and by their labour in the mine galleries, rendered invaluable, although unspectacular service in defence of that hard-won strip of territory to which our Forces clung precariously, while preparations were being made for further large-scale offensives—preparations, however, destined to be turned from an advance into a retreat, from promised victory, to failure, albeit a glorious failure.

On September 18th, the half-battalion garrisoning Pope's Post was relieved by the Nineteenth. It was on this same day that Captain Lonsdale was wounded by a Turkish bomb, and subsequently died. On the 23rd, General Birdwood visited Quinn's, remaining in that area sufficiently long to make a thorough inspection, both of the defences as well as of the troops manning them.

The General told Colonel Goddard he was very pleased with the way in which the Seventeenth had held Pope's Post. This compliment was received with gratification by all ranks.

The visit, however, did not prove to be such a happy augury for the Intelligence Officer of the Seventeenth, 2nd-Lieutenant Doull, recently appointed to that post. Doull was sitting in the sand-bag structure erected as an office, when it collapsed. One of the support-beams of the roof fell across one of his thighs and breaking it, eventually causing him to be invalided to Australia.

The Battalion had now been one month on Gallipoli and the losses incurred during the combat at Hill 60 had been made up by the arrival of the 2nd Reinforcements. Still the rigorous conditions prevailing on that unhealthy terrain were beginning

OCEAN BEACH, ANZAC.

to show in the tale of rapidly mounting casualties. Disease was entering the lists in competition with the bomb and the bullet, and whereas up to September 29th, one officer and twelve other ranks had been killed; seven officers and thirty other ranks wounded, and thirty-eight other ranks missing, in the same period disease and sickness had resulted in the evacuation of no fewer than two officers and one hundred and fifteen other ranks.

One of the officers, Lieutenant Nunn, a mere lad, who, although stricken with dysentery and suffering from a badly injured foot, which had caused him to be evacuated on two occasions, refused to remain away from the unit. But, on September 28th, he broke down altogether, and was evacuated to Egypt, and subsequently invalided to Australia. Recovering his health, he rejoined the unit in France, about the middle of 1916. After a few days, however, he had a relapse and was again returned to his homeland, there, eventually, to give up his young life.

The hard and almost unvarying rations of "bully-beef," biscuits, bacon and jam, soon became unpalatable and this factor, combined with the constant strain of work, with little time and few facilities for adequate rest, brought about a general lowering of physical resistance of which the spread of jaundice was symptomatic‡. Indeed, the physical condition of the troops was becoming so debilitated that the slightest scratch on the skin frequently would become septic, closely resembling the complaint, which, in Australia is known as "barcoo rot."

Most baneful of all the plagues were the swarms of flies that settled everywhere, even on the food as it was being passed to the mouth, while body lice, which, in the absence of ablution facilities, thrived out of hand.

Washing of clothes was almost out of the question, and whilst sea-bathing offered certain facilities for easing the problem of personal cleanliness, even this apparent boon was fraught with danger from enemy guns. These enfiladed the beach at Anzac Cove from positions further south, and caused many casualties amongst the bathers, as well as the troops drawing stores and materials from the huge dumps in the vicinity.

Sickness proved to be no respecter of rank. Between October 7th and 24th, Major Pye, Major (Temp) Brown, Captain Beiers, Lieutenants Spier, McCulloch, Shaw, McBride, Doone and Chaplain Colwell were evacuated. Though this was unfortunate for the officers concerned, the vacancies thus caused resulted in the promotion of junior officers and in the grants of commissions to several warrant-officers and sergeants. The

‡The ration scale is shown in APPENDIX and was extracted from 2nd Division Order No. 23 of September 1st, 1915.

following subalterns received their step in rank:—Lieutenant B. Holmes, who had rejoined early in October, to Captain, and Lieutenants E. T. Harnett and C. R. Lucas, to Temporary Captains. Those promoted 2nd-Lieutenants were Regimental Sergeant-Major F. B. Cheadle; Regimental Quarter-Master Sergeant C. Tims; Company Sergeant-Majors J. J. Fay, W. J. S. O'Grady, F. G. Rae, H. Ronald; Company Quarter-Master Sergeant A. S. Taplin; Sergeants F. W. Moulsdale, G. W. Norris. E. L. Lowther, W. A. Robertson, K. W. Mackenzie, W. H. Palmer, C. C. Finlay and G. J. Richards, the latter from 5th Brigade Headquarters.

Subsequently, further adjustments were effected by the transfer to the Eighteenth Battalion of Captain E. W. Kirke, Lieutenant H. L. Bruce (with rank of Captain) and 2nd-Lieutenants F. B. Cheadle and W. J. S. O'Grady, to replace casualties suffered by that unit in the August operations against Hill 60.

On October 12th an additional intake to the Battalion's strength occurred by the arrival of the 3rd Reinforcements in charge of Captain C. E. Cooke, and 2nd-Lieutenant J. P. Caddy, who, however, soon after his arrival fell ill and eventually was evacuated. But even this fairly considerable reinforcement only partially compensated for the steady decline in the unit's numerical strength, as will be seen by the following comparison between the strengths as at the date it landed on Galipoli and October 17th, the day on which the summary was made:—

	Officers.	Other Ranks.
Landed on Gallipoli	32	938
2nd Reinforcements	2	128
3rd Reinforcements	2	81
	36	1,147
Add Colonel Goddard	1	
Total	37	1,147

Effective strength as at 17/10/'15: 26 officers, 766 other ranks.

Despite the ordeal to which they were subjected, the troops readily forgot their trials on those occasions, infrequent though they were, which marked the arrival of parcels containing comforts from home, or, perhaps, a special issue of tinned fruit or strawberry jam. Mail-days were regarded somewhat in the light of feast-days, or, at any rate, judging by their frequent mention in the soldiers' diaries, events of such importance as to be worthy of special record and often comprising the sole entry for the day.

One such may be quoted, although, in this case, what promised to be a day of festival for the diarist, Corporal C. C. Brindley, proved to be one of mourning. Its succinct phrasing indicates the intensity of the writer's feelings. It ran thus: "Today some blighter pinched our issue of six tins of strawberry jam. I hope his guts ache."

Occasionally, opportunities would present themselves for individuals to proceed to Imbros, an island a few miles from Anzac, to purchase delicacies from the Expeditionary Force Canteen. Usually one man would be delegated the task of purchasing on behalf of a group of his comrades, and these occasions were regarded in the light of red-letter days by the troops. One such event was made memorable, though not in the way that the principals most immediately concerned could have wished. A member of B Company had been provided by his officers with a goodly sum of money wherewith to purchase whatsoever luxuries and extras could be obtained. He duly journeyed to the Island, but when he returned to the fold, in due course, sans luxuries, sans extras, sans everything—excepting two strings of dried figs and a handful of Egyptian piastres, there was gloom amongst his superiors whose trust he had betrayed and who had pinned their faith in him. The ingenious reason given by the defaulter for the non-fulfilment of his mission, combined with the wide personal popularity he enjoyed, caused his offence to be forgiven.*

The routine of trench-warfare went on from one day to another, relieved only by lively exchanges of bombs as an antidote to total boredom. One unusual incident on the morning of October 19th provided something in the nature of a relief from this monotonous situation when the Turks threw a weighted object into No. 3 sub-section. Wrapped round it was a note written in French requesting the Australians to throw them a tin of bully-beef. The request was promptly complied with.

Back came a second note, this time asking for a tin-opener. In response a jack-knife with such an attachment was tossed across to the enemy, but it fell short of the trench. A third note, asking for immunity while the knife was being retrieved, read: "We knew you were gentlemen, but why do you throw bombs?" It went on to congratulate the British on the recent victory in France (Loos) and the taking of 23,000 prisoners. The note also claimed that the Australians were not their enemies, but that the British were, and after wishing their opponents the compliments of the season (it was a Turkish feast day) concluded: "We are your brother soldiers," and was signed, "A Turkish Soldier"! †

This incident led to fraternisation between our men and the

---

*Private, later Lieut. H. J. Smith, one of the Battalion "hard cases," who subsequently earned the sobriquet "Smith of the A.I.F."

† From the Diary of Pte. J. C. Black.

Turks. During this period, Lieutenant Manefield walked across No Man's Land, unmolested, to the parapet of the enemy trench. But, acting upon a signal from the Turks, which indicated the approach of some one in authority, each side retired to its own lines. The whole affair occupied only a few minutes. A repetition of this unofficial armistice took place the following morning, but, thereafter, ceased upon instructions being received from 5th Brigade Headquarters.

Towards the end of October, rumours began to circulate that Gallipoli was to be evacuated. They gained some credence after the inspection of the position by General Monro, who had been sent out by the British Government to specially report on the situation.

According to the Australian Official War Historian, Monro's telegraphed report to the War Office, among other conclusions submitted, expressed the firm view that two main factors, the oncoming winter and the anticipated massing of heavy enemy artillery, which would be made possible as the result of the fall of Servia, would render Gallipoli untenable. In the meantime, Sir Ian Hamilton had been recalled to England, and Lord Kitchener, upon receiving Monro's report, decided to go to Gallipoli and personally examine the position. On November 13th he arrived at Anzac and the news spread quickly amongst the troops in the vicinity of the beach. Eagerly men jostled one another to get a close-up view of the great soldier. As his tall, bulky figure moved slowly through the press of men someone called for a cheer. He told them that the King had wished him to say how much he admired their conduct and bravery.

Lord Kitchener's inspection confirmed Monro's views, and as a result he ordered plans to be prepared with utmost secrecy for an evacuation. Birdwood, who was now in command of the forces on Gallipoli, instructed his chief-of-staff, Colonel White, to proceed immediately with their preparation.

It is now necessary to go back to late in October to pick up the thread of the story and refer to the Seventeenth's diary. This indicates that by this period the first bleak signs of approaching winter were manifesting themselves in chilly nights and some heavy rainfalls. It also records that on the 23rd Lord Kitchener sent a message stressing the need for the construction of deep shelters for protection against the elements, as well as enemy shells. This work was begun immediately. Soon, deep, underground chambers were excavated and fitted out as sleeping quarters immediately in rear of the front-line trench, but, they were not put to the full use for which they were intended. The imperative need at that time for such preparations was exemplified in the simple, expressive sentences recorded in Private A. Morris's diary, thus:—"It was very cold last night. The wind blows through the narrow trenches and is very keen. The food here, now, is very much 'off,' and the cooks are not much good. We get rice for breakfast, fat bacon for dinner and bully-beef stew for tea. No bread to-day." And a few days later:—"It is very cold here at night, now, and gales are blowing at sea. We had boiled onions for tea to-night. . . ."

The advent of winter produced no event of great importance. The records merely showed that on November 3rd, Lieutenant H. W. Johnson was promoted Temporary Captain, followed on the 9th by Lieutenants L. G. Fussell and E. T. Manefield, similarly elevated, while Sergeant J. Miller was given commissioned rank.

On the night of the 6th a diversion was caused by the Turks exploding a mine under number 6 sub-section, killing two men and wounding one. On the 9th, the Seventeenth retaliated by blowing up a section of Turkish trench. The enemy, about this time, began to use a stick-bomb projected from a mortar. It seldom did any damage, as almost invariably the stick, or tail, became detached from the bomb whilst in mid air, thereby rendering the missile very inaccurate. One, however, did score a direct hit on the cook-house, on the upper terrace, near Battalion Headquarters, wounding a cook.

Several previous attempts had proved ineffective, although they had contrived to instil in the mind of one of the assistant cooks, Pte. A. J. Meehan, known as "Tiger," a deep pessimism and a dark foreboding. On the morning in question, when he happened to be standing with a mate near the door of Colonel Goddard's shelter, and heard the "plop" of the Turkish mortar, Meehan's gaze was immediately directed to the skyline where it met the crest of Quinn's. With an accuracy of eye, bred of dodging previous similar bombardments, he saw that this time the Turkish gunner was about to score a hit. Thereupon, he began a running verbal commentary on the flight of the bomb. "Look," he cried, grabbing his mate by the shoulders and shaking him violently, while the bomb lurched upwards to its culminating point holding Meehan's fascinated gaze—"Here it comes—didn't I tell you? Right through the bloody cook-house—right through the bloody cook-house!"

Great was his consternation when he beheld that the man he had been misusing so forcefully was none other than Colonel Goddard, who had quietly stepped into the place hurriedly vacated by "Tiger's" mate. The latter had decided "to stay not upon the order of his going," or, in the more picturesque Australian phraseology—"to beat the gun."

The weather was daily becoming colder and the wind more boisterous, culminating in a violent storm on the night of November 17th. This struck the whole of the peninsula, causing many deaths through drowning, of Turkish, British and Indian troops in the trenches situated in the lower levels of the country north of Anzac, and at the same time turning the numerous narrow ravines intersecting the position into raging torrents.

In Wellington Gully the floodwater quickly undermined the terraces on the lower sides of the Gully sweeping away any material, food, arms or equipment that fell within its reach. The Battalion reserve, suffered particularly heavily, and when morning broke fine, the area presented a truly forlorn appearance. The sorely-tried residents did their best to salvage equipment and personal belongings from the river of liquid mud left by the angry waters, as they rushed to the sea, via the main drain of Monash Valley. With typically cheerful optimism the troops set in to rebuild their ruined bivouacs and terraces, and dry their sodden garments.

The incident provided a warning of what might be expected during the course of a winter campaign in that inhospitable

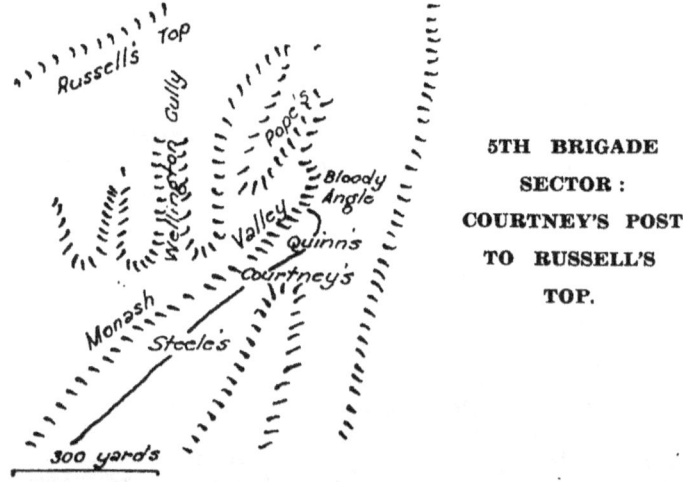

5TH BRIGADE SECTOR: COURTNEY'S POST TO RUSSELL'S TOP.

country. To make matters worse, the damage done by the storm was so widespread that the supply channels were seriously interrupted and the water position, always a source of anxiety, became most acute. Indeed, it was so critical that the only water issued during the week ended November 20th was one-quarter of a mess-tin per man, daily.

The arrivals of comforts were becoming both irregular and scanty, and, therefore, their advent was hailed with almost boyish delight by the luxury-starved troops, who, after their three months stay on the peninsula, were beginning to display increasing evidence of the strain, both on their morale and their physique. An entry in Private Morris's diary, dated November

11th, reads:—"We got our comforts to-day. They consisted of half a cake of chocolate, four small biscuits, two sticks of chewing-gum and two cigarettes (per man). This is not considered too bad under the circumstances."

Amidst this unpleasant prospect, there were consoling interludes in the fairly regular arrival of letters and reading matter. The diaries consistently mention the receipt of messages from loved ones far away in the homeland, almost invariably according first place in the record to "Mother."

In the middle of November it was notified to all and sundry that it was the intention of a Committee formed for the purpose, to publish a book entirely composed of contributions by the troops, in which would be included items of poetry and prose, besides illustrations, either serious or humourous in character. Several hundred contributions were received and the diversity of literary and artistic talent disclosed in the majority of these immediately ensured success of the production. It was called the Anzac Book, and, as the Editor said, "It called for an unusual degree of ingenuity on the part of contributors in making the best use of such materials as Anzac contained—any odd bits of white paper, red and blue pencils and even toilet brushes." Private V. N. Hopkins, of the Army Medical Corps details, attached to the Seventeenth, sent a short poem—a little gem—which was published under the title: "From Quinn's Post."

The Official History tells that the framing of plans for the evacuation of Gallipoli involved the consideration of two essential factors; firstly, the withdrawal would have to take place over a period of days in successive stages, and, secondly, the enemy must be tricked into believing, up to the last moment, that the position was being held in force.

The plan submitted by Colonel White, and subsequently adopted, provided for the withdrawal to be effected in two stages, covering a period of ten days. The first was to be occupied in the evacuation of men and material over and above the minimum required for the defence of the position, absolute secrecy being employed. The second, and final stage, would cover two days and entail holding the line to the last moment with a greatly reduced garrison, while a further gradual process of thinning out was being effected, no attempt, however, being made to save any material. In order to keep up the appearance of normal conditions, it was arranged that shipping in the offing would maintain their usual activity. Further, in order to delude the enemy into the belief, during this second stage, that the position was being strongly held, it would be necessary to begin at once to accustom him to the gradual reduction of activity consequent upon the thinning-out process.

The most critical period would be the last few hours, during which the troops left in the front line would be so thinly strung out that only a few hundred men would be holding the Anzac-Suvla Bay front, and consequently it would be impossible to maintain the normal activities carried out at night. As a precautionary measure mines were to be laid at various points on the central sector of the Anzac front, fifteen tons in all being subsequently placed ready for firing in case of emergency. It was decided to inaugurate this game of deception by ordering a complete cessation of bombing, rifle, machine-gun and artillery fire for two days along the whole front, which would be broken only if the enemy attacked in force. There also was to be a complete absence of movement during this period, which was set down to commence as darknness fell on November 24th and would last throughout the following day and night. All work underground was to cease at 6 p.m. on the 24th.

At nightfall on the 24th, the sudden complete cessation of the din of bursting bombs and the rattle of machine-gun and rifle fire to which they had been accustomed, nightly, for such a long period, produced a feeling no less eerie and strange in the minds of the defenders, as it must have proved mystifying to the Turks, whose feelings were indicated by the increased intensity of their bombing, several fusilades falling just short of the parapet in front of the centre sub-sections. Gradually, as the night wore on, the enemy bombing became intermittent, then ceased, and the silence that had descended like a pall seemed to be almost tangible. Dawn was welcomed as a relief from a period which had produced an unusual degree of nervous strain on the troops. On the other hand the Turks by this time were displaying much curiosity as to what might be afoot, for, as it began to get light, the men of the Seventeenth, behind their loopholes and "possies", observed numerous periscopes in the opposite trench, some of them being waved to and fro as though endeavouring to draw our fire.

Suddenly, observers on Steele's Post, next to Courtney's, which afforded an enfilade view of No Man's Land in front of Quinn's, saw a party of Turks emerge from the trench in front of number 3 sub-section and drop down into some old craters a short distance ahead. A moment or two later six of their number made straight for the bomb-proof screen in front of the sub-section. They pulled the screen aside, and then threw a bomb into the adjoining covered portion of the trench. Lance-Corporal J. Aitken of D Company, moving along the semi-darkness of the trench to investigate the cause of the explosion, saw a dim figure moving towards him and, thereupon, promptly challenged. To his amazement, he was greeted with the cry: "Allah!" Aitken, recalling the instructions to refrain from firing, lunged at the Turk with his bayonet. This his opponent grasped with his left hand, while with his right he tried to pull a pistol from the pocket of the greatcoat he was wearing. Aitken, although a powerful man, had only recently returned to duty after a bout of dysentery, and was still in a somewhat weakened condition. He soon found himself in difficulties with the Turk, who, still grasping the bayonet, was trying to shoot Aitken "from the hip," meanwhile calling out "Allah!"

At that moment, Aitken lost his balance and fell on his back into one of the safety saps leading from the rear of the trench. In the act of falling he dragged his rifle from the Turk's grasp. In a moment he was on his feet again and gave his opponent the point of his bayonet in the ribs.

The other five Turks threw bombs into the trench, slightly wounding three men, and then fled to the safety of their own trenches. Not a shot was fired at them, which speaks highly for the discipline of the troops, who refrained from opening up on such a tempting target.

The incident must have aroused wonderment in the minds of the Turks, numbers of whom were observed lining their trenches, their bayonets showing over the parapets, as though in preparation for a forward movement. It was hoped that the enemy would decide to attack, but as time passed it became evident that he was taking no risk in that direction. The Turk Aitken had bayoneted proved to be a non-commissioned officer and was wearing a decoration. He certainly was a brave man.

Once again the pall of silence fell over the British lines and continued throughout the daylight hours of the 25th. During the early hours of darkness the enemy again displayed a nervous curiosity opposite Quinn's, throwing flares in unusual quantities. The majority on the parados of our trenches, followed this up at 9 p.m. with heavy bursts of machine-gun, rifle fire and bombing. Ten minutes later a patrol of about twelve Turks moved towards the centre of Quinn's. Fired upon by a sentry group, they retired. Throughout the night sporadic firing continued from the Turkish trenches, and again bayonets were visible along their parapets, but nothing transpired.

The authorities considered that this "Silent Stunt" had been so successful that an extension for another day was ordered. The daylight hours of the 26th were uneventful, the enemy also remaining very quiet. At 9.50 p.m., a small party of Turks approached the centre sector of Quinn's but after being fired upon, retired. At 3 a.m. on the 27th another party approached the same point, but was driven off by rifle fire and bombs. Again at 4.45 a.m. six of the enemy attempted to occupy a crater in the vicinity, apparently with the object of establishing a bombing post there. They hastily retreated when a fusilade of bombs fell near them.

During the night a blizzard raged, and later, snow began to

fall, lasting well into the following afternoon. It covered the forbidding features of Gallipoli like a soft mantle. The next day the sun shone brightly, and the snow soon melted, leaving the scarred slopes and ridges, uglier than ever.

Subsequent events appeared to leave no doubt that this silent period had proved its value. It left the enemy confronted with the problem of discerning which was the real motive governing its employment. In the end he seems to have concluded that it was inspired by a desire on the part of the British to carry out their preparations for winter with as little disturbance as possible. As the Turks, themselves, had been observed making similar preparations the explanation could be deemed to be quite feasible.

Activity, both above and below ground, was resumed in normal fashion, especially in regard to mining and countermining. On the 27th the enemy had been heard working continuously at number 32 shaft, which was under the centre of Quinn's. The engineer officer in charge ordered that 75 lbs. of ammonal be laid and tamped in the right arm of the Y shape. It was estimated that the enemy was then five feet away. On the same day he had been heard from numbers 45A, 23 and 18 shafts, but sounded as though at some distance, and the next day he was still to be heard continuously at work at these three points. He, however, was quiet in 32. On the following day, the 29th, he was heard fairly close at 23, and, therefore, a charge was laid and partly tamped. At 32 it was still quiet.

Above ground, our artillery, on the 30th, shelled the enemy positions in the sector, and he replied by ranging with his guns on Steel's and Lone Pine, well to the right of Quinn's. It was subsequently learned that much damage was done and many casualties incurred at Lone Pine amongst units of the 6th Brigade. This was the first concentrated shelling by heavy calibre guns that the Australians had experienced, and it betokened the preparations for bombardments by such weapons brought to Gallipoli by the Germans. The result of this bombardment made it plain that the deep unrevetted trenches were virtual death traps, as the sides simply collapsed and buried the occupants; also that the shelters dug for sleeping quarters would not be able to withstand such heavy metal.

In the meantime, every opportunity was taken to harass the enemy. On one occasion five Lotbiniere bombs were thrown into the bomb-proof portion of his trench opposite the centre of Quinn's, but, although in each case they appeared to be well placed, the actual damage, if any, could not be estimated. In retaliation the Turks heavily bombed the central and northern sub-sections, but were soon silenced. At dusk the same day they again endeavoured to occupy the crater opposite number 3 sub-section, but were promptly bombed out of it.

On December 2nd, the 120 lb. charge of ammonal that had been laid in number 23 shaft on November 29th, was fired at 10.30 p.m. when the enemy was heard working about 5 feet away. The engineer officer reported that the blow was most satisfactory, no damage having been done to our surface works. The same day, 2nd-Lieutenant Lowther was wounded by a fragment of bomb whilst he was standing 50 yards in rear of the trenches On the following day, Lieutenant Chambers was evacuated sick

An indication of the inroads sickness was making into the strength of the Battalion may be had from figures extracted from the records and covering the period November 22nd to December 13th. The numbers killed and wounded during the same period are also given by way of comparison. It should, however, be explained that many of the sick were not evacuated further than the Field Ambulance at Anzac Cove. For these twenty-two days the figures were as follows:—Killed 4; wounded 20; sick 118.

Underground the miners continued their vigilance, and at 6 a.m. on the 4th, the Turks were heard working close to, and a little above the right arm of number 32 shaft, so at 7 o'clock the 75 lb. charge of ammonal laid on November 27th was exploded, while the enemy was about five feet away. For the rest of the day no sound of working underground could be heard. The following day the Turks put over a considerable number of stick bombs, but the Garland gun was brought into action and eventually subdued their fire.

It was during this period that the troops had their first experience of aerial bombing. At 3.30 p.m. on Dec. 6th, an hostile aeroplane flew over Quinn's from a south-westerly direction and dropped two bombs in the gully between it and Pope's. One proved to be a dud. The pilot then endeavoured to machine-gun the troops on the ground, but without causing any casualties. Finally, he flew off in a southerly direction, then turned north again, and threw out handfuls of darts, some of which fell near 5th Brigade Headquarters, slightly wounding one of the personnel.

The enemy's artillery fire was beginning to show a marked increase, and, judging by the unusual attention he was paying to the sector between Walker's on the left and Steele's on the right, he was evidently registering on positions selected as future targets. He was also actively engaged consolidating his own defences. On December 8th the result was noticeable in several places under observation from Quinn's, especially on the Razor Back and in front of Pope's. He was also seen to be busily engaged reinforcing the overhead bomb-proof of his trenches opposite to the northern sector of Quinn's, by means of steel rails and railway sleepers.

On December 11th, the first indication tending towards confirmation of the steadily spreading belief amongst the troops that an evacuation was to be carried out, was seen. The Seventeenth was ordered to take over that part of Courtney's immediately to the right, up to a point known as Observation Post, about one-third of the whole length. In addition, all work underground had been stopped. Then on the 13th the officers' baggage was sent down to the beach, and the men ordered to mark their packs with their regimental numbers and names; also to hand in spare blankets.

All other material and surplus ammunition, after having been rendered unserviceable, were dumped into a huge cess-pit that served the sanitary requirements of Quinn's; while between the front line and the beach, movement of stores and material had been observed for some days previously. Reserves of food supplies were drawn upon to augment the hitherto scanty rations and the remainder destroyed; thus, the troops lived like fighting cocks for two or three days. The medical details attached to the Battalion fared best in this respect, as they now had at their disposal comforts, such as oatmeal, jellies, tinned fowl, pea soup and milk.

Official confirmation of the determination to evacuate the Peninsula came on December 17th, when the troops were taken into the confidence of the authorities and told that the operation would begin on the night of the 18th. The news was received with conflicting feelings by the men, who, at first, sensible of a state of relief, quickly reacted with bitterness and regret. To them the decision was an acknowledgment of defeat, in which, moreover, they would be obliged to leave behind their comrades lying under the rows of pathetic wooden crosses in the cemetery in Shrapnel Gully, or elsewhere, in solitary graves on other parts of the Front. The feelings of the great majority of all ranks may be summed up in an extract from the diary of Private F. Brown, who later became the Signalling Officer. It read: "One thing that affected me, and many others, I am sure, was having to pass those quiet little spots, where the rows of rude crosses reminded us of the conditions under which we were leaving and of those vacant hearts at home. What would they who gave their all, think of us?"

The second and last stage of the operation, i.e., the evacuation of the forward area, including the front-line trenches was to be carried out in two days, the dates eventually selected were December 18th and 19th. What the troops had been witnessing for the past ten days, without knowing its actual meaning, were the preliminary and intermediate movements of the first phase. Meanwhile, on the Anzac front, on Plugge's Plateau in the centre rear, there had been constructed an inner line, or keep, which was to be held by 275 men under Colonel Paton of the Twenty-fifth Battalion, who would hold the position as a rearguard, which, in turn, would be covered by other posts, such as McLagan's, Ridge, on the right, Walker's Ridge in the centre, and No. 1 Outpost on the left.

The final phase of the withdrawal of the Seventeenth was subdivided into two stages, the first of which would be carried out on the night of 18/19 and the second on the night of 19/20, in the following manner:—

Date:	Time:	Party:	Officers:	Other Ranks:	Under:
18/19	5.20 p.m.	"A"	10	345	Major Martin.
19/20	5.20 p.m.	"A" 2	5	126	Major (Temp.) Griffiths.
„	11.45 p.m.	"B" 2	1	18	2nd Lt. Mackenzie.
„	2.20 a.m.	"C" 1	3	28	2nd Lt. Miller.
„	2.32 a.m.	"C" 2	1	14	2nd Lt. Moulsdale.
„	2.56 a.m.	"C" 3	2	21	Capt. Lucas.

Little remains to be told of this intricate operation and the success of the strategem upon which it was based, save to record that it was completed without the loss of a single soldier. Each party at the appointed time quietly wound its way to the beach, until there remained only Captain Lucas and his gallant band of volunteers.

Colonel Goddard and Captain Smith also stayed behind until almost the last moment and then went round and shook hands with the men. Earlier in the evening, Lucas had placed a record on a gramophone in Battalion Headquarters, ready to be played. It was a record of the popular "Turkish Patrol" march—a graceful compliment to a chivalrous foe.

The last two men to file out of the trenches on to the steep stairway of Quinn's were Privates S. A. Duggan and E. J. Martin.

The curtain had been rung down on one of the greatest war dramas in history—the Campaign of Gallipoli.

CHAPTER V.

Christmas at Lemnos—Return to Egypt—Colonel Goddard is invalided —2nd Division mans Suez Canal Defences—Anzac Corps to fight on Western Front—Seventeenth embarks at Alexandria—Marseilles, and train journey through France—Thiennes first billets—"The Nursery," Armentieres—First decorations awarded—General Birdwood presents Driver A. M. McLaren with a sovereign—5th Brigade Raid— Private W. Jackson wins the Victoria Cross—Move to the Somme.

BY 5.30 p.m., December 20th, both C2 and C3 parties had arrived at the camp, which was set upon a stretch of bleak, stony ground, open to the weather from all directions. But the ending of the strain of the past four months of fighting their physical enemies, as well as disease amongst their own ranks, left the troops in no mood to criticise the inhospitable surroundings. Excepting the lingering regrets at having parted from the mates they had left behind, the mental reaction generally was one of intense relief and a revival of hopefulness, although the incredible hardships endured would never be effaced from their memories.

Lemnos, in spite of its unattractive surroundings, seemed like a haven of rest to the men. They found, awaiting their arrival, stores of comforts from Australia. With such additional items of food that could be purchased in nearby villages, and at the Expeditionary Force Canteens, creature comforts were reasonably well supplied. Soon their spirits began to revive, and despite continuous rain and biting winds, preparations went forward for the celebration of that season of the year usually associated with "Peace and Goodwill." Christmas Day broke fine, and, excepting for the routine duties, all work ceased in order that as many as possible could enjoy the good fare provided.

For the next fortnight or so, platoon, company, and battalion drill, with regular route marches, were the chief items of training. All ranks soon began to show a marked improvement, physically and mentally, as the result of regular diet, proper exercise and adequate rest.

When it became known that the Battalion was to proceed to Egypt the projected change was universally welcomed. On January 4th, 1916, the Seventeenth embarked in the "Simla" for Alexandria, arriving there without mishap on the 8th. At Alexandria, Colonel Goddard found orders waiting for the Battalion to proceed to Tel el Kebir. On the morning of the 9th, the Seventeenth entrained for its destination and arrived there at about 8.15 p.m. The camp site was about half-a-mile from the railway station. The new arrivals were met by the Transport Section, which had been left in Egypt, under Lieutenant C. G. Johnston. Lieutenant R. V. Spier and a party consisting of various details were also present. The short march to the new camp was effected without incident, and by 10.30 p.m. the men had settled down for the night. On this date, 2nd-Lieutenants L. St. J. Allen and E. V. Smythe with a reinforcement of 102 ranks, reported for duty.

Egypt had been selected as the most suitable place in which to reorganize, refit and rest the Australian and New Zealand troops, and where reinforcements were waiting to replenish the 14,000 men Anzac Corps was short of its establishment.

Tel el Kebir, the new site chosen for their concentration, lay fifty miles or so to the north-east of Cairo, on firm, gravelled and gently undulating desert. It was served direct by a rail route which also connected Cairo with Ismailia on the Suez Canal. The place had given its name to a battle that had been fought in 1882 between the British forces under General Sir Garnet Wolesley and those commanded by the Egyptian rebel, Arabi Pasha. The neatly kept cemetery in which were the British soldiers killed in that action, bore silent witness to this episode in the Cavalcade of Empire.

North of the camp, the breastwork built by the rebels still stood, and the broad ditch along its front soon became the venue for the numerous devotees of that fascinating pastime—"Two-up." If the ghosts of Arabi's departed host could have returned to the scene, they might have concluded that it was occupied by the followers of some strange new religious cult.

It was in this setting that the units of the Anzac Corps were to recuperate, and once again fit themselves for battle. The chief reason for this concentration of troops was, however, strategical. Not only would the defence of Egypt be assured, but it would provide a large reservoir of troops which could be diverted to any part of the Empire, as required. The prospects of an attack on Egypt would be limited to the winter months of which there remained February and March. In January, 1915, the Turks had attacked the Suez Canal, moving across the Sinai desert. At that time the defences of the Canal were placed along the west bank. The attack, although abortive, illustrated what a resolute determined effort could achieve, and it was, therefore, decided to take up a defensive position on the eastern side in order to provide a more adequate measure of protection.

It was known that a force of 13,000 Turks was assembled on the Palestinian border of Sinai, and General Sir Archibald Murray, who had been sent out specially from England to organize the defence of Egypt, decided to take a series of positions on commanding ground eight miles east of the Canal.

Meanwhile, training programmes had been drawn up, and within a few days a definite degree of improvement was noticeable in the general bearing and physique of all ranks of the Battalion. It was during this period that the Seventeenth lost Colonel Goddard, whose health had given way under the heavy strain imposed upon it during the campaign on Gallipoli. Never physically strong, it was only the "Old Man's" indomitable spirit and high sense of duty that carried him through a critical period, which had broken stronger men. Now the reaction had set in, and no other course remained but that of a complete release from his heavy responsibilities as a battalion commander. Accordingly, he was evacuated on January 18th and sent to a hospital in Cairo, eventually returning to Australia.

Two days later, Major Griffiths, who had been holding that rank temporarily, was also evacuated through illness, the Battalion, thereby, losing another experienced leader. Griffiths also eventually returned to Australia, where he was discharged medically unfit.

The site selected by General Murray for a defensive position, although surveyed, had not been constructed at this date, and the protection of the Canal zone was entrusted to the 31st British Division, the 10th Indian Division and a recently arrived brigade from Australia, the 8th. To keep touch with any enemy movement, Arab agents operated across the desert.

The presence of 13,000 Turks on the eastern edge of Sinai caused General Murray to push forward his preparations. Accordingly, the 1st and 2nd Australian Divisions were ordered to move across the Canal to the front line, which was to be a series of defended localities sited so as to give supporting fire, each post to cover the one on either side of it. The bridgehead serving the 2nd Division front was at Ferry Post on the east bank of the Canal opposite Ismalia. On January 22nd, Major Martin, who had assumed command of the Seventeenth, entrained with A and B Companies for Ismalia, and after crossing the Canal, camped at Ferry Post until the 24th, when they marched to the newly-allotted positions at Canberra and Lithgow Posts, where they were joined on February 3rd, by C and D Companies under Major Maughan. Two days later the whole Battalion moved up to Gundagai Post, where it was joined by 187 reinforcements and twenty details.

It was at this period that the sad news arrived of the death of Captain (Temporary Major) Murphy, who had contracted meningitis on Lemnos after the evacuation of Gallipoli. Murphy's fatherly manner had won him the affection of C Company, which he commanded throughout the campaign, except for a few days, in the absence of Major Travers, after the latter was wounded.

The remainder of February was spent in constructing trenches and placing out barbed wire. The high winds caused the sand to fill the trenches, necessitating their continued clearance, much to the annoyance of the troops. During this period, General Legge, commanding the 2nd Division, and General Holmes, the Brigade Commander, inspected the positions held by the Seventeenth. The only incident, producing any cause for excitement, occurred one night when rifle shots were heard in the direction of the outpost line, resulting in the order "Stand-to" being given. It proved to be a false alarm caused by a sentry, who, mistaking a stray camel for an enemy patrol, had challenged. Receiving only a grunt in reply, the whole section opened fire, killing the unfortunate "ship of the desert."

By the end of February, General Murray had come to the conclusion that the best method of defending Egypt was to substitute reliance on a permanent garrison along the Canal Zone, with an advance to Katia, on the coast road, north, and pushing up the railway to that place, supplemented by mobile mounted columns pushed out into the desert a day's march east, prepared to strike. The present front line was to be held only lightly. He issued instructions early in March to give effect to his plans.

On the 5th, 2nd Division Headquarters sent a message that the Seventeenth would be relieved on the 6th by the Auckland Mounted Rifles. Early the next morning, the Battalion marched clear of the camp, piled arms, and detailed fatigue parties to clean up the lines. At 10.30 a.m. a squadron of Mounted Rifles appeared over the ridge from the direction of the Canal. The Battalion fell in, and as the New Zealanders moved in front of the line, Major Martin called for three cheers, which were heartily returned. The band played "Boys of the Old Brigade." The march to Ferry Post was completed by mid-afternoon and, after camping there for the night, the men the next day passed through Ismailia, to the tented camp at Moascar, about a mile to the west of that town.

En route to Moascar, in an open space alongside the road, the Battalion halted in order to exchange their Mark III rifles for those of the modern Mark IV pattern. Companies moved in single file to the issuing point, where each man in turn laid down his old rifle and picked up a new one. At Moascar, training and musketry instruction were immediately resumed with added zest by all ranks, in anticipation of an early move to the

Western Front, which, they had been informed, was to be their ultimate destination.

There was a reorganization of the A.I.F. decided upon soon after the return of the troops to Egypt, early in January. During the period between the landing on Gallipoli and the evacuation, recruiting in Australia had proceeded to such an extent that reinforcements, several thousands in excess of ordinary requirements, had accumulated in Egypt. In addition to this, the Australian Government had offered to raise a new division at home, and at the same time maintain a regular monthly quota of over 10,000 as reinforcements. This offer had been accepted, without hesitation, by the War Office, and these regular drafts, together with other details, ultimately presented a serious problem for the A.I.F. Administration in Egypt. It was solved by a decision to raise two additional divisions, the 4th and 5th (the one being raised in Australia was to be named the 3rd) by splitting into two each of the first sixteen battalions and incorporating the newly raised 8th Brigade, thus providing the nuclei of the additional twenty-four battalions required for the 4th and 5th Divisions. In addition, each division would have its own artillery, engineers, supply and medical services brought up to establishment. The 2nd Division would not be affected by this expansion. Some officers of the 2nd Division, however, were transferred to the 5th Division, the Seventeenth in this manner losing two—Captain C. R. Lucas to the 56th and Lieutenant B. Mendelsohn to the 55th. Mendelsohn was killed at Fleur Baix in July, 1916. In addition, 2-Lt. R. V. Smythe transferred to the 24th Battalion. Smythe, eventually, was rewarded with the Military Cross and Bar.

At Moascar, on the 12th, General Birdwood inspected the 5th Brigade, and addressed the troops about their relations with the French people, with whom, shortly, they would be brought into contact. He appealed to their honour to maintain the good name they had won on Gallipoli, particularly in their relations with the many old people and women and children whose men-folk were fighting in the trenches. At the time, some resentment was felt by the troops over the General's speech, but they soon recognised the motive underlying the appeal, and this combined with their affection for their leader, soon caused them to view the position in its proper perspective.

During the period of their stay in Egypt, alterations were made in the establishments of infantry battalions. Firstly, the machine-gun section, originally of two guns, expanded to four on Gallipoli, were taken away and formed into companies under brigade control; a Lewis Gun (an air-cooled automatic weapon) Section was substituted, comprising an officer and four sections, each of seven men, with four guns. There was also a Bombing Platoon of one officer and thirty-three other ranks, and a Scout

Platoon of one officer and thirty other ranks specially chosen for their skill at sniping, observing and scouting. Lieutenants J. L. Wright, and B. Williams, two reinforcement officers, who had joined in Egypt, commanded the Lewis Gun and Scout Sections respectively. The Bombing Platoon was temporarily commanded by Sergeant J. M. Lyons. Wright's sergeant was an Englishman, C. Blackford, and Williams's H. J. Smith, the same who had figured as one of the principals in "The String of Figs" episode on Gallipoli. Later, both were given commissions.

The 2nd Division, having been unaffected by the organization of the new divisions, was the first to leave Egypt for the Western Front. On March 16th, the Seventeenth entrained at Moascar in two detachments for Alexandria, the first consisting of ten officers and 210 other ranks, and the second detachment of nineteen officers and 701 other ranks. Arriving at Alexandria the same afternoon, the Battalion, less 24 other ranks and 57 horses, embarked on H.M. Transport "Arcadian," the details in charge of the horses embarking on the "Crispan." The "Arcadian" sailed at 5.30 p.m. on the 17th. All ranks were ordered to wear their life-belts during daylight, and at night-time sleeping next to them. The ship was built as a passenger liner, and had a swimming pool, which was a constant attraction for the troops. The voyage was rough but uneventful, although enemy submarines were known to be active. Gruesome evidence of this was furnished when the "Arcadian" steamed past a number of corpses, all with lifebelts on.

At 10.30 p.m. on March 22nd, Marseilles was reached, and at 11.30 a.m. the next day the troops began to disembark and march to the entraining station. Entrainment of troops of various arms is an interesting example of organization, the method varying with the particular circumstances. For instance, trains for a long journey, such as that from Marseilles to Northern France, were unusually long, and made up of compartment coaches seating eight other ranks or four officers. Lieutenant C. R. Maynard recorded in his journal that one of these trains was 350 yards long (measured by step) and hauled by a single engine.

For the shorter distances, trains were made up of closed-in waggons capable of accomodating either forty men or eight horses, together with drop-end and drop-side trucks for vehicles and a compartment coach for officers. Occasionally, waggons used for the conveyance of horses on one journey would carry troops on the return trip.

At 2.30 p.m. the long journey northwards, started. The weather was bright and warm. The troops looked with wonderment at the green foliage and pastures, and the farm houses surrounded by fruit trees, in full bloom. As the train wound its way up the valley of the Rhone, the feelings of the men may be best described in the words of Lieutenant F. Brown, who wrote: "Who could believe that a little more than a week ago our outlook was sand, sand, sand; not a blade of grass, and the only water was that brought by the camel train in ten-gallon fantasses (metal containers). Now the beautiful broad fields studded with daisies, buttercups and cowslips; the woods just burst into their Spring foliage; the red-tiled roofs of the farm houses; the warm sunlight, the fragrant breeze, which gave one the firm impression that come what may we would never forget our first day in La Belle France."

Three times each day the train stopped for an hour at some important station. These halts provided opportunities for the troops to walk to the engine to obtain hot water for the cafe au lait issued in tins, or exchange pleasantries, mainly by signs and gestures, with the residents who had gathered to greet the new arrivals. A sight that most deeply impressed our men was that of the large number of women and girls dressed in deep mourning garments. It was a striking reminder of the heavy price France was paying to save herself from being overrun by a remorseless enemy. Additional proof of this was observed subsequently in the towns and villages, for, rarely indeed, was a young man of military age to be seen.

As the journey proceeded the weather grew cold, and later, rain and sleet dampened the enthusiasm of the men not accustomed to such a climate. Nor was their condition mitigated by the draughty and dirty carriages. As one of the men with a distinct note of boredom, wrote in his diary: "This train is rather lousy, and we caught plenty of 'chats'." As the train approached Paris and the Eiffel Tower could be seen in the distance, the discomfort was temporarily forgotten by all in the eager speculation of the prospects of even a short interval spent in the Gay City. Their hopes soon receded as the train then turned away, skirting the western suburbs, and a few hours later, in the darkness, the tang of salt air let the men know that they were near the coast. Soon, Abbeville, near the mouth of the Somme, was reached. A little later, in sight of Calais the train turned east through St. Omer and Hazebrouck, then south again, finally stopping at its destination, the village of Thiennes, about twenty-five miles distant. The journey ended about mid-day on the 26th, after lasting just on seventy hours. The troops were joined by the Transport Section, which had detrained at Abbeville, where they drew their vehicles, and some additional horses. The Section had put up a highly creditable performance. In the seven days' voyage from Alexandria to Marseilles, followed by a train journey to Abbeville lasting four days, only one of the complement of fifty-seven horses was lost. Under his command, Lieutenant Johnston, the Transport Officer, had Sergeant H. E. Rentell, a veteran of other wars, and as fine a body of men skilled in horse-management a commander could desire.

Thiennes was a straggling village about half a mile long, and situated on the edge of a large forest which bore that name. In its single street of houses with their enclosed courtyards and barns the troops were billetted. The inhabitants were of a very friendly disposition, and although troops had been billetted on them since 1914, this was the first Australian unit they had encountered. They showed their hospitality in many forms. The big stove in the centre of madame's commodious living-room, with its comforting warmth, was much appreciated in the chilly evenings by our men, who endeavoured to repay their hosts in a practical form, by doing a variety of odd jobs about the place. The unaffected, carefree disposition of the Australians was something they could readily understand. A friendship was quickly struck, which, even two and a half years later, was vividly demonstrated by the inhabitants in the warm-hearted welcome they gave a party of the Battalion, which re-visited the scene of the first stage of their long sojourn in France.

Eggs, and the light wine of the country, were to be had at reasonable rates. The so-called champagne, sold at five francs a bottle was voted as possessing little more "kick" than the tasteless "penny-beers."

The frankness with which matters pertaining to sex was discussed, even by females of tender years, was at first a source of surprise and some embarrassment to the troops. One night, several men of a platoon were warming themselves round the stove in the living-room of the farm house which was their billet, drinking coffee with their hosts, and exchanging conversation through the medium of one of the men who spoke French fluently. Presently, the eldest daughter, a laughing, rosy-cheeked girl of about sixteen, came into the room, and addressed her parents, who immediately burst into laughter. Asked through the interpreter whether madame would consent to share the joke with her guests, she readily complied with the information that her daughter had just returned from a visit to a neighbour, a "grass-widow," dating from the early weeks of the war. This woman had had a child by a British dragoon billeted in Thiennes in August, 1914, another by an Indian sowar (trooper), and had just expressed her intentions of having a third child, this time with an Australian soldier as the father.

Training, including the use of the new gas helmets, was commenced immediately after the Battalion's arrival. On the 29th every officer and man passed through a specially constructed chamber filled with poison and lachrymatory gases. Steel helmets, which, recently, the authorities had decided to adopt as a protection against shrapnel, were not yet available in sufficient quantities for general issue. In the early stages they were virtually trench-stores, to be left for the use of the new unit taking over the line.

About this period, also, each battalion was called upon to furnish a number of men for the newly-formed trench-mortar batteries, medium and light. Among the personnel so transferred were Lieutenants F. G. Barnett and G. J. Richards. The heavy trench-mortar batteries, "flying-pigs," throwing a bomb weighing 152 lbs., were made up of volunteers from the artillery. The medium mortar threw a "plum pudding" bomb weighing 60 lbs., attached to a short steel bar, while the light Stokes mortar, a rapid-firing weapon was designed for use with infantry, two four-gun batteries being attached to each brigade.

From the sea to the Swiss frontier, a distance of about 470 miles, the Allied line was held by about 111 French Divisions on the right, with a frontage of 370 miles. Four British armies, under Field-Marshal Sir Douglas Haig, took up a further eighty miles, and between their left flank and the sea the small Belgian Army, reinforced by a French army corps stood in position. With the addition of the three newly-arrived divisions of the 1st Anzac Corps, Haig's four armies comprised forty-seven infantry and 5 cavalry divisions and the sector held by them stretched from Ypres to the northern bank of the River Somme just below the town of Albert. From right to left these armies were numbered as follows:—Fourth (Rawlinson), Third (Allenby), First (Monro), and Second (Plumer). Sir Douglas Haig's headquarters were at Montreuil, about 50 miles west of the First Army's sector.

The 1 Anzac Corps had been allotted to the Second Army. The area in which it was billeted was about twenty miles from the trench line, and immediately west of Armentieres, in front of which it ran. This part of the line had been the scene of fierce fighting in 1915, but at this period was very quiet, due, partly, to its strategical position and partly to the desire of the British not to damage the large manufacturing city of Lille, six miles east of Armentieres, or harm its population. Moreover, the country hereabouts was low-lying and intersected by narrow streams, ditches and hedges and did not lend itself to active operations. In consequence it had become what was called a quiet sector, and was used as a "Nursery" to accustom new troops to trench-warfare conditions and to rest tired troops.

Such was the position when, on April 7th, the 5th Brigade began its march to the sector of the line allotted to it, just south of Armentieres, at a place called Bois Grenier. The first day's destination was Oultersteene, and en route passed General Joffre, Commander-in-Chief of the Allied Armies on the Western Front, who stood by the side of the road watching the troops as they swung past. The second day's route lay via le Verrier, Steenwercke and L'Hallobeau to Erquinghem, and on the third day the Brigade took over the allotted sector from the 103rd Brigade of the 34th British Division.

Preceding the main body by three days, parties from each battalion, comprising four company officers, the grenade officer (as the bombing officer was then called) a proportion of Lewis gunners and signallers, were transported by motor buses to act as advanced parties and prepare the way for the incoming units. The dispositions of the 5th Brigade were: Eighteenth and Seventeenth Battalions in the front line, with the Twentieth and Nineteenth Battalions in reserve. During the movement of the advanced parties, Corporal E. Ikin, B. Coy. was hit by a piece of shell. He was, therefore, the Battalion's first battle casualty in France.

The new position was a continuous line to right and left, as far as the eye could see, of breastwork set in the dead flat country. This was strange to the men accustomed to the deep unrevetted trenches of Gallipoli, which were rather a series of defended localities than a continuous related line. A No Man's Land, intersected with ditches lined with blasted trees, stretched up to distances of 200 yards or more, in some places. The breastwork was constructed by digging a broad shallow moat, and heaping the earth obtained from it into a parapet about seven feet high and up to twenty feet in thickness, capped by rows of sand-bags. The inner side of the breastwork was supported by timber and wire revetments with wooden "duckboards," contrivances resembling lengths of ladders with the rungs a couple of inches apart.

This form of line was made imperative because of the lowlying nature of the ground. It was impossible to dig down more than a couple of feet without the ground becoming waterlogged. There was no parados and, therefore, the danger of back-blasts from bursting shells was much greater than in the ordinary type of trench. At intervals in the inner wall of the breastwork were shelters for the occupants. Invariably, company headquarters was a sandbag and timber structure offering comparative comfort.

About fifty to eighty yards in rear of the front line, ran a second parallel, or support, line, while perhaps half-a-mile again to the rear stood the reserve line. Connecting these were wide communication trenches, or avenues, also floored with duckboards set on V-shaped timber frames. In front of the breastwork, in the moat, or borrow-pit, barbed wire had been placed, and patrols moving into No Man's Land passed through sally-ports, carefully disguised and placed at intervals along the front. Battalion Headquarters was located generally in a specially constructed post leading off one of the avenues.

That part of the line to be taken over by the Seventeenth was about one mile distant from Bois Grenier. The avenues, just described, in each case lead off the main road from that village to Armentieres. It was at these junction-points that dumps of supplies, ammunition, and engineering materials were established. About a mile west of Bois Grenier the reserve battalions were billeted in farm houses scattered over a front of, perhaps, half-a-mile. In case of an alarm being sounded, each unit had allotted to it an "alarm-post."

The whole position was, however, commanded by the enemy from a low ridge behind their lines and with the aid of observation balloons, he could detect the movement of the smallest group of troops or transport. Such was the position around Armentieres when, on April 10th, the Seventeenth relieved the Tyneside Irish, a fine body of men, mostly hardy miners of few words, but, who in the characteristic warm-hearted fashion of the "Tommy," treated our advanced parties with all the hospitable means at their disposal. The officers, mostly professional and commercial men from Dublin, impressed their "opposite numbers" from Australia as being particularly good types, who seemed to be on terms with their men similar to those existing in our own forces. Nevertheless, outwardly at any rate they declined to take the war seriously—an attitude frequently observed by the Australians in their contact with British officers. This puzzled them until they realised that it was characteristic of the Britisher not to take anything seriously until he was really angry; and how could a man possibly be angry with an enemy he had not yet seen, excepting, perhaps, at a distance through field-glasses?

It was quite a usual performance for the subalterns of a company to go for a stroll, nightly, in that part of No Man's Land immediately fronting their sector, armed only with revolvers and stout walking sticks. When on one occasion their guests expressed surprise at this somewhat casual procedure, they assured them that "this is a home from home; if you leave the Boche alone, he'll leave you alone." British officers invariably referred to the Germans as "Boches," or "Huns." To the "Tommies" they were "Jerries" and to the Australians "Fritzes."

If this attitude betokened in the minds of the more seasoned Australian troops a regrettable lack of enterprise, it must at the same time be remembered that these regiments belonged to the New Army, and that few, excepting, perhaps, the senior regimental officers, had any previous experience of war. It would certainly have been a mistaken notion that it was due to any "stickiness" on the part of these splendid battalions, every man of which, like the Australian soldier, was a volunteer, and who subsequently displayed the greatest gallantry in their first action—The Battle of the Somme.

The Armentieres sector was also used by the Germans to rest their tired troops and to give experience to untried units.

Apparently they, too, observed the convention of refraining from annoying their opposite numbers in the British lines. It remained for the newcomers to demonstrate that this static view-point differed widely from their concept of war, which was to harass and hit the enemy at every conceivable opportunity. The Australians soon engaged in active patrolling of the length and breadth of No Man's Land, and before a fortnight had elapsed, enemy movement outside his wire was limited to a narrow strip bordering his own entanglements.

A brief description, taken from the diary of Private W. H. T. Burrell, one of B Company's men, who was about to experience his first tour in the front line, was typical of the Australian soldier's flair for perceiving the humorous side of a situation. The writer noted: "April 10 to 12, Armentieres. Instructed during day as to our position in the line, after which we had a good clean up. Private ———— reckoned he was not 'chatty,' so we got him down and had a look. He was crawling with them, so we sentenced him to a bath—and helped him to have it, too. Some fun. There were plenty of balloons and 'planes up, and some shelling going on. Fell in at 6 p.m. and moved off for the trenches; passed through a village completely destroyed, near which we entered a communication trench, and after a long walk we reached the front line. Owing to the flat, wet nature of the country the 'trenches' are built up like breastworks, instead of being dug down. They are very muddy and wet, so we had plenty to do making them ship-shape. It is a peculiar feeling to know that one is actually in the front line—a feeling of curiosity, more than anything else. Out in No Man's Land is a yellow flag, but it is suspected of being a trap. The last two brought in by patrols had 'damned English' written on them. . . . Plenty of rats, and they are very big; they crawl over us when we attempt to lie down. Old Fritz is fond of playing his machine-guns along our parapets, so it does not do to show one's head too often. The trenches here are about 300 yards apart."

During this period the first awards of decorations for bravery to members of the Seventeenth were announced. They were for the action at Hill 60 on Gallipoli. Sergeant (then Lance-Corporal) J. E. Bennett, Privates A. H. Hamilton, J. H. Green and W. Deonck, who received Military Medals. Thus the gallant conduct these men had displayed in that sharp, but bloody combat, was rewarded.

Two nights after taking over the front line from the Tyneside Irish, the Seventeenth was relieved by the Nineteenth Battalion, a rotation carried out, thereafter, whilst in this sector every third day, during the hours of darkness.

Good Friday fell on April 21st. On that day the Battalion received its first experience of a heavy bombardment by artillery. About twenty-five 5.9-inch shells fell on B Company's front, without causing casualties. On Easter Sunday, Padre Fernie held a Holy Communion Service in A Company's headquarters. The solemn celebration was accompanied by a steady shelling on the part of the enemy's artillery, eighty-seven 4.2's falling between 10 a.m. and 1.0 p.m., increasing to 292 between 1.0 and 1.30 p.m. Again there were no casualties. Although the breastwork was breached in several places, it was repaired during the hours of darkness. Late the same afternoon a British Airman, known to the troops as the "Mad Major," gave the men in the trenches one of his customary displays of daring and skilful flying. He was literally only a few feet above and parallel with the enemy's front line trench, machine-gunning the occupants.

On the 25th, the Anniversary of the landing at Anzac, C Company's billet at Hushi Farm was heavily shelled during the afternoon, 184 5.9's falling on, or near, the building, which, with the adjoining outhouses, was completely destroyed. Four men were wounded, including Company Sergeant-Major W. H. Watson, who gallantly returned to the burning house while it was being shelled and brought away the company's records. For his gallantry and devotion to duty Watson was awarded the Military Cross. He was subsequently invalided to Australia.

Apart from local incidents of the kind just mentioned, life in the Nursery was much to the liking of the troops, despite the unremitting night fatigues, carrying engineering material, or the construction and revetting of breastworks by the "resting" battalions. The long summer days provided ample opportunities for excursions into nearby Armentieres and the adjacent villages, to sip cafe au lait, drink the light white or red inexpensive wines; or yet, perhaps, partake of an omelette, cooked by madame, the estaminet keeper. Taking it as a whole, it was voted by all ranks to be a good war, and, notwithstanding the unbroken tours of trench duty, varied with night fatigues, both the physical condition and the spirits of the troops thrived under the influence of the warm sunny weather, adequate food and comfortable billets.

Casualties had been very light. Occasionally there would be had a sharp reminder that a war was in progress by news of the death, perhaps, of a well-known and popular identity. Two followed closely on one another, both the men concerned were held in high regard by all ranks. The first was Lieutenant Frank Cheadle, who had been transferred to the Eighteenth Battalion after his promotion, the previous October. Cheadle was struck by a stray bullet as he was getting into the trench after returning from patrol on May 12th, a year to the day after the Battalion left Australia. He was buried in Erquinghem Cemetery. As Regimental Sergeant-Major of the Seventeenth, his unobtrusive zeal and devotion to duty, combined with the possession of a pleasing sense of humour and a reputation as

Brig.-Gen. E. F. MARTIN, C.B., C.M.G., D.S.O., V.D., C.O. 1916-1918.

Pte. Wm. JACKSON, V.C.

HUSHI FARM.
After the shelling on April 25th, 1916.

BEHIND THE BREASTWORKS, BOIS GRENIER.
Pts. T. Graham (with periscope), G. H. Gallogly (Lewis gun),
and N. J. Dulhunty.

BATTALION COOKS.
(Foreground)—Sgt. L. Lillis and Pte. J. Cusack (hats),
Pte. H. S. Baty (civilian cap).

an international footballer, made him highly respected by superiors and subordinates.

Five days later, on the 17th, Lieutenant R. A. Pye, a fine specimen of country-bred Australian and an officer of sound promise, was killed while on patrol. Pye, who was a cousin of Major Pye, had only rejoined the Battalion before it left Egypt after having recovered from the wound he received at Hill 60.

Another reminder had been received earlier. At 7.40 p.m. on May 5th, the Germans raided the Twentieth Battalion's sector, killing or wounding four officers and ninety-one other ranks, besides taking eleven prisoners and two Stokes mortars. The preliminary artillery and mortar bombardment by the Germans had been so intense that at one period 2nd Division Headquarters thought a general attack was about to be launched. The reserve battalions were moved into position in preparation to meet any such threat. About an hour later the shelling ceased and the situation again became normal.

A period of regular activity ensued. The usual tours of duty, turn about, were carried out on the brigade front. On the 18th, General Birdwood, accompanied by Brigadier-General G. N. Johnston, commander of the 2nd Division artillery, inspected the Seventeenth's billets. The corps commander said he was very pleased with the Transport Section; the horses were in excellent condition, the harness very satisfactory, the waggons clean, and the parking arrangements very good. He was particularly pleased with the turn-out of Driver A. N. McLaren's harness, remarking: "This man's harness is the best I've seen." He shook hands with McLaren, and, turning to his orderly officer, told him to give the young soldier a sovereign. He next instructed General Johnston to send his officers to personally view this fine example of a high standard of harness maintenance. McLaren, who had received his early training in a hunting stables, in Scotland, was heard to remark after the General left: "The quid came in very handy, for I was broke at the time."

By the beginning of June the sector became lively, starting on the night of the 6th with a retaliatory bombardment by the enemy's artillery against ours, which had been engaged in support of a raid by parties from the Twenty-sixth and Twenty-eighth Battalions of the 7th Brigade, holding the sector immediately on the left. The Seventeenth's losses were five killed, and five wounded. The raid, the first of a series launched by the Australians, proved entirely successful in its objective, which was to give confidence to the troops, foster their fighting spirit, obtain identification, and strike at the enemy's morale.

It was now the turn of the 5th Brigade to carry out a raid, plans for which had been prepared at the instance of 2nd Division Headquarters. It was timed to take place on the night of June 25th and would comprise a party of sixty-eight of all ranks drawn from the four battalions and organized in the following manner:

 O.C. Attack Party: Major R. J. A. Travers, Seventeenth.
 Deputy O.C. Attack Party: Lieutenant R. R. Harper, Twentieth.
 O.C. Scout Party: Lieutenant C. Wallach, Nineteenth, and 5 other ranks.
 O.C. Assault Party: Captain K. Heritage, Nineteenth.
 Deputy O.C. Assault Party: Lieutenant L. B. Heath, Nineteenth.
 O.C. Right Party: Lieutenant J. J. Fay, Seventeenth, and 21 other ranks.
 O.C. Left Party: Lieutenant J. B. Lane, Nineteenth, and 22 other ranks.
 O.C. Covering Party: Captain E. W. Kirke, Eighteenth, and 12 other ranks.
 Fourteen additional details comprising engineers and stretcher-bearers made up the party's total to eighty-two of all ranks.

All the officers and men participating were volunteers. In the Seventeenth, as doubtless also with the other battalions, practically every man applied for inclusion. Much disappointment was felt by those who failed to satisfy the critical scrutiny of Colonel Martin and the Medical Officer, Captain Smith, but every one wished good luck to those fortunate to be included in the Battalion quota.

Three weeks prior to zero day, the brigade party was concentrated in a suitable spot, some miles behind the front line. From aerial photographs there was constructed a full-size replica of the sector of enemy trench which was to be the objective, thus permitting practical rehearsals of the operation to be carried out. A syllabus of rigid and intensive training, designed to improve skill-at-arms and promote physical fitness, was also drawn up. The following indicates the nature of the work: Reveille, 5 a.m., coffee served, after which a smart walk of several miles. Breakfast 8 a.m. Training commenced 9 a.m., bayonet-fighting and bomb-throwing practice; barbed-wire cutting with specially designed snips; Lewis gun and signalling in their specialised roles. After a couple of hours a short march, then a hot shower followed by a cold douch and rub down. Then lunch. In the afternoon: rehearsals of the actual raid, interspersed with appropriate lectures. Smoking and drinking were prohibited. By "zero day" all ranks were literally bursting with high spirits and eager for combat.

Just after dark on the night of the 25th the party moved into the sector opposite the objective, the scout party under Lieutenant Wallach moving out ahead into No Man's Land in order to reconnoitre the position. Soon they returned and reported that the enemy was working on his wire. The raiders then filed out of the sally-port and crawled to their allotted position in No Man's Land. At 11 p.m. the 18-pounders opened on the enemy line and soon the bombardment grew into a deafening roar as guns of heavier calibre joined in. Immediately, up went constellations of red, green, and blue alarm rockets from the German line, calling for artillery retaliation, while No Man's Land was transformed into day by dozens of starshells. The enemy, by this time, was thoroughly awake and was sending over shells which crumpled on our parapets, but, fortunately, caused little damage and few casualties. His machine-guns added their harsh chatter to the din of the combat as they swept our breastworks.

Half an hour later our barrage lifted on to his support line immediately in the rear and a curtain of shells was also placed across each side of the objective to prevent reinforcements moving up from the rear, or flanks, to the support of that portion of the garrison which, thus, would be held as though in a box. The attack-parties then went in and cleared up the strip of trench 30 yards each side of the point of entry, while the covering-party guarded the flanks. The scout-party had previously dealt with any enemy listening posts in the vicinity, after which it ran out a line of white tape to guide the returning raiders to their own trenches, on completion of their tasks.

The raid was entirely successful, each man doing his part with clock-work precision. Telephone communication was maintained throughout with Major Travers in the Command Post. It was estimated that at least thirty Germans were killed, and four captured. One who became recalcitrant whilst being escorted through No Man's Land had to be killed. Altogether the raiding party spent only five minutes in the German's trench, which was part of the sector held by the 231st R.I.R. of the 50th Division.

The raiders suffered some casualties, one being killed and thirteen wounded, the majority occuring on the return journey to our trenches. Sergeant J. L. Mitchell, of the Seventeenth, was the man killed. By his death the Battalion last one of its finest non-commissioned officers. He held the Military Medal. He was buried next day in the tiny cemetery at Bois Grenier. In addition the Seventeenth lost Company Sergeant-Major E. F. Edwards, severely wounded.

An act of outstanding gallantry was performed during the raid by Private William Jackson, of the Seventeenth, a boy of eighteen, one of the scout-party. Jackson was assisting in carrying the wounded, when, on his third journey, his left arm was shattered by a piece of shell. Despite his frightful injury, he refused to go to the rear, because two of his mates were still lying wounded in No Man's Land, to which he returned and assisted one of them back to the trenches. For this brave deed Jackson was awarded the Victoria Cross. The official citation will be found in the Appendix. Major Travers was awarded the Distinguished Service Order.

Five days later—that is, on June 29th—the 5th Brigade was relieved by the 4th Brigade of the 4th Division, which had recently arrived in France. The Seventeenth marched to the pleasant little village of L'Hallobeau, about three miles distant, where, for ten days, it was to enjoy a respite from the discomfort and monotony of trench routine and fatigues, quartered in hutments in the green fields adjoining the village. But there was no relaxation of normal routine, "physical jerks," games, and close-order drill were judiciously dispersed in a syllabus designed as a tonic for physique as well as for discipline. Inter-platoon competitions in drill and marching were organized, the winning platoon in each company striving in its turn to gain the Battalion Championship. All ranks entered whole-heartedly into the spirit of these contests, no one more so than the popular young commander of B Company, Captain L. G. Fussell. He had only recently returned from a course of instruction at the 2nd Army School, where he had imbibed deeply of the British Army's traditional insistence on precision in all matters pertaining to drill and ceremonial movements. With fiery zeal and unflagging enthusiasm he exercised his platoons in the true Guards' manner, until they literally groaned, like the children of Israel under the yoke, and fervently wished themselves back in the trenches.

Two entries in the diary of Private Burrell reflect in cogent terms the general opinion of the devoted rank-and-file regarding their too ardent commander. The first entry records that "old Captain Fussell is a military maniac, and had us drilling like a machine"; and the second: "Still plenty of drill by old Fussell." The keenness of all ranks, however, enabled them to overcome such minor ills and when the competitions started everybody "were on their toes" for the honour of their Company. Five platoons, one from each Company, plus one comprising details from Battalion Headquarters, took part. So keen was the enthusiasm aroused over the final event that Lieutenant E. H. McCulloch, Signalling Officer, wagered £30 that the last-named platoon would win. Unfortunately for him, it was placed last with forty-five marks out of the possible 100. Its personnel, however, received warm congratulations from General Holmes on their good performance. A Company won first place with 100 marks.

The testing time was near at hand. The great offensive had opened on the Somme on July 1st. Already the 1st Australian Division, which, hitherto, had held the right sector of I Anzac, in the Nursery, had entrained on the journey southwards, and the next in line would be the 2nd and then the 4th Division. These men from the land of the Southern Cross—citizen soldiers—were about to be pitted against the best trained and equipped soldiers in the world, and by the courage, dash and determination displayed in one of the bloodiest battles, were to establish their title to rank with the elite of any army.

CHAPTER VI.

Position of Allies in 1916—Seventeenth en route to Somme—Pozieres —Bomb-fight in Munster Alley—Privates T. Ridley and "Scotia" McLeer display great courage and endurance—Privates "Leggy" Ford and "Chiller" Craig have a contretemps with a German officer— First attempt on OG lines—Gallantry of stretcher-bearers—Enemy's sustained bombardment—Private "Spud" Murphy invites General Birdwood to tea—Capture of O.G. lines and windmill—Out for a rest—Immediate awards.

THE costly and abortive offensives by the French and British in the Champagne and at Loos in the autumn of 1915, had demonstrated to the Allies the futility of launching piecemeal assaults on the centralised positions of Germany and Austria.

In December of that year, France, Britain, Russia and Italy (the latter country had declared war on Austria in May, but it was not until August 28th, 1916, that she declared war on Germany) decided on plans for a series of joint offensives during 1916. At this period no unified command existed. It was agreed that on the Western Front the French and British would attack together on the Somme, on a forty-mile front between Bapaume and St. Quentin, with a total of about sixty-five divisions. The plan was to be mutually arranged between the French Generalissimo, Joffre, and Sir Douglas Haig.

The German General Staff was also planning to deal in detail with these two powerful opponents in the West, first France and then England.

On February 28th, after a series of feint attacks along the whole front from Ypres to the Swiss border, the enemy hurled masses of troops against the fortress of Verdun, 160 miles east of Paris. The object was to compel the French army to exhaust its reserves in defence of the fortress, thus virtually putting France out of the war, after which Germany could settle her score with England, the power that was holding together the Allies. The tempo and weight of the attack was maintained virtually unabated until the end of June, with extremely heavy casualties on both sides. The French losses were much greater than the German.

The intensity and violence of the assault before long compelled the French to draw heavily upon their reserves. These, by the end of June, had become dangerously depleted. The French and British between them now had only twenty-nine divisions available for their Somme offensive. This fact necessitated a modification, both in the weight and scope of the proposed operation, and it was eventually decided that it would be carried out on a twenty-three mile front. The British took over portion of the French front.

The part of the German line selected for the assault lay about twenty miles to the east of Amiens, and consisted of two strongly fortified trench systems about two miles apart. The second system followed the crest of a ridge known as "Second Line Ridge" on which stood the village of Pozieres. The plan was for the British to smash through these lines to Bapaume, a town eight miles distant, thence turning northward and rolling up the German line, while the French would protect the British right flank. The British attack was to be made by the Fourth Army (Rawlinson) and part of the Third Army (Allenby) on the left. It was hoped to breach the enemy's line in two or three days. To exploit this success a Reserve Army (Gough) consisting of cavalry divisions and an infantry corps was formed.

On July 1st, after a seven-day bombardment by concentrations of artillery, totalling on the British front alone more than 1,200 guns, ranging from 15-inch howitzers to 18-pounder field-guns, the attack was launched. The French, who met with less resistance, early thrust deeply into the enemy positions, but, on the British front, the Germans held a system of deep dug-outs. In many cases these withstood the bombardment, thus enabling the enemy machine-gunners to shelter until the barrage had lifted, then man their guns and cut down the advancing waves of infantry. Despite the great gallantry displayed by the untried soldiers of the new armies, every man a volunteer, the objective was not attained, and, when the 1st Australian Division entered the battle on July 23rd the advance had reached only the western outskirts of Pozieres.

Towards this battlefield, sixty miles to the south, I Anzac commenced to move early in July. On the 9th the Seventeenth marched from L'Hallobeau to Rouge Croix, where it billeted for the night, on the following day moving to Eblinghem. St. Omer, the quaint old town about thirty miles west of Armentieres, was the next stage and was reached on the 11th.

The weather was extremely hot, and the troops, weighted with full marching order, soon began to get footsore on the cobbled roads, despite the easy stages in which the move was being carried out. Still, neither the heat nor the physical discomfort it caused failed to dampen the spirits of the men. Down the long column, sometimes by platoons and sometimes by whole companies, snatches of songs and choruses, like "Tipperary," "Mother May I Go Out to Swim," and "What Will We Do With the Kaiser," resounded along the tree-lined roads, as often before they had echoed to the marching songs that inspired the thousands of other soldiers who had passed before on these self-same roads to the bloody Somme battlefield.

Lieutenant Maynard described in tabloid form the complicated problem of large troop movements as follows: "The movement of a large formation of troops, such as a division,

Maj. R. J. A. TRAVERS, D.S.O.

Maj. J. M. MAUGHAN, D.S.O.

DRAWING RATIONS.

Maj. B. HOLMES, D.S.O.

C.Q.M.S. R. C. AUSTIN, M.S.M.

Pte. (afterward Lieut., M.C.)
~~W. M. FLOOD, D.C.M.~~

Sergeants (afterward Lieuts.) J. P. TAYLOR (standing) and J. M. LYONS, M.C., M.M., M.S.M.

en route to an entraining point, provides an interesting example of the degree of organization and control called for in order to pass troops, guns and transport along the available roads in the allotted area. A strict schedule laid down by a special section of the Staff has to be observed. Certain roads are allotted to units and only by these may they travel; it may not be the most direct route. Problems of time, space and rate of movement are resolved very much as in a railway timetable. The country through which the Seventeenth was passing was plentifully supplied with roads, which presented little difficulty in this respect, and on several occasions the troops found themselves marching parallel with other units, and at other times, as the head of the column approached a cross roads, would see the rear of another column that had just cleared that point."

At 4 p.m. on July 11th the Battalion entrained, and after a tedious journey pent-up in horse trucks marked "Hommes 40, Chevaux 8," arrived at Longeau, just outside Amiens, at 2.40 the next morning. The destination for the day was Argoeuves, about five miles distant, and the route to the village lay through part of the city. Here the troops obtained their first view of the beautiful Picardy country, second only to Paris in the heart of every Frenchman. Except for the dull muttering of artillery twenty miles to the east, there was little to suggest that the rolling countryside, filled as far as the eye could see with golden grain crops strewn with red poppies and corn flowers, hedgeless and studded with green copses, was but a false Paradise, where men paused for a brief respite before being flung into the hell of battle.

The country folk showed eagerness to dispense hospitality. Frequently they thrust presents of fruit and strawberries in the hands of the men as they marched. The inhabitants of Argoeuves greeted the troops with a warm welcome, reminiscent of a similar gesture by the good villagers of Thiennes. In more than one diary the warmth of this welcome has been commented upon, and which left pleasant memories.

The Battalion stayed at Argoeuves for three days. Advantage was taken of the respite to apply treatment to the men's sore feet. The billets were comfortable and leave to Amiens was liberal. Ere long, in the streets of that city the slouch-hatted soldiers from the land of the Southern Cross were exploring the sights down the tree-lined side walks and viewing with reverence the beautiful cathedral.

July 16th found the Battalion en route to Cardonette, the next stage, the warm sunshine reminding the men of their own homeland. A full day was spent at Cardonette. The march was resumed the following morning with Rubempre the destination; and then on the 20th to Warloy, about ten miles from the battlefield. The artillery bombardment could now be heard more distinctly, another indication of the impending clash.

Warloy itself bore all the traces of the tragic effect of war on a civilian population. In the partly deserted village, with its wall-enclosed houses standing back from the road, only an old man or two and a few elderly "madames" were to be seen. The rest of the inhabitants had departed, leaving these poor people equipped with only the bearest conveniences. Late in the afternoon of the 22nd the Battalion moved out of the village to a position on the high ground overlooking Albert from the west, and bivouacked in a brickfield. The town, situated on the Ancre, had been much battered by shell fire and its population long ago evacuated. The tall cathedral tower, surmounted by a huge gilt statue of the Madonna and Child, now pointing earthwards, stood up starkly in the surrounding ruins, as if in defiance of the hate and fury of the enemy.

As the long summer evening closed, the troops prepared to settle down to get what sleep they could on the bare earth. All blankets had been withdrawn to regimental store. All ranks were, however, far too interested in the news that had just come through to bother about any physical discomfort. Pozieres was to be stormed that night by the 1st Division. This key-point, hitherto, had withstood every assault. This time thorough preparation would leave no doubt as to the outcome.

With nightfall, the British bombardment began. Against the glaring curtain of red flame that lit the sky-line far away to the east was patterned the bright reds and greens of signal-rockets and star-shells, while the thundering of hundreds of guns, including the nearby 15-inch howitzers, combined to create a macabre picture, fascinating and unbelieveable in its intensity.

This was the first experience our men had of a big scale bombardment. They were silent with wonderment that human beings could exist in such a hell-storm. The sudden realisation that soon they, too, would have to pass through a similar ordeal, produced a markedly sobering impression on their mind, though their spirit was in no way affected.

With the dawn came word that the assault had been successful. It served as a filip to the universal desire to emulate the splendid performance of the gallant 1st Division.

The day being Sunday, a church parade was held in a quarry near the bivouac. General Holmes and his staff attended. Padre Fernie officiated at the service, which acquired a greater degree of solemnity by the simplicity of its order and the attention paid to the Padre's brief but earnest exhortation.

During the course of the day all ranks were issued with diamond-shaped pieces of bright tin to be worn on the back to facilitate identification by our aircraft flying over the front trenches. This day, too, Captain B. Holmes, commanding C Company, was evacuated sick, his second-in-command, Captain E. T. Manefield, assuming the command. The waiting period was spent by many of the men writing letters home, whilst others took the steep road to Albert in the valley below to explore its ruins. A budget of newspapers had just arrived from England, and in the Paris edition of the London "Daily Mail" there appeared the following items of Australian news which excited much amusement and not a little ribald comment:

"July 21: A movement is on foot in Sydney having as its object the sending of a military band to take part in the London celebrations on the declaration of peace."

"July 22: The closing of hotels at 6 o'clock was enforced yesterday evening. This sudden official action caused great indignation amongst workers who were on their way home."

One officer was moved to make the following comment: "We were, of course, deeply interested in the news. It is so nice when one is so far away to know what is going on at home. It would be interesting to know when the Peace Band anticipates having an opportunity to play. It is too bad that the workers should have such cause for indignation."

During the afternoon, instructions were received for the Seventeenth to detail a party of two officers and fifty other ranks to report to 1st Brigade Headquarters in Sausage Valley, about two miles east of Albert, to carry ammunition, rations and water to the battalions holding the front line in the brigade sector. This party, under the command of Lieutenants K. W. Mackenzie, H. Ronald and fifty other ranks, moved off, and, in due course, arrived at its destination, "Gordon Dump," near the entrance to Sausage Valley, where it picked up its load and proceeded to "Casualty Corner." There the party was to meet the guides from the 1st Brigade, but no guides were present when the party reached Casualty Corner. The brigade was heavily engaged in beating off furious counter-attacks by the Germans.

The party stood-by nearly all night and just before dawn returned to Gordon Dump for further instructions. At about 7 o'clock the enemy put down a terrific bombardment on the whole of the sector held by the 1st Division. It was kept up throughout the greater part of the day, and eventually Mackenzie and his men were ordered to "stand-down." That evening the party rejoined the Seventeenth, which had moved into Sausage Valley after dark, and bivouacked there.

The following morning, the 25th, orders were received for the 5th Brigade to relieve the 3rd Brigade on the right of Pozieres, the Seventeenth taking over that portion of the line held by the Ninth Battalion. The relief was to take place during the same night. The waiting period was spent by the troops exploring the area in the vicinity of their bivouac over which the opening phases of the pressent battle had been fought. Not far from the entrance of Sausage Valley ran the old British and German front lines. Portions of the German trenches with many of the dug-outs still in a fair state of preservation. Some of the latter were twenty to thirty feet deep and their sides securely timbered. Each was capable of holding a considerable number of men in the series of connected chambers and alternative exits providing quick means of manning the trench to meet an attack. There were also avenues of escape should the main entrance be blown-in or otherwise blocked. It was the policy of the Germans to shelter in these dug-outs until the fury of the British barrage had passed, and then rush up and meet the advancing infantry with machine-gun fire. That they were driven out of these strong-holds reflects grea tcredit on the British troops, that same 34th Division which the 2nd Division had relieved in the Nursery earlier in the year.

In the high ground between Sausage Valley and the Albert-Bapaume road, a patch of rubble and pulverised bricks marked the place where the tiny village of La Boiselle once stood, just behind the old German front line. The whole of the surface of the surrounding area as far as the eye could see was cratered and seamed with lines of trenches, with here and there the jagged stump of a tree stuck up forlornly from the battered earth. Under La Boiselle itself the Germans had constructed elaborate dug-outs, which housed the local garrison. It is estimated that their capacity was 2,000 men.

The unburied bodies of numbers of British and German soldiers in the vicinity bore grim evidence of the dreadful slaughter before the village was taken. Our men, inspecting the vast crater caused by the mine the British had exploded on July 1st were able to enter portions of the underground galleries, and in one place alone they counted the bodies of eighty-three Germans—a veritable community tomb.

From the crest of the ridge nearby, Pozieres and the Second Line Ridge, along which ran the German second system of trenches comprising two lines about 150 yards apart and called O.G.1 and O.G.2, respectively, could be identified by the pall of smoke and dust of the intense bombardment by the artillery of both sides.

At this period, the British had almost complete command of the air, and in consequence rarely was an enemy plane to be seen over our territory. This, added to the fact that we now dominated the high ground in the vicinity of Pozieres, troop movements could be carried out without hindrance in our own back areas, even during the hours of daylight. An amazing spectacle, which confronted our men, was the large number of guns of all calibres, super-heavy, heavy, medium and light. Across Sausage Valley itself stretched several rows of 4.7's,

18-pounders and 4.2-inch howitzers standing practically wheel to wheel.

During the course of the morning, Colonel Martin conferred with his officers and issued orders for the carrying out of the relief. He explained that, although Pozieres was in our hands, the enemy opposite the sector to be taken over by the 2nd Division was still in possession of that part of O.G.2 trench for a distance of about 500 yards south of the village. The corresponding strip of O.G.1 was by this time only a straight shallow depression, blocked at the northern end. In the earlier fighting, the 3rd Brigade had bombed up O.G.1 and the 1st British Division up O.G.2 to a point where a cross-trench connected the two lines. Here they had established blocks, after their efforts to advance further had been frustrated by the stubborn German defence. About fifty yards south of the cross-trench, Pozieres Trench, or Suicide Alley, as it later came to be known, joined O.G.1, while a little to the south of the cross-

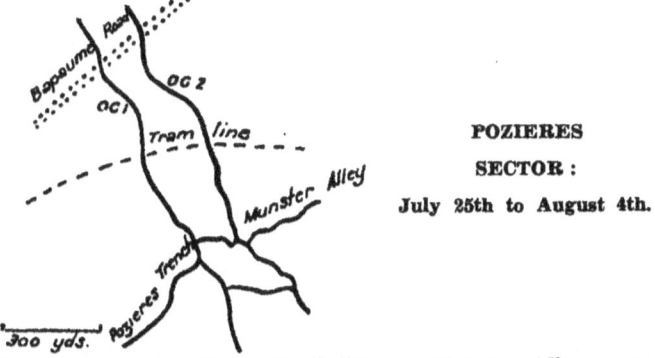

POZIERES SECTOR:
July 25th to August 4th.

trench at its junction with O.G.2 ran Munster Alley, a switch trench held by the enemy. O.G.2 at this point was so badly battered that it was difficult to identify.

The Seventeenth had been allotted the task of taking over part of O.G.1 and Pozieres trench to Walker's Avenue. Colonel Martin, then announced the following disposition of companies in the new position: B. (Fussell) in the cross-trench and part of O.G.1; D. (Maughan) less two platoons, and A. (Beiers) Pozieres trench to Walker's Avenue; C. (Manefield) in support in O.G.1 in the vicinity of its junction with Black Watch Alley, a communication trench running back to the head of Sausage Valley. Battalion Headquarters and the Signalling Section would be located in a group of old German dug-outs in O.G.1 near the junction. The battalion nucleus, Transport Section and regimental cookers were to be located at Gordon Dump under command of Major R. J. A Travers.

Late in the afternoon, the Seventeenth moved forward to Contalmaison, a little to the north of Sausage Valley, and middle weights W. L. ("Leggy") Ford, C. H. ("Chiller") Craig file up Black Watch Alley in the following order of companies —B, C, D and A. Progress was painfully slow, owing to the Alley being used as a two-way traffic route down which numbers of wounded were being carried to the Advanced Dressing Station at Casualty Corner. Moreover, its whole length was littered with abandoned material and equipment, further impeding movement. There were frequent halts of considerable duration. During these intervals, the troops were able to estimate the heavy price paid for maintaining this vital communication link, the route being lined with bodies of Australians, many belonging to the First Pioneer Battalion. To add to the congestion, the Germans started their regular evening "hate" on our communication trenches, causing further casualties and the Alley being blown-in and blocked with earth in several places.

About 250 yards from O.G.1, Walker's Avenue led off from Black Watch Alley in the direction of Pozieres. Into that trench D. and A. Companies were diverted to their new positions, B. and C. Companies moving straight up Black Watch Alley. By midnight the relief of the Ninth Battalion was completed and the men of the Seventeenth set about further consolidating the line. Dawn found the Battalion "standing-to," and all ranks straining their eyes in the direction of Pozieres, now a tumbled heap of rubble. On the south side of the scarcely recognisable remains of the village the stumps of trees, all that remained of an orchard, appeared forlorn and grotesque in the half-light and bore a weird resemblance to human shapes.

Suddenly on D. Company's sector the cry was heard: "Look out, they are coming over!" On the left front, moving straight towards A. Company, appeared a line of men advancing at the double. Orders were immediately given to D. Company to prepare to give rapid fire. Every man strained his vision to pick up a good target and waited tensely for the word. It did not come. Captain Beiers of A. Company had almost immediately observed that the oncoming troops were Australians, and a message was shouted down the whole length of the two Companies not to fire. His quick thinking prevented an awkward situation. The supposedly enemy soldiers turned out to be the remnants of a detachment of the Twentieth Battalion returning after a gallant but abortive attempt to capture O.G.'s 1 and 2 south of the main road by a frontal raid, without any special artillery barrage.

The Seventeenth's companies had received no previous warning of this attack. Denied the opportunity, either for reconnaissance or for organisation, the men of the Twentieth had been launched on one of the most difficult of military operations, a night assault against a resolute enemy, and which, in consequence, was foredoomed to failure.

With the advent of daylight, the situation once more became normal. It also afforded our men the opportunity of an uninterrupted view of the scene. Everywhere the soil had been rendered friable by the sustained artillery bombardments, and the pleasant green countryside churned into a mass of shell-holes. The dead of both sides lay thickly, while broken weapons, twisted wire and abandoned equipment littered the whole area.

In this waste and featureless strip of territory it was difficult to locate the enemy's position. One of the few remaining landmarks was the battered base of the windmill standing on the main road 600 yards north-east of Pozieres. As Sergeant H. J. Smith, of the Scout Section, was heard to remark, when he cast a critical eye on the landscape, that the visit of the Seventeenth to the village of Pozieres had been signalised by a hopeless dawn.

The morning passed quietly, there being little artillery activity on either side. An ominous calm prevailed on the whole of the 2nd Division sector. However, about mid-day, companies were warned that the British unit on the immediate right of the Seventeenth intended to launch a bombing attack on Munster Alley. The assault was to be made from the Australian position.

Accordingly, at 2.30 p.m. the British bombing platoon made its way into position at the junction of Munster Alley and O.G.2, which was guarded by a section of B. Company under Corporal A. H. Edwards. On the signal from their leader, the bombers climbed out of the trench and advanced in fine style, their concerted rush pushing the enemy back about 150 yards.

Quickly recovering, the Germans came back with a solid bombing counter-attack, supported by machine-gun fire, and eventually the hard-pressed British were forced to yield ground. Captain Fussell, the commander of B. Company, observing their plight, sent a message to Colonel Martin suggesting that the Seventeenth's Bombing Platoon should be put in to reinforce the Tommies. The Commanding Officer agreed, and before long the platoon, led by Sergeant J. M. Lyons, was on the move in the direction of Munster Alley to take up the fight.

A few moments in which to reconnoitre and then it went into action. Every man had been picked for his toughness and skill with bayonet and with bomb. They forced the enemy back over a further fifty yards; but the Germans were also tough and skilled in trench warfare, and, moveover, their supply organization was very good. Recovering from the first shock of surprise, they fought back, and before long the contest developed into one of sheer physical endurance, in which our men more than held their own.

Stripped to the waist, sweating and cursing, big men like Privates J. E. ("Scotia") McCleer, T. Lawler and C. S. Holland; middle weights W. L. ("Leggy") Ford, C. H. ("Chiller") Craig and W. A. Fraser; with A. E. Doling, F. McNair and F. Jefferson representing the light-weight class, continued to hurl their bombs with a precision acquired on the cricket field. Their advance down the Alley was grandly supported by the riflemen, Sergeant J. E. ("Bluey") Bennett—he who had won the Military Medal at Hill 60—Lance-Corporal H. D. McKenzie, and others. Later, both Bennett and McKenzie were killed. The brave Lyons was himself severely wounded and had to drop out of the fight, but the remainder of the platoon, under Corporal E. J. O'Keefe, carried on.

Many fine deeds were performed during the bloody combat that was now joined, and, perhaps, the most outstanding of these was the display of courage and endurance by Private T. Ridley. Wounded early in the fight, Ridley went to the rear to have his wound dressed. He returned to the firing line and again began to throw bombs, and to encourage his comrades. For three hours he continued thus, although in the meantime he had received two more wounds. Unable to throw any more bombs, he lay on the bottom of the trench and passed them forward, until, finally becoming exhausted, he was carried out of the line.

McCleer, one of the toughest of men, also displayed magnificent courage and stamina, and, like Ridley, gave a marathon display of bomb-throwing lasting for three hours.

Without exception every man in the platoon fought bravely. The casualties were heavy. On the other hand, the enemy continued to throw in fresh bombers, and as the afternoon waned, weight of numbers, added to the physical strain, began to tell against our men, who were gradually forced back. Stubbornly contesting every foot of ground, parched with thirst and choked with fumes from the bursting bombs, they called for more bombs and water. Captain Fussell immediately organized a chain of carriers, which eventually stretched for the best part of a mile down O.G.1 and Black Watch Alley to the supply dump. Padre F. Clune, the Brigade Roman Catholic Chaplain, who was ever to the fore when trouble was brewing, enthusiastically bore a hand in the task, the while shouting words of encouragement to the sweating human links forming the chain, pausing only to administer reproofs to those who used strong language.

Meanwhile, reinforcements arrived in the form of the Nineteenth's and, later, the Twentieth Battalion's Bombing Platoons, who took over the contest from the exhausted remnant of the Seventeenth, at a point about 50 yards down the Alley. Their advent was the signal for a renewal of the intensity of the struggle, with the Germans, however, displaying no sign of weakening in their counter-thrust. Casualties began to mount, and Fussell, observing the plight our men were in, called for volunteers to go to their assistance. Immediately Lieutenants H. G. Matthews and E. L. Lowther came forward and with them Sergeants A. Lorimer and J. P. O'Toole, Corporal R. Jolly, Lance-

Corporal N. R. Bailey and Privates W. A. Negus, J. J. Fahey, T. Brown, R. Palmer, J. Hubbard and A. C. Berry.

Fussell ordered Matthews to establish a bomb-block, which work that fine young leader proceeded to carry out, directing the operation while exposed to bombs and bullets. His coolness inspired all, and under cover of a hail of bombs from his men the block was completed and the enemy's thrust held. Matthews and his brave band manned the block until towards sundown, when they were relieved by the Eighteenth Battalion's Bombing Platoon.

And now to the two companies D. and A., in Pozieres Trench. Immediately following the opening of the attack by the British bombers, the Germans, evidently fearing a general attack, put down a blanket barrage on the whole of the 5th Brigade sector; as the afternoon progressed the bombardment was intensified. Pozieres Trench was enfiladed from both northwest and north, in consequence of which its garrison suffered severely. In many places its sides were blown in and men buried in the debris.

The stretcher-bearers performed prodigious deeds of bravery and self-sacrifice. All that hot afternoon, under the guidance of Sergeant H. Rockliff, the band-sergeant, they toiled like Trojans at their humanitarian task. Late in the afternoon, Rockliff, that cheerful, lovable character, was killed by a shell. The rest carried on.

Private A. Grix, a stocky, red-headed bandsman, was one of the coolest and pluckiest performers. The cry of "stretcher-bearers" invariably found him near at hand. During the brief respites between carries, he would return to his "possy" in the trench and set-to darning his socks, while he crooned to himself a sentimental ballad, utterly unperturbed by the terrific bombardment. Grix's fortitude and endurance were typical of the rest of the stretcher-bearers, who, every man of them, worked heroically throughout the whole of the period of eleven days the Battalion remained in the sector.

Pozieres Trench was by now a veritable shambles. Both A and D Companies had suffered heavily. The Lewis guns, under Sergeant C. Blackford, on the left of the trench, were hit and rendered useless, the majority of the crews becoming casualties, including Corporal L. Batt, who had a thigh broken. After Sergeant Blackford had put on a couple of splints, Batt dragged himself down the trench until, exhausted, he could not move any further. He lay there for some time uncomplaining until the stretcher-bearers could remove him.

The Scout Section lost nearly every one of its members, including Lieutenant B. S. Williams and Sergeant H. J. Smith, both of whom were severely wounded. By now it was evident that the trench was untenable. On D Company's sector, of the two platoons that originally formed the garrison, there remained unwounded Major Maughan, Lieutenant Mackenzie,

Sergeant J. W. Raitt, Corporals J. R. Felan and C. C. Brindley, Privates W. H. Griffiths and T. W. Johnson. Realising the futility of hanging on in such circumstances, Major Maughan decided to report personally to Colonel Martin and recommend that the trench be evacuated.

Maughan had previously observed that any attempt by the Germans to launch an infantry attack against Pozieres Trench could be met by enfilade fire from the cross trench linking O.G.1 and 2, which was held by B Company and where Lewis and Vickers guns were posted. He concluded that to remain in the position any longer would involve an unnecessary sacrifice of lives. Receiving Colonel Martin's assent to his proposal, Maughan returned to Pozieres Trench and ordered the withdrawal of the survivors to O.G.1. The move coincided with the arrival of the Eighteenth Battalion's Bombing Platoon to relieve Matthews at the bomb-block in Munster Alley.

The garrison of the cross trench and O.G.1, in the vicinity of the former, were fortunately not affected by the heavy bombardment. Evidently the German gunners were afraid their shells would fall on their own positions in O.G.2 and Munster Alley.

About 100 yards further down O.G.1 towards Black Watch Alley, the trench had been flattened in many places by the huge weight of metal that had pounded it for four hours. C Company, engaged in passing grenades to the embattled bombers during that long, terrible afternoon, also suffered severely. Eventually, O.G.I. for a considerable distance was littered with bundles of sand-bags, tins of water and cases of Mills bombs dropped by carriers who had been hit. Lieutenant L. S. Allen, of C Company, observing that this congestion would serve to interrupt the chain of supply, himself assumed the responsibility of giving orders for its discontinuance until such time as the scattered cases of bombs and supplies could be collected and formed into dumps ready to be passed forward when required.

Meanwhile, in Munster Alley, the bombers of the Eighteenth had relieved Matthews and had set about consolidating the position during a lull that had occurred in the fighting. Just after dusk a big explosion was heard near the bomb block in the Alley. Under cover of the smoke and the temporary confusion thus caused, the Germans, supported by a barrage of rifle-grenades, overran the defenders at the block and pushed down the cross-trench to a point about half way down its length.

Captain Beiers, who had taken over the command of the sector from Captain Fussell, called for volunteers to repel the Germans. Lieutenants Mackenzie and Lowther, who were standing near Beiers, immediately organised a party of bombers, which, headed by a couple of bayonet-men, counter-attacked. Lowther fell mortally wounded and gallant young Sergeant J. P. O'Toole was killed.

Presently, Mackenzie and a man of the Eighteenth, Lance-Corporal R. Wilkins (for his fine performance in this engagement Wilkins received his commission), found themselves at the junction of Munster Alley and O.G.2. The enemy had been cleared from the trench, but in all probability would again attack. It was decided, therefore, to establish a block at the junction. This task Mackenzie's party successfully accomplished, despite the showers of rifle grenades and bombs accompanied by gusts of machine-gun fire. When it was reported to him that the Germans had broken into the Seventeenth's position in the cross-trench, Colonel Martin sent for Major Maughan and instructed him to take charge of the operations in that portion of the Battalion sector. Maughan arrived on the scene while the bomb-block was being built, and with the aid of a Verey pistol illumined the area in which the enemy might attempt to group for a fresh attack.

Casualties among the defenders began to mount, but, despite the danger to which he was exposed, Maughan continued to direct and encourage his men. Whilst so engaged, he was struck in the forehead by a bullet and compelled to retire. The position, however, had been secured, and our men had the situation in hand, despite the night-long exchange of bombs. With the advent of daylight, this bickering ceased, as though by mutual consent, no doubt due to exhaustion.

The outcome of the desperate and costly struggle into which the Seventeenth, as well as the bombing platoons of the other three battalions of the Brigade had been drawn, remained in military parlance, "as you were."

Later in the morning, by mutual agreement, the 68th British Brigade took over the whole of the cross trench hitherto manned by B Company without incident. But about mid-day a fresh outbreak of bombing was heard in the direction of Munster Alley, followed by a call for "Anzac officers." Captain Beiers, at his headquarters near the junction of the cross-trench and O.G.1, heard the call and at once instructed Matthews and Mackenzie to investigate. These two officers made their way to the bomb-block at the mouth of the Alley, where there appeared to be some confusion amongst the defenders at that point. They learned that the situation was once more in hand. A sergeant of the West Ridings had mounted a Lewis gun in the vicinity of the block and had repelled an attempt by the enemy to advance up Munster Alley under cover of rifle-grenades and bombs. The explanation given by the sergeant for the appeal for Anzac officers was that both the officers of the West Ridings in that post had become casualties. The two Australians remained with the Tommies until another officer of the West Ridings arrived to relieve them.

Thus ended the fight for Munster Alley, one of the fiercest of its kind in the whole of the war, and into which the Seventeenth, as well as the bombing platoons of the 5th Brigade, had been thrown at a very heavy price. During its fifteen hours it was estimated that 73,000 bombs were passed up from the rear, for the gain of not one single yard of ground.

Munster Alley was to be the scene of more bombing assaults in the ensuing ten days, though not by Australian troops. The British units which attempted its capture also failed, and the position remained in German hands until August 4th, when together with O.G.2, it was taken as part of a general attack by the 2nd Division.

During the fight in Munster Alley there was an incident possessing a humorous aspect. Privates Ford and Craig, bombers, were the principals. These two worthies, who in civilian life were coal-miners, had retired during a lull in the fighting to slake their thirsts. Upon rejoining the platoon, they found the situation still quiet, so they decided to further explore the Alley "just to see what was doing." Both had their tunics slung on their arms as a relief from the intense heat, but neither carried weapons nor bombs. Rounding a bend in the trench they came face to face with a German officer, probably on a reconnaissance mission. The three men stood as though rooted in their tracks. Ford was the first to act. "Go for your life," he yelled, as he leapt on the parapet of the trench, Craig following suit by a split second. There each man grabbed a clod of earth and hurled it at the startled German, and then fled incontinently back to our lines. In the course of their hurried departure both dropped their tunics, and in the pocket of Craig's garment reposed his pay-book with a credit of £30 recorded therein. In narrating this tragic episode, Craig said: "I did not hesitate to run away from the Fritz, but I went 'butcher's hook' at losing my pay-book."

The incident had a pleasant sequel. Craig, together with Privates Mansell and McNair, also bombers, were wounded later in the day and eventually found themselves in hospital in Cardiff, "stone motherless broke." What could be done to raise some cash?

Suddenly remembering a public pronouncement by the Lord Mayor that no Australian soldier in that city would want for anything while he could help, the trio decided to "touch him for a few bob." For this purpose lots were drawn. It fell to McNair to act as spokesman, and he duly departed on his mission. After a full half hour's suspense, during which hope began to fade in the breasts of his waiting companions, McNair reappeared (and again to quote Craig) "with a grin on his dial, waving a five pound note in his hand and with two whiskies and soda under his belt."

Additional officer casualties incurred on the 26th, included Lieutenants C. C. Finlay, W. A. Robertson, H. G. Matthews and 2nd-Lieutenant R. V. Shields.

The 27th passed quietly, although the Seventeenth's position was subjected to some intermittent shelling, which appeared to come from a point north-west of Pozieres and thus enfiladed O.G.1. No further infantry action took place on either side. The opportunity was taken to remove the debris of bombs and material that littered O.G.1, and to deepen the trench where it had been almost levelled by shell fire.

Late the same afternoon, Colonel Martin received instructions from 5th Brigade Headquarters to organize a bombing attack up the unoccupied strip of O.G.1 between the sand-bag block and the tramline, where the enemy had established a similar block. On the map the operation appeared feasible enough, but evidently one thing not realised by the powers higher up was that the so-called trench was then only a straight shallow depression entirely devoid of cover. Gravely concerned, the Commanding Officer ordered Lieutenants Spier, Fay and Mackenzie, who were thoroughly acquainted with the position, to carry out a reconnaisance and report to him their views on the likelihood of the success of the proposed operation.

In due course, these three officers submitted their reports in person. They indicated that it was their firm conviction that the attempt would be disastrous. There was no vestige of cover under which to approach the objective and that the attackers would be exposed to machine-gun fire both from the front and from O.G.2. The report confirmed Colonel Martin's opinion, but he was faced with the necessity of making a grave decision, involving his personal position on the one hand and on the other a proper regard for the security of the men under his command. He did not hesitate. "Gentlemen," he said, "I know it will cost me my command, but I shall decline to undertake the operation until the Brigade Commander is personally acquainted with the result of your reconnaissance." It was a serious matter, involving the possibility of an end to his military career.

General Holmes was not only a first-rate soldier, he was also an understanding man. The following morning he went up to O.G.1 and saw the position for himself. He turned to Colonel Martin and said "I uphold your decision, Martin. It is now entirely my pigeon." But for the Commanding Officer's courageous attitude, it is morally certain that the Battalion would have suffered further heavy casualties, and, as in the Munster Alley affair, with no commensurate gain.

Plans were maturing for the next important step in the task allotted the I Anzac and II British Corps, of rolling up the German second line in the vicinity of Pozieres and to secure the high ground to the north and north-east of that place. The 1 Anzac Corps would advance along the crest of the Second Line Ridge. First it would be necessary to capture the two O.G. lines on the high ground already mentioned, on which stood the ruined windmill. The 2nd Division was ordered to carry out this operation on the night of July 28/29. The attack would be made on a 1,500 yards front and all three brigades would take part, from right to left the 5th, 7th and 6th. The sector allotted the 5th Brigade extended from the right of the Seventeenth's position to the main road and the inter-battalion boundary for the two attacking battalions, the Seventeenth and Twentieth, was the clearly defined tram-line. The Twentieth's objectives were O.G.1 and 2, while the Seventeenth (less two companies) would play a subsidiary part by capturing O.G.2, thus swinging into alignment with the Twentieth. The centre and left attacking brigades would be supported by the artillery of two British divisions and six Australian artillery brigades. The role of the right brigade, the 5th, was a minor one. It would be covered by one Stokes and one medium trench-mortar battery. Zero hour was fixed for 12.15 a.m. on the 29th.

The dispositions of the Seventeenth were five waves, each of fifty men, under the command of Captain Fussell, the first four to capture O.G.2 and the fifth to carry tools in order to consolidate the position. The first and second waves would form up in the cross-trench now held by the British and then move into No Man's Land in succession, doing a right form to bring them parallel with the objective. They would then lie down and await the signal to attack. The remaining three waves would form up in O.G.1, south of the sand-bag block, and move into position behind the two leading waves. Captain Beiers was in charge of the operation.

During the morning of the 28th, Captain G. J. Richards brought up a section of Stokes mortars and emplaced them in C Company's sector. The mortars had fired only a few ranging shots on the German positions in O.G.2, when an enemy shell scored a direct hit on one emplacement, wounding Richards and 2nd-Lieutenant W. H. Ravell of C Company, and temporarily disabling Captain Manefield. A little later the second emplacement also received a direct hit, which exploded the mortar-bombs stowed there, killing Lieutenant W. S. Kemmis and the whole of the crew of seven.

As a preparatory measure the British heavy and medium artillery pounded the trenches to the east of Pozieres all day. The 12- and 8-inch shells raised a dense curtain of dust, and hurled huge clods of earth into the forward position of the Seventeenth, hundreds of yards distant. Occasionally German soldiers could be seen running to the rear to escape the terrific shelling, giving our men the opportunity of indulging in some snap shooting at long range.

Soon after the close of the long summer evening, the attack-waves commenced to take up their positions in readiness to go over the top. In the limited space available for this purpose some confusion and delay resulted, added to which the enemy started his usual evening hate. This menaced the ranks of C

Company's detachment strung out in readiness in O.G.1 towards Black Watch Alley. Fortunately there were only a few casualties, although the trench was blown down in several places.

Finally, all were set for the assault, straining for the seemingly unending interval before zero to elapse. Suddenly, from the direction of Sausage Valley and Contalmaison the sky was aflame. Almost simultaneously there followed the roar of our guns and swishing of the shells speeding on to their marks. This was the signal for the first two waves to swing into position in the shell holes of No Man's Land. The Germans were ready. They had seen the Twentieth Battalion's waves as the latter left their trenches to line-up in the shell-holes ready to charge. Their S.O.S. rockets brought down a strong barrage, which was supported by a hail of machine-gun fire, while flares lit up the whole area, turning it into day. The third wave attempting to move out of our trenches was caught in a deadly traversing machine-gun fire, many men being hit as they climbed to the parapet. Lieutenant Maynard, in command of the third wave, had gone only a short distance when he was severely wounded in the leg. He lay all night and part of the following morning helpless in No Man's Land. His plight was then seen by one of his men, who went out in broad daylight and brought him in.

In the two preceding lines some confusion had been caused by casualties and difficulty in keeping touch on the shell-torn ground. Captain Fussell led the lines forward, but many fell and the attack petered out a few yards from O.G.2, where, from a shell-hole in which Fussell and a group of B Company men found themselves, they could see the Germans throwing grenades at our men. Many were hit, including Corporal Edwards, who was wounded in the neck and had his rifle smashed to bits. Privates Griffiths and Fahey were killed and Lieutenant L. K. Chambers, leading the second wave, was also shot dead as he attempted to lead his men forward.

Disorganized and subjected to a galling fire, the men waited for an easement of the murderous hail of lead. It was plain, however, that the attack had failed, and Fussell gave orders for the remainder to make their way back as best they could to our lines. In the meantime, due to the misunderstanding of an instruction, the fifth wave, commanded by Lieutenant Ronald, was ordered to move forward before the fourth, under Lieutenant Allen, and in consequence this officer, who had received explicit instructions not to move until he received the word, was left with his party in O.G.1 quite ignorant of what was happening to the other waves. They took no actual part in the attack.

On the other hand, Ronald, part of whose task was to maintain touch with the Twentieth, was unable to find the right flank of that battalion. At that time he was not aware of its failure to get forward. He decided to hold on where he was while he endeavoured to find the Twentieth and ascertain the position. For this purpose he sent out a patrol in its direction.

Back at his headquarters, Colonel Martin, unaware of Ronald's very proper decision, was becoming anxious, and this anxiety increased as time went on and no messages were received either from him or the Twentieth. He, therefore, ordered out a patrol to ascertain the position. The patrol returned and reported that it had located Ronald, who, by that time, was aware of the set-back received by the Twentieth. Colonel Martin thereupon issued instructions for his recall. The party returned. It had fortunately suffered comparatively light casualties.

Once again the Battalion was obliged to metaphorically lick its wounds. And the price paid was not light. All night the stretcher-bearers worked without respite bringing in wounded. The Regimental Medical Officer, Captain Smith, and his two capable assistants, Corporal E. Hall and Private J. C. Black, calmly dressed the wounded, all the time exposed to very heavy shelling in the vicinity of the Aid Post.

Of the stretcher-bearers, Privates W. Davis, A. Grix, P. A. Fahey, C. H. Childs, F. J. Hardy and G. Shuck showed an utter disregard for their personal safety while bringing in the wounded from No Man's Land. Sergeant C. Castleton, of the 5th Machine Gun Company, who was stationed at the sand-bag block in O.G.1, observing the plight of several men lying wounded well out in No Man's Land, went forward alone and brought two of them in. Whilst endeavouring to bring in a third man he was struck by a bullet and killed. He was posthumously awarded the Victoria Cross. In the vicinity of this sand-bag block, two other Australians had won the Victoria Cross during earlier operations. They were Lieutenant A. S. Blackburn, Tenth and Private J. Leak, Eighth Battalion.

Runners also behaved with conspicuous bravery. Among these were Privates A. W. McGlashan and M. Sharman, H. H. Rath and C. W. Ogilvie, who never faltered nor seemed to tire. The Signalling Section, under Lieutenant McCulloch, assisted by Sergeant D. H. White and Corporal F. Brown, worked unceasingly to maintain communications by telephone, an almost heart-breaking task requiring consummate nerve and coolness.

Battalion Headquarters, near the junction of O.G.1 and Black Watch Alley, was a hot spot from which Colonel Martin with his Adjutant, Captain H. W. Johnson and Regimental Sergeant-Major G. King, carried out the direction of the Battalion during the whole of its long and trying tour in that sector. King, a dapper little ex-British regular soldier, had sailed with the Seventeenth from Sydney as a lance-corporal.

The Seventeenth had now been in the line three days, and, while the task of capturing the O.G. Lines remained unfinished, there was little prospect of an early relief. Some temporary respite was secured by arranging that detachments in turn would proceed to Sausage Valley and have a spell for twenty-four hours. Another eight days ordeal had yet to be endured before the Battalion itself was relieved.

In the trenches conditions were making existence almost unbearable. In addition to the almost continuous shelling, intensifying periodically into the barrages, which the enemy put down over the very congested sector held by the 2nd Division, the heat and the stench of rotting corpses of Germans combined to make life miserable. In the vicinity of the sand-bag block in O.G.1, where the 3rd Brigade had had heavy hand-to-hand fighting, the enemy dead lay so thick that parties were detailed to bury the bodies. A few yards ahead of the block was a large dug-out with the entrance partly choked with debris. It had been bombed by 3rd Brigade.

One of the Seventeenth, engaged in the task of disposing of the enemy dead, on July 30th was amazed to see a young German soldier, little more than a boy, emerge from the dug-out and give a sign of surrender. He seemed to be on the point of collapse. Soon he revived under the stimulus of a tot of rum, and was then escorted to the rear. He had been in that foul dungeon for five days in the company of four of his dead comrades, whose bodies were later found by Lieutenant Mackenzie and Private M. J. McKay.

A human sidelight on these terrible conditions is revealed by a lad, Private J. Hutton, who had had the misfortune to be one of a number of reinforcements that joined the Battalion in the trenches about this time. In his diary, Hutton has briefly recorded his reactions to the mental strain to which he, an untried soldier, was being subjected. He wrote:—On July 25 ". . . it's just hell!" July 26 ". . . murder, bloody murder!" July 29 ". . . God in Heaven—how awful!" August 1 ". . . how long O Lord, how long!" Nevertheless, despite his mental anguish Hutton evidently found time to divert upon the part the pestilential body louse plays in the life of the soldier in the trenches. On August 1st he recorded that "Chats are sweet little crawling animals that make me take off my shirt four times a day!" Something in the nature of anti-climax, but typical of the Australian soldier's ability to fit into his surroundings and quickly forget the "rough stuff."

In Black Watch Alley, near its junction with O.G.1, the medical staff of the Battalion was kept busy attending to casualties. Walking wounded were directed to the Advanced Dressing Station near Casualty Corner, happy in the thought that they received only a "blighty."

Even in such circumstances the irrepressible humour of the Digger was much in evidence. Corporal (afterwards Lieutenant) F. Brown has recorded one such incident as follows:

"One poor cove, who was wounded in the thigh, was making his way down O.G.1, minus his breeches, which had been cut off so that he could be bandaged. One of his mates seeing the wounded chap wearing only his shirt, boots and tin hat, called out: "Hello, Chidley, what about 'The Answer'?" To which the wounded man replied: " 'The Answer'—I'm it!"*

The end of July found the Seventeenth still in the trenches and carrying out the routine duties of repairing and strengthening the defences, as well as clearing away debris in the form of engineering material, broken rifles and equipment. Lieutenants Ronald and Allen were detailed to take a party to conduct salvage operations in Suicide Alley, where they retrieved hundreds of picks and shovels. They were complimented by 5th Brigade Headquarters. During this period three Reinforcement officers joined the Battalion in the trenches. They were 2nd-Lieutenants J. C. Donaldson, J. E. Mawdesley and J. J. McDiarmid.

At Gordon Dump, where the Battalion nucleus, cookers and Transport Section were located, speculation was rife amongst the men on the subject of relief from the ordeal their mates in the front were undergoing. In normal times three days was the customary tour for a battalion, but now while a battle was raging, the Seventeenth had been kept in the front line for six days.

It transpired that during the afternoon, General Birdwood happened to be passing the Battalion kitchens, and observing the cooks and their off-siders at work, he paused to give them a few words of greeting. The General was about to move on when up spoke Private "Spud" Murphy with an invitation "to have a mug of tea with the mob." Being in a hurry Birdwood courteously declined and gave the men his usual friendly salute in farewell. Again Murphy spoke, and this is what he said: "Hey, Mr. Birdwood, don't you think you're making it a bit hot keeping the boys in the front line for so long?" The General did not reply. He simply had not heard the question. He was famed for his tact and wide understanding.

The long travail of the 2nd Division was about to end. A thoroughly prepared attack was to be mounted with its objective, the O.G. Lines and the windmill east of Pozieres. Profiting by the experiences of July 28th, jumping-off trenches would be dug under cover of darkness close enough to the enemy to allow our men to go into the attack before his machine-gunners could come up from their shelters and man their guns after our barrage had lifted. The order of attack and the objectives would be the same as those during the previous action, but in the 5th

---

* Chidley was a citizen of Sydney and an advocate of the "simple life," who was wont to appear in public, his sole outer apparel being a sleeveless white linen tunic reaching to the knees. He embodied his theories in a book the title of which was "The Answer."

Brigade the Eighteenth would this time go in on the right of the Twentieth Battalion, the task allotted the Seventeenth being a purely holding one in its present position and providing carrying parties for the Eighteenth. Zero was set for 9.15 p.m. on the night of August 4/5.

This time the attack was completely successful, all objectives being taken. At about 3.30 a.m. on the 5th the enemy threw in a heavy counter-attack, mainly on the 7th Brigade front. It was repulsed and the enemy left several prisoners in our hands.

At last relief was at hand. On the morning of August 5th, the Forty-fifth Battalion, of the 4th Division, arrived to take over the position which the Seventeenth had held for eleven consecutive days, the Battalion filed down O.G.1 and thence through Sausage Gully to Tara Hill, where it bivouacked for the night.

The following day General Birdwood made an inspection and congratulated all ranks on their good work. He also told them that they had "hearts of gold." He was sorry he could not promise them a long rest, as they were wanted back to kill some more Bosche. The same afternoon the Seventeenth moved on to Warloy and on the following day to la Vicogne. A stay of one night in this pleasant village and then on to Halloy to rest and recuperate for a short period. Sports and concerts were organised for the recreation of the troops, whose jaded spirits quickly revived under the warm sunshine and the peaceful surroundings of a place remote from the sound of battle.

During the Battalion's stay in Halloy, the following promotions of officers were announced: Captain H. M. Beiers to be Major and Lieutenant R. V. Spier to be Captain.

August 16th and 17th found the Seventeenth once more on the move to the forward area, in the vicinity of Pozieres. After a night in Sausage Gully the Battalion took over the Sunken Road Trench, near Pozieres village, and remained there until the 23rd, when it was relieved by the Nineteenth Battalion, in the front line. Two days later the 5th Brigade was withdrawn to Tara Hill to act as Divisional reserve. On the 28th the Battalion moved back to Warloy, where it stayed until the 31st.

Here immediate awards of decorations were promulgated. The Military Medal was bestowed on the following:—Lance-Corporal G. Kirkpatrick, Privates H. H. Rath, C. W. Ogilvie, A. W. McGlashan (who subsequently died of wounds), F. J. Hardy, E. Day, N. R. Bailey and G. Shuck.

Casualties suffered by the Seventeenth were as follows:— Officers: two killed and eleven wounded. Other ranks: sixty-four killed and 339 wounded. One other rank was reported missing.

CHAPTER VII.

North to Ypres—A comparatively peaceful sector—Back to the Somme—Rain, mud and freezing cold—A batman receives a surprise packet—Corporal A. McDonald repels a flammenwerfer attack—Private T. Crawford interrogates a Guards' colonel—A new Brigade Commander appointed—The second Christmas in bleak surroundings.

THE three Australian Divisions, which took part in the operations at Pozieres, suffered nearly 23,000 casualties—the 1st, 7,654, the 2nd, 8,114, and the 4th Division 7,058, an enormous total in relation to the strictly limited advance made. The losses sustained by the British, Canadian and New Zealand Divisions, which also participated, were correspondingly heavy, averaging nearly 7,000 per division. Such was the result of the policy of the British High Command, of dealing sustained heavy blows at a resolute enemy behind formidable entrenchments.

Looking back upon the series of limited operations in the Somme battle, in which the part played by the I Anzac Corps was typical, it may be questioned whether these attacks were too often not launched without adequate preparation. It may also be doubted whether the principle of economy in the expenditure of man-power was sufficiently well appreciated. Frequently trenches were over-manned, or the intervals in the attacking lines or waves too narrow. The mass of artillery of all calibres employed by the British to cover the comparatively narrow sector, together with the possession of an increasing number of machine-guns and light automatic weapons, should have made it possible to thin-out the trench garrisons and to utilise lesser numbers during attacks. As it transpired the congested area provided an almost wide-open target every time the enemy put down a barrage on it; while the assaulting infantry afforded unusual opportunities for the German machine-gunners, as they endeavoured to pick their way over the shell-cratered ground. In the circumstances heavy casualties were inevitable. The lessons drawn from this drastic experience resulted, however, in a modification of the tactical employment of the machine-gun and the Lewis gun, as well as infantry formations in the attack.

In its first major combat, the Battalion had acquitted itself in a worthy manner, and despite the heavy casualties and the great strain on their morale, all ranks were now in a position to claim veteran status. They were confident, too, that they could give measure for measure in combat with a scientific and resolute foe, whose fighting spirit, though severely tried, had not perceptibly diminished in strength.

The operations of the French and British armies were about to enter a third phase, representing the renewal of attempts to break through the German defence system on a wide front. For the operations, Haig, on the British sector, had been gathering fresh strength. He decided to use the Canadian Corps, then in the Ypres area, and send I Anzac to replace them. On August 28th, the 1st Division relieved the 1st Canadian Division in the Salient, with the 2nd Division moving in that direction.

September 1st found the Seventeenth in Beauval, a large village about fifteen miles due north of Amiens, the first stage en route to Ypres. Here, four days were spent in resting and refitting. Major Maughan reported back for duty, resuming command of D Company.

On the following day additional honours and awards for the operations around Pozieres were announced, Major J. M. Maughan receiving the Distinguished Service Order, Lieutenants K. W. Mackenzie and H. G. Matthews the Military Cross, and Distinguished Conduct Medals were awarded to Privates C. H. Childs, W. Davis, P. A. Fahey, A. Grix and T. Ridley, and the Military Medal to Private K. Filbey.

The occasion was celebrated in the form of a concert in the spacious Town Hall, and it produced unexpected talent from within the Battalion's ranks. The gallant Grix, whose cheery, ruddy countenance, masked a fondness for sentimental ballads, gave a soulful rendering of "In the Heart of a City that has no Heart." "Spud" Murphy, as an anti-climax provided a stirring, if somewhat ribald rendition of "La Marseillaise," which brought down the house, and by way of encore "Antonio Spagoni, the Toreador." Privates J. C. Black and Archie Baldwin gave an amusing topical sketch "The Soul of Anzac"; Major Beiers displayed his skill at sleight of hand and card tricks, and Lieutenant Ronald's imitation of the Pioneer-Sergeant sawing wood was well received.

On September 4th marching orders arrived, and on the following day the next stage, the march to Doullens, a large town, and entrainment there for Poperinghe seven miles west of Ypres, was completed. This pretty little town, once the centre of the lace making industry, though partly destroyed, was still inhabited by a considerable number of civilians of Flemish origin and with keen eyes as to what the soldiers wanted. There were the stationers' shops stocked with post-cards and writing materials, and even the London "Daily Mail" could be purchased. The fighting man, desiring a change from army diet, could buy himself an appetising dish of fried eggs and chipped potatoes.

The next move was in the direction of Ypres, where the

Seventeenth relieved the 11th Somersets in the Cavalry Barracks, on the 7th. The following day it relieved the 1st Rifle Brigade at Zillebeke Lake, south-east of the city. Compared with the conditions they had recently experienced the troops found the new sector a comparative haven of rest. Indeed, the "Bloody Salient" seemed to belie its terrible name. As a fact, both sides, during this period were sending their battle-worn divisions there to rest and recuperate; hence the change. The Germans appeared to be conserving their artillery, and refrained from any regular concentrated shelling. The main bombardments were by trench-mortars, throwing missiles which the troops called "rum-jars."

The tour at Zillebeke Lake was without incident, and on the 10th the Seventeenth moved back to Ypres after being relieved by the Twenty-third Battalion. A few days spell in billets in the Cavalry Barracks, and then orders were received to relieve the Nineteenth Battalion in the front line. This tour of duty passed uneventfully, and, except for a constant look-out that had to be kept for the rum-jar bombs, the troops devoted their attention to strengthening and draining the trench systems, and laying duck-board tracks. Out in No Man's Land, nightly, patrols worked with vigilance and energy, and soon gained a mastery in that sphere over their opponents. Mining operations on both sides were pursued with great activity. Even at that early date the Second Army was preparing the mines, which, nine months later, were touched-off as a curtain-raiser to the battle of Messines.

The only events of note in the life of the Battalion at this period were the wounding of Major Beiers, who was subsequently evacuated. There was also the announcement of the award of the Military Medal to Privates A. M. Dick and J. E. ("Scotia") McCleer for their bravery at Pozieres.

On the 21st, Captain Holmes, who had been evacuated ill in July, rejoined the Battalion and resumed command of C Company. The 26th was also a notable date, for it signalised the visit of Mr. Andrew Fisher, late Prime Minister and at that time High Commissioner for Australia in London, to the Ypres sector. It was quite a novelty for the troops to see a civilian in the front line trenches. Of necessity he could not tarry on the journey. The men were able to get only a passing glimpse of the stateman, who, at the call of the Motherland, had pledged Australia "To the last man and the last shiling." Certain military appendages to his civilian attire, necessitated by the exigencies of the situation, gave this grave and dignified elder statesman an unusual appearance. They were the subject of comment by Lieutenant Allen, who wrote in his diary: "Andy Fisher made a tour of inspection of our trenches, yesterday. He looked 'some nut' in 'civvy' clothes, with his slacks shoved into gum boots and a 'tin-hat' on top of his soft felt hat, not to mention his gas-helmet satchel strung round his neck. As he moved along the trenches all he would say was: 'Good-day— Good luck, boys.' "

Just at this period a mild out-break of scabies occurred. A highly infectious, but not dangerous, skin disease, easily cured, it had a distinct nuisance value. It temporarily rendered hors-de-combat forty of all ranks of the Battalion.

On the 27th the Nineteenth Battalion took over the front line, and the Seventeenth returned once more to Rampart Barracks. Here, after a stay of nine days, orders were received to proceed again to the Somme, where, on September 15th, Sir Douglas Haig had launched his second great break-through attempt. He had the assistance of the new "tanks," whose existence had been kept a secret up to the last moment, and which caused great consternation and panic amongst the enemy.

The attack was carried through nearly all the original German defence lines; but by October 7th the British found themselves still short of their original objective, Bapaume, and confronted by three additional defence-lines between them and that town and beyond it. The British line now extended from Morval, on the right, where it linked with the French Sixth Army (Foch) along the forward slopes of the Second Line Ridge, to Thiepval, north of the Albert-Bapaume road. Bapaume itself lay on the crest of the opposite slope of the valley some five miles distant.

Haig believed that the German losses had been far heavier than his own, and moreover, that their morale was showing signs of deterioration. In addition, the entry of Roumania into the war, and the gradual realisation that the great Verdun offensive had failed, would, he believed, further depress the enemy's spirit. He, therefore, decided to continue his policy of delivering sustained blows at the enemy, despite the lateness of the season. Early in October he issued orders for I Anzac to return to the Somme.

The Seventeenth was relieved by the Twenty-fifth Battalion on October 6th, and entrained for Godwaervelde. The following day it moved into Winnezeele, where, after a stay of five days, it marched into St. Lawrence Camp, Poperinghe, on the 12th. Three days later it moved to Alberta Camp, Reninghelst, where a stay was made until the 17th.

During the Battalion's stay in Alberta Camp the first referendum vote relating to conscription in Australia was taken. The votes cast by the A.I.F. were in favour of conscription by 72,399 to 58,894, but the total vote of the nation, by a slight majority, rejected the proposal.

At 9 a.m. on the 17th the Battalion moved to Arneke, via Winnezeele, where it remained until the 21st, then on to Bayenghem, and two days later to Rocques, which was left behind on the 24th, with Audruicq as the next point en route to its destination—that sector of ill-omen, the Somme. The following day the Battalion entrained for Pont Remy, eight miles from Abbeville, near the mouth of the Somme.

The weather was now becoming cold and the autumn rains were beginning to fall. When the Seventeenth marched out of that village to Les Haut Cloches, four miles distant, where it had to embus for the next stage of the journey, it encountered a heavy downpour, which drenched the troops, and did not tend to elevate their spirits. To make matters worse, the motor-bus column was three hours late. The journey was commenced under the most uncomfortable conditions of cold rain and damp, which chilled to the bone men sitting for a long period in cramped positions.

Once again the city of Amiens was traversed and then northeast along the main road leading to Albert, the long column coming to rest at Ribemont, about nine miles short of the former place, nine hours after it started. Ribemont, where the Seventeenth stayed for eight days, was a most uncomfortable billeting area. The barns in which the troops were quartered were verminous, draughty and leaky. It was a foretaste of the terrible conditions which they were destined to encounter during a winter afterwards said to have been the coldest in Europe for forty years.

During their stay in Ribemont the usual exercises and tactical formations were practised in weather that was wet and chilly. For the next six weeks, until the advent of the snowfalls and the frosts, the area of the Somme battle-field was literally a sea of mud, the continuous attacks of the preceding three months, accompanied by heavy shelling, having turned the countryside into one vast crater-field, for a depth of seven miles from the line where the great push had started on July 1st. The villages with their orchards that had dotted the landscape, were reduced to mere heaps of rubble, and of trees and hedges there remained hardly any trace. It was, indeed, a scene of utter desolation, presenting a seemingly unending vista of shell-holes. While the weather had been dry and the going good, the trenches required neither flooring nor revetting, and both troops and motor-lorries could make their way across country to any point desired, but the wet weather had changed all that. Trenches became drains, sometimes feet-deep in mud, which made it impossible to lay duck-boards on their floors; vehicular traffic was forced to keep to the few roads that existed, with the result that they broke down and made the going extremely heavy. This caused serious congestion in the endless lines of lorries, suplying ammunition and food. Even off the roads progress was difficult for men and horses, because of the boggy ground.

The heavy demand for labour in prosecuting the offensive of the preceding six weeks, had made it impossible to make adequate provision, beforehand, for an eventuality of this kind. For the time being, therefore, the question of bringing up engineering materials for strengthening the trenches had to be abandoned. The farthest point forward to which heavy transport could go in the area was just behind Second Line Ridge, two miles in rear of the front line. Here, depots were established and the regimental transport organized into pack-trains. Similarly, the artillery emplaced on the unsheltered forward slopes of the ridge had to receive their shells by pack-horse.

To provide for evacuation of wounded, relays of posts, each manned by groups of stretcher-bearers, were organized, and later, sledges were brought into use to carry the wounded.

In the whole of this wide area practically no head cover existed, excepting here and there in the form of old German dug-outs. It was far too risky to attempt to use what doubtful shelter could be found in the cellars of the ruined villages. The enemy regularly shelled these spots, which, in consequence, were studiously avoided by the troops.

Such were the conditions, the Battalion, refreshed by its rest at Ypres, found awaiting them. Strategically, also, the position had changed, Haig having once again modified his policy of breaking the enemy's resistance to one of maintaining a constant tension and meanwhile striking him at selected points along the pressure-line. In pursuance of this policy he had drawn the 5th Australian Division, which was part of II Anzac, from the Armentieres sector and brought them south, where it was incorporated with the I Anzac Corps, which was now under the Fourth Army. His intention was to attack across the valley in front of Bapaume and capture positions about a mile on the opposite slope, in the middle of October, in conjunction with the reserve (later Fifth) and Third Armies on the left carrying out subsidiary supporting actions. After several attempts, which were rendered abortive owing to the sodden nature of the ground greatly reducing the effectiveness of our artillery bombardments, he decided that the enemy's line could not be pierced that year. He was, however, still determined to maintain a constant pressure on his opponents in order to be in a position to renew break-through operations in the spring. He cancelled the operations of the two other Armies, and decided to give effect to his intention of hitting hard and often, by employing the Fourth Army for that purpose, incidentally securing for itself better wintering positions and be more favourably situated for the projected spring offensive.

The Fourth Army sector extended from Morval, on the right, to Le Sars, on the Albert-Bapaume Road, where it joined the Fifth (late Reserve) Army. The Fourth Army front was held by the XIV, I Anzac, and III Corps from right to left, each corps having two divisions in line, one in reserve and one in the back area, training. The front held by I Anzac was about 4,000 yards.

Towards the end of October the 1st and 5th Divisions took over the front line on I Anzac sector, with the 2nd Division in reserve and the 4th behind it. Already, by the time the 2nd Division had arrived in the area the 4th and 1st Divisions had been involved in a series of attacks. These had ended in stalemate, partly owing to the exhaustion of the infantry, which was greatly impeded by the boggy condition of the ground at the bottom of the valley, and partly to the enormous difficulty in maintaining food and ammunition supplies.

In the early days of November the 5th Division was withdrawn and the 2nd put into its place. Conforming to this movement, the Seventeenth marched out from Ribemont on the 4th, and, after a painfully slow approach along the congested road through Fricourt, reached Montauban, or rather, the place on which it once stood. The troops were billeted in wooden huts, affording them shelter from the biting wind and the rain. On the night of November 6/7, the 5th Brigade relieved the 7th Brigade, which had suffered heavy losses in seemingly useless attacks carried out in heavy rain. For two days the Battalion remained in the front line trenches, existing under conditions difficult to adequately describe. There was no overhead cover, other than that which could be "scrounged" from odd places for use as company or post headquarters, or by spreading the men's waterproof sheets over vertical "possies" scooped in the trench wall.

The trenches themselves in many places were feet deep in mud, in which men frequently were bogged and had to be dug out with shovels, often after much labour. A private of D Company was nearly three-quarters of an hour in such a position before being released in a state of semi-exhaustion. Captain Spiers found one of his men, Private H. G. Thornborough, stuck waist deep, and had to lay a folded stretcher across the trench to enable Thornborough to pull himself out of the mire. Extreme care had to be taken by the men in order to keep the mechanism of their rifles from becoming clogged and their ammunition dry and clean.

No hot food could be supplied, although hot tea was brought up in petrol tins. The troops, in consequence, had to carry on with dry rations, frequently fouled by contact with the mud. Communications with flank companies and the supports was difficult and hazardous, runners preferring to work along the top of the trenches at the risk of being sniped, to the slow exhausting process of ploughing through the gluey slime on the trench-bottoms.

The signallers and runners performed splendid feats of endurance and courage, maintaining communications, repairing broken telephone lines and carrying messages between Battalion Headquarters and the front line. In this hazardous work the signalling-sergeant, D. H. White, who originally played the tenor horn in the band, and Signaller J. T. O'Neill were killed, and two of their comrades, Privates Wilson and Kelly, severely wounded.

Sergeant M. Sharman, then a battalion runner, has left a vivid description of the prevailing conditions. He wrote: "I had a job as battalion runner between headquarters and companies. Part of my job was to guide ration parties up to the front line on pitch dark nights. So that I could find my way I kept my eyes on the muddy waste in order to pick up the track, which shone whenever the flares went up. I used to have a new pair of socks every trip, otherwise I could not have kept going. I got them from the number of dead men lying about, each of them had a spare pair in his haversack. One blessing the mud brought was that the enemy shell-fire was largely ineffective; it nearly took a direct hit to bowl one over, because the shells just threw up a spout of mud when they landed. I heard of one officer who had a Verey flare pistol in each hand when "Fritz" made a local attack. In the excitement of the moment he fired both at once, only the pistol in his left hand was pointing downwards, the result being that he shot his own batman in the back-side . . . Getting up the line used to take hours; one got bogged and had to get out of one's gum boots to get unstuck. Rifles and Lewis guns had to be wrapped up and the trench wall to be constantly shovelled out when it collapsed. I made myself a shallow hole in No Man's Land to save me from having to stand in the mud. Back in rest areas it was nearly as bad—Nissen huts with narrow duck-boards in between and mud everywhere. I remember seeing a man trying to cross a road and getting stuck. Finally a mule had to be ridden out to him and he had to hang on to its tail to be pulled out. In the front line, drinking water was scarce and we had been warned not to use the water in shell-holes. That was all very well, but thirsty men had no option; some of us found a nice clean pool in No Man's Land and after using it again and again we found a dead Hun in it. Soon the mud gave way to intense cold; the water in our bottles froze, and the bully beef and tea had become ice cream by the time they reached the front line."

The forward area was under constant and heavy shell-fire, most of which, luckily, fell to the rear of the front trenches. One shell, however, got right into B Company's trench on the right, killing 2nd-Lieutenant W. G. Devitt and wounding Lieutenant J. J. Fay. Devitt was a promising young officer of more than average ability. He had received his commission direct from the rank of lance-corporal, for his courage and leadership during the Pozieres operations. The Seventeenth had lost a promising young officer. Fay was ultimately invalided out of the army as the result of his head wound, and with his departure the Battalion was deprived of the services of one of its best platoon leaders, fearless as he was meticulous in carrying out every detail of his duties. He had been a tower of strength to B Company, and was subsequently awarded the Military Cross.

The two-day tour of duty in this unwholesome spot was also the occasion for an unusual experience, in fact one which it is doubtful befell any other battalion of the A.I.F. It was in the form of a flammenwerfer attack made by a small party of Germans, just before daybreak, on the 8th on a post held by No. 16 Platoon under Sergeant R. Wilson and Corporal A. McDonald. Wilson, with a party of riflemen and bombers was holding a portion of the trench some 60 yards to the right of McDonald, who was in command of a Lewis gun section posted at the mouth of an unoccupied stretch of trench leading to the German lines. He had with him Corporal W. H. Rowe and Private T. A. Kelly, one of the lightest and toughest men in the Battalion.

The enemy made a feint attack on Wilson's post while the flammenwerfer party stole along the disused part of the trench leading to McDonald's post. The enemy operator had the machine trained on McDonald and his gunners, who were intent on watching developments on their right and, therefore, had not seen the move. With a hiss and a roar the contents of the flammenwerfer were launched at the gunners, who instinctively ducked below the level of the parapet. But they kept their heads, and moving back along the trench they waited for the Germans to appear, when McDonald opened fire on them with his gun. That finished the attack and the enemy withdrew under cover of semi-darkness, and bombs, which, however, caused only one casualty, a man in Wilson's party being slightly wounded.

It was not possible to ascertain whether the enemy had suffered any casualties, but the incident was a close shave for our men who had to withstand the terrific heat of the flames and were covered in oil-spots. Some webbing equipment lying on the parapet was incinerated, and had the German, who operated the flammenwerfer used it from the top of the trench instead of the bottom, it is certain that the Lewis gun section would have suffered a horrible death. But even this ordeal by semi-immersion in muddy drains, and exposure to chilling wind and soaking rain, that frequently induced a state of physical nausea, ended for the time being. It was to be repeated on several occasions in the ensuing eight weeks, but none of the subsequent tours during that dreadful winter left such a deep impression on the minds of the men who were subjected to those unforgettable experiences.

During the night of November 9/10, relief came in the form of the Nineteenth Battalion, and the Seventeenth withdrew to Carlton Camp, about two miles distant. Many men were so exhausted that they fell asleep in shell-holes, rejoining the unit after day-break. Morning revealed a camp of tents, stained with mud to camouflage them. There were no facilities for drying clothes, or for reasonable comfort. After a scratch breakfast, a roll-call was held, and one officer and 107 men were subsequently evacuated, the majority with trench-feet; others were suffering mainly from the effects of exposure. Many of the latter after receiving treatment at the Field Ambulance rejoined the Battalion in a day or two.

The Seventeenth "rested" at Carlton Camp all that day, and on the following morning sixty more of all ranks were given attention by the Field Ambulance. At 4 p.m. it moved to Mametz Camp, a collection of Nissen huts, designed to hold about one platoon to each hut. Here, in the comparative comfort afforded by protection from wind and rain, and the warmth enjoyed from the fire in braziers made out of oil-drums, the troops soon recovered their spirits. At this period the use of whale-oil was introduced as a preventive against trench-feet. Standing orders were that commanders should be responsible to see that it was applied daily. Except for the beneficial effects derived from the massaging part of the process, it is questionable whether the oil itself was of any value for this purpose; at any rate, its use was subsequently discontinued. Three days were spent at Mametz Camp, and on the 15th the Battalion moved to Montauban Camp about a mile and a half distant.

The conditions described were the common ills of the Fourth Army, but there remained another serious problem. That was the tactical situation arising from the boggy nature of the countryside, and the few roads that were rapidly becoming unusable, rendering it extremely difficult to maintain communications and supplies to the troops in the front line and supports. Had the enemy attacked during this period troops holding these positions ran a grave risk of being isolated. Orders were issued for an intensive works programme and soon there sprang up in this wilderness of shell-churned mud, wooden hutments, roads, watering-points and light railways, while miles of duck-board tracks were laid running right up to, and along the parados of the front trenches. New trenches were also dug forward of the crest-line of the ridge.

The Germans on their side of the valley were also suffering hardships similar to that being borne by our troops, though, perhaps, not to the same extent. The slopes on the German side still retained their greenness and comparatively level condition, while the villages in the immediate rear, as well as the town of Bapaume, with its numerous cellars, provided a reasonable degree of shelter for the troops withdrawn from the front line. In the trenches their troops also suffered much hardship, as was subsequently proved to be the case.

At this period the British artillery was superior in weight to the German, although much of its effect was neutralised by the boggy condition of the ground into which the shells plunged, throwing up columns of mud and steam. It did not screen the advance of our troops from view of the enemy machine-gunners, who, in consequence, were able to inflict heavy casualties on the lines of attackers laboriously wading towards them through the morass. This was responsible for the abortive results of the many piecemeal attacks delivered on the Somme, between the middle of October, and which finally caused Haig to refrain from further operations during the winter.

Only one of these attacks had proved successful, that one being by the Fifth Army, which captured Beaumont Hamel, on November 13th after a brilliantly executed operation, resulting in the capture of 7,500 prisoners. This action, the last of a series of bloody encounters, brought to a close the Battle of the Somme, which had been launched four and a half months earlier with the object of breaking the German defences on a frontage of about sixteen miles, and a depth of eight miles, within the compass of a few days, but had failed in its immediate object and at the tremendous cost of nearly 500,000 casualties of which the Australians losses totalled 7,487 killed and 23,277 wounded. The number of casualties inflicted on the Germans has not been made known, but 38,000 prisoners were taken with 125 guns and 514 machine-guns.*

Although the objective aimed at in the great Somme offensive had not wholly succeeded, the tremendous blows rained on the Germans had a marked effect on their morale, which was showing signs of strain. On the other hand, however, a corresponding effect, though to a lesser extent, was also manifested in the British armies. The tremendous losses suffered and the extreme rigours of a prolonged campaign could not fail to result in some degree of deterioration. But out of that stern ordeal of blood there arose an army that man to man was a match for the German soldier, trained to war, and entrenched in seemingly impregnable positions though he was.

The men of the New Armies raised in the British Empire were mostly only partly trained, when they entered the battle. Every man, however, was fired by the volunteer spirit that upholds courage in the face of danger and hardship, supported by the firm conviction that the cause for which he was fighting was right.

The rival armies settled down to the task of consolidating

---

* The Australian Official History, Vol. III, page 946, gives the estimate of 2.3 British to 1 German put out of action.

their respective positions in the sea of mud and dead, brown wilderness, which once was part of beautiful Picardy. On November 18th, the Battalion moved out from Montauban Camp and relieved the Twenty-Seventh Battalion in the front line, losing 2nd-Lieutenant New, who was slightly wounded. After another three days of exhausting front line trench duty the Seventeenth was relieved by the Royal Sussex Regiment, and moved back to Carlton Camp, and thence to Quarry Siding, the rail-head of the newly-laid line just north of Montauban, and entrained for Meaulte, a village a few miles south of Albert, where, after detraining it marched to Ribemont, arriving there at 3 p.m. the same day. At Ribemont all ranks found relief from the strain of trench duty and the seemingly unending fatigues of the forward areas, despite the dirty, damp and draughty billets. There was added satisfaction when it was announced that leave to Amiens would be granted.

Driver McLaren has recorded his impressions of the conditions prevailing in the rear areas, thus: "The first fall of snow (November 18). Boots are frozen and, oh, the misery of this sloshing about in the frozen mud! It is beyond me to describe it. And when the poor horses' work is finished they stand on the lines, knee-deep in the mud and we can do nothing for them. The boys in the trenches share the same fate. It is cruel. Very rarely nowadays is there a smiling face; but the sun will shine again."

Allusion to the congested state of the roads in the forward zone recalls a pithy incident in which a Guards' colonel and Private T. C. Crawford of A Company were the principals. Crawford, who was too old for the front line, had been assigned traffic duty in this area, regulating the manner in which horse, foot, guns and vehicles should move along the route, in accordance with instructions handed to him by a higher authority. One day a battalion of Guards marching in fours approached Crawford's point, colonel in front, adjutant half a horse-length in rear, and so on down the column. Up went Crawford's arm signalling "Halt!" Then addressing the colonel he said: "Sir, you will have to march in single file on the side of the road."

Colonel: "We are the Guards."

Crawford: "It don't matter to me, you've got to march on the side of the road. Them's the orders."

Colonel: "Get out of the way. We are the Guards."

Crawford: "I don't give a damn if you are the bloody engine drivers, you've still got to march on the side of the road."

And history will probably record that they did march on the side of the road.

While the Battalion lay at Ribemont, Captain Smith left in order to take up an appointment at a base hospital. This genial and capable officer had given fine service during his eighteen months stay with the Seventeenth. At the outset he earned a certain degree of unpopularity because of his attitude to those men whom he felt were malingering. After the troops had observed his coolness under fire, and his untiring attention to the wounded, especially during the battle of Pozieres, where his Aid Post was constantly under shell-fire, their opinion of this imperturbable giant, who, in unofficial moments was wont to address everyone, including senior officers as "George," changed to one of esteem and respect. The Battalion was fortunate in the appointment of his successor, Major R. M. McMaster.

Orders were received on the 29th to move to Cardonette, twelve miles further west and about five miles north-east of Amiens, the move being completed by 5 p.m. on the 30th. Two days later the Divisional Commander, General Legge inspected the Battalion, and complimented it on its good showing, while, on the following day, General Holmes reviewed the 5th Brigade for the last time before proceeding to take over the command of the 4th Division.

The general had early gained the confidence and respect of all ranks of his command by his courtly manners, utter disregard of danger and soldierly bearing. Holmes was frequently to be seen in the front line during the hottest period of an action, the red band of his gold-laced staff cap being conspicuous as he moved along the trenches, spurning urgent invitations by the occupants to "keep his head low." His untimely death in 1917 was a heavy loss to the A.I.F. He was succeeded by Brigadier-General R. Smith, who had commanded the Twenty-second Battalion, 6th Brigade.

Smith was a Victorian and both in physique and temperament was the direct opposite of Holmes, being large of stature, forthright of speech and manner, hard-swearing and possessed of a broad humour; but prone to allow his judgment of individuals to be swayed by personal prejudices. Like Holmes, he was a man of great personal courage, and his forceful character soon made itself felt throughout his new command. His military career was an unusual one. Receiving his first commission in the Commonwealth Military Forces in 1910, when 33 years of age, he had, six years later, attained the rank of brigadier-general. He was fond of recounting the story of a youthful British subaltern whom he met whilst on leave in London. This young officer complained to Smith of the language used by an Australian soldier, whom the officer had reprimanded for failing to salute him. "What did he call you?" asked the general. "Why, Sir, he called me a bloody 'one-pip' artist," the subaltern replied. "Is that all," exclaimed the general. "My boy, do you know what my men call me? They call me 'Bob the bastard!'"

The Battalion stayed at Cardonette for seventeen days, during which period it was exercised in the new "artillery formation"—that is, sections advancing in single file and widely dispersed in intervals and in depth. This had superseded the system of lines or waves, during the attack. Part of these exercises comprised practice in moving to the attack under a "creeping" barrage. The role of barrage was taken by transport horses, led back and forth along the front about one hundred yards in advance of the infantry, for the allotted three minutes or so, when the barrage would "jump" another hundred yards allowing the troops to advance a further stage under its protective screen.

On December 16th, the Battalion marched out of Cardonette towards Franvillers, where it stayed one day, and on the next moved to Dernacourt, its destination once again the forward area. Here, Colonel Martin fell ill and was evacuated to hospital, Major Travers assuming temporary command. The following day, Sydney Camp, Fricourt, was reached and the first snow-fall encountered. The next day, the 20th, "E" Camp, Trones Wood, was made and here the Battalion remained until the afternoon of the 25th, which had broken fine and clear although the ground was still wet and muddy.

The forbidding aspect of the surroundings in which they were about to spend Christmas Day, however, had little effect on the spirit of the troops, which was further cheered by the distribution of reading matter and a liberal issue of plum-puddings, on a scale of 16 pounds to every 22 men. Thus their second successive Christmas Day was spent on a bleak wind-swept country side, in conditions calculated to depress even these cheerful warriors from the land of the Southern Cross, accustomed to celebrating that season of the year on the warm sunlit beaches, or picnicking in the fragrant bush. If occasionally their spirits were dampened by the extreme hardships to which they had been subjected during a winter said to have been the severest on record in Europe for forty years, their inveterate humour invariably rose to the surface inspiring all ranks to "give it another 'go'."

The same afternoon the Battalion moved to Delville Wood, where it relieved the Eighteenth Battalion, in brigade reserve. Here, quartered in damp old German dug-outs and "possies" which they had done their best to make habitable, the troops bivouacked for three days in weather that was cold but bright and clear. On the 28th the support line at Switch and Needle trenches were taken over in a heavy fog from the Nineteenth Battalion, thus marking the occasion of yet another spell of duty in conditions no whit more comfortable than on their previous visits.

Fortunately, the position was relieved to some extent by

an issue of "tommy cookers" (small tins filled with solidified alcohol) which proved a distinct boon to the troops. These cookers had been sent by the Seventeenth Battalion Comforts Fund from Sydney, and never was any of the numerous gifts forwarded by this devoted band of women workers more gratefully received. Nor could they have arrived at a more opportune time, for conditions made it impossible to keep up a regular supply of hot food to the front trenches.

If these devoted women could have been present to witness the expressions of pleasure with which these simple, but practical gifts were received, assuredly they would have felt themselves amply repaid for their assiduous attention to the needs of their menfolk, who were experiencing such mental and physical discomfort.

It is recorded that on this date General Holmes handed over command of the 5th Brigade to the new brigadier, and that a billeting party from the Seventeenth was detailed to proceed to Albert. The 29th and 30th were devoted to improving communications and front-line trenches, the weather still being foggy and the situation normal.

On the night of December 30/31, the Seventeenth relieved the Nineteenth Battalion, the change-over being completed without incident. On the 31st the Germans shelled the forward area heavily, once again leaving the signallers hard put to it, dodging from one shell hole to another, locating and repairing breaks in the telephone lines, sometimes even wading through saps up to the men's waists in water. In retaliation, and also, perhaps, as a farewell to the old year, the artillery on the British side opened a very heavy bombardment on the German trenches at 11 p.m., which lasted until 1.5 a.m. on New Year's Day. In this manner the year 1917, a year of more bloody battles, with their attendant heavy casualties, made its debut.

CHAPTER VIII.

Advent of 1917—Allies retain initiative—Plans for early resumption of the offensive upset by appointment of new French Generalissimo—Seventeenth in Switch and Needle trenches—Bitter frosts and snowfalls—Lieutenant J. L. Wright trains Lewis gunners—Battalion inspected by new Divisional Commander—Life in the outposts near Butte de Warlencourt.

THE advent of 1917 found the contending armies on the Western Front in a position similar to that of two powerful adversaries who had just completed a hard-slogging round in the prize ring, and were waiting for the gong to sound in order to resume the contest. The enemy, although thrown on the defensive by the unrelenting, hard-hitting armies of France and Britain, his morale shaken, and his material losses great, had, nevertheless, extracted a very heavy price for the territory he had been forced to give up. But he was still strong, and, furthermore, was buttressed by the knowledge that both Russia and Roumania were virtually out of the war.

The Franco-British Armies, on the other hand, possessed two clear advantages over the Germans, first, an ever mounting strength, and second, the initiative, which had passed to them during the preceding summer campaign. Joffre and Haig, jointly, had agreed to press on with the policy of hitting the enemy hard and without respite, thereby obviating any attempt on his part to wrest the initiative by a forestalling offensive. Their plan was to deliver a blow early in February on a front of sixty miles extending from Vimy Ridge, north of Arras, to the River Oise in the south, while further south another powerful French army would be waiting to go in and exploit any success. At a later date British armies would launch offensives in Flanders with the object of driving the enemy away from the region of the Belgian coast.

Unexpected political events occurring in France, about this period, caused a complete overthrow of the proposed plan. The French Generalissimo, Joffre, was replaced by General Nivelle, who held different strategic beliefs to Joffre and Haig. He was an exponent of the principle of the massive break-through at a single selected point, therefore, their plan was totally unacceptable to him. Finally, it was agreed between Haig and himself that the French armies, early in April, would deliver the main blow at a point to be selected, while the British armies and part of the French would launch powerful subsidiary assaults with the object of pinning the enemy's reserves. To give effect to the new plan, Haig agreed to take over ground to the south and thus make an additional army available to Nivelle. At this period the Allied Armies on the Western front were operating under dual control. It was not until early in 1918 that a unified command was established.

We now return to the narrative. We find the Seventeenth still in the line on January 1st. On the following day a readjustment took place, whereby the Twentieth Battalion took over the front line and the Seventeenth Switch and Needle Trenches in reserve. On January 3rd, it was relieved by the Nineteenth Battalion, and moved back to "E" Camp, Trones Wood. During this tour 2nd-Lieutenant W. R. Haigh was wounded. The Battalion remained at "E" Camp, where it was relieved on the 7th by the Twenty-Seventh Battalion, Seventh Brigade. Montauban Camp was the next stage, and there the Seventeenth stayed for six days. In this camp new devices were installed to serve as gas alarms and S.O.S. signals in case of attack. They were in the form of Strombos horns and coloured flares fitted to rifle grenades, but tests revealed that owing to the high winds the horns proved ineffective. Here, Lieutenant W. H. S. Sheppard, who had been evacuated ill from Gallipoli, rejoined in company with 2nd-Lieutenant T. R. Reid, a reinforcement officer, and Major J. M. Maughan, who had recently completed a senior officers' course in England, was transferred to the Twentieth Battalion. His departure was regretted by all ranks, especially junior officers and the men of D Company, who regarded him as a true friend and wise counsellor. His cool bearing in all circumstances attracted the confidence of every one with whom he was brought into contact, and none more so than the subalterns and non-commissioned officers of the company, among whose ranks was a liberal sprinkling of men of either Scottish birth or descent, a fact of which he was very proud.

The long period of foul weather which had proved such a bane to the existence of the troops, now gave way to bitter frosts, followed by heavy falls of snow. The ground became firmer, and in the trenches, hitherto water-logged, men could now move about freely, thereby reducing the number of casualties arising from trench feet. For additional comfort all ranks were issued with two pairs of gloves, per man, one pair being of worsted and the other of sheepskin lined with wool. In the rear areas, however, there was no improvement in the damp and draughty billets to offer even the barest comfort. This condition was responsible for a crop of casualties, for the War Diary states: "The weather conditions at this period were exceptionally severe . . . From December 29 many cases of severe frostbite were experienced and casualties were heavy."

On January 16th the Battalion moved to Dernancourt, a three-hour march. In this miserable spot it was billeted for twelve days. The opportunity afforded by the spell from front line duty was devoted to reorganization and training. A new batch of reinforcements had just arrived and from these a number were selected for training as Lewis gunners under Lieutenant J. L. Wright, the Lewis gun officer. Lieutenant Maynard has described the enthusiasm and zeal displayed by this capable officer: "We had recently received reinforcements, and we had to put in a lot of training with them under difficult conditions. Lieutenant Wright has a passion for training his people to be good Lewis gunners, and we have hardly arrived at a bivouac—or camp, before we hear his guns rattling away right by our front door. In no time runners arrive from neighbouring battalions complaining that bullets are flying about amongst them, and will we please stop. Our sympathy is always entirely with our neighbours; indeed we are always a little apprehensive that we shall be shot-up ourselves."

At Dernancourt, on January 25th, the Battalion was inspected by the new Divisional Commander, Major-General N. M. Smyth, V.C., who subsequently informed Major Pye, who was temporarily in command, that the Seventeenth appeared to him to be the best turned-out battalion, as regards personnel.

About this time a reorganization of the establishments of infantry battalions took place. Instead of specialists, such as Lewis gunners, scouts and bombers, being attached to either battalion or company headquarters, as hitherto, they were now to be distributed between platoons, which would comprise one Lewis gun section, the members of which could be identified by a narrow band of yellow cloth worn on the shoulder straps; one rifle, with white; one bomber with red; and one rifle-bomber section with red and green distinguishing tabs. Each section comprised one non-commissioned officer and seven other ranks. The new field formation, or battle drill, as it was called, which has been previously mentioned, consisted of groups of men, mainly sections, advancing in single file with wide intervals between sections, thus offering a much smaller target to enemy artillery and making for better control by junior leaders. It was called "artillery formation."

On January 29th the Battalion departed from Dernancourt for Albert, at which place it stayed until the 31st, when it moved to Shelter Wood Camp, near Fricourt, where it relieved a battalion of the Highland Light Infantry. The following day it moved up to the front line and relieved the Gordon Highlanders, at Le Sars. On that part of the front there was no continuous line of trenches, the defence system comprising a series of strong posts sited so as to give covering fire to each other; they were linked by systematic patrolling during darkness. This patrolling proved to be ticklish work on account of the heavy blanket of snow that covered the ground, making even night movements discernible at comparatively long distances.

An admirable account of the conditions prevailing during this period is to be found in Lieutenant Maynard's intensely interesting "Letters." Maynard's description of the weather, terrain, conditions of life in the outposts, and the hazardous work of patrolling, is given in his usual breezy and vivid style, in which hardihood, courage and devotion to duty displayed are sharply underlined. It is slightly edited.

"Looking across these peaceful snowfields one finds it hard to realise that but a few months ago they were the scene of some of the fiercest and bloodiest fighting of the war. Here were villages, factories, woods, cemeteries, roads and railways; now all have been levelled and what traces there still are of former days have been covered by a couple of feet of glistening snow. The wet weather has caused most of the old trenches to fall in, and even where a particularly well made trench has withstood the weather it is now full of frozen water, and being snowed over, is unrecognisable as a trench.

"As one gets closer to the present firing line, however, this peacefulness gradually merges into activity of a military nature. The French population have not been allowed back and no attempt has been made to rebuild villages, but in their place are camps, workshops, dumps, railways and the thousand and one things required behind an army in the field. Streams of vehicles of all classes occupy the numerous strategic roads, day and night, carrying ammunition and supplies to the armies in the line. Baths have been erected where men from the trenches bathe and obtain clean underclothes. Soup kitchens are dotted along the roads to the front line, where tired troops returning from the trenches may obtain a mug of soup any time during the day or night free of charge. Everywhere is activity and everywhere are soldiers, all hoping that this will be the last year of war.

"A visit to the battlefield of Pozieres is of interest, even though not many of the old spots are recognisable. Occasionally a familiar object would be found, such as a heap of trench mortar bombs on the side of a sap, or the remains of an old French farming cart which had been in No Man's Land in front of us. By these means, guides are able to locate the trenches which we occupied and out of which we attacked on 28th July. Not much of the trenches remain now, and by the time spring comes they will be entirely obliterated, and over all will be a growth of grass and field flowers. Nature is a wonderful healer; woods, such as Delville Wood, High Wood, Fricourt Wood, Bazentin Wood, etc., which now are only represented by stumps and blasted undergrowth, will be leafy glades of the Christmas card variety in a month or two, and shell-holes of earlier days will be overgrown with yellow charlock, like so many golden fairy rings.

"As the battle line moves on, so do the names given by the soldiers to the various trenches, saps, crossings, sunken roads, corners, etc. In many cases the old notice boards are carted along and put up in new positions. From the names it is easy to recognise whence the original occupants came. London troops stick to Shaftesbury Avenue, Leicester Square, Bow Bells, Tottenham Corner, Charing Cross, Old Kent Road, etc. East Coast Scottish troops stick closely to Princes St., Carlton Square, William Street, etc., whilst the Glasgow men christen their spots Sauchiehall St., St. George's Square and so on. Australia never had much chance to identify herself with the custom of name-giving, as we generally occupied trenches which had already received the necessary attention. One typical Australian name only I remember, and that was at the intersection of two main saps in the Armentieres District which rejoiced in the title of 'Belfields Corner.' Dugouts also come in for a variety of names. We have 'Rose Villa,' 'Berlin View,' 'Leicester Lounge,' '10 Downing St.', 'The Cecil'; whilst 'Little Grey Homes in the W_{et}' abound. But only one of them really lingers with me as having possessed both feeling and appropriateness—it was called 'Latrine View.'

"Major Pye, is now relieving C.O. of the Battalion, to which he brings an alert mind, enthusiasm and guts. By profession a medical man, he chose the fighting side of the army. His cousin was killed with us at Bois Grenier.

"This land in winter alternates between hard frost and mud. For three weeks we have continuous frost, during which the ground is so hard as to defy the men's efforts to dig trenches. All food is frozen, including bread, and the Brigade Band can't play for fear the men's lips will freeze to the mouthpieces of the instruments. Then suddenly, a thaw sets in and the country in one day is transformed into a sea of mud in which horses and men struggle and flounder. Whilst the frost is on, conditions are very severe, both in and out of the line. Every procurable article of clothing is put on, but still we are cold, whilst underneath the chats (body lice) keep us in constant torture. It is far too cold to strip off and look for them, and the weight of clothing nullifies the satisfaction which scratching usually affords. Braziers in dugouts and huts invariably smoke, and in any case only warm those in their immediate vicinity. Rum is a solace — when we can get it.

"Let us follow a battalion into the trenches. An officer and a couple of N.C.O.'s from each company have gone up to the line the night before to obtain full particulars as to how it is held and the disposition of the troops in the various posts. They return and are able to divide their companies up accordingly, so that on arrival at the trenches each party can move to its appointed place without confusion. A heavy frost is on and the road is slippery, so the men wrap a sandbag round each boot to help them keep their feet. Steel helmets are chalked white so as not to show up against the snow. Rations and water being served all round, we push off. For a mile or so we follow the road, and then branch off on to a duck-board track and here our troubles commence. The duckboards are frozen and are very slippery. I used to think that walking with carpet slippers on polished lino was a perilous matter, but frozen duckboards beat all. It is moonlight and the duckboard track shows up well across the snow as it winds about the shell-holes. Falls are frequent and the language is vile. Once a man falls it requires a considerable struggle for him to get to his feet again so great is the load on his back.

"After three hours of walking and slipping we arrive at our area and each party moves off to relieve the post to which it is allotted. Half an hour goes by and then the report comes through 'relief complete,' and we are left in possession of that section of the line whilst the relieved battalion winds its weary way back to the camp from which we came. Fortunately, a few clouds have come over to obscure the moon, and the relief is accomplished with trifling casualties. The battalion settles down to get the hang of its new position, to improve the existing cover and to do as much damage to Fritz as possible.

"On the occasion which I have in mind we take over from the 8/10th Gordon Highlanders. The company commander appears to be a Jew, but as he is very elated he might be anything. It seems that they are still celebrating a raid which they have made on the Butte de Warlencourt, near the Albert-Bapaume road, the night before. With white nightshirts (procured from Amiens) over their kilted uniforms, a big party of them crawled out over the snow, and as the moon was partially obscured by clouds, they proceeded quite a way before they were spotted, whereupon they made a rush for the hill which was known to be honeycombed with dugouts and used to house troops. Down the dugouts they threw tins of petrol and kerosene, followed by bombs, and gathering up a few prisoners, they beat it back to their own lines. The Butte smoked for days and the 'Scotties' claimed to have trapped a lot of Germans in the dugouts.

"Outside the company headquarters are eight or ten frozen Scotsmen still in night-shirts. Their company commander says that owing to the ground being frozen and the shell-holes full of ice, they have been unable to bury them (which would be quite true), and he makes us promise that if a thaw sets in we will bury them. I have a parting drink with him and off he goes, quite happily. However, a thaw does not set in during our occupancy, so we hand the Scotsmen over to the next incoming tenants.

"The Manchester Regiment had previously made an attack on this Butte of Warlencourt, but got badly mauled in getting there, though I believe they held it for a while.

"But let us return to our own war.

"During the winter months it is often impossible to hold continuous lines of trenches, owing to the swampy nature of the country, and on these occasions the line is held by posts arranged along the trench line, or elsewhere, just where the ground is suitable. The intervening spaces are covered by machine-guns, and in addition, patrols watch the gaps by night. The enemy holds his line in the same manner, and for a time the raiding habit was popular, each side trying to cut off one or more of his opponent's posts. Food has to be carried out to the various posts by night, taking advantage of any clouds which may be about in the event of the moon being bright. On this occasion the moon is at its full and this, in conjunction with the snow-covered ground, makes movement very precarious, as the enemy is quite close. We take full advantage of it to worry the Boche, but this is poor comfort to you when you are crawling along on your stomach through the ice and snow, on your visits from post to post. The available officers split the time up so that each has only a few hours' crawling to do each night. Accompanied by your patrol corporal you set off to visit the posts. All is well until you top a bit of a rise just behind the first line of posts, and now you are on a sort of plateau which is a salient into the enemy's lines. This makes it very awkward, as Fritz snipers and machine-gunners on the left are able to 'moon' you against his flares, which are being sent up a mile or so to your right and rear. Usually it is only necessary to drop down flat when flares go up in your immediate vicinity, but now you must keep your eyes open for distant flares lest they expose you. By walking doubled up we reach the first post unobserved.

" 'Good night, Sergeant.'

" 'Good night, Sir,—everything is O.K. here, except for the cold. That tea you sent up last night was frozen solid by the time we got it (tea and water are carried in two gallon petrol tins) and as all our water bottles are frozen, we have been unable to get a drink. I've had the men sitting on the tins in turn in the hopes that the heat of their bodies would melt the ice, but this only yielded a trickle after the whole personnel of the post had had a turn at the hatching business.'

" 'That's bad luck, Sergeant, but we may be able to fix you up with something before daylight, as we have sent to try and get some 'Tommy Cookers' (a small spirit lamp operated by solidified spirit), and if these are procurable you shall have one.'

" 'Thank you Sir. Good night.'

" 'Good night, Sergeant.'

"We crawl over the parados and make for No. 2 post.

"We have not gone more than about thirty yards when a couple of rifle shots whiz close by us, so knowing that we are spotted, we finish the journey on hands and knees, in which attitude we are scarcely likely to be visible from the German line, about one hundred and fifty yards away.

"As a preliminary precaution we have wrapped sand-bags round our knees and put on leather gloves, so that crawling about in the snow would not inconvenience us too much.

"No. 2 post reports the same trouble with the tea, and also that, being unable to move about, the men are finding difficulty in keeping up the blood circulation in their feet. Here the sergeant is instructed to make each man responsible for the condition of the feet of the man on his immediate left. This has been found to work well before, each man taking the bare foot of his neighbour between his knees in the manner of a man shoeing a horse, and by constant rubbing and chafing, restoring and keeping up the circulation. If something of this sort is not done, frost-bite, or trench feet (these are not the same thing), will surely result, with painful consequences to the soldier, often finishing with the loss of a couple of toes, or a foot.

"No. 3 Post is further out towards the enemy line and we have not crawled half the distance before a machine-gun spots us and we both dive into a shell-hole for shelter. These shell-holes contain about four or five feet of water, which is just now topped with ten or twelve inches of ice, and therefore, carries us well. It is rather a cold resting place and, after a few minutes, we decide to push on, but he has seen us go to ground and is waiting for us to come out. Tut! tut! tut! goes the gun and we slide back into the hole to wait awhile. After a few minutes we hear him firing again, but as the bullets do not appear to be coming our way he must have sighted someone else moving about, so now is our chance and out we scramble and do our best crawling speed to No. 3 Post.

" 'Good night, Sergeant.'

" 'Good night, Sir. Very bright to-night. We could see you crawling along fully one hundred yards away, and against the snow you looked the size of horses.'

"This is a poor compliment to our crawling abilities, but still we let that pass and enquire after the war as far as that post is concerned.

"The frozen tea is uppermost in this sergeant's mind— Fritz is quite a secondary consideration. After consoling with him about the tea and the frozen bread (which cracks like biscuit) he reports that Fritz has been troubling them a lot tonight with a couple of machine-guns.

" 'I've tried to get the one opposite here with the Lewis gun, but he's rather difficult to locate and so far I haven't been able to silence him.'

" 'Well, try and locate him definitely next time he fires, Sergeant, and I will get the Stokes Mortar people on to him.'

" 'Very good, Sir.'

"As we are talking, a figure can be seen wallowing along in the snow from the direction of No. 4 Post. On scrambling in he explains that they have seen us come to No. 3 and the sergeant has sent him over to report that a man in his post is in a fit and has been in that condition since four o'clock in the afternoon. He asks for instructions. Beyond recalling that you should put something in the man's mouth to keep him from biting his tongue, and rub his hands vigorously, none of us knows quite what is the correct treatment for fits. As the messenger explains that they have tried both these remedies without effect, I decide to go over and have a look at him.

"A bit of an old sap runs part of the way to No. 4 and, although full up with ice, the old parapet still stands up about two feet, so that by crawling along the ice we do not expose much of ourselves, and, beyond a few shots from a sniper who seems exceedingly close, we are left alone until when, just as we have to expose ourselves rather much in crawling over the parados into the post, a machine-gun fires a couple of bursts at us without effect.

"The man in the fit still shows no signs of coming round, despite the fact that one man is assiduously pushing an entrenching tool handle down his throat, and another is smacking him vigorous blows on the palms of the hands. After consulting with the sergeant, it is decided that he must be got back to the Aid Post in the rear, and that two men should go with him, one to crawl with the patient on his back, and the other to crawl alongside and hold him on, as the man is quite helpless.

"So as to avoid as far as possible the risk of them being shot on the way back, I send my Corporal back to Nos. 3 and 2 posts telling them to fire a few rifle grenades over at the Boche and to rattle up the Lewis Guns a bit in order to attract attention down that end, whilst the strange stretcher party get away. This works well. Several times they must have been sighted and fired on, for we suddenly see them flatten out —this is done by the crawlers just straightening themselves out flat, allowing the inert man to roll off into the snow. After a few minutes they hoist him up again and carry on. They get him safely down to the Dressing Station, and I hear afterwards that it wasn't a fit he had, but some rather serious affair. I don't suppose that lying on ice with an entrenching tool handle between his teeth from four in the afternoon until nine at night did him much good, but still, at last report, he is getting along very well.

"Number 5 is the most exposed post of the lot, being only about eighty yards from an enemy post, and to get to it from No. 4 takes us just on three-quarters of an hour, although the journey is under one hundred and fifty yards. The moon seems to be brighter than ever, and the only way we can get along with safety is to lie flat and wriggle along. The least attempt at crawling brings the machine-guns and snipers on to us, causing hurried scrambles into shell-holes. Some of these shell-holes have recently been the landing-place of other shells, with the result that the ice has smashed up, but the water thus exposed has frozen immediately, cementing the whole together in such a manner as to leave the jagged pieces of ice sticking up like almonds on top of a cake. To have to suddenly dive in on top of this, or even to have to crawl through such shell-holes is no pleasantry.

"After much wallowing, during which the Corporal will bring up the old joke about an army moving on its stomach, we at last wriggle into No. 5 post.

" 'Good night, Sir,' says the sergeant. 'A lovely night for a harbour picnic.'

" 'And a lovely night for a sniper,' adds my Corporal, with feeling.

" 'There is one sniper who appears to be only about fifty yards out from here,' says the sergeant. 'I've swept all the ground round about there with the Lewis gun, but I fancy he must be in a shell-hole and just sticks his head up to fire.'

" 'Well, get your rifle grenades ready; keep a careful watch to locate his flash, next time he fires, and then pour a couple of dozen grenades into the vicinity.' (On a night when the moon is not so troublesome, such a sniper would be dealt with by two or three men wriggling out and settling Mr. Sniper with hand grenades.)

"By now the enemy's artillery has opened up in reply to the disturbance created down at Nos. 2 and 3 posts and things are merry for awhile. Soon our own artillery joins in and the Boche quietens down again.

"Our return journey to No. 2 is just a repetition of the outward trip, and here the relieving patrol should meet us. We wait half an hour, but as no sign of the patrol appears, we set off to look for them. No. 1 reports that the patrol has been there and left again an hour ago. Soon a messenger turns up and tells us that the patrol corporal has been sniped through the head between Nos. 1 and 2 and that the officer, not having been over the ground before, has been compelled to return to Company Headquarters for a fresh guide. He turns up about half an hour later and we are both held up in No. 2 whilst Fritz puts over some minenwerfers (large trench mortar shells, making a trenendous noise in exploding and having great tearing effect). One of these landing in a post would mop up the whole crew, but, fortunately, although some come dangerously close, we have no casualties from this little 'hate.'

"We start for home (Company Headquarters) and are within thirty yards, when Fritz, evidently mistaking all the movement about our lines for a relief in progress, puts a barrage across us with surprising suddenness. 'Five-nines,' 'four-twos,' 'whizbangs,' shrapnel, etc., scream and crash around in salvos, all falling about the places where reliefs would have to pass. Something hits me on the steel helmet (probably a bit of ice thrown up by an explosion) making it ring like a bell, and causing my corporal to poke his head up from the neighbouring shell-hole in which he had taken shelter, to enquire if I am all right. For a quarter of an hour we are held here, and by that time our 'heavies' are seeking out the German batteries which are doing the firing, and continue to pound them for half an hour or so.

"There is one thing we can always rely on our artillery to do and that is never to leave off until they have had the last say, and it's wonderful what a comfort just a little thing like that is to the men in the trenches. You will hear them remark such things as—'That's all right, Fritz, but you'll get about ten back for every one of those'—this quite cheerfully, when the enemy's shells are knocking their parapets about.

"We finish the last thirty yards at a run, and, cold and hungry, we climb down into the evil-smelling old German dugout which is being used as our Company Headquarters.

" 'A wire from Headquarters for you, Sir,' calls the signaller.

" 'Well, what do they want? The number of tins of raspberry jam we had last Thursday week?'

" 'No, Sir, worse than that. They want to know the number of men in the Company who come from Wagga Wagga.'

" 'What on earth do they want to know that for?'

" 'I expect,' says the signaller, 'that the Wagga Wagga Mothers' Association wants to get a list of all their men in the A.I.F. so that they can send them a Xmas billy, next year!'

" 'Well, I'll be damned!' "

CHAPTER IX.

Seventeenth parades at Memorial Cross, Pozieres—Corporal G. Masterton assumes an unusual role—Beginning of German retirement—Malt Trench and Layton Alley—Loupart Wood—Bapaume Falls—Germans halt on Hindenburg Line—Once again in the outposts—"Greater love hath no man"—Lagnicourt—A hero's death —Heavy casualties.

THE Seventeenth remained in the line until February 5th, and then moved to Scots Redoubt Camp, where it was joined by two reinforcement officers, Lieutenants H. T. Allan and 2nd-Lieutenant R. C. Worthington. On the same date 2nd-Lieutenant T. J. Reid was evacuated, ill.

Whilst at Scots Redoubt Camp the Battalion paraded for a solemn ceremony at Pozieres, on the sector held during the fighting which took place the previous July and August. Here a large wooden Memorial Cross had been erected. Chaplain Fernie conducted a short but impressive service, at the conclusion of which, Privates A. Foot and D. Gillett, who had joined as buglers, in 1915, sounded "Last Post." The erection of this cross originated in a suggestion by Regimental Sergeant-Major V. J. Sullivan, who secured the timber from the 5th Field Company Engineers, and co-opted the services of Pioneer-Sergeant T. Beer and Private Shipway to fashion it and write the inscription, which read: "In proud and loving memory of Officers, N.C.O.'s and Men of the 17th Battalion A.I.F. who Fernie conducted a short, but impressive service, at the confell in action at Pozieres, July 25 to August 5, and August 21 to 28. 'Then are they glad because they are at rest': Erected by their comrades of the 17th Battalion, February, 1917."

In 1932 the cross was brought to Australia and subsequently enshrined in St. Thomas's Church, North Sydney. Some years before, the dead warriors it commemorated had been re-interred in one of the many cemeteries controlled by the Imperial War Graves Commission.

The Battalion stayed at Scots Redoubt until the 9th, when it moved to Acid Drop Camp, and whilst there the following promotions to the rank of lieutenant were announced: 2nd-Lieutenants E. C. New, H. O. Busby, T. L. Adam, C. R. Maynard, W. R. Haigh, R. V. Shields, J. J. McDiarmid and H. S. Ramsay; and on this day, also, 2nd-Lieutenant A. S. Brown left for England for a tour of duty with the 5th Training Battalion.

Two days later the Battalion relieved the Eighteenth Bat-

THE MEMORIAL CROSS, POZIERES.

Sgt. T. A. H. BREADEN, M.S.M.

"A" COMPANY SERGEANTS:
A. W. Carter, T. L. Ryan, M.M.,
—. Campbell, G. J. Chick, M.M.,
F. M. McDonald, M.M.

(Left)—R.Q.M.S. (afterward Hon. Capt.) A. J. R. Davison.
(Right)—R.S.M. (afterward Lt.) V. J. Sullivan, M.C.
(Seated)—Sgt. A. J. R. Baldwin.

(Seated)—C.S.M. (afterward Lieut.) A. F. Gilbert, L/C. W. Davis, D.C.M., M.M.

Lieut. E. F. EDWARDS.

THE BATTALION TRANSPORT SECTION.
Captain H. O. Busby, O.C., fourth from left, second row.

talion in front of Warlencourt, on the left of the Bapaume Road, and it was here that an unusual incident occurred, which involved an Australian corporal, a British soldier and a group of Germans. The Australian was Corporal J. Masterton, of the Seventeenth, attached to 5th Brigade Headquarters as observer. This is the story. Two days before the attack scheduled to be launched by the Fifth Army, on Pys, which lay well to the left of the Seventeenth's sector, Masterton, in pursuance of his duty, had made his way to one of our forward posts. Just after early morning "Stand-down," as, with his binoculars, he was sweeping the enemy position, several hundred yards on his left front, he observed a solitary British soldier, with full equipment and slung rifle, plodding heavily across the crater field of No Man's Land towards the German line. Masterton concluded that the soldier must have missed his way in the bank of mist still lying in the hollow ground between the opposing posts. Alarmed at the possible consequences if the Tommy were taken prisoner, Masterton, who possessed a strong sense of duty, decided that there was only one course to take—shoot him. In the act of unslinging his rifle, however, the Corporal saw a group of Germans rise from their post a few yards in front of the British soldier, and beckon to him to join them. In a moment he had disappeared into the enemy post, leaving, as it subsequently transpired, the amazed Masterton the sole witness of the incident on the British side of the line. The conscientious Masterton immediately reported the matter on his return to 5th Brigade Headquarters, and by the time the report reached Fifth Army Headquarters, consternation must have been the dominant note. The upshot of the affair was that Masterton was ordered in arrest by the Brigade Commander, General Smith, and in due course faced a court-martial on a charge of "Neglect to the Prejudice of Good Order and Military Discipline." In these proceedings he performed the dual role of informant, and sole witness for the defence. The unfortunate fellow was so genuinely concerned over the episode that, when asked by the President of the Court how he pleaded to the charge, he replied: "Guilty." However, the President, exercising his prerogative, declined to accept the Corporal's plea, and ordered that it be recorded as "Not Guilty," which, of course, permitted accused to give evidence on his own behalf. The Court brought in a finding of "Not Guilty," so all was well with the conscientious Masterton.

In connection with this unusual episode there is one feature which appears to call for comment: it was, perhaps, ironical that the very authority responsible for charging Masterton with "neglect" should itself neglect to arrange that he be represented at the trial by an officer to act as "Prisoner's Friend," which it is the duty in such cases for the convening authority of a court-martial to ensure.

Pys, the last German stronghold on the Somme, was taken in a brilliant assault, and almost immediately after its fall the enemy began the great retirement, which had been in preparation for several months and which completely deceived the Allies, so closely guarded had been the plans. The Germans, during the winter months had constructed a formidable system of field-works called the Hindenburg Line, which stretched for 100 miles between Arras and Soissons, and which, while shortening their line, at the same time conserved manpower, a move made imperative by the huge losses incurred during the Somme battle and at Verdun. The enemy also constructed three intermediate systems of trenches which he named R1, 2 and 3 respectively. R1 stretched from Loupart Wood to Le Translay; R2 through the south-western edge of Bapaume; and R3 between Bapaume and the main positions upon which he was falling back. Each of these three systems was protected by broad swathes of barbed wire and manned by rear-guards, consisting mainly of groups of machine-guns.

The enemy withdrawal was observed on the night of February 21/22, whereupon orders were issued to pursue and push him with the utmost vigour; and for this purpose, on the 5th Brigade front, the Seventeenth was ordered up in support of the Eighteenth Battalion, which was to advance in the Butte de Warlencourt sector, while the Twentieth Battalion on the left worked up the Albert-Bapaume Road.

Progress, however, was slow, for the foggy weather hampered aerial observation, thereby compelling the advancing troops to "feel" every yard of the way. But by the night 26/27 the Eighteenth's patrols had worked along Malt Trench, an intermediate line between the German forward posts and their R1 Line, to a point north of the main road, where a communication trench, Layton Alley, linked it with the R1 system. As there was no sign of the battalion that was to operate on the left, the Eighteenth constructed a barricade in the vicinity of Layton Alley, in order to secure its flank. The same night the Seventeenth relieved the Eighteenth in both Malt and Malt Support Trenches, the latter beginning south of the Bapaume road. A distance of about 150 yards separated it from Malt Trench.

In Malt Support an amusing example of the German psychology was displayed in the form of a declaration posted on a board found by our troops when they entered the trench. It read: "If we not will that you here, you was not here."

During these operations the Battalion lost two fine soldiers, Company Sergeant-Major F. M. Thomas and Corporal G. S. Black, both of whom were killed, and 2nd-Lieutenant G. M. Dickens and four other ranks wounded. Dickens was hit by machine-gun fire and was lying helpless in No Man's Land, when his plight was observed by Corporal T. R. Knight, who, in broad daylight, went out to the wounded officer and brought him back to safety. During this period Knight was subjected to enemy rifle fire.

On the night of March 1/2, the Seventeenth took over the whole of Malt Trench north of the Bapaume road up to the barricade in Layton Alley. Thus, the 5th Brigade front was now held by a single battalion, the remainder being disposed in depth in other portions of the old German trenches which now lay to the rear. The 7th Brigade continued the line on the left of the 5th Brigade.

It was known that the Germans were holding Layton Alley in some strength, not far from its junction with Malt Trench, and General Smith decided to drive them out. Major Pye, temporarily in command of the Battalion, was entrusted with the task. Pye arranged that the position should be assaulted by two parties, one to bomb up Layton Alley and the other moving across the open to take the enemy in the rear. On the night of March 2nd, 2nd-Lieutenant J. M. Lyons, advanced up the Alley under a supporting barrage of Mills bombs and completely surprised the enemy guarding the barricade set across that trench. Those Germans who endeavoured to escape were accounted for by the flanking party. A bomb-block was then erected in the Alley several hundred yards in advance of Malt Trench, and flanking posts thrown out to link with the company on the right and the 7th Brigade on the left. Our loss was one man wounded.

Towards the morning of the 3rd, a heavy fog descended, in consequence of which patrols were doubled in order adequately to cover the flat stretch of No Man's Land to the east.

Just before daylight the enemy laid down a heavy artillery barrage on the whole of the Battalion front, but mainly in the vicinity of Layton Alley, following it up with a strong counter-attack on Lyons's party holding the barricade. The sudden rush forced our men back, fiercely contesting every foot of ground. Lyons was wounded, but big Sergeant H. J. ("Snowy") Pearson took charge and held the men together, ordering their steady withdrawal, until himself wounded. Here another big man stepped into the breach. He was Corporal T. L. Ryan, who encouraged his team by his coolness and the physical endurance he displayed in throwing bombs for nearly two hours. Another fine non-commissioned officer, Sergeant W. L. Flood, also did excellent work prior to the attack, reconnoitring the position, and subsequently, during the counter-attack, carrying out the wounded Lyons through the heavy artillery barrage. The fine work of Corporal E. G. Cowcher should also be mentioned. During the attack he lay out in No Man's Land directing the fire of two Lewis guns, and when later on men were forced back, Cowcher held the barricade with his gun, while bombs were falling near him. He was ably assisted by Private W. McKinlay, who although exposed to shell- and machine-gun fire, showed a total disregard for his personal safety, by moving out into No Man's Land with a Lewis gun and keeping up a continuous fire on the enemy.

Other fine deeds were performed. There was 2nd-Lieutenant B. Bradford, who during attack up the Alley, was in command of the blocking party, and by his coolness and sound judgment carried the task through successfully. Later, when the enemy counter-atacked, Bradford organized the defence by building a new barricade, his confident direction and fine personal example resulting in the enemy advance being held. Bradford was one of the original members of the Seventeenth.

Two privates, C. R. Nicholson and L. Buhl, also were in the forefront of our attack on the Alley. This powerfully built pair acted as bayonet men and they were always in the thick of the fighting. Subsequently they were given well-deserved commissions.

An outstanding performance was put up by Private James Fenwick, one of the bombers. Suddenly confronted by five Germans, he hurled a bomb with the safety pin still in position, at the foremost man, knocking him out. Fenwick then dashed in and grappled with the next in line and took him prisoner. The remainder fled.

One of Fenwick's comrades, Private M. P. Gibbons, also showed great gallantry as first bayonet man during the attack, and when the enemy launched his whirlwind counter-attack, Gibbons coolly covered the withdrawal of a Lewis gun that had jambed. Despite heavy shelling he stuck to his post, until the wounded were cleared from the Alley.

Another fine feat during the counter-attack was by Private J. K. Campbell. Campbell, like Gibbons, helped to cover the withdrawal of wounded. In this work he displayed great courage and devotion to duty. Throughout his service this soldier, although still quite a youngster, had done excellent work.

At the barricade in Layton Alley, to which point the enemy had pressed our men back, Corporal B. H. Hembrow showed his prowess as a bomber, while the block was being erected under Bradford's direction. He sustained his effort for two hours, until wounded.

Sergeant G. R. McPhee, in charge of one of the flanking parties during our attack, showed sound judgment and leadership. Together with Lance-Corporal H. W. Barnes and Private H. G. Bell, he held the post for over an hour, until his party was reinforced, although attacked by bombs and heavily fired on by machine-guns.

The task of keeping up supplies of bombs and ammunition

was under the direction of a very fine young non-commissioned officer, Sergeant R. P. Little, who by his personal example and disregard of danger, ensured a continuous and steady flow to the front line.

The heavy shelling of our positions caused repeated breakages of the telephone lines. But, as ever, the signallers were out exposing themselves unconcernedly, intent on keeping communications uninterrupted. Of this devoted band two showed conspicuous gallantry and devotion to duty. They were Privates E. E. J. Brooks and G. C. D. Stone.

The stretcher-bearers also played their part during this lively operation; one of their number, Private F. Smith, going forward several times to bring in wounded men while exposed to bombing and machine-gun fire. Smith's devotion to duty undoubtedly saved the lives of several men.

As evidence of the stout defence, only one of our men was taken prisoner. He was Private T. Lawler, a bomber, one of the Battalion's hard cases, and a man of iron constitution, who had served with the Seventeenth since its inception, and had fought in Munster Alley on that stifling July afternoon seven months previously. When the enemy counter-attacked, Lawler was seen to fall, and it was thought he had been killed. But later, when the enemy was found to have evacuated the Alley, a party, under Regimental Sergeant-Major V. J. Sullivan, found definite evidence of a struggle that had been waged for some distance along the trench. Apparently the gallant Lawler, although desperately wounded, had fought it out to the last. Later in the month, when the enemy had evacuated Bapaume, our men discovered a cross which the Germans had erected over a grave near the village of Behagnies. The cross bore the inscription: "Tim Lawler, Australian"; a simple tribute to a brave soldier. As a tribute from his mates, Sergeant C. H. Craig, also one of the original Bombing Platoon, affixed the Battalion's black and green cloth shoulder patch to the cross.

The main weight of the enemy's attack had fallen on that portion of Malt Trench north of the Albert-Bapaume Road; nevertheless some anxious minutes were endured by the defenders south of this point, as there existed a wide gap between the Seventeenth and the Fourth Battalion on the right. However, the attack was not pressed home here, although elements of the assaulting troops, under cover of the fog and smoke screen, came very close to Malt Support Trench. One very stout German non-commissioned officer, however, ventured too far down the road and was well past the left flank of the trench. Suddenly he realised his position. He turned and fled incontinently, greeted by a "View halloa!" from our men as they followed hard on his heels. But he succeeded in eluding his pursuers, and disappeared in the mist.

Among the casualties was an officer, 2nd-Lieutenant A. Young, who had been with the Battalion for only a little while, but who had made himself popular with his brother-officers as well as his platoon by his cheerful manner and the lively quips by which he helped to sustain the spirits of all with whom he came in contact. Young was mortally wounded by a piece of shrapnel.

After reconnoitring the position, Major Pye, ordered a fresh attack to be launched with the object of driving the enemy away from where he had established himself in Layton Alley, near its junction with Malt Trench. However, a piece of bold patrol work carried out by 2nd-Lieutenant H. E. Clifton, disclosed that the enemy had evacuated the position, and, indeed, the greater part of the Alley itself.

Once again the Battalion had done an excellent job of work, which brought a warm note of appreciation from that hard-bitten soldier, General Smith; he was never known to be lavish in the distribution of encomiums.

Under the calm and inspiring leadership of Major Pye, all ranks had faithfully carried out their tasks. But the account of the Layton Alley fight is incomplete without a comment on the part played generally by the non-commissioned officers, of whom four may be quoted as being typical examples of their fellows. They were Company-Sergeant Major J. P. Taylor, Sergeant H. F. Didcote, and Corporals C. C. Brindley and F. J. Coombes; all original members. Their consistently fine example and devotion to duty had earned the confidence of officers and men.

The work of the runners is also deserving of mention. In this action the part played by Private C. C. Brown is cited as being typical of the faithful manner in which they performed their extremely dangerous tasks. Brown had displayed bravery during the Pozieres battle, and his cheerfulness, willingness and disregard of danger on that and subsequent occasions, raised him high in the estimation of his comrades.

The following night, 3/4, the Twenty-fourth Battalion relieved the Seventeenth, which moved back to Shelter Wood Camp, where it stayed for three days before moving on the 7th to Bazentin Camp. Here the following awards were promulgated: Lieutenant-Colonel E. F. Martin received the Distinguished Service Order, Lieutenant J. J. Fay the Military Cross, and 2nd-Lieutenant J. M. Lyons (as Sergeant Lyons), the Military Medal. Lyons had previously been awarded the Meritorious Service Medal.

The Seventeenth left Bazentin on the 11th for Le Sars, where it relieved the Twenty-seventh Battalion, and the following night moved across the valley to Warlencourt. The Battalion had hardly time to settle down when orders were received to probe for the Germans, who, it was reported, were falling back in their R2 Line north of the Albert-Bapaume road. That night, the Seventeenth established a line of outposts between Loupart Wood and Grevillers Village. A solitary German was taken prisoner.

Here the country to the east appeared refreshingly green and almost unmarred by shell fire, in striking contrast with the bare, brown crater-field over which our troops had been operating for many months. The change of scene was quickly reflected in the spirits of all ranks.

The Battalion War Diary reveals that under date March 13, Lieutenant K. W. Mackenzie was promoted to rank of captain.

The Seventeenth was not involved in any close fighting during the operations in the vicinity of Grevillers, but vigorous patrolling and probing of the enemy's position was kept up. This onerous duty provided opportunities for the display of individual courage and initiative. Among those deserving special mention was Captain R. V. Spier, one of the elder members of the Battalion, who exercised sound judgment in controlling his command during a period when prompt decisions had to be taken. Throughout his service Spier had shown himself to be a capable and reliable leader, who had earned the full confidence of his men. As a fitting reward for his services he later received a staff appointment.

Another fine young officer, Lieutenant L. S. Allen, commanding C Company, displayed commendable coolness and skill in handling his platoons on the outpost line. His personal example greatly encouraged his men, and he insisted on satisfying himself as to the position by personal reconnaisance. On one occasion, in company with Sergeant H. F. Smith and a youthful runner, Private F. J. Dearie, he led a patrol through Loupart Wood in the Seventeenth's left front. Later, when his company held the outpost line east of Grevillers, he continually moved amongst his platoons, although at times they were subjected to heavy machine-gun and trench-mortar fire. During one of these rounds of visits Allen observed one of his men, who had been on patrol, lying in an exposed position well in front of his posts. Allen went out and brought the man back. He was dead.

A young subaltern, A. T. Doig, behaved with conspicuous gallantry throughout the operations, carrying out reconnaissances under heavy shell fire. On one occasion he penetrated the enemy's line and captured a German. Doig had been with the Battalion since it left Australia, and his work had always been marked by zeal and efficiency.

Four sergeants, J. A. Barnier, G. Chick, Finley Macdonald and R. P. Little, also displayed daring and enterprising leadership in command of patrols, often under heavy machine-gun and shell-fire, and always subjected to a galling fire from snipers. Their conduct inspired all ranks under their command.

But it was a humble private, James Marsden, who performed the most daring feat of all in this period. On the 16th, he took out a patrol of three men in broad daylight, and worked his way into the enemy trench for about sixty yards, until he ran into a strong post. Noting its position he withdrew his patrol, which, while on its way back to our lines, was fired on heavily by machine-guns and snipers, but got back safely. This plucky venture secured useful information about the enemy's dispositions.

The Seventeenth moved back to Martinpuich on the 16th, after being relieved by the Nineteenth Battalion. But by the 20th the Seventeenth was moving forward again, this time to Biefvillers, a tiny village on the north-east outskirts of Bapaume, which had been evacuated three days previously. Before they left, the Germans carried out a systematic destruction of buildings, orchards and anything likely to afford shelter to troops, guns or horses. Wherever possible, they used the debris from these demolitions to block the roads, necessitating the employment by their opponents of hundreds of men in clearing-up work. The only building left intact when they pulled out of Bapaume, was the town-hall, under which they had planted a delayed action mine. A few days later the mine exploded, killing a number of troops and two French deputies. Colonel Maughan, who was acting as Town Commandant, had a narrow escape. He had only left the building a short while before it was blown up.

In Biefviellers the Seventeenth set about effecting repairs, and quickly made it sufficiently habitable, while craters blown in the road were also filled in. Such work was well within the scope of the Seventeenth, for the personnel of a battalion includes experts in many trades and callings accustomed to adapting themselves to work with a minimum of tools. This aptitude was especially valuable because the enemy always destroyed all the wells, either by blowing them in or filling them up with stable refuse. But well-sinkers were forthcoming, and even divining-rod experts were found in the ranks. The latter calling possessed a special fascination, and before long everybody from the colonel to the cooks were walking around with bits of forked stick. Actually water was found easily anywhere in that district, but the divining-rod experts claimed a win when the spot they chose yielded water at seven or eight feet, and the other members of the Battalion marvelled at their skill.

The main Albert-Bapaume road presented a remarkable scene. Day and night an unending procession of troops, guns, ambulances and vehicles of all kinds, moved in a gigantic stream. Every couple of miles the enemy had blown huge craters in the road, some measuring fifty feet in diameter and thirty feet deep. It was found to be much quicker to build a road round each side than to repair damage to the original road.

The Battalion transport was brought up and the animals

turned loose to grass. Veteran limber horses and mules which, for months had toiled in the mud and as a result they had difficulty in keeping their heads up, in a day or two took on a second lease of life, they galloped over the fields, kicking their heels in the air. The devoted beasts had merited the change; they had worked wonderfully all through the extremely severe winter.

The maintenance of supplies to the fighting troops was of prime importance, and in the new Transport Officer, Lieutenant H. O. Busby and Regimental Quartermaster-Sergeant A. J. R. Davidson (the latter an original member), the Battalion possessed as efficient a pair as might be found in any unit. It was mainly due to thier devotion to duty that rations and supplies never failed to reach the front line. In this achievement the stout-hearted transport drivers and quartermasters' assistants must be given full credit for their part.

Six days were spent in Biefvillers, and then the Battalion moved back to Bazentin with orders to rest and refit. Here, on the 31st, the Corps Commander presented ribbons of decorations

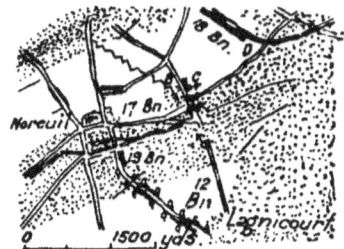

5TH BRIGADE SECTOR,
NOREUIL.
April 15th.

awarded the following officers and other ranks: Major C. R. A. Pye, Distinguished Service Order; 2nd-Lieutenant B. Bradford, Military Cross; and Sergeant H. J. Pearson, Corporal T. L. Ryan and Private M. Gibbons, the Military Medal.

Here, also, changes occurred in the Battalion staff; Major Pye being promoted Lieutenant-Colonel and appointed to the command of the Nineteenth Battalion. Major B. Holmes was appointed second-in-command, vice Pye. About this period the brigade commander proceeded on furlough and was relieved, temporarily, by Colonel Martin.

April 11th was the date on which the 4th Division launched its gallant but ineffectual assault on Bullecourt, the key position of the Hindenburg Line, on which, as previously stated, the enemy had decided to halt and fight. The following day the 2nd Division was on the move with orders to relieve the 4th, which had suffered very heavy losses.

It was the intention of the Fifth Army Commander, General Gough, to renew the assault on Bullecourt, this time employing the 2nd Australian and 62nd British Division. The First

Australian Division on the right would have a "holding" task and therefore, a very thinly held front, extending for over 12,000 yards south of Noreuil Valley. This front was covered by artillery pushed well forward, while the intervals would be protected by groups of machine-guns. The 2nd Division sector would be held by two brigades, the 5th right, and 6th left, in the front line, with the 7th Brigade in reserve. The 5th Brigade was disposed as follows: Seventeenth, the Hirondelle Valley, inclusive, to a point in the railway cutting in front of Queant, where the Eighteenth Battalion continued the line northwards to its junction with the 6th Brigade. The Nineteenth Battalion was held in support on the high ground south of Noreuil village and a little in rear of the road connecting it with Lagnicourt. This position was actually in the 1st Division Sector, but subsequent events proved it to be a fortunate choice. The Twentieth Battalion was placed in reserve at Vaulx-Vraucourt, a little to the south-west of Lagnicourt.

The Hindenburg Line at this point was ideally situated for the enemy. It gave him a complete "gallery" view of the gently undulating country to the west entirely devoid of cover and of the two valleys of Noreuil and Lagnicourt leading directly towards the German positions and offering no concealment for our batteries, which, in consequence, suffered severe losses from the opposing artillery fire.

The dispositions of the Seventeenth's companies were as follows: C (Sheppard) and D (Mackenzie), in the outpost line; B (Ronald), support, in the trench covering the two forward companies, with A (Spier), in reserve just south of Noreuil Village, and adjoining the left of the Nineteenth Battalion. Battalion Headquarters was situated in the southern end of the village, with the field-kitchens in the sunken road nearby. 5th Brigade Headquarters was also located in Noreuil. The marginal sketch shows the position of the Seventeenth's companies as well as those of the rest of the 5th Brigade, and it will be observed that D Company in the railway cutting was pushed much further forward than its neighbour C. Moreover, owing to the formation of the ground in this locality the only position of the latter Company visible from D Company's position was the left-hand post under the command of Sergeant R. H. S. Thompson. This fact should be noted in view of subsequent developments.

The relief of the sorely tried 13th Brigade of the 4th Division, by the 5th Brigade was effected without incident, and the following day, the 14th, spent in improving its positions. The whole countryside as far as the eye could see, lay green and virtually unscarred by shell-fire, and both sides seemed to be quiescent. The weather was cold, but clear, and our men were able to observe the formidable nature of the enemy's defences, and to estimate the stern task that lay before them.

Realising that his thinly held posts, strung out over a line more than 1,600 yards in extent, were devoid of any protecting barbed wire, Colonel Martin (who had rejoined the Battalion only a day or two previously) gave orders that, in addition to local patrols, a fighting patrol should be sent out with the specific object of reconnoitring towards Queant. The patrol was placed under the command of 2nd-Lieutenant H. Ellis, who had enlisted as a private and served with the Battalion since its inception. During the course of this hazardous operation, there was an example of heroic self-sacrifice on the part of one of the men. Attached to the patrol were two stretcher-bearers, Privates E. S. ("Bluey") Watkins and W. Foster; they were mates. The patrol moved out and had almost reached the heavily wired defences of the German positions, when, from somewhere in the rear, a cry rang out in the stillness of the night. It was the voice of Foster calling on Watkins to come to his aid. The unfortunate fellow had evidently been cut off by a German patrol, or, perhaps, stumbled on to one of their listening posts. In the pitch darkness it was impossible to see more than a yard or two around, but Watkins had heard his comrade's urgent call, and that was sufficient. Swiftly, and entirely unarmed though he was, he dashed in the direction from which Foster's voice came, and in a moment had disappeared from the sight of his fellows. Ellis's patrol carefully searched the vicinity for some time, but without success. Both men had completely vanished, leaving no trace whatsoever of the manner of their going out. Watkins's act was indeed one of sublime heroism and typical of the Digger's staunch regard for a mate. The names of Watkins and Foster are included in the Imperial War Graves Commission's records with thousands of other Australian soldiers whose graves are not known.

Just before daybreak on the 15th, the patrol returned through D Company's lines, and Ellis proceeded direct to Battalion Headquarters to report in person to Colonel Martin. Except for the incident just related there was nothing to report, though on the right some small-arms fire had been heard towards dawn. But the lull was but the prelude to a violent storm, for at the moment Ellis and his patrol were moving back to their lines, an enemy concentration of twenty-three specially selected battalions, with its right flank facing the mouth of the Hirondelle Valley, was creeping forward under a ground mist to the attack. The main weight of the blow was directed against Lagnicourt situated in rear of the 1st Division's sector. His purpose was twofold; the operation would disrupt the British plans for a further attack on Bullecourt and would also assist in restoring the morale of his own forces, which had shown a marked degree of deterioration in the past few months. The attack was to be a complete surprise. Therefore, it was decided to dispense with an artillery barrage.

The first indication received by the Seventeenth that something unusual was afoot, was the sporadic rifle and machine-gun fire across the valley to the right of C Company. It happened that the two picquets of this company stationed in the mouth of the valley, were in charge of experienced men, Sergeants H. F. Smith and W. L. ("Leggy") Ford, who, after consultation, decided to jointly investigate the cause of the firing. Proceeding cautiously in the direction of the spur on which was situated the left-hand picquet of the Twelfth Battalion of the 1st Division, they suddenly observed in the half-light a large group of Germans. Realising the urgency of the situation both men ran back to their own posts and although fired on, succeeded in reaching them safely. There was not a moment to be lost. If they stayed where they were they would be cut off; thereupon they ordered their men to fall back on the supports on the northern slopes of the valley. They were only just in time, for hardly had they reached the new position when they saw large numbers of the enemy advancing directly on the posts. Smith's and Ford's men opened up a hot fire with both Lewis guns and rifles which caused heavy casualties. For about thirty minutes the group held on until a message was received from Captain Sheppard to fall back on his position in the sunken road. As the men infiltrated to the rear, they came under heavy machine-gun fire from the Germans, who were by now on the spur south of the valley. Several of our men were hit. As the survivors reached the sunken road they saw the Germans in large numbers advancing directly across the valley towards them. Already, forward elements had seized the lower end of the road leading to C Company's Headquarters, where a desperate fight was in progress. Here, Lieutenant R. V. Shields and his platoon were engaging in hand-to-hand combat with the enemy who, after over-running the left post of the Twelfth Battalion were endeavouring to roll up C Company's right flank. Shields, revolver in hand, coolly directed and encouraged his men until struck down by a bullet in the leg. Lance-Sergeant G. H. Gallogly was killed and several men who had been cut off in the first surprise, were taken prisoner. The southern end of C Company's position was strewn with dead and wounded men, both ours and Germans. Nearby lay the bodies of the crews of our machine-gun sections posted so as to command the mouth of the valley. They had been enfiladed by the fire from heavy machine guns posted by the Germans on the commanding ground of the opposite spur. Dakin, the young commander was also killed. The situation was now critical. Sheppard's posts (all but the extreme left hand one under Sergeant Thompson) were falling back steadily, as ordered, to the sunken road.

These platoons, under Lieutenants F. W. Smith and R. T. Phelps, had also put up a splendid defence, Smith being conspicuous for his disregard of danger and for the manner in which he inspired his men. Both these officers were subsequently wounded, thus Sheppard had only his sergeants to fall back on. But these were staunch men and one, Sergeant G. Kirkpatrick, showed outstanding courage and tenacity, which contributed greatly towards the stemming of the German assault on that flank. Kirkpatrick, who had won the Military Medal at Pozieres, was instructed to hold on in the sunken road and thus enable the remainder of C. Company to complete the withdrawal in that direction. Rallying some men in the vicinity, the gallant sergeant and his band kept the Germans at bay with rifle fire and bombs. Showing an utter disregard of personal danger while shouting defiance at the enemy, the stout-hearted Kirpatrick, a country man (an original member of the Battalion) engaged single-handed four Germans, three of whom he killed, before he himself was shot dead. His sacrifice, however, had not been in vain. The position had been held sufficiently long to enable Sheppard to reorganize the remainder of the company, which he now ordered to fall back into the old 4th Division outpost trench in rear of the sunken road. Undoubtedly Kirkpatrick's magnificent devotion and leadership had redeemed a very nasty situation, for not only did his action cover the retirement of the remainder of C Company, but it gave time for supports to be brought up to reinforce the position. The brave fellow's action resulted in a recommendation by Colonel Martin for the award of the Victoria Cross. Kirkpatrick's deed ranks amongst the highest of the many performed by individual members of the Battalion. It was a shining example of courage in the face of desperate odds.

Back at Battalion Headquarters, Colonel Martin was for some time left in complete ignorance of the fact that C Company was being heavily attacked. It can only be assumed that the reason why Sheppard, the company commander, had failed to communicate with the Commanding Officer was that the telephone lines had been cut, or that his runners had failed to get through with their messages. Be that as it may, the first intimation Colonel Martin received that his right company was being sorely pressed was through the direct agency of Lieutenant J. L. Wright who was then serving in the triple roles of Scout, Intelligence and Lewis Gun Officer. It was Wright's duty to have his daily Intelligence Report completed by 6 o'clock every morning. Just before daybreak he was working on this report when he heard a considerable amount of small-arms fire to the right front. He, therefore, decided to investigate the cause. At this stage there was no artillery fire on either side. To his amazement he saw groups of Germans advancing very quickly and boldly up the floor of the valley as well as along the spur on the southern side. Obviously the enemy had over-run the 1st Division's posts in that sector, for their machine-guns posted on the spur were bringing plunging fire to bear on C Company's position which was thus enfiladed. Wright, with the quick intuition which was one of his notable attributes, saw what was wrong. He, therefore, immediately ran forward towards C Company's position, and dived into the shallow outpost trench occupied by Sheppard's men. He also observed that a detachment from B Company, whose commander, Ronald, was by now fully seized with the situation, was reinforcing the left of C Company. The enemy was then holding the sunken road only about seventy-five yards from that Company's right flank. Wright judged that the position was capable of being held. He, therefore, dashed back to Battalion Headquarters, and on the way there could see groups of Germans moving up the valley in the direction of Noreuil, under cover of the embanked sides. On the receipt of Wright's report Colonel Martin ordered him post-haste to deliver the news to the Brigade Commander, General Smith, whose Headquarters was only a short distance away. The Brigadier immediately issued instructions for the Nineteenth Battalion to extend along the road in front of its bivouac and also directed the Twentieth Battalion to move up from Vaulx-Vraucourt and close the gap between the 5th and 3rd Brigades. As previously related, the placing of the Nineteenth in the 1st Division Sector showed sound tactical judgment, for although the German attack had succeeded only in bending back the Seventeenth's right flank, his occupation of the spur south of the valley would have permitted him to pour through to the Noreuil Valley and behind the village itself, causing havoc amongst our artillery and communications. As it transpired, he was met by a wall of fire and cold steel two hundred yards from the Nineteenth's and A Company's position nearby, and was ultimately routed, leaving behind many dead and prisoners.

In its advanced position in the railway-cutting in front of Queant, D Company had just "stood down" and its commander was about to report by telephone to Battalion Headquarters, when he was informed that Colonel Martin urgently wanted to speak to him. The Commanding Officer told Mackenzie what was happening and instructed him to order D Company to forthwith stand to arms, as even then the enemy was moving in on Battalion Headquarters, after having worked behind C Company. Hurrying to his right-flank in the cutting, Mackenzie observed that C Company's left-hand post, the only portion of that Company's line visible from the cutting, was intact. Its commander, Sergeant Thompson, intimated that neither he nor his men had seen any sign of the enemy. In fact it was the first indication they had received that an attack was in progress. Mackenzie then ordered two platoons of D Company together with two Vickers guns of the 5th Machine Gun Company, to man the rear face of the cutting and simultaneously informed Captain Hobbs of the right company of the Eighteenth Battalion as to what had happened. From the rear of the cutting, groups of Germans could be observed working along the front of B Company, which was keeping up a hot fire on them from Lewis Guns and rifles. There were still traces of fog which occasionally obscured the view, and doubtless aided the enemy. However, it was soon evident that B Company had the situation in hand, and as it was feared that casualties might be inflicted on them by our fire Mackenzie ordered his company and the machine gunners to refrain from firing for the time being.

B Company's view of C Company's position was partly obscured by a slight rise on the former's right flank. Curiously, as in the case of Battalion Headquarters, no intimation of any attack was received by Ronald until Sheppard's men, only a few hundred yards to the right, had become fully involved with the enemy. It happened that one of Ronald's corporals, A. H. Edwards, in charge of a Lewis Gun on the extreme right of B Company, hearing an unusual amount of firing just before daybreak, decided to investigate the cause. Taking with him a private named Lovegrove, he moved up the slight ridge, separating the two companies. There on the slope to their right front they saw considerable numbers of Germans moving in their direction. The two men returned with all haste and reported to Ronald, whose company in the ordinary course of events was standing to arms. Ronald immediately ordered his men to withhold their fire until the enemy was clearly visible.

It was now about 5.30. The attack had been in progress for about three-quarters of an hour and C Company was being sorely pressed. Colonel Martin, who had just received Wright's report ordered Ronald to detach two platoons to reinforce Sheppard. This small force under the command of Ellis moved off, but soon came under heavy fire from the front and right, losing a number of men, including Ellis. But the remainder, with two additional Lewis guns reached C Company, which by now had fallen back into the outpost trench and thus formed a continuous line with B Company.

Battalion Headquarters staff and various details, including runners, cooks and batmen, were also involved in the fighting. Immediately Colonel Martin received Wright's report, he ordered Captain Barnett, the Adjutant, to rouse out everybody, and to take up a suitable defensive position. At that moment Regimental Sergeant-Major Sullivan reported to Barnett, who ordered him to collect a party and carry ammunition to C Company. Sullivan was about to depart on his mission when he was stopped by Colonel Martin who told him that C Company was surrounded, and therefore, it would not be possible for the ammunition supply to get through. He intimated that he had ordered Ronald to reinforce C Company. Sullivan thereupon organised a detachment armed with rifles which included the effervescent Private "Spud" Murphy, and with Company Quartermaster-Sergeant E. J. Tidmarsh proceeded to the outskirts of Noreuil facing the sunken road leading to Queant. By this time our artillery had laid down a heavy barrage. It was subsequently revealed that the Germans got so close to our guns that on the 2nd Division front the gunners manhandled their pieces out of the pits and fired over open sights, tearing great gaps in the enemy's ranks. Sullivan, using Barnett's glasses, could see large numbers of Germans surrendering on the opposite ridge near Lagnicourt. Their advance had been halted. The time had arrived to launch our counter-attack. About this time Sullivan's party was reinforced by Lewis guns of the Twenty-fourth Battalion of the 6th Brigade, but they were not needed. Sullivan, who was directing the fire of his detachment noticed groups of Germans who had taken cover behind mounds of manure; his men enjoyed much good shooting, when the enemy attempted to retire. Our men shouted and danced as their shots found the target. So infectious was their mood that Colonel Martin, who in the meantime, had joined the party, made just as much noise as the rest of the men.

Our artillery by this time was again in action, and as enemy movement in front of Noreuil appeared to have ceased Colonel Martin ordered Sullivan to move forward and to mop up any stray Germans in the locality. The party had advanced a couple of hundred yards when they encountered six Germans, one of whom Sullivan shot, but immediately afterwards was himself wounded in the leg. Tidmarsh then took over the command and cleaned up the remainder. The whole job was neatly done but not without several casualties, as the ground over which the party advanced was exposed to heavy rifle-fire.

The situation on the 5th Brigade front was by now well in hand. On the right, across the valley, the enemy could be seen retiring in haste, while a considerable number surrendered to the Nineteenth Battalion, which was now advancing along the spur in the direction of the Twelfth Battalion's posts. Simultaneously B and the remnant of C Company advanced and reoccupied the sunken road and all the other positions from which they had been forced back. In the sunken road were lying several of our severely wounded, including Shields. The enemy had had no time to remove them. Several Germans also surrendered, including an officer, who Shields pointed out to Sergeant H. F. Smith as being the person who had taken Shield's eye-glasses from him as he lay helpless with a shattered leg. Smith immediately went up to the German and retrieved the glasses, and for good measure relieved the German of his own spectacles.

By 8 a.m. the position was again normal and the Battalion

was able to take stock of the position. The casualties, especially, those of C Company, had been heavy. Twenty-nine other ranks, including that fine soldier Company Sergeant-Major F. May, another original member of the Battalion, were killed, and five officers (Ellis subsequently died) and ninety-six other ranks wounded. Fifty-one other ranks were posted as missing, making a grand total of 181 of all ranks. C Company could only muster one officer and twenty-seven other ranks, at the end of the combat.

On the other hand the enemy had suffered very heavy casualties, although, as is frequently the case, these were much exaggerated at the time. German accounts of the operation, however, admit the loss of nine per cent. of their forces engaged, a fairly high rate. The I Anzac Corps suffered 1,010 casualties, of which about 300 represented prisoners. Of the Germans, four officers and 358 men were taken by the Australians.

As usual, the runners and stretcher-bearers did great work, especially of the former, Privates A. H. Chambers, S. H. Thompson and F. J. Dearie. Several times in the height of the action these three ran their messages back and forth between Battalion Headquarters and the front line, often under a hail of machine-gun fire. They showed great courage and devotion to duty. A very gallant stretcher-bearer deserves a special mention for his work. He was Private J. Sheehan, who, with three others, went out to bring in a wounded man who was seen endeavouring to crawl back to our lines. When the party got to this man they discovered several other of our wounded in the locality. Sheehan ordered two men to attend to the original case and, with Private Buckridge, stayed to succour the remainder. All this took place not more than 100 yards from the enemy. Buckridge was killed while dressing a wounded man, but Sheehan completed the task and then waited until some other bearers arrived, himself remaining to see the last of the wounded cleared.

The 5th Brigade Commander, General Smith, summing up in his official report of the engagement, attributed the successful repulse and counter-attack largely to the following circumstances:—

1. The fire service of Lewis guns.
2. The excellent barrage that was arranged at such short notice.
3. The skilful use of ground by subordinate commanders.
4. The resource and initiative of Lewis gun crews.

To which he might well have added a fifth factor: "The dauntless courage and resolution of the garrisons of the outpost positions."

CHAPTER X.

Attack on Bullecourt postponed—2nd Division withdrawn to rehearse its part—Second Bullecourt—Seventeenth suffers heavy casualties—The long rest in St. Omer area—Battalion excels in sports—Training in forest fighting—General Plumer "is not amused"—Sir D. Haig inspects 2nd Division—Northward again to the Bloody Salient.

THE German onslaught at Lagnicourt was sufficiently weighty to cause General Gough to call a temporary halt in his plan of hitting the enemy hard and often at a time when he believed his opponent's morale was low. He decided to postpone any further attempt to capture Bullecourt until adequate artillery supplies could be accumulated.

The 2nd Division was withdrawn from the line and concentrated in the Bapaume area to rehearse its part on ground similar to that over which it would operate in the actual attack. Unfortunately, during the whole of the fortnight these manoeuvres were carried out, they were under direct observation by German balloons. Thus, the enemy was fully aware of the intention of the British to launch a further attack in that sector.

During its temporary sojourn in this area the following awards were announced: Lieutenant L. S. Allen and 2nd-Lieutenant A. T. Doig, the Military Cross; Sergeants F. McDonald, R. P. Little and Private J. Marsden, the Military Medal.

During the last days of April, the 2nd Division began to concentrate in the Noreuil area for the attack, which was set down for May 3rd. On the 1st the Seventeenth moved into Vaulx-Vraucourt.

The general plan of the Fifth Army's attack comprised an advance of abut 3,000 yards, and as stated in the preceding chapter, by two divisions, the 2nd Australian, right, and the 62nd British, left, with the object of capturing Reincourt and Hendecourt. The sector allotted the 2nd Division was the re-entrant between Bullecourt and Queant. The objectives were: first, O.G. 1 and 2; second, the Fontaine—Moulin—Sans Souci road, and third, Reincourt itself. For artillery support the Australians would have thirty-one heavy and medium batteries, in addition to thirty field-batteries. The 2nd Division was to attack with two brigades, 5th and 6th, in line, with the 7th in reserve. The frontage of the attack would be 700 yards for each brigade which would be drawn up two battalions deep, and divided into eight waves. The dividing line between the 5th and 6th Brigades was the Central road, which was covered from Queant was a broad flat feature sloping gently upwards in the direction of the German trenches. It was on this feature that the 5th Brigade was to deploy for the attack. The jumping-off tape was laid down 400 yards from the zero barrage line. All units were to be in position by zero minus fifteen minutes. At zero hour the first wave was to close up to the barrage. By zero plus two hours and twenty minutes all objectives should be taken. The two forward battalions of the 5th Brigade were

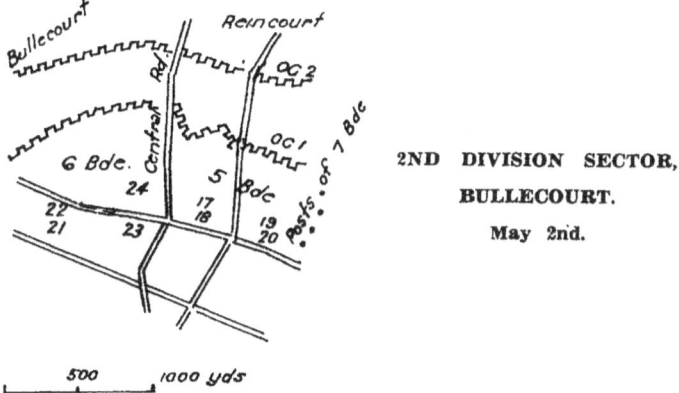

2ND DIVISION SECTOR, BULLECOURT.

May 2nd.

Nineteenth, right; Seventeenth, left; while in rear stood the Twentieth and Eighteenth. Bayonets would not be fixed until after our barrage had started, so as to avoid the glint of mono on the steel. The dispositions of the Seventeenth's companies were as follow: A (Nalder), right; and B (Ronald), left, in front. In rear, C (Maynard) and D (McDiarmid).

From battalion commanders to privates, all ranks of the 2nd Division were aware of the formidable nature of the German positions and the ground over which the attack was to be made. The majority possessed sufficient battle experience to convince them that they required a lot of luck in an operation which bore such a close resemblance to the unsuccessful earlier attack by the 4th Division on April 11th. The approach march across ground almost entirely devoid of cover from fire, and the deployment on an elevated strip of territory under a clear moon, within a few hundred yards of the enemy, and with their right flank semi-enfiladed from Queant, in itself would be a delicate manoeuvre. Moreover, as late as May 2nd, the day before the attack was to be launched, Lieutenant Wright, who was acting as Battalion Intelligence Officer, had reconnoitred the enemy's position from various points well forward of Noreuil, during daylight, and through his field-glasses had observed that the wire on the 5th Brigade sector was insufficiently cut; the effect of many of our shells had been wasted through their falling in the spaces between the three main belts of wire in front of the German front line trench. Wright took the earliest opportunity of communicating the result of his observations to the artillery Forward Observation Officers, who, however, preferred to rely on the conclusion they had reached from their position in the high ground east of Norauil over a mile short of the target area. Unfortunately Wright's report ultimately proved to be starkly true, and many gallant lives were to be sacrificed unnecessarily because of the ill-conceived belief held in certain quarters that the enemy's will to fight had considerably weakened.

At 11 p.m. on the night May 2/3, the Seventeenth moved out of Vaulx-Vraucourt in the direction of Noreuil. Soon after its arrival the 5th Brigade's approach march began, the Battalion leading. There was light shelling which resulted in a temporary hold-up when a shell fell near the head of B Company, killing 2nd-Lieutenant C. Houston and wounding several men. Slowly, but steadily the advance continued, each man in fighting order and wearing either a sheepskin or cardigan vest and carrying a rolled ground sheet. Each man also carried an additional 120 rounds of ammunition in his pouches, six Mills bombs, and four sand-bags, plus forty-eight hours rations. In addition, a proportion of picks and shovels was carried by each wave, while wire-cutters and mats for crossing were borne by the first and fourth waves. At the forward battle-dump the Seventeenth's quota of 100 Mills bombs packed in canvas buckets was deposited as a reserve.

Shortly after clearing the forward battle-dump the head of the Battalion entered Central road a little distance up which Lieutenant Wright was waiting to direct the companies to their positions on the high ground on the right of the road. This manoeuvre was successfully carried out, and by 3.40 a.m. the four battalions of the 5th Brigade were ready on their jumping off tapes. Wright, after seeing the Battalion moving in orderly fashion on its mark, ran back to report to Colonel Martin, who had established his Headquarters in a railway embankment several hundred yards to the rear. Just after Wright's arrival there our barrage commenced, and was almost immediately answered by the enemy, whose protective barrage was laid down behind the 5th Brigade. It was now growing light and the attack should have been developing according to plan. But there was an ominous lack of news, so Colonel Martin ordered Wright to go forward again and obtain a report as to what was occurring. Accompanied by Corporal Masterton,

Wright started on his hazardous mission. Pausing awhile near the Regimental Aid Post situated in a sunken road, which was being heavily shelled, he and his faithful henchman hastened forward through the enemy's barrage. Here the corporal was hit and after dressing his wound and making him as comfortable as he could in a big shell hole, Wright signalled some passing stretcher-bearers and went on alone. Soon he observed a short distance ahead groups of men in the prone position near the enemy's wire. Obviously they had been held up. And the reason was obvious. To the right and left, too, he could see the spurts of earth thrown up by a perfect, text-book, enfilade, machine-gun fire on the right. Shortly afterwards he himself was severely wounded and compelled to drop out of the fight.

What had happened is precisely what Wright had anticipated. Immediately the 5th Brigade rose to advance on the first objective it was met by a hurricane of machine-gun bullets from the direction of Queant. In a few minutes hundreds of men were struck down, the casualties among officers and sergeants being very heavy in proportion to their numbers. Nevertheless, small groups moved forward until they were held up by the wire in front of O.G.I. In most places this was impassable; our artillery had hardly damaged it. A number of bodies of men killed in the earlier battle were hanging on the wire. A. and C. Companies were somewhat more exposed to the scourging machine-gun fire from Queant than were B. and D. Nalder, the gallant young subaltern in command of A Company was killed soon after the advance began, as was his batman, Private E. H. Dawson, who had declined the opportunity to remain with the battalion nucleus, preferring to be at his officer's side. Lieutenant A. S. Taplin was also killed. The number who reached the enemy's wire was pitifully few, so Lieutenant Maynard ordered them to take cover in shell holes, hoping to be found shortly by supporting units of the brigade; but unfortunately these did not materialise, as the two rear battalions also had suffered grievously by the hail of fire from Queant. In the circumstances confusion was unavoidable. Lieutenant J. Donaldson of D Company, who himself was later wounded, estimated that eight minutes from the time the German artillery and machine-gun retaliatory barrage came down, the 5th Brigade ceased to be an organized formation. Those who were able to do so, made their way forward either singly or in small groups under corporals, or even senior privates. In this manner, elements of B and D Companies who were partly protected by the gentle slope of the ground to the left, gained a footing in O.G.I. Here McDiarmid was killed, but 2nd-Lieutenant J. M. Dickens and a small party cleared the enemy from a stretch of trench. Shortly after this Dickens was wounded. Sergeant M. J. McKay coming up, took charge and with a rifle grenade knocked out a German machine-gun; then leading twelve men, with Private J. P. Francis as first bayonet man, he bombed his way 300 yards along O.G.I. Here the party ran into a German counter-attack from two directions which forced them back a distance of 100 yards. McKay then constructed a barricade and held it until relieved, his party being ultimately reduced to five in number. McKay was greatly assisted by Sergeant E. G. Cowcher, in charge of the Lewis guns of D Company. One of his crew was knocked out by a shell, but Cowcher, after salving the gun, went forward in support of McKay. His ammunition ran out, but he seized a German machine-gun and brought it into action. Throughout the fight his conduct was admirable.

Many gallant deeds were performed that were not recorded. Among those that have been noted were the actions of Corporal S. Oakley, who, in charge of a carrying party, went back and forth through the enemy barrage several times. Privates S. Edwards, H. W. Brown and F. Wilson, stretcher-bearers, showed splendid devotion to duty bringing in the wounded. Big Private W. S. Bothamley was wounded during a bombing attack, but he stuck to his post. Later he assisted a wounded comrade to the Regimental Aid Post, afterwards returning to the fight. Subsequently he was seriously wounded. Private R. S. Davies, a Lewis gunner, also displayed courage and tenacity in fighting his gun after all his crew were killed.

When Colonel Martin received a full report as to the situation he immediately sent a message to Captain R. V. Spier, who with Major B. Holmes, was with the battalion nucleus, to report immediately with every man available. It was his intention to direct Spier to attack along O.G.I. to the right flank; but on arrival at Battalion Headquarters Spier learned that the arrangement had been cancelled, as in the meantime the 1st Brigade of the 1st Division had been brought up to take over the task.

On the night 3/4 the 5th Brigade was relieved and the exhausted remnants of the Seventeenth filed back to Battalion Headquarters where Sergeant J. M. Rigby was stationed in order to take a tally of the numbers. Rigby's original tally-sheet, which has been preserved, shows:—Headquarters, fifteen; A Company, thirty-three; B, twenty-six; C, eleven, and D Company, twenty-six—111 of all ranks. The total casualties of the Seventeenth were eleven officers and 331 other ranks.

The Seventeenth moved back to Biefvillers on the 6th and on the 8th entrained for Albert, en route to Fricourt. Here, on the 12th, the sergeants held a dinner to celebrate the second anniversary of the Battalion's departure from Australia. A generous menu comprising cold viands, vegetables, sweets, coffee, wine, beer, stout and spirits, with a limited quantity of lemon-squash and lime-juice, were important contributions to the enjoyment of the entertainment. There was an appropriate toast list, as follows; and the proposers were all members of the original Battalion:—

The King—W-O. V. J. Sullivan.
The Day We Celebrate—C.Q.M.S. E. J. Tidmarsh.
Fallen Comrades (In silence)—Sgt. J. H. McClure.
The Ladies—"Smith of the A.I.F." (Sgt. H. J. Smith).
The Visitors—R.Q.M.S. A. J. R. Davison.

It is a matter of regret that there is no record of the speeches, especially that by the dashing cavalier, Sergeant Smith, he of the "figs" episode on Gallipoli; however his elegant gestures and colourful imagery were in perfect accord with the importance of the occasion.

The next move was on the 17th to Senlis, for one night, and then on to Rubempre. Here a stay was made for nearly a month, to provide an opportunity for rest and relaxation after the strenuous campaigning of the preceding twelve months. During this period, sports were held at Contay, the Battalion being well represented amongst the prize-winners; Private W. Johnson taking first place in four foot-running events, and Private Reg. Sproule the heavy-weight boxing contest. Here, also, further honours and awards were announced: Lieutenants J. L. Wright, R. V. Shield; F. W. Smith, and Regimental Sergeant-Major V. J. Sullivan, the Military Cross; Company Quartermaster-Sergeant E. J. Tidmarsh, the Distinguished Conduct Medal; and Sergeants J. A. Barnier and G. Chick, and Privates A. H. Chambers, F. J. Dearie, J. A. Sheahan and S. R. Thompson, the Military Medal. These awards were for the operation at Lagnicourt. Sullivan's was the second award of its kind for the Battalion; the Military Cross was rarely given to Warrant Officers.

Training and recreation went hand in hand, and with the influence of the warm days, the spirits of the troops were soon restored, whilst the intake of reinforcements to repair the heavy losses of Bullecourt, laid the way open to rebuilding an efficient Battalion. Among the recreational attractions during this period was a grand fancy-dress carnival, of which, unfortunately, there exists no detailed account. However much ingenuity was exercised in the selection and style of costumes worn; J. Black and A. Preece of the Army Medical Corps details, looked and acted their parts as a French dude and mademoiselle, respectively, while A. McLaren, Transport Section, must have travelled a long distance outside the area, to obtain his Black Watch turnout. The first prize, however, went to a trio of officers, representing a French family—Lieutenants H. E. Clifton, father, and E. R. Raine, mother. Lieutenant L. S. Allen, child. Good British beer and succulent goods purchased from the nearby Expeditionary Force Canteen helped to provide for all ranks a temporary surcease from the strain of war.

An interesting sidelight on the character of the Australian soldier, is given in an extract from Lieutenant Maynard's "Letters." It reads:—"At Rubempre most of us heard a nightingale for the first time. Soon afterwards quite a procession of men could be seen wandering off about half a mile to a clump of trees, where one of these remarkable song-birds, nightly, lifted up his perfect notes to thrill his lady-love. Some of our troops would stay for an hour or two, lying in the field listening to the love-song, comparing their position and that of the bird, and thinking how we humans have retrograded."

The following awards of the Military Medal for bravery at Bullecourt were promulgated: Sergeants M. J. McKay and E. G. Cowcher, Corporal S. Oakley, Privates S. Edwards, H. W. Brown, F. Wilson, J. P. Francis and W. S. Bothamley.

On June 14th the Battalion, with the rest of the 5th Brigade, entrained for Bapaume, and was quartered in tents, just outside Biefvillers. Training continued. But there was also cricket, and, despite the hot weather, football. Every evening boxing bouts were held, which brought to light some unexpected talent. A contest was arranged between the Battalion's lightweight, "Paddy" Le Brese and a British soldier, T. Mayberry, and there was heavy wagering on the result. To a man the Seventeenth's money was on Le Brese, but, alas, the Tommy knocked-out their champion in three rounds. There ensued a period of financial drought amongst the personnel of the Battalion, both officers and men. To add insult to injury, that night a heavy thunderstorm broke and under its weight, many of the tents collapsed, leaving the bewildered occupants in a state of semi-nakedness to retrieve their sodden garments from the tangle of blankets and equipment.

A brigade inspection by the Corps Commander had been ordered for the 29th, but as the day was wet, the parade was cancelled. General Birdwood, who was accompanied by the Hon. W. A. Holman, Premier of New South Wales, contenting himself with visiting Brigade Headquarters and presenting ribands to recipients of decorations.

On July 3rd a memorial service was held for the late brigadier, General Holmes who was killed by a shell whilst accompanying Mr. Holman on a visit to the 4th Division near Messines. The 5th Brigade paraded for the occasion, and the Divisional Commander, General Smythe and his staff were also present. Chaplain Fernie paid a high tribute to the soldierly and humane qualities of the late General, and at the conclusion of the service the combined bands gave an impressive rendering of Chopin's "Funeral March."

About this time the award was announced of the Military Cross to Captains L. G. Fussell and H. W. Johnson, whilst the following promotions were promulgated:—Captain L. G. Fussell to Major; Lieutenants L. S. Allen, J. L. Wright and H. O. Busby to Captain; 2nd-Lieutenant W. A. Robertson to be Lieutenant; and Sergeants R. P. Little, J. H. McClure and H. J. Smith to 2nd-Lieutenant. Hon. Lieutenant and Quartermaster C. Tims was placed on the Supernumerary List, his place being taken by Regimental-Quartermaster Sergeant A. J. R. Davison, promoted Honorary Lieutenant. It is also recorded that Lieutenant E. C. New, who had been wounded, reported for duty, and that 2nd-Lieutenants T. H. E. Harries, M. Davis, reinforcements, and H. E. Warner and V. H. Hopkins, from the Officers' Training Corps, were taken on the strength.

July 28th marked the end of the Battalion's stay in the Somme area. The tide of war was setting northward, and with it went I Anzac with orders to move into General Headquarters Reserve and to concentrate in the St. Omer area. The Seventeenth marched to Beaucourt, to entrain for its destination, Westbecourt, about twelve miles from St. Omer. The march was carried out in the heat of the day and a number of men fell out, en route, several fainting. St. Omer was reached at 10 p.m. that day, the Battalion marching to Malhove about three kilometres distant, where it stayed for three days. On August 1st it proceeded to Westbecourt; and on August 7th to Arques, where it camped in tents. Three days later, the camp having been flooded by heavy rain, orders were issued to move into billets in the vicinity of the Forest of Clairmarais, Battalion Headquarters and A Company being quartered in a hamlet and the remaining three companies in a seminary about a mile distant on the outskirts of the forest. Here, the troops were excersied in close-order and in wood-fighting. The change from the routine tactical training was welcomed by all ranks, especially as no undue physical exertion was required in moving through the woods, which, moreover, provided cool shelter from the hot August sun. Word had been passed that this type of training was intended as a preparation for operations at a later stage in the forest-covered country north-east of Ypres. Credence was given to the rumour when it was notified that a divisional exercise would be held under the eye of no less a personage than the Second Army Commander, General Plumer. Everything went well for a start, and the successive lines, fifty yards in depth from each other advanced silently on a wide front through underbrush and leafy glades, while General Plumer and his staff, mounted, moved up and down one or other of the numerous rides, or tracks, that intersected the forest, watching the manoeuvres. At the edge of a narrow clearing the General waited to observe the Seventeenth's first wave debouch into the open. Everything was going according to plan, when suddenly, along the front of the advancing line sped a startled deer. In a moment good order and military discipline were tossed to the winds. Shouts of "there goes the cow!—stick it into him," made the welkin ring, while the bewildered animal was subjected to a barrage of steel helmets and other handy missiles. It took some minutes to restore decorum and to get the troops moving again in proper formation. The Army Commander rode off, his florid countenance registering undisguised displeasure. As one officer later remarked "The General was not a bit impressed, and we understand that we are not exactly on drinking terms with him at the moment.—After this performance perhaps he will not let us in on the Houthulst Forest proposition. Or will he?"

With the object of fostering the team spirit and increasing efficiency, an inter-company drill competition was held on the 8th and was won by C Company, Captain Allen. The Brigade Commander was so pleased with the idea that he ordered a similar test between a picked company from each of these four battalions, the Seventeenth, represented by C Company gaining first place. The display of arms drill and close-order movements by the competing companies demonstrated that the Australian soldier, when the occasion called for it, could equal in ceremonial drill the performance of trained regulars. An unusual and quite unrehearsed incident occurred, which exemplified the high standard attained. The four companies had marched past the Brigadier and were drawn up in line standing at ease, bayonets fixed. General Smith instructed Allen to pile-arms and break-off. Allen called his men to attention, but instead of first unfixing bayonets, he, in a moment of aberration, gave the order: "Pile arms." Unhesitatingly the left-hand man in the front rank rapped three paces forward and without further word of command led the remainder through the six movements of the "unfix." A pause, and then both ranks clicked into the first of the four movements of pile-arms, the whole being completed with a swing and in unison, leaving the Brigadier and his staff with amazement writ large on their features.

Shortly afterwards orders were received that the 2nd Division would be inspected by the Commander-in-Chief. The Divisional Commander ordered a rehearsal parade and it was announced that only one battalion in each of the three brigades would march-past. On the 29th the whole Division was drawn up on an extensive field, about 18,000 strong. The general salute was given, and as the Field-Marshal, astride a splendid

GROUP OF OLD IDENTITIES. Lieutenant V. J. Sullivan, M.C., in centre.

THE BATTALION'S BILLETS AT CLAIRMARAIS.

THE BATTALION SWIMMING TEAM.
Captain L. S. Allen, M.C.   Chaplain E. H. Fernie.

charger, galloped on the ground, the massed bands played "Australia Will be There." After the inspection the march-past took place, the Seventeenth representing the 5th Brigade. Subsequently Sir Douglas Haig shook hands with Colonel Martin. The Official War Historian relates that: "the Field-Marshal, after his scrutiny of the march-past, remarked to Sir Brudenell White, Chief-of-Staff of the Corps, that the men could not have marched better if they had had years of training."

The following day was observed as a holiday which was celebrated by the holding of a series of swimming matches between the Army Service Corps unit in St. Omer and the Seventeenth, which resulted in an overwhelming victory for our men; they won nine of the ten events. S. Riddington (champion of New South Wales) took the fancy diving event; Murray, the 50 and 100 yards; and Rollison, the 440 yards. The opposing team included an old Manly swimmer, Tartakover.

The warm weather and beautiful green countryside, combined with the respite remote from the scenes of their fifteen months continuous campaigning on the Western Front, were now showing their beneficial effects both on the health as well as the morale of the troops, which, perhaps, was never better than at that period, despite the stringency in food rationing. The German submarine campaign was then at its height, taking a serious toll of Ally shipping; indeed, so critical was the situation in food supply, that the High Command co-opted the services of culinary experts with the object of finding dietary substitutes, to alleviate the situation. Whether or not this experiment proved to be generally successful is a matter of speculation, but, certainly, so far as the Australian troops were concerned it was definitely not so. For, after a variety of experiments (including a soup concocted from the leaves of the dandelion plant) designed to appeal to their palates, the project was abandoned, doubtless, much to the relief of the regimental cooks, whose professional pride had been outraged by the very suggestion that the common "leontodon taraxacum" should be deemed worthy of inclusion in a diet designed for dinkum soldiers.

However, in nearby St. Omer and the surrounding villages, the men discovered means of augmenting the army ration and such social amenities as were afforded by this comparative haven from the turmoil and din of war. Thiennes, the first village in which the Seventeenth had billeted, was a popular rendezvous for those who could borrow horses or bicycles, or, perhaps, "wangle" a ride in an army lorry, they were certain to receive a hospitable reception from the kindly villagers who retained a warm-hearted interest for the first Australian soldiers quartered on them. One such reception was, perhaps, typical of this hospitality. It marked the occasion of a visit by 2nd-Lieutenant H. J. Smith and three boon companions, who, firstly, paid individual calls, on their former hosts and then repeated the process in the company of each other, Monsieur "Smeeth," whose lively personality had remained a pleasant and vivid memory with the kindly populace, was made especially welcome. Everywhere food and liquid refreshment were lavished on the party, whose members, in the gloaming, returned to billets, gastronomically replete and mentally at peace with the world. The subsequent accounts by Mr. Smith of this red-letter day, the quality and quantity of the champagne, the fish and the fruit consumed, lost nothing in the re-telling.

But the time for serious work was again at hand. I Anzac had received orders to concentrate in the area south of Ypres, preparatory to taking its part in the operations that were about to be resumed in that sector. On September 12th, the Seventeenth, now thoroughly rested, and with all ranks in the highest of spirits, marched away from Clairmarais Forest and its beautiful surroundings. With the band playing the rousing quick-step "El Abanico," they headed once again for the "Bloody Salient."

CHAPTER XI.

The scene moves north to Flanders—Haig launches Third Battle of Ypres, July 31st—I Anzac joins Second Army—"Set-piece" attacks skilfully prepared—Menin Road, September 20th—Operation a complete success—Many brave deeds performed—Transport Section does excellent work—Out for a brief rest.

IN an earlier chapter it has been narrated that following the supercession of Joffre by Nivelle, the policy of the big breakthrough was substituted for the existing one of hard and frequent blows and the British armies were thereby relegated to a relatively subsidiary role in the projected spring offensive. In April Nivelle mounted a tremendous attack on the German centre between Soissons and Rheims, and though at first successful, it ultimately proved a complete failure with a cost of very heavy casualties and with serious effects on the morale of the French Army. Nivelle was replaced by Petain, but unity of command had not been achieved.

This development left Haig free to give effect to a longcherished plan of his which was to strike in the northern sector, with the object of freeing the Channel ports. In anticipation of these events the Field-Marshal, had had prepared months previously, plans for such an operation. The intended method of execution was his favourite one—a succession of sledgehammer blows at limited objectives. The part of the German line selected lay to the east of Ypres, where an advance of a dozen miles or so would squeeze out the German garrisons on the Belgian Coast and deprive the enemy of access to the English Channel and the Strait of Dover. Haig now had a plentiful supply of artillery which he could mass at any given point to overwhelm the enemy artillery and at the same time provide maximum cover under which his own infantry would advance.

As a preliminary to the main operation the enemy had to be cleared from the Messines—Wytschaete Ridge, a commanding height a few miles south of Ypres. This position was captured after a brilliant operation on June 7th, in which the 3rd and 4th Divisions played an outstanding part.

On July 31st, after a bombardment lasting fifteen days, the British Fifth Army which had been put in on the left of Plumer's Second Army, together with a French Army, were launched into the Third Battle of Ypres. The attack, however, met with only a moderate degree of success, mainly due to the heavy rains turning the low-lying countryside into a quagmire, through which even men on foot found difficulty in advancing. The bad weather continued throughout the month of August, but in spite of this Haig persisted in the attack. Finally, after extremely heavy losses, he decided to wait for favourable weather and for the ground to dry. He decided that Plumer's

Second Army would be entrusted with the task of continuing the operations, which was planned to commence about September 20th, and for this purpose I Anzac would be placed under Plumer's command.

The writer recalls that, early in September, Colonel Martin told him the metereological experts at G.H.Q. had predicted that the first twenty days of the month would be free from rain.

The first day's march from Clairmarais brought the Seventeenth to Steenvoorde, fifteen miles distant, and the next day, the 13th to Dickebusch, about three miles south-west of Ypres. Here the Battalion was quartered in tents. The weather was fine and warm, no rain having fallen for about a fortnight and the ground drying fast. As far as the eye could see the flat back area of Ypres was packed with troops, transport and animals, offering a target, which the Germans, with their new aeroplane, the Fokker, were not slow in bombing. At this period the enemy had a temporary ascendency in the air, and it was galling to our troops to have to watch his 'planes coming over in broad daylight, virtually free from molestation by our own aircraft, to drop their bombs on a motor park or horse-lines. Some very heavy casualties were thus caused amongst both personnel and material, although, fortunately, the Seventeenth did not suffer.

Meanwhile, preparations for the renewal of the offensive were reaching the final stages, and all ranks soon after their arrival in the area had ample evidence of foresight and attention to organisation to a degree they never had experienced before. At the village of Busseboom, a few miles distant, there were constructed relief models of the sectors over which the divisions of I Anzac were to operate, and each unit in turn marched there to view, in tabloid form, every feature of the ground. In addition, all leaders, from brigadiers to lance-corporals, attended lectures by Royal Flying Corps Officers on liaison work between air and ground forces. They were shown reproductions of aerial photographs and instructed how to identify in the shell-pitted terrain gun-emplacements and concrete "pill-boxes" which the Germans had built in dozens. Copies of these photographs were freely distributed amongst leaders to be studied in detail. This was the first occasion the troops had been given a close-up view, so to speak, of a projected operation, and in consequence they were inspired with confidence in the outcome of the battle.

The attack was to be launched from Westhoek Ridge, the furthest point in that sector reached in the August operations. About a thousand yards distant the enemy's line ran along a spur known as Anzac Ridge, and between the two positions the ground formed a shallow depression, through which ran a small stream, named the Hannebeek. The ground itself was a mass of shell-holes, and on the aerial photographs resembled a gigantic sponge. In the bottom of this depression could be seen the bare shell-stripped remains of what was once a wood, and scattered chequer-wise along the churned-up terrain were scores of pill-boxes, designed as a forward zone of defence, some being used as machine-gun posts and command centres, while others served as medical-aid posts.

As already stated, the attack was to be of the "set-piece" type, limited to the extent of artillery-barrage cover capable of being given as a protection from counter-attack, while the infantry were consolidating the newly-won positions. It was to be launched by the X British Corps on the right, Anzac Corps centre, and the 25th Brigade, 9th (Scottish) Division of the Fifth Army, on the left. The sector allotted I Anzac was 2,000 yards wide, and the attacking divisions of the corps would be 1st, right; and 2nd, left; each division having a two-brigade front and each of the latter being formed up in a one-battalion front. The operation would be carried out in three stages, the assaulting battalions leap-frogging one another.

On the 2nd Division sector the 7th and 5th Brigades would comprise the assaulting brigades, with the 6th in reserve. The order in which the battalions of the 5th Brigade were to form up was Twentieth, first objective; Eighteenth, second, and Seventeenth, the third objective, with the Nineteenth in reserve. The three stages were known as the Red, Blue and Green Lines respectively, and were identifiable mainly in the form of map references.

A feature of the operations would be the unprecedented weight of artillery concentrated on this narrow sector, comprising forty-six-and-a-half siege or heavy batteries (208 guns) and nine brigades of field artillery (216 guns), the equivalent of one gun for every five yards. In addition, there would be 112 machine-guns, one half of which would provide a creeping barrage while the other half would be responsible for counter-barrage fire. The assembly position of the Seventeenth was to be on Bellewarde Ridge, a few hundred yards west of Westhoek Ridge, where the Twentieth and Eighteenth Battalions would be drawn up. The dispositions by the Seventeenth for the attack were as shown in the diagram:—

D	C	B	A	
(Mackenzie)	(Allen)	(Haigh)	(Wright)	
———	———	———	———	1st and 2nd
———	———	———	———	assault platoons.
———	———	———	———	3rd mopping-up platoon.
———	———	———	———	4th carrying platoon.

The distance between platoons was seventy yards.

Companies would be in position one hour before zero, which was set down for 5.40 a.m.

As an example of the thoroughness, even in minute details, with which the operations had been planned, it was notified that at assembly places and jumping-off lines, notice-boards would be erected on the night previous to the attack, showing where the right of companies would rest, while, green lamps would indicate the right boundary and red lamps the left boundary of the 5th Brigade. In addition to this, sign-boards were erected showing the way to Brigade Headquarters, Regimental Aid Posts and Brigade Dump. Each man of the Seventeenth would wear a green patch of cloth on the back of his helmet corresponding to the Green Line, or Third objective. Bayonets would not be fixed until Westhoek Ridge had been crossed. For support, a section each of Vickers guns and Stokes mortars would move forward with the Battalion to the Green Line so as to cover the approaches by which it was considered counter-attacks were likely to be delivered. When the Green Line had been captured, the Twentieth Battalion would be withdrawn, the Eighteenth taking its place, while the Seventeenth would then become responsible for both Blue and Green Lines. The remaining details were also clear and simple: the dress, as usual, was battle order, with waterproof sheets carried rolled on the back of each man, who, in addition, would carry 220 rounds of ammunition, two rifle-grenades, four sandbags, one iron ration, one emergency ration and two full water-bottles. It was also provided that each mopping-up platoon would carry one tool per man. Three green flares would be lit as a signal that the Battalion had attained its objective.

The pattern of the preparatory artillery shoots, as well as for the actual barrage covering the attack, was designed to suit the peculiar conditions, already narrated, under which the enemy had disposed his defences in depth in the form of concrete pill-boxes and strong points, necessitating the provision, not only of a curtain of fire, but a barrage several hundred yards deep, blanketing his posts and stifling retaliatory fire from artillery and machine-guns, as well as disorganizing his communications and preventing the assembly of counter-attack troops. To quote the Australian Official War Historian: "This barrage comprised five successive lines of shells, or bullets, with 200-yard intervals, the nearest lines being laid down by 18-pounders combined with 4.5-inch howitzers, and the other three by the machine-guns, the 6-in howitzers, and the 8- and 9.2-inch howitzers and the 60-pounders. At the end of each stage of the attack, in order to catch any counter-attack that might approach while the troops dug-in, all lines of the barrage, except the first, would move steadily ahead 2,000 yards into the enemy's country. They would suddenly return and the whole barrage would then conduct the next line of infantry to the next objective, until the final objective had been reached."

The morning of September 19th dawned bright and warm, and the ground was dry and firm. If the rain held off the going would be good, even in the shell-pitted terrain over which the approach-march would have to be made. The four company commanders had just returned from reconnoitring the route along which the Battalion would move to take up its position on Bellewarde Ridge. While companies were completing their preparations, Colonel Martin brought together the officers and non-commissioned officers and explained once more the details of the forthcoming operation. Whilst he was addressing them, an enemy plane was seen to approach, flying low. A few hundred yards distant was a large wagon-park and horse-lines. These were targets for the Fokker, which dropped a couple of bombs right upon the closely packed vehicles and animals, causing heavy casualties amongst the latter and killing several soldiers. The plane then flew away in the direction of its own lines.

At about 11 p.m. rain began to fall in a steady drizzle, and the prospect of an attack under wet weather conditions cast a temporary damper on the spirits of the men, who had been anticipating a fine day and a good barrage for the "hop-over." However, the feeling was dispelled the moment the Battalion formed up near midnight to move up to its allotted position, and although it was still raining when the march commenced the mind of every man was too concerned with the task in hand to feel the physical reaction caused by this inconvenient intrusion of Jupiter Pluvius into the proceedings.

Slowly, past the south-eastern outskirts of Ypres, the Seventeenth moved in single file along the slippery duck-board tracks laid over the uptorn country-side, towards the Menin Road. Just before reaching the road a heavy shell fell on the rear of C Company, killing 2nd-Lieutenant W. K. Seabrook and two men, and wounding three others. (Seabrook's two brothers, both in the Seventeenth, were also killed in this action.) But the remainder of this unavoidably slow journey was completed without incident, and at 3.35 a.m., on the 20th, Bellewarde Ridge was reached. There were two clear hours in hand before the barrage would begin. The darkness began to fade. It was still raining steadily. The men huddled together for warmth, turned their gaze in the direction of Ypres. Zero hour was at hand. To use one of their favourite expressions: "The balloon was about to go up."

Suddenly, on the horizon, there shot up a vast unbroken sheet of flame. The ground trembled, and then a few seconds later came the simultaneous thunder of hundreds of howitzers and field-guns, roaring their prelude to the accompaniment of the ear-splitting chatter of the barrage machine-guns. The balloon had gone up!

Never before had our men experienced such an overwhelmingly concentrated barrage, not even at Pozieres or Bullecourt. This was, indeed, a new experience, vast and awe-inspiring. But what about the fellow opposite? How was he faring under that dreadful hail of steel and lead? Could his gunners face the storm and lay down a retaliatory barrage along Bellewarde Ridge where the Seventeenth awaited the moment for their part in the drama on which the curtain had been raised? This interval of tense expectancy, of being heavily shelled in turn, and not being able to do anything about it, imposed a tremendous nervous strain upon all ranks. But to-day, fortunately, it was different. The supporting battalions were not getting any "back-wash"; the enemy's artillery had been virtually abolished. A few heavy shells did fall in the area occupied by the Battalion, causing some casualties, among them 2nd-Lieutenant V. N. Hopkins, who was mortally wounded. He was a fine specimen of young Australian, and had shown his worth by qualifying for his commission from the ranks, where he had served as one of the medical details attached to the Battalion.

In due course the barrage lifted, and later a message came through that at 6.11, the Twentieth Battalion had captured its objective—the Red Line. That was a good start. By 7.55 a.m., the Eighteenth had taken the Blue Line. Eeverything was going well—in fact so well, that at 7.40 a.m., before the scheduled time to move, Colonel Martin obtained permission to go forward. The four companies quickly shook themselves into artillery formation, and the signal to advance was given. The rain had ceased and a high wind was blowing. The spirits of the men were high. The intervening distance to Westhoek Ridge was covered quickly and without incident. As the four companies, in lines of sections disposed in depth, topped the rise, company commanders' whistles shrilled for the signal to fix bayonets. It was as though the Battalion was carrying out an exercise during manoeuvres, and to quote from the report of the Brigade Commander, General Smith, who watched operations from Advanced Brigade Headquarters: "The advance of the Seventeenth Battalion was one of the features of the operation."

As the Battalion moved down into the dip to the Hannebeek it was seen that the enemy had managed to lay a light curtain of shell fire along the bottom to the edge of Hannebeek Wood, on which no shells were falling. D Company, therefore, performed a left incline which took it on to the 9th Division's sector, swinging back into their original position immediately it had cleared the flank of the shelled sector. The Battalion suffered only a few casualties, and the advance continued up the further slope, passing through the Twentieth and later the Eighteenth Battalion, which unit had advanced well beyond its objective. Under a perfect barrage the Seventeenth moved on to the Green Line, which was occupied without opposition. Colonel Martin, who arrived at the newly-won position almost as soon as his leading platoons, observed that some of these had pushed too far forward and were in danger of being caught in our own barrage. From his Advanced Headquarters, which he had established in a shell-hole a little in rear of the objective, Colonel Martin directed a re-alignment of the position, and ordered it to be consolidated. The enemy by now had partly recovered and began shelling the area fairly heavily, while his low-flying aeroplanes machine-gunned our men, wounding two. A shell killed two other ranks of Battalion Headquarters staff, which soon afterwards was moved into "Garter Point," a pill-box lately used by the Germans as a medical aid post. It was stoutly built and roomy, and its existence subsequently saved the lives of many of our wounded, who were collected under its shelter whilst awaiting a favourable opportunity to be evacuated.

The work of consolidation proceeded apace, and as by 1.30 p.m. no counter-attack had materialised, our protective barrage was switched off. The savage pounding of the enemy's assembly places by our artillery evidently had been completely effective.

But during the course of the afternoon the Germans kept up a steady shelling of the Seventeenth's position, causing many casualties, including Lieutenant C. A. Hannaford, killed. Earlier in the day 2nd-Lieutenant T. L. Ryan had been killed during the advance across the Hannebeek, and thus the Battalion lost two of its finest junior leaders, both of whom had won their commissions in the field. Both men were also splendid physical specimens and of gigantic stature, Hannaford being 6 ft. 4½ in. in height, and Ryan 6 ft. 3 in. The possessors of opposite temperaments, they were nevertheless close friends. Hannaford, despite his great stature and strength, was in reality a warm-hearted boy, radiating laughter and good cheer wherever he went, and like all healthy boys was ever ready to participate in a harmless practical joke. Ryan, on the other hand, retained a simple dignity and poise, both mental and physical, behind which, however, there lurked a droll wit and pleasing sense of humour. It will be recalled that he won the Military Medal at Layton Alley, when a corporal. The Battalion could ill-afford to lose two such capable and courageous officers.

Late in the afternoon, the enemy's shelling slackened, and by nightfall it had almost entirely ceased.

The Seventeenth had acquitted itself well, all ranks having been imbued with a confidence arising from the knowledge that they were participating in an operation planned with such unusual care and forethought, that its success was ensured from the outset. However, heavy casualties were inseparable, and had it not been for sound leadership on the part of the company and platoon leaders, these would have been much greater. A Company on the right flank was led by its commander, Wright, across the enemy's barrage line in the Hannebeek Valley, between salvoes, at the double, and that officer, on approaching the objective, observed the line our smoke-shells were marking for that purpose. Thereupon, he signalled Lieutenant H. T. Allan and the leading platoon of the Company to halt and commence digging. During the whole of the action Wright displayed conspicuous determination. Eventually he was the only officer left in A Company.

B Company under its impetuous leader, Haigh, was not so fortunate in identifying the objective on that featureless terrain, and as a result his right flank was pushed forward under our protective barrage and suffered severely. Lieutenant R. W. Pettit, who during the advance, was in charge of the last wave of men carrying tools and ammunition for the Company, observing the error, immediately took steps to remedy the situation. Coolly moving into the barrage he personally supervised the withdrawal on to the proper alignment, and in the process was himself wounded, but he refused to quit. Noticing one of his men named Etheridge lying wounded and unable to move, Pettit, a powerful lad, lifted up his comrade and carried him back to safety. Shortly afterwards Haigh was wounded, but Pettit carried on until hit a second time; then he was compelled to retire from the fight. This movement by B Company's right-flank sections, unfortunately, influenced some men of the left sections of A Company to follow their example and in consequence several were hit, Sergeant McDonnell being killed.

C and D Companies under Allen and Mackenzie respectively, reached their objectives with comparatively few casualties, as the enemy's barrage seemed to be less concentrated in the vicinity of Hannebeek Wood on the left flank of the advance.

Three subalterns, H. T. Allan, H. E. Clifton and E. W. Dark, were conspicuous for their good work that day. Allan, a man of strong personality concealed under a cloak of irresponsibility, took over the command of B Company when all its officers and the company sergeant-major were casualties, and his calm and confident bearing and total disregard of danger inspired all ranks. Clifton, who although wounded during the advance by a bullet from a German aeroplane, continued to lead his men, and during the process of consolidation showed a complete disregard for his personal safety. He only retired when ordered by Colonel Martin to report to the Regimental Aid Post for treatment. Clifton had left Australia as a lance-sergeant, and after being invalided back to that country from Gallipoli, had rejoined his old comrades in 1916. Dark, who was acting as Assistant Adjutant, also displayed resolution in the task of keeping touch between Battalion and Company Headquarters— a task which often necessitated his moving in the open, thus exposing himself to the enemy's fire. In addition, his knowledge of the Lewis gun proved very valuable in assisting companies in the selection of suitable sites during the process of consolidating the line.

Additional officer casualties were Lieutenant S. M. Blackshaw and 2nd-Lieutenant A. E. Warner, both efficient leaders. Warner had enlisted in the original Battalion as a private.

During this and the following day all ranks showed a splendid determination and restraint under the gusts of concentrated shell-fire that came down on them, as the enemy began to recover from the heavy initial blow. All branches—non-commissioned ranks, signallers, runners, Lewis gunners, riflemen and stretcher-bearers, participated equally in the many fine deeds that were performed. No one present, however, would begrudge a special meed of praise to the work of the stretcher-bearers. Compelled to carry the wounded for long distances, picking their way laboriously over the friable earth fringing gigantic shell-holes and exposed to the full view of the enemy, these men, generally the "hard-doer" type, shortish, but "nuggety" in build, displayed a tenacity of purpose and physical endurance over sustained periods, that were the admiration of their comrades. Lance-Corporal W. Davis, who had won the Distinguished Conduct Medal at Pozieres, personally tended the wounded unable to be moved because of the heavy drain on the supply of stretcher bearers. For thirteen hours he toiled unremittingly at this work, almost all the time in the open, thereby undoubtedly saving many lives. The gallant fellow died of cholera in Persia, in 1918, whilst serving with the Dunster force.

Then there was Private L. R. Gibson, who, throughout the whole of the action carried casualties from the front line to the rear, through intense shell-fire. On two occasions this plucky lad went forward from our line during the period that our barrage was covering the task of consolidation, and bandaged and carried back men who had gone too far into the barrage and had been hit. Gibson worked tirelessly, refusing to rest, all the while showing an utter disregard for danger. Yet another of this hardy band, Private W. H. Burrell, did a continuous stretch of "carries," through heavy shell-fire, also careless of his own safety. He, too, went into our own barrage to rescue the wounded and subsequently was himself hit. Burrell's own experience, as recorded in his diary, provides a fine example of that devotion to duty which marked the work of the stretcher-bearers, and also illustrates the deep loyalty of the Digger to his mate. He states:—"The rain had cleared, and we went about 1,000 yards without losing a man. It was so easy that I stopped to take a photo. Then we struck it rough and the boys went down like nine-pins. We had a case on a stretcher, and a shell landed alongside killing one of my squad and wounding the other two. 'Morrie's' (Private E. J. Morris) was only slight, so he kept on with me up to the front line. Dead and wounded lay everywhere, both Fritz's and our own. Some of our boys had gone too far and had been wounded and left in No Man's Land, including Alf and Watson. Morrie and I went out and got them in, while low-flying German 'planes machine-gunned us. We took Watson down, as he was badly wounded, and left Alf in a trench. It was heavy work carrying through the swamp (the Hannebeek) as old Fritz was putting down a barrage of five-nines. Went back for Alf, but another shell had got him and taken both legs off. I put on a proper tourniquet but he had lost too much blood. When he saw me he said: 'Well, Bill, I knew you would come back for me'."

Burrell goes on to relate that just as he was going to put his dying comrade on a stretcher, a shell landed just behind him, wounding him in the thigh and back. Despite considerable loss of blood he made his own way back on foot to Hellfire Corner, two miles away, rather than add to the burdens of his grievously overworked comrades; and how, at Hellfire Corner, a mounted officer, observing his plight, dismounted and had Burrell lifted into the saddle, himself leading the horse carrying the wounded man right into Ypres. But Burrell's thoughts were for his wounded mate, for after describing the foregoing incident he adds:—"I hope someone is able to get poor Alf., as he is one of the best."

Private Morris, Burrell's mate, who although hit by a shell before the advance started, refused to go to the Aid Post, moving forward with the attacking troops. Wounded a second and a third time, he insisted on continuing duty, and stayed with the Battalion until it was relieved.

Two other stout-hearted lads, Private H. Targett and A. E. Doling, both showed almost unexampled endurance, tending and carrying the wounded, with little rest or food. Nor was this the first occasion that they had displayed such unselfish devotion to duty; whilst another comrade in D Company, Private J. T. Rowan also worked untiringly without a break for twenty-four hours, bearing his wounded mates over the shell-torn

Capt. J. L. WRIGHT, M.C.   Pte. A. E. DOLING, M.M.

Pte. W. H. T. BURRELL, M.M.   Pte. C. J. BURTON, M.M.

THE MENIN ROAD — SEPTEMBER 1917.

ground. His cheerfulness and endurance did much to relieve their suffering.

In the ranks of the riflemen, one of the best deeds performed was by Sergeant J. H. Evans, who took charge of a section of carriers, and led it through heavy shell-fire and established a dump of his valuable material. He then went back and supervised the task of bringing up additional supplies. When this was completed he took command of a post in the line, after most of the officers and non-commissioned officers had become casualties. Evans gave an inspiring display of leadership, which was in keeping with the traditions of the wearers of the coveted three stripes. Another fine soldier, Sergeant T. R. Knight, showed an excellent example of courage, cheerfulness and initiative. Knight took command of a platoon when his officer was hit and remained with it throughout the operation, during which he displayed sound ability in the siting and construction of posts which he personally supervised, encouraging all ranks by his cheerful manner and high devotion to duty. On several previous occasions his work had been marked by the same degree of determination, thoroughness and ability to handle men. Lance-Corporal R. C. Worthington also proved to be a leader of resource, for when his seniors became casualties, he assumed command of the platoon and led it to the objective, despite heavy shell and machine-gun fire.

Another who displayed fine leadership was Sergeant C. J. Sewell, who organized and led carrying parties, regardless of personal danger; and although these parties suffered casualties, he saw that the supplies reached the front line. Afterwards he took command of a post and was twice wounded before he left the line.

The work of Sergeant R. C. White illustrated the courage and initiative typical of the junior leader. He was one of the carrying platoon of his company and after his officer was wounded, took command. When the objective was reached he established a dump under heavy shell and machine-gun fire. On the return journey, to fetch additional ammunition and supplies, he organized stretcher parties to carry wounded. Later, he lent valuable assistance in the work of organizing and consolidating the Company front.

The work of the Lewis gunners was also good. Corporal T. A. Corbett displayed conspicuous gallantry and devotion to duty. Corbett brought his gun-team to the objective and having set them in position, he assisted his company commander to supervise the other gun-teams, during the course of which he was wounded, but refused to leave the line. Later, he was buried through a shell blowing down his post, and when extricated had to be ordered to rest. However, hearing that casualties among the gun-crews were fairly heavy he crawled to a post and carried on until the Battalion was relieved. His courage and tenacity went a long way to keeping up the spirits of the men. Corporal G. S. Dryden displayed conspicuous bravery and devotion to duty whilst in charge of four Lewis guns. His gun-crews were depleted by casualties, but he nursed and encouraged the remainder without rest or respite for twenty-four hours. His guns inflicted many casualties on the enemy while his coolness, cheerfulness and endurance kept his teams together and filled them with confidence.

Lance-Corporal R. S. Davies was in charge of a Lewis gun section during the advance, when a shell burst, burying the gun and knocking out the crew with the exception of himself and another man. He recovered the gun and magazine and took them forward to the line, where he soon had the weapon in action inflicting casualties on the enemy. Later, he crawled forward alone from our line through heavy shell-fire and successfully dealt with two enemy snipers who were causing casualties amongst our men. Throughout the operation he showed great dash and courage. It will be recalled that Davies displayed conspicuous gallantry at Bullecourt, for which he was recommended.

Private W. A. Brogden showed coolness and resourcefulness in the way he handled his gun throughout the action; despite heavy shelling his weapon was always in action and dispersed several parties of Germans, inflicting casualties on them. Two young riflemen, Privates E. Scott and A. Thomas, also showed their mettle. Scott, during wiring operations in front of the trenches, disregarding personal danger, although under heavy shell-fire, worked rapidly and coolly throughout; while Thomas displayed determination, initiative and devotion to duty, and when his platoon commander and several of the carrying party became casualties, Thomas came forward and led the remainder to their objective. Afterwards he formed a post in the line and did fine work under heavy shell-fire, and although wounded remained there for many hours during a period when a counter-attack was expected. He did not report to the Aid Post until ordered to do so.

The work of the runners and signallers was also of the highest order, of which fine examples were given by three young privates, C. J. Burton, G. R. Millthorpe and Lance-Corporal B. G. Starr. The two former revealed conspicuous gallantry and devotion to duty whilst running messages through barrages and the fire of snipers, Starr, equally gallant, sent messages visually, in the open, under heavy shell-fire, during the course of which he was badly wounded in the hand, but carried on as lineman all the following day, until ordered to report to the Aid Post. He had continually repaired lines under heavy fire, and by his conduct set a fine example to the men under his charge.

The part played by the Transport Section under the command of Captain H. O. Busby cannot be allowed to pass without mention. In conditions calculated to test the courage and endurance of the bravest and toughest, the men on whom the troops depended for rations and supplies never failed to get through, despite the appalling difficulties. Indeed, it was with them a point of honour to fulfil every task allotted without any fuss, every such job being carried out in the customary matter-of-fact way of the Australian soldier. To these men, mainly country-born and bred, the indescribable conditions with which they had to contend were regarded merely as being part of the day's work. Even before the Battalion went into the attack, and after it had been withdrawn for a rest, the Transport Section, along with those of other units, was continually moving up supplies of ammunition and material to the forward zones, with the aid of their faithful horses and mules.

An extract from the diary of Driver McLaren gives a glimpse of these conditions. It reads:—"I got my first trip to the line (Sept. 18), a four-horse trip with a limber load of bombs, one limber from each battalion. At Hellfire Corner, the Nineteenth Battalion limber was blown to pieces killing the driver, his mate and the four horses of the team. . . After one leaves the main road running from Ypres to Menin, the mud is impassable, even for pack-horses. There is only one way, that is to make a sleeper track. Each of these sleeper tracks has its avenue of dead animals, harness, vehicles and even ambulances, stacked along its sides. When anything is knocked, it is just bundled off the track, and fresh sleepers put down. And so the game goes on amidst some awful sights here." Four days later, that is the 22nd, he records: "Been up the line to 'Anzac House.' The liveliest day of my life. Fritz shelled the track up and down and all over the place. He blew up the bomb-dump and killed and wounded a lot of our boys. I did three trips through the heaviest barrage I was through."

We now return to the description of the action. The afternoon wore on without incident from the time our protective barrage ceased. About 2 p.m. groups of Germans were observed in the vicinity of Zonnebeke, to the north-east, moving southwards across the Seventeenth's front, but these groups quickly dissolved when our artillery fire was brought to bear on them. Late in the afternoon the Germans began a fairly heavy shelling of the whole of the 2nd and 9th British Division sectors, and at about 6.30 this was intensified into barrage proportions, apparently the preliminary to a counter-attack. But no such movement developed, and after an hour or so the shelling died down.

All through the night unusual quiet reigned, and the only incident that occurred was when a young German soldier walked into one of the Seventeenth's posts. He had been lying "doggo" in a shell-hole throughout the hours of daylight. He was only a lad and very frightened, but when questioned in kindly tones by Colonel Martin, while 2nd-Lieutenant Raine was examining papers taken from the prisoner, the lad spoke freely of what he knew of enemy troop movements and the identity of his own as well as neighbouring units. However, when he was handed back the few letters and a photograph or two of the folks at home, the youth burst into tears, and said he never expected that these personal mementoes would be returned. He could speak English well, having served in trans-Atlantic liners prior to the War.

At dawn on the 21st our artillery placed a heavy barrage all along the newly captured front, in accordance with a prearranged plan. This barrage was intended to catch any counter-attack that might be launched at such a favourable time. Field-guns which had been moved up during the interval to the Bellewarde and Westhoek Ridges, as well as the machine-guns, played for some time, both laterally along our front and to a depth of 2,000 yards, but as daylight broke and it was clearly evident that the enemy was not in an attacking mood just then, the barrage was switched off.

During the morning German aircraft flew up and over the position endeavouring to harass our troops with machine-gun fire, but casualties were negligible. The day passed in comparative quiet, until the late afternoon, when advanced parties from the relieving battalions began to arrive. Whether the Germans, who must have observed them, concluded that they were elements of an attacking force, is not known, but at 6.30 that evening they began a very heavy bombardment along the whole of the front. On the other hand, as there appeared to be some movement on his part along the Battalion front, S.O.S. signals were sent up, which brought an immediate and equally heavy response from our artillery. The din went on for over two hours, but the only casualties were one other rank killed and two wounded. Colonel Martin's Headquarters repeatedly received direct hits but its concrete roof proved a perfect protection, and apart from the inconvenience the occupants were put to re-lighting candles extinguished by the concussion of shells, no material damage was done.

During the night 21/22nd the Twenty-first Battalion took over the line from the Seventeenth, without incident. By 2 a.m. the relief was complete and the Battalion moved back into Ypres, where it rested all day, moving to Halifax Camp, on the 23rd, and the following day to Whippenhoek Camp, where the opportunity was taken to rest and recuperate, after the trying, though successful operations, just concluded. Not every man in the Battalion, however, had the luck to enjoy this well-earned respite, for the following day instructions were received to detail two officers and fifty other ranks for duty as stretcher party with the Fifth Division, which was scheduled to carry the operation a stage further in the Polygon Wood sector.

It was at Whippenhoek Camp, on the 28th, that General Birdwood presented ribbons to those men who had been awarded the Military Medal. The recipients were: Sergeants H. J. Evans, T. R. Knight and C. J. Sewell; Lance-Corporals R. C. Worthington and W. Davis; Privates W. A. Brogden, H. Targett, A. E. Doling, L. R. Gibson, B. G. Starr, C. J. Burton, G. R. Milthorpe, E. Scott, G. S. Dryden, A. Thomas, E. J. Morris and W. H. T. Burrell. It will be recalled that Davis won the Distinguished Conduct Medal at Pozieres.

Thus ended that phase of the Third Battle of Ypres, known as the Menin Road. It was an almost perfect example of the set-piece type of operation, although attained at heavy cost to the Seventeenth, four officers being killed and five wounded; fifty other ranks killed and 186 wounded, while twenty-one other ranks were posted as missing.

The evening of the 28th found the Battalion facing once again in the direction of Ypres and the rolling tide of battle to the east and north.

Two days previously, that is, the 26th, a brilliant operation by the 4th and 5th Divisions had advanced the line another thousand yards, or so, from Polygon Wood to the outskirts of Zonnebeke.

After a night's stay at Halifax Camp the Battalion moved into a bivouac of tents outside the ramparts east of Ypres, and remained there until October 3rd, when it moved back into the old infantry barracks. The following day orders were received to proceed up to Westhoek Ridge in support of the 6th and 7th Brigades, which had the same day assaulted and captured Zonnebeke and the Broodseinde Ridge south of the Ypres-Roulers railway. At the same time, the ridge north of the railway was taken by II Anzac, which included the 3rd Division, its capture giving the British over 3,000 prisoners and also possession of a commanding height which had been in the hands of the Germans for nearly three years. Haig's third blow of the series commencing September 20th was the most powerful he had yet delivered, and the result indicated that the enemy's morale had been further gravely impaired and his organization badly mauled. Another blow or two of similar intensity and he might well be ousted from his position to the north, under threat of being cut off.

Rain had begun to fall on the 4th, after an almost unbroken period of six weeks, and continued until the 7th without ceasing. The lower portions of the salient reverted to a series of bogs, thus throwing a great strain on the supply and communication services required to feed the advance with artillery shells and ammunition, and provide for the evacuation of the wounded. Great numbers of troops were employed in laying duck-board tracks and corduroy roads, while every available item of transport was ordered into this service. Some of the difficulties encountered by the men responsible for keeping up the necessary supplies, is recorded in a further entry in the diary of Driver McLaren. Under date October 2nd, he writes: "I got a trip to Westhoek Ridge with S.A.A. and was held up on the track alongside our batteries for twenty minutes, while they sent a barrage over to Fritz. The noise was dreadful and I got quite deaf, but the horses stood it well." Again on October 10th, McLaren writes: "We have had the worst experience, which is beyond my power properly to describe. What with rain, soupy mud, cold and confusion and 101 other things that go to make life unbearable. I'll give one instance. I was shifting some S.A.A. on pack-horse, at times wading anything from knee-deep to waist-high in mud on, perhaps, the coldest and wettest day you could imagine. We started off and had to do two trips east from Zonnebeke to an advanced dump. I had not gone far when my poor old horse slipped into a shell-hole. I got him out again after an hour's hard work and wasn't I a mass of slime and mud from head to foot, and soaked to the skin! Meantime, my mates had gone on their trips, while I still had mine to do. The Huns were heavily shelling the track I had to go, which in places had trees lying across it and dead Huns and horses everywhere."

The work of the Transport Section was highly commendable, and under the cool leadership of Captain Busby, assisted by Sergeant J. G. Mackie and Corporal E. G. Brewer, laboured efficiently and unceasingly, carrying forward ammunition to newly-formed dumps in advance of Zonnebeke, despite heavy and constant shelling. Brewer, who had charge of the pack-animals, showed sound leadership, and ability, getting the best out of his teams. He worked tirelessly to ensure that they kept together and when on occasions the shelling became too heavy he sent back the animals and personally led the carrying of supplies by hand. Brewer was born and raised on the land. His devotion to duty under similar conditions on the Somme, a year earlier, showed that he possessed courage and resourcefulness. By good fortune the section suffered no casualties, but Captain Busby relates that one man was suddenly seized with a violent colic and asked Busby what he should do. Busby replied laconically: "Carry on."

The exhausting work of the carrying and pack-animal parties soon began to manifest itself in the form of the increasing number of the troops parading sick. Exposure to the rain and the mud of that completely devastated area also added its quota to the casualty list, some units finding it difficult to muster fifty or sixty men to each company. The medical services were hard put to it to establish suitable aid-posts and stretcher-bearers with wounded men lined up in long queues in the vicinity of the limited number of captured enemy pillboxes available for that purpose.

Perhaps the greatest problem of all was that involving positions for the artillery in that vast chain of waterholes separated by narrow ridges of soddened earth, which frequently collapsed under the weight of the ordinary infantry soldier. To emplace adequately the concentrations of guns required to support further advances necessitated resourcefulness and ingenuity on the part of all ranks comprising that arm. (An Australian Artillery officer told the writer that in this sector a gun from his battery was overturned into a huge water-filled shell-crater and completely submerged.)

With this unpleasing prospect the Battalion faced its next period of front-line duty.

The night of the 4th passed without incident, and the daylight hours of the 5th were spent in standing-by until darkness and then moving up to a position in front of Zonnebeke, where the support line lay. It was occupied by the Twenty-seventh and Twenty-eighth Battalions. Orders received on the evening of the 6th caused the Battalion to move back about a mile into the reserve position at St. Joseph's Institute west of Zonnebeke, where, according to the records, many S.O.S. signals were thrown up by both sides, and the resultant barrages added further to the discomfort of the troops. Fresh orders received on the 7th required the Battalion to occupy the front line trench on Broodseinde Ridge, taking over from the Twenty-seventh, which had moved up the previous day. That night, led by guides, each company moved across the featureless water-logged ground, in places knee-deep in mud, painfully and slowly, the long strung-out lines pausing every now and then, while an unfortunate soldier was retrieved from a muddy shell-hole into which he had slipped. Or, the guide, perhaps, not sure of his way, would halt for a few minutes to try and pick up his bearings. In fact, C Company was led by its guide right past our front-line positions before the mistake was discovered, fortunately in time to rectify it without incurring any casualties.

Weary, and with garments soddened by continued exposure to rain and mud, the Seventeenth took up its new position on the broad sandy ridge which was about a quarter of a mile wide in this sector. The Battalion had a frontage of about 500 yards south, and inclusive of the Ypres-Roulers railway. The line at that point ran through a fairly deep cutting in the north side of which was a large dug-out. The night passed without incident and when day broke on the 8th the rain had ceased, and the sun shone brightly. A high wind greatly assisted the troops to dry their soddened garments.

CHAPTER XII.

First attempt on Passchendaele—Seventeenth plays subsidiary role—All ranks display great gallantry—Very heavy casualties—A brief rest—Trench-holding in the Salient—Lieutenant Maynard displays a taste for light literature—Christmas in the front line—Move to Colombey rest area.

AFTER their exhausting experience of the past three days, the comparative dryness of the sandy ridge, which the men of the Seventeenth now occupied, was consoling. At daybreak, work was begun consolidating the position.

A mile to the north-east, Passchendaele could be seen standing in its setting of green fields, its red roofs glaring in the bright sunlight. In the distance, the green fringe of the mighty Houthulst Forest was clearly visible.

Passchendaele was the next objective in Haig's drive, and although he was fully aware that he was risking an imminent break in the weather he decided to deliver another mighty blow, this time with the Fifth Army with its right resting on the Ypres-Roulers railway. I Anzac, of which the 2nd Division was the left flank formation, would be used in the subsidiary role protecting the advance of the right of the Fifth Army. The date of the attack was set down for October 9th.

Late on the morning of the 8th, Major Holmes, who was acting-Commanding Officer, issued a warning order to companies, and after darkness fell the four company commanders repaired to Holmes's headquarters situated in a pill-box several hundred yards to the rear. The orders were both brief and lucid. The 5th Brigade with the 6th Brigade on its right, would move parallel with the railway line, conforming to the movement of the Fifth Army. The 5th Brigade would attack on a single battalion front, utilising the Twentieth for this purpose, with the Seventeenth in immediate support. There were to be two objectives—the "Red Line," 600 yards and the "Blue Line" about 600 yards further on. The four companies of the Seventeenth, each averaging less than 100 rifles, would be drawn up in line in the following order: A (Allan), B (Doig), C (Allen), and D (Mackenzie). Zero was timed for 5.20 a.m. on the 9th.

In order to adjust the position so as to permit the Twentieth to take post and also to give the artillery a straight line on which their barrage would fall, a withdrawal by the Seventeenth of about 250 yards, one hour before zero was arranged.

The men were disappointed that the anticipated early relief was to be a "washout," but they soon settled down to put the best face on the situation. Though cold and wet, their morale was still high.

The withdrawal was carried out without incident, but a few minutes before zero a shell burst, killing Lieutenant E. C. New and Private C. A. Maloney.

Punctually at 5.20 a.m., the barrage opened, and though not so heavy as on September 20th, it was of considerable volume. Unfortunately, owing to the boggy terrain our artillery found it impossible to place their shells in line, with the result that the Twentieth Battalion found themselves moving inside the barrage. The Seventeenth, following closely, found itself in a similar predicament, and for a little while there was some loss of cohesion, and the advance was slowed down. However, hardly had the companies reached the crest of the ridge, which was their original line, when they came under heavy rifle-fire from nearby enemy posts; Captains Mackenzie and Allen both being hit and Sergeant W. R. Hood of D Company, killed. Approaching Defy Crossing, a nest of machine guns was located and rushed, five guns and several prisoners being taken. Mopping up, however, was being rendered difficult because of our numerical weakness, and a galling cross-fire from the sector on the left, which the right brigade of the British 66th Division had failed to reach, having being bogged in swampy country during the approach march.

The right and centre of the Seventeenth also advanced steadily, but ultimately came under heavy machine-gun fire from Dairy Wood on the right front. Here, again, owing to the failure of the left battalion of the 6th Brigade to come up, our men were subjected to a fierce semi-enfilading fire. Allan quickly grasping the situation, detached groups of men of A Company to form a defensive flank, in which task he was assisted by the gallant Lyons, who had led the bombers in Munster Alley. When B Company lost all its officers, Allan and Lyons took it under their care. The first objective—the Red Line—was reached, but the advancing line soon after came under a hot fire from Assyria, a fortified farm house not far to the front. Lyons collected fifteen men and led them in a headlong charge on the place. So sudden and determined was the attack that the garrison barely resisted, several being kiled and fourteen taken prisoner. Unfortunately, later in the day, when the enemy counter-attacked, Lyons was seen to fall severely wounded. A subsequent search for him and his companions proved fruitless.

Private P. J. Broder, who was one of Lyons's party, distinguished himself by capturing the crew of a machine-gun. Later, he attacked a group of the enemy, single-handed, killing an officer. Another gallant action was performed by Corporal R. E. Massey, who, with his Lewis gun, gave protective fire on the right flank. Massey's alertness and his prompt action, helped to break up several attempts by groups of the enemy to assemble in order to counter-attack. Later, thirty-five dead Germans were counted on his immediate front.

B Company had also suffered severely, its commander, Lieutenant Doig, being wounded. But Lance-Sergeant R. Moffatt took charge of the remainder and by his good example and skilful handling led his men on to the objective.

One of the finest deeds performed that day was by Corporal W. O. Rabey, who reorganized his platoon on the first objective, and then supervised a similar procedure with neighbouring groups which had suffered severe casualties. Later, during the advance, he captured a machine-gun post and seven Germans by cleverly working round the position. With his party reduced to two men beside himself, Rabey took up position in shell holes and sniped the enemy with deadly effect.

Another man, Private P. R. O'Connor, went on alone and captured twelve Germans who were holding up the advance of his company, and latter, in company of an officer of the Twentieth, captured another six. O'Connor, who was number two on a Lewis gun, was later severely wounded whilst bringing up ammunition for the gun.

C Company, like D, came under heavy fire from Defy Crossing soon after it topped the ridge, where, as already stated, its commander, Allen, was wounded. Shortly afterwards, two fine young subalterns, A. R. McDowell and E. J. Verrills were killed, and the command then devolved on Company-Sergeant-Major R. Bagnall, who himself was subsequently wounded. A party was detailed to deal with the offending post at Defy Crossing, and this was carried out successfully, thirty prisoners being taken. In this action two Sergeants, H. L. Appleton and F. G. Grange, showed their capabilities as leaders, but both were severely wounded. Another sergeant, J. Graham, also showed dash and leadership, and although severely wounded saw his men well on the first objective before he consented to leave the line. Sergeant J. Young, also of C Company, showed sound judgment and leadership, inspiring all near him by his fine example.

In this action, perhaps, more than in any other, the work of the non-commissioned officers stood out. When most of the officers were casualties, these men calmly took command, and by their coolness and soldierly initiative both encouraged and inspired their men.

Lieutenant J. M. LYONS,
M.C., M.M., M.S.M.

R.S.M. J. W. RAITT,
M.M.

HELL FIRE CORNER, YPRES, 1920.

DESPIERRE FARM, 1917.

THE BATTALION FOOTBALL TEAM.

On the left, D Company was also having its share of trouble. Earlier it had lost all its officers but one, and had suffered heavily from semi-enfilade machine-gun fire from the left front. Major Holmes, becoming anxious over the failure of the British brigade on the left flank, sent his adjutant, Barnet, up to examine the position and to ensure the taking of adequate measures to protect that flank. Barnet encountered Lieutenant J. M. Dickens and Sergeant J. W. Raitt on the railway line, where it ran through a cutting. Observing a number of dugouts in the sides of the cutting, Barnet ordered Raitt to take a party and clean up any of the enemy found there. Raitt collected a few men and with Sergeant C. G. Schwonberg, proceeded to bomb the dug-outs, during the process of which they accounted for a machine-gun and its crew. A little later Schwonberg was severely wounded, and as Raitt bent down to tend his wounded comrade, a party of Germans came up behind him and took him prisoner. He endeavoured by signs to secure the permission of his captors to carry Schwonberg, but this they refused, and soon Raitt was being escorted by two of the enemy towards their positions. The party had proceeded several hundred yards when a shell burst close by them, one of the Germans falling wounded. With great presence of mind the sergeant swung a lightning right fist on to the jaw of the other German, and then turned and fled back to his own lines, discarding his greatcoat as he went. Although heavily fired on, the plucky fellow got back safely. Two other sergeants of D Company displayed courage and initiative in leading forward the remnants of D Company on to the first objective. They were Sergeants C. Neville and D. Roberts, both original members. During a hold-up at one stage of the advance, Roberts took two men with him and captured a machine-gun and its crew.

The only means of communication was by runner, and here two Privates, W. D. Hume and A. S. E. Earnshaw did fine work. Time and again they made trips through the enemy barrage, braving heavy machine-gun fire. These two lads showed extraordinary courage and endurance. Both were original members. Another runner who distinguished himself was Private G. R. Millthorpe, who had won the Military Medal at the Menin Road action. Like his two comrades, he displayed great pluck and tenacity and seemed to bear a charmed life.

As the day wore on our casualties began to mount. The enemy, after recovering from the initial set-back, concentrated his attention on the Twentieth and the Seventeenth, which were well "into the blue" as the result of the failure of the British on the left, to come up with them. The advance on the second objective was, as a result, held up. During the course of the day, several attempts by the enemy to group for the counter-attack were broken up by our Lewis gun fire. But except for A Company's move towards Assyria, which it cleaned up, the advance did not progress beyond the Red Line. Allan, fearing for his right flank, wisely withdrew to a position more secure.

In his Aid Post, which he had established in the railway cutting, Major R. M. McMaster and his capable staff efficiently tended the wounded. As may be expected the spot was a target for enemy shells, but despite the casualties requiring their attention, they showed an utter disregard for their own safety. McMaster's right-hand man, Corporal J. E. Abbey, displayed great coolness. Subsequently, when the Battalion was relieved he volunteered to stay behind and supervise the clearing of the remainder of the stretcher cases.

The stretcher-bearers had a very trying task, and because of the terrible condition of the ground, four men were required to man each stretcher. One of this devoted band was Corporal S. J. Nimmo, who, while in charge of five parties of bearers, assisted in carrying wounded for thirty-six hours.

The main attack had failed, and the Battalion, although it had partly achieved the objectives set for it, had done so at the heavy cost of twelve officers and 177 other ranks, equal to about two-thirds of its effective strength.

At 3 a.m., on the 10th, the Seventeenth was relieved by the Forty-Fifth Battalion and moved back to the Ypres area. The following day it marched to Abeele, thence to billets at Steenvoorde, where, on the 25th, General Birdwood presented ribbons of decorations awarded for the Menin Road operation, as follows:—Captain K. W. Mackenzie, a Bar to the Military Cross; Lieutenants W. R. Haigh and H. E. Clifton, Military Cross; and Corporal T. A. Corbett and Lance-Corporal R. S. Davies, Distinguished Conduct Medal.

At 4 p.m. on the 26th the Battalion embused for Dickebusch, en route once more for Ypres. On November 4th the Seventeenth took over a quiet part of the line six miles east of that place. Continuous rain had converted the shell-torn ground into a vast morass. The operation of taking over from a battalion in the front line was in itself an ordeal, which Lieutenant Maynard describes as follows: "From the point where the guides of the battalion in the line are picked up, that is, provided they have not become casualties, or mislaid, progress is maddeningly slow, despite which, however, there are frequent cries from the rear of the column that it has lost touch, so you must wait. Men become casualties or fall into shell holes, or get stuck in the mud and have to be hauled out. Some are night-blind, and have difficulty in keeping up. If your guide becomes a casualty, you are indeed in difficulties. Somewhere in the murky darkness, a mile or two ahead, a company is in a collection of muddy shell-holes waiting to be relieved, and they must be got away by sunrise . . . If everything goes well, a relief between companies who know their job will be completed in half an hour."

The sector taken over by the Seventeenth was opposite Moorslede. On the left front stood Passchendaele, now badly battered. The Canadian Corps had been put in opposite there and was destined, a few days later, to capture it.

The new position was merely a series of unconnected posts, without overhead shelter of any kind, though an occasional captured German pill-box offered facilities for establishing a company headquarters. In most cases, the tops of the structures were only a few feet from the ground, and to enter them one had to crawl on one's belly. The interiors were mostly evil-smelling and wet underfoot. Here we again refer to Lieutenant Maynard who thus records his impressions of his occupancy of one of these noisome shelters: "I occupied an ex-German concrete pill-box about half the size of a domestic bathroom and with the top almost flush with the ground. The previous tenant had left the pill-box clean (very unusual, this) and with two books on the bench—one 'The Life of Christ,' by Dean Farrar, and the other 'Five Nights,' by Victoria Cross. We had nothing to do, so there was time to read one of them—Five Nights, which concerned an amorous lady who entertained the representatives of five different nations on five consecutive nights and described her reactions. Maybe, I should have read Dean Farrar's work first. Perhaps the next occupant of the pill-box will probably show better taste.

"During daylight on November 5th, I was called to Battalion Headquarters, which was in some concrete pill-boxes 300 yards to the rear, and on the way across I was swooped on by a German aeroplane. Three times he turned and dived on me, and on each occasion I had to dive into a muddy shell-hole for protection. I eventually arrived at my destination, covered in mud, out of breath and highly indignant, to be met with yells of laughter by the Headquarters people who had watched my predicament and been much entertained. I am afraid that I was rather rude to them."

The Battalion's tour of duty ended on December 6th, and by the 8th it was quartered in Steenvoorde. For the Australian troops, the bloody campaigns of 1917 had ended.

About this period additional awards were promulgated, Major R. M. McMaster receiving the Distinguished Service Order; Lieutenants J. M. Lyons and R. P. Little (attached 5th Brigade) the Military Cross; Sergeant W. O. Rabey, the Distinguished Conduct Medal; Private G. R. Millthorpe, a Bar to the Military Medal; Sergeants J. W. Raitt, H. L. Appleton, R.

Moffat, F. G. Grange and D. Roberts; Corporals S. J. Nimmo and E. G. Brewer; Privates W. D. Hume, A. S. E. Earnshaw, P. J. Broder, P. R. O'Connor and R. E. Massey, Military Medals; and Sergeants J. Graham and J. W. Raitt received the French and Belgian Croix de Guerre, respectively.

Staples, in France, was the Battalion's destination, on November 11th; thence to Moolenaere, on the 18th, and the following day, Menegate Camp, near Steenwerck in the Armentieres sector, at which place Sir Walter Davidson, Governor designate of New South Wales, accompanied by General Birdwood, inspected a guard of honour comprising three officers and 100 other ranks drawn from the Seventeenth. It was commanded by Captain J. L. Wright and the subalterns were Lieutenants C. Blackford and H. E. Lane. Sir Walter carried out a critical inspection, on completion of which he remarked that he had inspected guards in many parts of the world, but had not seen a finer one than the Seventeenth's.

As the result of its trying experiences in the Ypres campaign the Battalion was considerably under strength; moreover, the men were tired and their morale severely strained. Company commanders, therefore, held a meeting, at which it was decided to organize inter-company football games (Rugby Union). Immediate interest was created, and a plethora of talent forthcoming. Later, an inter-battalion competition was held within the 5th Brigade for a trophy—a shield. The Seventeenth's name was the first to be inscribed on the shield. The Battalion team was light but very fast, and carried no "passengers"; its forwards were always on the ball. It was coached by Lieutenant F ("Poss") Courtney, and much of its ultimate success was due to his knowledge of and enthusiasm for the game.

By the middle of December the Seventeenth was back in the Salient, this time holding a subsidiary line on Westhoek Ridge. The 23rd of the month found the Battalion once more in the Armentieres sector, where, as in the preceding year, Christmas was spent in freezing mud and chilling rain. Fortunately it was a very quiet period. January 1st was marked by the despatch of two officers and 100 other ranks to Ploegsteert Wood, as a wiring party. The party returned to camp the following day. On the 4th the Battalion moved into Le Rossignol Camp, and four days later relieved the Twentieth Battalion in the front line.

On the 9th, a visit of inspection was paid by Generals Birdwood, Smythe and Smith; and the records disclose that on the 14th a standing patrol at Moat Farm was attacked by a party of the enemy, but after sharp fighting, our men inflicted several casualties without loss to themselves.

Increased flooding caused all works, except draining, to be suspended, the water in some of the communication trenches being three feet deep in places.

On the 16th the Battalion moved back to Le Rossignol Camp, after being relieved by the Twentieth Battalion, and the following three days were spent in musketry practice, cleaning equipment and bathing.

The 24th of the month found Major L. G. Fussell in his new appointment as Second-in-Command of the Battalion, vice Major B. Holmes, who together with Captain R. C. Anderson, in November, 1917, left to take up a commission in the Indian Army. Holmes was awarded the Distinguished Service Order for his sound leadership during the recent operations. Fussell had for some time been Commandant 2nd Division Wing, of the Corps School. His place was taken by Lieutenant W. R. Haigh. Major Fussell assumed temporary command of the Seventeenth in the absence of Colonel Martin, who, on the 31st, relieved the Brigade Commander. Earlier in the month Colonel Martin had had conferred on him the Order of Companion of Saint Michael and Saint George, as a mark of his sound leadership and devotion to duty.

February 1st found the Battalion in Colombey, a pleasant village in the well-back areas, where the opportunity was taken to indulge in sport and recreation as a handmaiden to serious training. Here, on the 4th, the officers who left Australia as members on 12th May, 1915, celebrated a notable event. It was the occasion of the thousandth day of the Seventeenth's departure from Australia and it took the form of a dinner in the Hotel Chemin de Fer, at Lumbres, not far from Colombey. The names of those present appear in the appendix.

A Brigade football competition was organized, the Seventeenth beating the 5th Machine Gun Company, 5th Field Ambulance and Twentieth Battalion, and playing a draw with the Eighteenth. However, it was beaten three to nil by the Nineteenth Battalion.

But it was not all play, for on the 19th a Brigade inspection was held, the Seventeenth receiving high commendation for its turn-out and steadiness, a special word of praise being accorded the Transport Section under Captain H. O. Busby. This was followed by intensive training in field operations, including battle practices with ball ammunition, under the personal supervision of that hard-bitten soldier, General Smith. The Battalion was also tested in gas efficiency by details of a Special Service Company of the Royal Engineers.

Two other events which merit recording, occurred at this period, the first being the arrival of a new Chaplain in the person of Padre Tugwell. The advent of Frederick William

Tugwell as spiritual adviser to the Battalion was, indeed, a happy one, for he possessed all the simple, though ardent Christian attributes which, before very long, attracted and held the affection and respect of men of every denomination. He was a thorough sportsman, and on the football field played a hard, clean game, and showed a commendable turn of speed. With his fellow-chaplain, Father Clune, he demonstrated, both by precept and example, the virtue of the Christian faith. The 5th Brigade was fortunate to have two such splendid padres at one and the same time, and the influence for good which they exerted upon all with whom they were brought into contact, was incalculable.

The second event was a gala day. It began with a fancy-dress and costume parade through the long, straggling village main street to a large level field, where marquees had been erected and stocked with food and liquid refreshments designed to promote cheer and good fellowship. Much ingenuity was displayed by those participating in the fancy-dress parade, in which they received ready assistance from the mademoiselles of the village, who entered wholeheartedly into the gala spirit of the occasion, and also turned out in full force. Lieutenant Courtney and his party of "Cockneys," in a light cart hauled by "Tibby," Captain Wright's hack, won first prize in its section, while Privates "Spud" Murphy and Thomas Murnane secured the first place in the "most original subject" class, in the characters of Australian black-fellow and gin, respectively. Lieutenant F. A. Mailler so effectively took the part of a charming mademoiselle that he attracted the admiring gaze of many a hard-bitten veteran, while Private J. Studds, of C Company, won the prize of 100 francs donated by the officers for the best turned-out soldier. It was a memorable day.

CHAPTER XIII.

Germans regain the initiative—Russia out of the war—Ludendorff's great offensive, March 21st—Australian Corps ordered south—Defence of Amiens—Sergeant M. Sharman experiences the lighter side of war —The crisis reached.

THE first day of March dawned disappointingly for the 5th Brigade, for on that day it had been planned to hold a grand carnival and sports meeting, embracing pedestrian as well as horse events; while tug-of-war, drill and small-arms contests were included in a truly attractive programme, which aroused much enthusiasm when announced. The senior officers of the 2nd Division had been co-opted for service as judges, and the day was to be given over entirely to the carnival spirit, to ensure which, money and forethought had not been stinted. The coming event was the talk of the town, so to speak, and much wagering and speculation were indulged in on the chances of the competing teams and individuals.

But rain commenced to fall during the night of February 28th and continued steadily throughout the following day, necessitating the abandonment of the meeting, to the intense disappointment of all ranks. However, some consolation was afforded the following day, when, the rain having ceased, the Seventeenth and Eighteenth were lined up as rivals in a keenly contested game for the Brigade Football championship, which ended in a draw, leaving our team the runners-up.

A few days later—on the 8th—we find the Battalion back at Le Rossignol Camp, and split up into working parties, less A Company, which was detached to protect bridges over the Lys, near Armentieres; and here, two days later, General Smyth, the Divisional Commander, attended a church parade held by the Battalion and presented the football team with the Challenge Shield, of which they were the winners in the first competition held during the previous November.

Here the Battalion lost its popular medical officer, Major McMaster, who went to the 5th Field Ambulance, his place being taken by Captain L. M. Piggott. Like his two predecessors, the new "Doc" possessed in full a strong sense of duty, but in temperament he differed markedly from them; he never attempted to conceal the boyish spirit, which found expression in a droll humour that was a source of inspiration to his brother-officers. His sharp features wore a perennial expression of impishness, and he was richly endowed with that typically Australian attribute—the love of a "leg-pull." Always the good companion, he was ever ready to share the good things of life with his neighbours, thereby earning their affection and infecting all who were brought within his sphere with his own happy disposition. As a moral factor, "Doc's" presence was a valuable asset.

Already it has been narrated that, since the beginning of the year, much of the time spent by the Seventeenth during its tours of duty in the line, was occupied in strengthening existing positions and in the construction of additional zones of defence, in anticipation of the launching of a great offensive by the Germans. For the first time since the middle of 1916, the initiative had passed into the enemy's hands, mainly as the result of the collapse of Russia, whose armies, corrupted by revolutionary propaganda, assiduously applied over a number of years, and aided by maladministration and the bitter hardships suffered by the people, had, during the winter of 1916-17, been the victim of a slow paralysis. In March, the Czar abdicated, and a Provisional Government with Socialistic tendencies was formed. The anticipated better conditions resulting from this change gave hopes that Russia could be kept in the war. But when, in July, the Germans launched a great offensive, the Russian armies commenced to disintegrate. The soldiers were tired of fighting, and the people were crying for bread. The following November the Provisional Government fell, and the Bolsheviks took over the country. The treaty of Brest Litovsk followed, and Russia was irrevocably out of the war, thus releasing Germany's Eastern forces for a concentrated assault in the West, and giving the Central Powers yet another chance of winning the war. In October, Italy had been crushingly defeated at Caporetto, and it was thought that Germany might get in a decisive blow before America, which country had declared war in April, 1917, was able to throw in her full weight.

During the winter of 1917-18 the Germans were training and massing for this purpose, while the French and British armies (the latter since early 1917, having borne the brunt of the war in the West), were forced on to the defensive until American reinforcements began to arrive in sufficient numbers. The bloody struggles in Flanders and at Cambrai had left the British at a low ebb in numbers and training, so it became necessary to build new armies and strengthen the defence system. Late in January, Sir Douglas Haig took over more line from the French, the Fifth Army extending its front to a distance of forty-two miles. Such was the position at that period of the fateful year of 1918.

During the night 13/14 March the Seventeenth relieved the

Twentieth Battalion, and during the hours of darkness carried out active patrolling. The following evening, at dusk, the enemy opened up with his light artillery on D Company's position, but the only casualty was Lieutenant F. A. Mailler, wounded. Later, the same night, an enemy patrol of seven men was observed near the post at Estaminet Farm, the occupants of which opened fire, whereupon the patrol retired leaving their leader, an under-officer, wounded and a prisoner. He belonged to the 102nd Saxon Regiment.

The rest of the Battalion's tour was fairly quiet, excepting for the discharge by our engineers of 700 gas shells from projectors planted in groups forward of the line and fired by electric contact. The enemy retaliated with gas shells and trench mortar bombs, but caused only slight casualties.

On the night 21/22 the Twenty-seventh Battalion took over the line, and the Seventeenth returned to Kortepyp Camp, where, on the 23rd, it was inspected by Colonel Martin.

At last the anticipated blow fell. It was while the Seventeenth was resting at Kortepyp Camp that news was received that the Germans had launched their offensive, designed to knock their opponents right out of the war. Massing thirty-four divisions on the sectors facing the British Third and Fifth Armies, and heralded by a tremendous bombardment and aided by mist, at 5 a.m. on the 21st Ludendorff struck with sixty-four divisions, against the nineteen thinly strung-out divisions opposing him. The unexampled fury of the attack seemed to give no hope of being stemmed, and by the 26th it had carried the German armies within a dozen miles of the key city of Amiens. The grievous loss by the Fifth Army, not only of ground, but men and guns was, to a good extent, offset on the 28th, when a second attempt to break through the Third Army, on the left of the Fifth was shattered with very heavy loss to the enemy.

To the officers and men of the Seventeenth, who had participated in the long-drawn-out battles, over that selfsame ground, not very long before, where progress had been marked by mere hundreds of yards, the news came as a painful shock. To them it seemed that all the blood and agony with which that experience was fraught, had been in vain. Territory painfully wrested after months of bitter fighting from an enemy thought to have lost the initiative, had been recaptured by him in a few days. Even veterans, accustomed to the sudden fluctuations of fortune in battle, and therefore, not prone to pessimism in such circumstances, realised that only in a supreme effort lay the hope of stemming the onward rush of a seemingly irresistible enemy. However, the initial shock of surprise spent, there came a settled determination to wipe out the score;

and behind this the knowledge that, man for man, they had the measure of the Hun, inspired all ranks with a supreme confidence in their ability to deal adequately with him when once again seconds were out of the ring. That conclusion reached, everything proceeded as before, without fuss or flurry. In due course, their turn would come. Descriptive of this mood, blended with a note of prophecy, was the entry by Driver McLaren in his diary at this time. It read: "April 1. We left Neuve Eglise for Meteren on our way to the fight. Poor Grundy's grave is now a long way behind the German lines; but let us hope we will restore our mates' last resting-places before the year is out. But it is hard to have to fight over the old ground again."

On the 24th, the Seventeenth relieved the Thirteenth Battalion in the vicinity of Warneton village—or, what was once Warneton—a little south of Messines. There was little activity, other than patrolling, in evidence during the two-days' tour in this part of the line. Here the Battalion lost one of its original members, Corporal H. Davis who was killed by a bullet while out on patrol. Davis was a young Englishman who was the life and soul of his section. His death was a blow to the comrades whose spirits he sustained by his wit and unfailing good humour.

It was during this period that the Seventeenth acquired a new commanding officer, the third since its inception. Rupert Markham Sadler was one of that splendid band of youthful senior officers who had gained promotion through sheer ability, zeal and talent for leadership. He was twenty-six years of age, and like his predecessors in the command, had absorbed his early training in the Citizen Forces of the Commonwealth. He was Signalling Officer of the New Guinea Expeditionary Force, and later was posted to the Eighteenth Battalion upon its formation. He served with the Eighteenth on Gallipoli and in the subsequent campaigns in France. Displaying gallantry at the Battle of Pozieres he won the Military Cross, and, in due course, well-deserved promotion. Six feet tall and of cornstalk build, he outwardly affected an easy going manner, which belied a strong underlying determination. A splendid athlete, he loved nothing better than a hard, clean game of football; and was also no mean performer with the willow or the boxing-gloves. He was both affable and a good mixer, while insisting on a high degree of discipline, and he quickly gained the confidence and esteem of ranks.

We now take up the story at the point where the Australian Corps (on November 1st, 1917, the titles I Anzac and II Anzac were abolished, the five Australian Divisions being constituted "The Australian Corps") had been ordered to move south. The 4th and 3rd Divisions, already were in contact with the enemy in the Somme area, the former at Hebuterne, north of Albert, and the latter opposite Morlancourt, north-east of Villers-Bretonneux. They were to be followed immediately by the 2nd and 5th Divisions. The Seventeenth embused for Meteren, ten miles west of Warneton, remaining there until the night of April 2/3, when it marched to Caestre, four miles to the west, entraining in the early hours of the morning for Amiens, and arriving there at 11.25 p.m. the same day. There followed a seven-kilometre march to Allonville, which, after their long journey in the cramped and crowded troop-train, and without proper sleep, the troops felt severely. By 11 a.m. on the 4th, the Battalion was billeted, fed and settling down to enjoy a good sleep, when orders were received to move at once. On the outskirts of the village a convoy of motor 'buses was drawn up. In a biting wind and chilling rain, all ranks had to endure a depressing journey to Bussy-les-Daours, a few miles north-west of Villers-Bretonneux, through the eastern suburbs of Amiens. On leaving that city and striking east, the convoy passed a long column of British cavalry moving in the opposite direction, the large number of riderless horses denoting that they had been in action. These British units were moving out of the line, after a brilliant piece of co-operation with the infantry in the defence of Villers-Bretonneux, which defence had been entrusted mainly to the 9th Brigade under the Seventeenth's old commander, Lieutenant-Colonel Goddard, now commanding the Thirty-fifth Battalion. That same morning the enemy had launched yet another determined attack in an endeavour to capture the town, but was staunchly resisted by the hard-pressed battalions of the 9th Brigade, which although forced to give some ground under sheer weight of numbers, eventually had stopped a little to the east of the town. But it had been a near thing, and the position in fact, was still so critical that the 5th Brigade was rushed up to support this hard-pressed brigade holding the sector south of the Roman road.

Villers-Bretonneux was the key to the tactical situation on this part of the front. Situated on the edge of a plateau, it looked across the intervening flat country to the city of Amiens, the spire of the great cathedral standing clear against the sky several miles to the west. Possession by the enemy of the town, would have opened the gate to Amiens, the great strategic nerve-centre at the junction of the French and British armies, or failing its capture, enable him to destroy by shell fire the network of railways which radiated in all directions, and were vital to the Allies. The town itself was the centre of the home manufacture of woollen goods, and it contained several fine storehouses, stocked with soft-goods, foodstuffs, wine and grain. When the Australians arrived, they found the place deserted, the towns-people having departed in haste, carrying only their most easily portable belongings. Already, it was pretty badly knocked about by shells; the only remaining living things were the horses, cattle, poultry and domestic rabbits straying amongst the ruins and the rubble-filled streets.

Arriving at Bussy-les-Daours, the men of the Seventeenth proceeded to settle down into their billets. Bussy, like its larger neighbour, had been a prosperous, neat village, hitherto untouched by war, but the new arrivals found it to be entirely deserted. Only that morning the inhabitants had hurriedly evacuated their homes and taken to the roads leading to the west, a melancholy procession with their household goods piled on any kind of vehicle that could be pressed into service. The partly-eaten breakfast meal, hurriedly adandoned, bore mute and pathetic testimony to the urgency of their going, leaving behind an atmosphere of utter desolation. There had not been time to let the cattle and horses out of the stables, a task our men had to carry out, in order that the animals could find water and forage for themselves.

But hardly had the tired troops eaten a meal and proceeded to relax in expectancy of a comfortable night's rest, when orders were received to stand-by, ready to move up in support of the 9th Brigade. Meanwhile, company commanders were to go forward, mounted, in order to reconnoitre the line of approach, and the positions allotted to their companies.

In Bussy-les-Daours occurred an incident which reflected in a manner highly praiseworthy, the discipline and trustworthiness of the Australian soldier in times of stress. D Company was billeted in the local hall, the cellars of which were full of cases of wine, a fact not known to the troops. Realising the potential danger, Mackenzie, the company commander, prior to moving out to take part in the reconnaissance, instructed Captain Finlay, his second-in-command, to get the men together, tell them of the existence of the stocks of wine and place them on their honour not to touch it. Not a man succumbed to what must, in the circumstances, have been a strong temptation.

Shortly after the return of company commanders, the Battalion fell in, and by 11 p.m. was in position on the northern edge of the Bois L'Abbe, half a mile or so to the west of Villers-Bretonneux where it remained until the following night, 5/6, when it relieved the Thirty-third Battalion in the front line, a thousand yards east of the town, on an abandoned aerodrome. The ground to the east was quite flat as far as Warfusee-Abancourt, the twin village on the Roman Road, three and a half miles distant. An almost unbroken view could also be had in a radius of a mile or more north-east to south-east. The relief was completed without hindrance, and the night remained quiet. By daybreak on the 6th, the dispositions of the force covering Villers-Bretonneux were as follows : Between the Roman road and the village of Hangard, 6,000 yards to south, where it joined the French, stood the 18th British Division (Lee), to which was attached the 5th Brigade, with all its four battalions in the front line. Northwards, stretching to the Somme, the ground was held by the 5th Division (Hobbs). Thus the whole of the front line was held by Australian infantry. In the centre of the 5th Brigade sector was Hangard Wood, and here the line curved inward, passing through the centre of the wood. Behind the wood the ground was scored by a ravine, with more timbered country on the north-east.

The line itself comprised a series of unconnected platoon posts, as yet very shallow, while the absence of cover from view made movement by day extremely risky. To add to these discomforts there were an almost-continuous light rain and a cold wind. But all ranks were extremely alert, for, although so far, all had been comparatively quiet, warning had been circulated of further impending attacks by the enemy. Colonel Sadler, going the rounds of companies, impressed on each commander in turn the necessity for constant and vigilant patrolling, and that in case they were attacked, to hold on at all costs. At 6 o'clock on the morning of the 6th, a message was received from 5th Brigade Headquarters intimating that two Germans captured about four miles to the south, where the British and French armies formed a junction, had said that it was certain the enemy intended to attack Hangard that day. All ranks were immediately extra alert and keyed up to a higher pitch of resolute expectancy. Grim though the position, now, at any rate they would be the marksmen and not the targets, as hitherto, for not since Lagnicourt, a year before, had the Battalion been put to it to repel an attack. And the men were buoyed up with the memory of how they had "slathered" the Huns that day. Cramped, wet and hungry in their pot-hole posts, their spirits nevertheless revived when they heard that action was imminent. But nothing of that nature transpired, although at 4 p.m. an observer reported enemy cavalry to be moving south from Marcelcave in the direction of Aubercourt, directly in rear of Hangard.

At 7.50 p.m., the same day, the enemy put down a fairly heavy barrage along the 5th Brigade front, but no infantry action followed. A German who was captured the same night, said that the enemy themselves were expecting to be attacked. The only other incident was the capture of a sergeant-major and a private of the 14th Bavarian Regiment, who had lost their way and wandered into one of B Company's posts. On the flat, featureless ground, it was a very easy matter to lose one's direction, during darkness, and oft-times difficult to locate our own posts. Indeed, one of D Company's officers, 2nd-Lieutenant C. Robins, had an alarming experience of this kind during one of his periodical visits to neighbouring posts. Robins, in the inky blackness, lost direction, and after wandering in No Man's Land for half an hour, saw looming before his anxious gaze the outline of a building. Was he in the German lines, or in the proximity of our own posts? Forthwith, he would resolve the situation, which by now had become intolerable. Robins possessed a powerful baritone voice, which presently penetrated the eerie silence, its stentorian tones addressed to the gloomy shape of the structure immediately in front of him, demanding to be informed as to his exact whereabouts. Fortunately he had wandered in between our own posts and had brought up in front of a hut—the only one left standing on the old aerodrome—and now being used as D Company's Headquarters. So all was well, though Robins himself confessed, later, that he had the "wind-up" badly.

During the course of the night, Colonel Sadler again visited his company commanders and warned them that they might be attacked at any moment; he repeated his orders of the previous night, that there was to be no retirement. However, again the night passed without incident, and on the following night, the 8th, the Battalion was relieved by the 12th London Regiment and moved back several miles to Gentelles, to the south-west, where it was ordered into billets. During the three-days' tour in the line, casualties had been light, only eight other ranks wounded. Soon after its arrival at Gentelles, instructions were received to bivouac in the nearby wood, as it was deemed too risky to occupy the village on account of the enemy's propensity for shelling such likely sheltering places. By this time the majority of the troops were beginning to feel the physical and mental reaction from the high nervous tension, and lack of warm food and regular sleep, for since leaving Meteren they had not spent one night under shelter. However, despite the entire lack of protection from the misty rain, the exhausted men threw themselves on the wet ground, under the gaunt, leafless trees, with an occasional layer of brushwood under them. But they were not to have even this cold comfort for very long, for towards noon, Colonel Sadler sent for company commanders and warned them that preparations were being made for an attack on Hangard Wood, which, as already stated, formed a salient menacing Villers-Bretonneux from the south-east. On the morning of April 7th, companies of the Nineteenth and Twentieth Battalions had made a gallant but unsuccessful attempt to capture the eastern portion of the wood, and the broken country to the east, losing 161 officers and men. The operation lacked both sufficient preparation and adequate numbers for its execution, but several gallant deeds were performed, one by Lieutenant P. V. Storkey of the Nineteenth, earning that brave officer the award of the Victoria Cross.

Quickly the news that the Seventeenth was to go in to the attack spread through the ranks of the exhausted men endeavouring to snatch some sleep. The result of this unwelcome information manifested itself in a few requesting to be paraded sick before the medical officer. By the time the company commanders' conference with Colonel Sadler was over, these fragmentary groups had increased to a line of men awaiting examination. Immediately, company commanders issued orders for their companies to fall-in without arms, and then addressed the men appealing to them to "stick it out," as otherwise some equally tired battalion would have to do the job that lay ahead. As in every instance where an appeal was made to either the intelligence or the sporting instinct of the Australian soldier, the response was effective. The men returned to their bivouacs, where a hot meal quickly helped to repair the temporary dent in morale.

During the afternoon, company commanders went forward on foot to reconnoitre the position to be attacked, but upon their return were informed that the operation had been cancelled and that the Battalion had been ordered into billets at Gentelles, the authorities evidently deciding to run the risk of the place being shelled. The warm, dry straw in the barns and the shelter they afforded from the rain, gave the men the long-desired opportunity of a good night's rest. Fortunately, the enemy refrained from shelling, and throughout the next day all ranks rested in comparative comfort until evening, when his artillery threw some shells into the place, killing one man and wounding three other ranks. Thereupon the Battalion returned to the former bivouac in the dreary wood, until 8 p.m. on the 12th, when it moved up to the front line opposite Hangard Wood, relieving the Thirty-fourth Battalion, which had lost its headquarters staff by a direct hit from a shell, the majority being killed. The situation was quiet, but active patrolling was carried out along the whole of the front. There was some heavy shelling by the enemy of the rear areas, some of which caught the Transport Section billeted in Boves, to which place it had moved on the 10th, together with the regimental quartermaster's store. One man, Private G. Fisk was killed; and some horses belonging to the Army Service Corps were knocked out.

On the 15th the Seventeenth was relieved by the Nineteenth Battalion and was ordered into position, less D Company, just in rear of the junction of the French and British armies, a little north of the village of Hangard, the 5th Brigade being the extreme right formation of the British Army. D Company was held at the disposal of Colonel Bennett of the Twentieth Battalion, which had suffered severely in the recent attack on Hangard Wood.

For liaison duties, an officer of the Seventeenth, Lieutenant F. W. Tindale, was attached to the neighbouring French brigade. Tindale, who although of Australian parents, was born in New Caledonia, where he lived for some years, could speak French fluently. He soon became very popular with his French confreres, and was eventually rewarded with a decoration by our gallant Ally for the services he rendered during the period of his attachment. Tindale had left Australia as a sergeant in the original Battalion.

The day after the Seventeenth took up its new position, after a reconnaissance by aeroplanes, the enemy started to shell heavily. This continued from 2 to 4 p.m., but the only casualties were two other ranks killed and five wounded. After the shelling had ceased, a German airman flew over to observe the result of the afternoon's "strafe." He was flying so low under a heavy bank of cloud that his features could be plainly seen as he leant over the side of the machine observing our positions. He flew up and down the area for a short while, the only 'plane in view, when, suddenly, out of the bank of overhead cloud, a British machine swooped like a hawk straight at the German's flank. When within what seemed to be only a few yards of his opponent, the British airman fired two short bursts from his guns, and the German machine plummeted to earth, a mass of flame and smoke. Aerial combats were common sights, but never had the surprised troops immediately below witnessed such a "close-up" view of an amazingly neat piece of work.

On April 18th, the 2/2 London Regiment took over the position, the Seventeenth moving back to bivouac in the Bois de Blangy, and the following day marched to Querrieu, where, on the side of a large white house at one end of the street, some wag had painted, in large capital letters: "Pessimists will be shot at sight." Here, in this pleasant village, the troops were to find warmth, rest and comfort for the second time since they left Meteren sixteen days before.

During the latter part of its tour in this sector, the 5th Brigade had come under the control of the 58th British Division, whose commander Major-General Cator, sent to General Smith a letter conveying his warm thanks and appreciation for the work of the Australians whilst under his command. The general said that the 5th Brigade was "quite one of the best fighting units I have come across." And from the 29th French Divisional commander General Smith received the following letter:

"Dear General,—I was extremely sorry at not being able

to call on you on the evening of the 16th instant, at your Headquarters at Bois de Gentelles, before my departure from this sector. Lieutenant Tindale has already conveyed my regards on that score. With all my heart I want to thank you for the thorough and cordial co-operation that I have personally met from you, from the 2nd to the 16th April, as also have my men from their brave British comrades. The memory of this will always remain. We came to Hangard and stopped the Boche. Our two countries will exploit still further what we have done on a small scale, and victory will be ours.

"I have submitted Lieutenant Tindale's name for a decoration from our Army. The French Croix de Guerre will be a fitting reward for this gallant officer.

"Good luck to you and your splendid Brigade.

"C. LE BOUHOOLOO, Colonel,.
"29th Division."

At Querrieu, the resting troops were able to observe the disturbance in the lives of the civil populations of the surrounding districts, caused by the sudden irruption of the Germans, which gave them only the barest space of time to evacuate their villages, and perhaps, to suffer the irreparable loss of their property and household treasures.

Amiens itself, by this time, was largely depopulated as the result of bombing and shelling. The truly pathetic condition of these civilians, mostly either very old or very young, was an ever-present reminder of the stark tragedy of war. Private A. C. Goodwin, in his "journal memories," has recorded his impressions thus: "Amiens no longer bears that calm and prosperous appearance; within range of the enemy's guns, with the majority of its citizens evacuated, the remainder cowering in cellars, it resembled a city of the dead. Shells and bombs were continually falling into the town, spreading ruin and destruction in homes and public buildings, and damaging the beautiful cathedral. Homeless wanderers even strayed as far as Allonville to seek relief and food from their more fortunate countrymen. The neighbouring villages of Vignacourt and Querrieu were also finding means to accommodate these broken-spirited refugees, who were uttering words of condemnation of the Boche."

The bombardment of Amiens by German long-range guns, indeed, caused an almost entire evacuation of the city, and ultimately the cancellation of civilian railway-passenger services. In this connection, an incident recorded by Sergeant Mark Sharman in his diary reveals the lighter side of the dark drama of war. Sharman writes: "One morning I was ordered to report to Battalion Headquarters, where I was told that I had to go Ypres to attend the court-martial of a fellow from my platoon charged with inflicting a wound on himself. After reporting to Brigade Headquarters, I went on to Amiens, and saw the Station Master, who was so delighted when he learned that I could speak French, that he gave me a French railway pass, a yellow document about two feet long and of three pages. He added a written footnote to the effect that I could also take four men and eight horses, if need be, with me. I don't know why he put these down—perhaps he thought it might be handy. Whilst at Brigade I had been given the 5th Brigade Concert Party's concert 'girl' (probably 'Tiki' Carpenter) to deliver safely at St. Omer. I suppose we were some of the last to leave Amiens by train. We duly got into a passenger coach with three mademoiselles and their mother, and when I told them that the fellow with me was the Brigade concert 'girl' they were highly amused, and I think would have liked to do a bit of investigating. We had several days on the train and after I delivered him I continued to Ypres. One experience, at least, is worth recording. We were stopped about four miles outside Ypres, when an English officer came along and banged at the door of our carriage and yelled: 'The Boches are on you!' My carriage mates consisted of two New Zealanders without equipment or rifles, a Chinese policeman and a missionary looking after Chinese workmen. He had been telling me about them making razors out of nails. I got my rifle, loaded it and said: 'Well we have a good railway embankment and there should be a few dead Fritzes before we finish' . . . Just then the British officer came back past our carriage, so I said: 'What are your people doing? Shall I come in with you?' He looked at me and said: 'Where are you going?' and I replied: 'To Ypres.' He said: 'Well, you had better go on there.' It appears he was only trying to get his troops out quickly. He would have got a wonderful reception had they been Australians."

However, the writer's lacerated soul was ultimately solaced when the Warrant-Officer to whom he had to report, produced a bottle of whisky and at the same time informed Sharman that the accused awaiting court-martial had all gone, and that in any case their papers had been lost.

The gallant sergeant's final experience before entraining to rejoin the Battalion is recorded by him thus: "I camped in a house at Ypres, and a soldier there said to me: 'Do you know that there is a battalion on the road trying to get rid of its money? They are paying anyone who wants any.' I replied that I could always do with more cash, so I went up and got a good reception from the C.O., and twenty francs, for which I signed a special sheet."

The weather was getting warmer, and under the influence of the genial sunshine, the vigor and spirits of all ranks were quickly restored, while the additional recreational facilities offered in the form of games and bathing enabled them to forget, for the time being, the strain of their recent experiences. On the 20th, a move was made to Bazieu, a lovely village where the Battalion remained for five bright warm days. But by the 24th, orders were received to be prepared to move at short notice, because that morning the Germans had made a violent attack on Villers-Bretonneux from the south-east, and succeeded in capturing the town, as well as the high ground to the north and south. But on the following day, the third anniversary of the landing at Anzac, a brilliant counter-attack delivered by the 5th Division during the hours of darkness, completely restored the position. Their drive on the 24th marked the concluding phase of the Germans' spring campaign, which, although it had brought them considerable gains in terms of territory both in the north (Lys, April 9th) as well as on the Somme, had failed to achieve its immediate objective—the splitting in two of the French and British armies.

It also marked the beginning of a new chapter for the Allied armies, which were about to exchange the role of a holding defence for one of active defence, penetrating here and cutting-out there; harassing the enemy with artillery fire and bombing, giving him no rest; while, all the time, behind the rapidly consolidating Allied line, there was being prepared a gigantic counter-offensive under the direction of the new generalissimo of the Allied Armies, Foch, which eventually was to hurl back in disorder, and to ultimate defeat, the Kaiser's seemingly invincible armies.

Although the German offensive had temporarily exhausted itself, at least two important considerations presented themselves to the British command, the first being the need for more room for defence, and, secondly, information as to the probable direction of the enemy's next stroke. And the most direct method of obtaining this information was by the capture of German prisoners. On the Australian Corps front, stretching from Albert southward to Hangard, the ground was fairly open, except between the rivers Ancre and Somme; country, which, in places, lent itself to active, offensive patrolling. The enemy, on his side, had adopted a system of defence in depth, but had purposely refrained from placing any barbed wire in front, in order to keep the Allies guessing as to the sector in which he would make the next attack.

The ground between the two rivers had been held by the 3rd Division ever since its arrival on the Somme a month earlier, and it was now decided to replace it with the 2nd Division; thus we find the Seventeenth in the village of Warloy, on May 1st, just in rear of the new sector to be taken over. The following day, it moved on to Behencourt, in the same area, remaining there until the 5th, when it marched to Allonville. It was while the Battalion was billeted at Allonville that the corps commander, General Birdwood presented awards to members of several units of the 2nd Division at Querrieu—Lieutenant Tindale and Sergeant Graham receiving the French Croix de Guerre. Tindale's award was for efficient liaison work of recent date with the French, and Graham's for gallantry in action at Ypres, the previous October.

During this period a change occurred in the command of the 5th Brigade. Owing to the illness of General Smith, necessitating his evacuation to hospital and eventually to Australia, his place was taken by Brigadier General Martin, the Seventeenth's old commanding officer. Under General Smith's command, the 5th Brigade had attained a high degree of efficiency, and his departure was regarded by all who were able to discern the human qualities that lay under the forthright manner and blunt speech of the big Victorian, as a distinct loss. "Bob" Smith, as he was known to all ranks, recognised no middle course; either a thing was good or bad, an officer efficient or inefficient; and Heaven help the officer who did not size up to his standard of efficiency; it invariably meant "outski," to quote a popular slang expression. That he made serious errors of judgment cannot be denied, and, being a creature of marked likes and dislikes, his estimates were sometimes coloured so strongly as to lead him to unjust decisions, as in one or two notable instances.

Whilst at Allonville training was carried out intensively, especially in Lewis gun work, despite the prevailing bad weather, until May 6th, when orders were received to reconnoitre the position to be taken over from the Thirty-fourth Battalion holding the extreme right of the 3rd Division's sector. The next day came fresh orders, this time to be prepared to move at twenty minutes notice, as it was expected that the enemy was about to launch another attack. However, nothing happened, and the Battalion was still at Allonville when Colonel Sadler carried out a detailed inspection preparatory to the move forward.

It was also in this village that the Seventeenth made its first contact with a representative of the great American Republic, in the person of Lieutenant Baldwin of the 306th Regiment, United States Army, who had been attached to the Seventeenth for experience as an Intelligence Officer. Later, additional contacts of a more individual character, were to be made when sub-units of American infantry were attached (one platoon to each company), resulting in a warm friendship and mutual understanding and admiration between the Australian soldier and his counterpart from across the Atlantic.

An interesting record of the impressions created by the new arrivals has been preserved by Lieutenant C. Maynard who wrote in July: "American troops were now seeking experience in the line associated with more experienced soldiers . . . a big platoon came to my company and our fellows made them welcome. Their Commander was Lieutenant Fritz, and he arrived wearing a six-shooter on his right thigh, suspended by straps from his waist. I asked him what it was all about, and he said it was to enable him to be 'quick on the draw.' He seemed perplexed when I told him that I had never fired my revolver in anger. I think he imagined that war was waged after the cinema idea of gang-feuds in Chicago.

"The Americans' kit, however, was scandalously unsuitable. Their breeches were of thin khaki serge, their boots were of thin glace kid, with soles as light as civilian walking shoes, whilst most of them possessed only one pair of socks—and cotton at that. We are always well equipped with good boots and socks, apart from the socks which are sent from the various women's organizations in Australia, and we were able to fit out the worst equipped of the Americans.

"They are a nice lot of chaps and willing enough, but although they had been enlisted nearly twelve months, their training fell far short of being fitted to hold a section of the line by themselves. Why they should take so long to accustom themselves to the requirements of army-life, was something our fellows could not understand."

On the same day that the American officer reported for duty, Colonel Sadler was ordered to report for a rest to the battalion nucleus, which was located at Berteaucourt, a pleasant village surrounded by woods. Here were located other similar details from the 2nd Division. It was an ideal spot for resting tired troops. The command was temporarily handed to Major S. A. Middleton of the Nineteenth Battalion.

On the 9th the Battalion marched to La Houssoye, arriving there at 11 a.m. on a hot day, and taking over from the Forty-second Battalion. Slightly damaged, La Houssoye was one of the many well-ordered villages whose one street branched off at right angles to the main highway, and finished in a dead end at the gates of a big chateau. Here the men of the Seventeenth prepared to settle down, and make themselves comfortable in the empty cottages and barns. But shortly after the mid-day meal, urgent orders were received to vacate the place within half an hour, as information had been received that it was anticipated the enemy would shortly start shelling the village. The Battalion was ordered to move out to a switch-trench about 600 yards distant, and bivouac there for the night. The move was nearly completed when the simultaneous whine and impact of a long-range "rubber" gun shell was heard. It fell on a billet killing four men and wounding one. For twenty minutes the shelling continued, but caused no further casualties.

That night and the next two days, were spent in the switch-trench. The weather was warm and the ground dry, and the occupants provided additional comfort for themselves from the nearby village. Meanwhile, the positions to be taken over were duly reconnoitred by company commanders. Just after darkness fell on the 11th, the move forward to relieve the Thirty-fourth Battalion was commenced. Because of the subsequent events in the new sector, the position to be taken over by the Seventeenth will be described in detail.

As already related, the 3rd Division's sector lay between the Rivers Ancre and Somme, the ground being high and broken by a series of hollows and steeply-crested folds, running at right angles from the river flats. Despite heavy losses, the 3rd Division had advanced its line along these physical features by a series of well planned and executed night-operations, to a point about one mile west of Morlancourt, about midway between the two rivers. Along the main ridge of this high tongue of land, ran the road from Corbie, eastward to Bray. It was from a point on this road overlooking a plateau that marked the left of the Battalion sector, which stretched for about one thousand yards towards the Somme. Just north of the river the Twenty-ninth Battalion of the 5th Division, continued the line. The dispositions of the Seventeenth's companies were as follow: D (Mackenzie) right and B (Ronald), left; C (Small), support, and A (Wright) reserve. Between the two forward companies was an unentrenched gap of about 500 yards, D's position being sited a little below the crest of the ridge on our side. This, combined with the fact that the intervening ground was covered in barley crops, rendered impossible, observation between the two companies. In the rear, the ground fell away into a re-entrant leading up to the main road, and here C Company occupied a strip of trench, previously dug by the Thirty-fourth Battalion. "A" Company, on a ridge about 1,000 yards in rear of the forward companies, commanded the approaches from the southern side of the Bray-Corbie road, while Battalion Headquarters was situated at a point near this road in the vicinity of A Company.

CHAPTER XIV.

Consolidating new position—Captain J. L. Wright engages in duel, Lewis v. machine-gun—The combat at Morlancourt—Junior leaders' boldness and enterprise—Private R. S. McGovern has a date with death—Lance Corporal D. Gallway does some salvage work—Back to Villers-Bretonneux—"Peaceful penetration"—Americans attached for training.

THE relief of the Thirty-fourth Battalion was completed without a hitch, and immediately thereafter the work of linking the two positions was begun by parties belonging to the forward companies. The diggers put their backs into this urgent task, but with only a few remaining hours of darkness, were unable to make any appreciable progress. During the night the enemy indulged in some scattered shelling of the area. killing one and wounding one other rank. A survey of the position by daylight revealed that the gap between the two companies had not been reduced sufficiently to provide a reasonable margin of safety, for, excluding a small post a little to the south of B Company's right flank, there remained an unbridged space of about 500 yards. The danger attending the situation was quickly recognised by Major Middleton, who gave orders for A Company to complete the task.

Soon after night-fall on the 12th, A Company filed out through the left of D Company's trench, and commenced digging. All night they toiled, the diggers being silhouetted against a background of star-shells, which the enemy kept dropping well to the rear. A German machine-gun on the nearby ridge kept up a harassing fire, causing some casualties. In addition, the Germans fired about 100 rounds of 5.9-inch high-explosive shells on B Company's position, killing three and wounding three other ranks.

The following day, the 13th, being comparatively quiet, efforts were made to locate the offending machine-gun's position. After long and careful observation, it was detected on the crest at a point about half way between the gap. Arrangements were thereupon made to bombard it with 4.5-inch howitzers in the early hours of the 14th, and then to endeavour to carry it by assault.

That night, A Company resumed its digging operations. Hardly had it got into full swing, when it again came under fire from the same gun. Soon men began to fall, causing serious interruption of the work. Wright, the commander, on learning what was afoot, went out alone, to reconnoitre. It was not long before he located the gun by its flash; thereupon he ordered up three Lewis guns, with the object of silencing the intruder. Wright, himself an expert in the use of this weapon, took one, and crawling out, lay down in the young barley crops, a little to the left flank of the enemy gun. Each time he saw a flash, he replied with a burst from his weapon. Presently the enemy gun ceased firing, and Wright, after waiting some time until he was satisfied that his opponent had had enough, withdrew to our line. The digging continued without further interruption until 3 a.m., when the party was withdrawn. Almost immediately afterwards, two of our 4.2-inch howitzer batteries shelled the post for five minutes, and then a detachment, under Lieutenant A. S. West of A Company went forward, but were stopped by fire from other enemy posts in the neighbourhood. The bombardment had been ineffective, the shells falling well to the rear of the target. West, thereupon, withdrew his men, but hardly had they got clear when, at 3.45, the enemy commenced shelling D and B Companies' positions, accompanied by intense machine-gun fire.

One of the enemy's 'planes flew slowly up and down the line evidently observing the effect of the shoot, and was

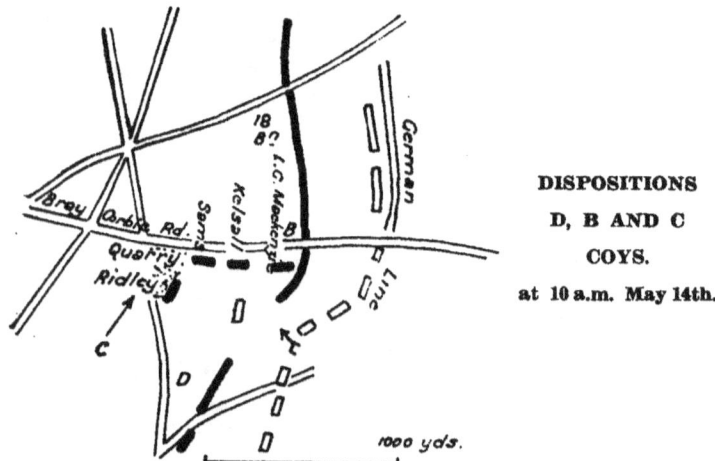

DISPOSITIONS
D, B AND C
COYS.
at 10 a.m. May 14th.

promptly subjected to fire from D Company's Lewis guns. The fire was so accurate that our men could plainly see pieces of the fabric, torn from the 'plane, descending to earth. The shells fell well to the rear of D Company, but B Company was subjected to a gruelling time and all telephone lines were severed. Moreover, the intervening crops rendered it impossible for either company to observe what was happening on the other's front. As no move had been made on his sector by the enemy when the shelling ceased, Mackenzie assumed that the bombardment had been merely a retaliatory one on the part of the Germans, and, therefore, contented himself by sending a written message to Battalion Headquarters, giving the position as he saw it. Small, C Company's commander, had arrived at a similar conclusion. But just before daybreak, Corporal A. H. Edwards of B Company, and three men entered one of Small's platoon posts, where they met Company Sergeant-Major J. H. Murphy. Edwards informed him that B Company was being heavily attacked, and that some of the enemy had penetrated to the rear of its position. Edwards reported that his Lewis gun section was manning the detached post in B Company's right flank, when at dawn it was rushed by a party of Germans. After firing one magazine from the gun, Edwards ordered his men to fall back. His Lance-Corporal, W. H. L. Pearce, was actually grabbed by a German but wrenched himself free. At first Murphy doubted Edwards's story, but eventually guided him to a quarry at the top of the re-entrant, where he knew Small to be. Looking over the edge of the quarry, Small observed the enemy digging in, between him and Ronald's company.

What had happened was this: The commander of the German regiment opposite the 5th Brigade Sector, sought, and obtained permission to attack and drive the Australians from the crest of the ridge, and thus remove the re-entrant "which was like a thorn in the eye, and to bring their untried reinforcements into touch with the enemy." (Australia in the War 1914-1918.) His plan was to employ one company to attack in an oblique direction, and get round the right flank of B Company, while one battalion would make a frontal attack along the main road. The advance would be prepared by a barrage from twenty field-batteries, as well as by trench-mortars. Unfortunately for his untried re-inforcements, the plan did not quite work to schedule.

On B Company's front the enemy advance had been observed north of the road, and Lieutenant L. G. Mackenzie's platoon, firing at point blank range, compelled it to halt. On the southern flank, despite the resolute stand by Corporal C. F. Cracknell and his Lewis gunners, the attackers swept round to the rear, over-running Corporal Edwards's detached post, as already related. A small party under an officer, endeavoured to charge B Company's trench in the rear, but all but two were shot, and two taken prisoner. The remainder seemed to be disorganized, and commenced to dig themselves in in the green crops. From one of the captured Germans, Ronald learned that about 150 men had attacked through the gap between his company and D, so he immediately ordered Lieutenant C. P. Kelsall to form a defensive flank parallel with the road, thus protecting his rear.

It was at this juncture, that Small, peering over the edge

of the quarry, observed what had happened. Quickly he summed up the position, and as quickly acted. Ordering up Lieutenant T. Ridley's platoon, he placed it in position in an old strip of trench, a little to the front of the quarry. He then directed Lieutenant C. J. Sams, with his platoon, to extend along the main road facing south, which move, as it transpired, brought him on to Kelsall's right flank. Thus, as the result of Small's prompt action, the Germans in rear of B Company, were securely pocketed. Small also ordered Company Sergeant-Major Murphy to get into touch with Ronald, by using the partly-dug strip of trench running parallel with and north of the road, and to tell him that he, Small, intended to counter-attack as soon as possible. He would also explain to Ronald the dispositions taken to support B Company. Subsequently, the two commanders arranged that zero hour for the counter-attack should be ten o'clock.

Back at Battalion Headquarters, just as day was breaking, the first news of the attack, received by Major Middleton, was from stretcher-bearers bearing casualties to the Regimental Aid Post. Simultaneously, a message was received from Colonel Murphy of the Eighteenth Battalion, confirming this report, and at the same time offering to counter-attack with one of his companies. Middleton immediately ordered Wright, in reserve, to move forward to the re-entrant at the rear of C Company's position, and at the same time instructed Lieutenant E. W. Dark, the Lewis gun officer and Sergeant A. McDonald, to endeavour to get in touch with either Ronald or Small.

On the right, when day dawned, Mackenzie, D Company, had observed stretcher-parties, under protection of white flags, moving to the rear along the road, and sensing that perhaps the enemy had attacked, despatched a small patrol under Sergeant E. Cowcher crawling through the crops, to try to get in touch with B Company. He immediately ordered D Company to stand-to-arms. About 9.15, Cowcher and his party returned, and gave the first account of the morning's events. A little later Lieutenant Dark arrived, and gave Mackenzie a verbal message from Small that the latter intended to counter-attack in the direction of the gap nearest to B Company's southern flank, and asked for supporting fire. Ronald's company was to assume a similar role, and also bomb down the captured portion of his trench at the southern end. The right company of the Eighteenth Battalion, which was on Ronald's left, would co-operate by extending its front to the right. A message had been sent to Battalion Headquarters, requesting artillery support to keep the enemy on his front pinned down where his troops had commenced to dig in. Small also indicated that the attack would be preceded by a three-minute bombardment by a Stokes mortar, which had been brought up by Lieutenant U. K. Walsh, to the quarry behind Ridley's platoon. Mackenzie immediately issued the necessary instructions to his two front line platoon-commanders. It will be recalled that the lay of the land in this part of the sector, with growing crops between D and B Companies, obscured the view each of the other; nor could the German posts on the plateau in front of D Company be seen by the latter company. But they knew that somewhere in the vicinity was located the gun—the one Wright had engaged in a duel. Particular attention would have to be paid to it.

Suddenly, the watchers in D Company's trench saw Walsh's Stokes mortar shells lurching in quick succession in their high-trajectory flight to the target area; and, simultaneously with the first burst, the heads of half a dozen Germans showed on the skyline about a hundred yards away from the left of the company's position. They were too intent on watching the bursting mortar-shells to observe that, a little distance down the declivity, between forty and fifty Australians were crouching ready, with fixed bayonets. At last the position of the offending enemy post had been revealed. But it was possible that there might be other posts along the crest, so Mackenzie decided to clean up the situation there by sending over the two forward platoons, under Lieutenants R. R. F. Willard and J. G. Edmondson. Hardly had the mortar ceased firing when the order was given to charge, and with a yell, the two platoons raced across the intervening space to the crest. But the gunners in the offending post did not wait for D Company; they fled incontinently for the safety of their main positions. And the reason for this was presently made plain to the assailants, for, under a rubber sheet beside his gun, the breech-block of which was shattered, a German lay dead—shot clean through the temples. He had been dead some hours. The gallant Wright had already written "Finis" to that chapter.

The occupants of nearby enemy posts did not wait to join issue with D Company; they also fled, while the laughing, excited attackers took pot-shots at them from both the standing and kneeling positions. But the Germans had had a flying-start, and few were seen to fall.

Immediate steps were taken to link the captured post with D Company's trench, and thus prevent further interference with the work of connecting D and B Companies' trenches.

On returning to their trench, D Company's men noted that Company Sergeant-Major J. Glenday had, on his own initiative, placed a Lewis gun and a section of riflemen out in the long crops, in order to form a flank to the left, but events proved that this wise precaution was not necessary.

C Company's part was carried out efficiently, as though on parade. Immediately the mortar ceased firing, Small ordered Ridley's and Sams's platoons to advance and clean up the Germans in the pocket behind B Company, and the two remaining platoons to move up into the gap at a left incline and cut off any of the enemy trying to get out. The movement was well timed, and when the Germans realised their own predicament, most of them decided to surrender rather than fight. Those who tried to escape were quickly shot, either by the advancing platoons of C Company, or by B Company's men engaged in the task of cleaning out those remaining in the southern portion of their trench.

While this operation was in progress, Wright brought up A Company, and occupied the position vacated by C. But this was not needed as the enemy had had enough, and by 10.30 a.m. the position was restored to normal. Sixty-nine prisoners were taken by our men, and in addition it was estimated that about eighty had been killed. Our casualties were Lieutenant Kelsall and fifteen other ranks killed, Lieutenant Sams and thirty-six other ranks wounded and eight other ranks missing.

Many fine deeds were performed that day. The brave but impetuous Kelsall was shot during a futile premature attack he had ordered, and Sergeant E. T. Oberg and Lance Corporal W. G. Knight, were also amongst the killed. Corporals C. G. Williams and C. F. Cracknell, Lance-Corporals L. C. Clarke and G. H. Taylor, and Privates S. Edwards, A. Makin, W. A. Walsh, A. J. McCaffrey, H. G. Murrell, J. T. Gregory and H. J. Compton were amongst those whose conduct set a fine example to others.

Thus ended the combat at Morlancourt, an action of a type being waged daily in a score of places from the sea to the Swiss border, and revealing the resource and initiative possessed by subordinate commanders cut off from communications and with no superior to lean upon. Undoubtedly, it was the competent handling by company platoon and section leaders which saved the day. On the rank and file, however, fell the main burden, and right well did they acquit themselves of the task. But to Small, the quick-witted, courageous, young subaltern, temporarily in command of C Company, must go the chief credit for the ready perception and the prompt and effective measures taken to retrieve our extremely awkward situation. Like so many of his colleagues, Small had gained his commission from the ranks, having served with the Seventeenth since its inception.

But before we close the account of this episode, four incidents directly concerned with it are narrated, because of their unusual character. The first concerns Private R. S. McGovern, who, on the 13th, was one of Cracknell's section of B Company, when a shell hit the trench completely burying McGovern; he was saved from suffocation by his steel helmet, which was forced down over his face, thus giving him breathing space.

Pinned helpless by the crushing weight of earth, McGovern suffered the ghastly ordeal of being buried alive. He could hear his comrades' voices and movements as they searched for his mangled remains, as they thought, but he himself was quite helpless. On the point of losing consciousness, he heard Cracknell say:—"By God, he might be buried under here! Dig like hell, blokes!" Before long they had extricated their comrade, bruised and very shaken, but otherwise unhurt. But it had been a near thing.

Then there were Privates E. C. Ralphs and A. R. Saundercock, who belonged to Corporal Edwards's section manning the detached post on the right of B Company. Both men were captured when the Germans over-ran the post. Two of the enemy marched Saundercock towards their own lines, and one man remained with Ralphs, who had been disarmed. Presently the German made a sign that he was going on, and indicated that Ralphs should make his way along to the German line. But as soon as his captor's back was turned, Ralphs seized a rifle and shot him, then made a bolt for our line, which he reached safely.

Saundercock had a still more unpleasant experience. Half way across No Man's Land, his two captors were killed by bullets, but he himself, unharmed, dropped into a convenient shell-hole, where he remained all day, returning to our lines after dark. To his disgust, he learned that his mates had given him up for lost, and had proceeded to divide amongst themselves the contents of his haversack, including the unexpended portion of the day's rations. The indignant Saundercock was obliged to spend a considerable amount of time retrieving his lost possessions.

The third instance was a tragic one. Lance-Corporal H. W. Gane and two of his comrades, Percy Rice and another, were standing in B Company's trench on the night of the 12/13, when a bullet passed through Gane's head, killing him and then passing on struck Rice and his comrade, inflicting serious wounds.

The final episode concerned Captain Ronald. After the fight had ceased, some prisoners were brought to him; among them was one whose face seemed familiar. Questioning of the man revealed that, just prior to the outbreak of the war, he had been a drink-waiter at a well-known Melbourne hostelry patronised by Ronald, whom, the prisoner declared, he clearly recalled having regularly served.

What the German regimental commander, Major von Lossberg, who persuaded his superiors to allow him to attack, thought after he had finished casting up the figures of the profit and loss account of the combat, has not been recorded. But the comment of the Australian Official Historian, after quoting extracts from official German accounts is interesting. He writes:

"The report of the undertaking sent to the army commander, however, stated that the raid by the assault troops of the 31st I.R. had been successful. The German front, it claimed, was advanced 400 metres on a front of 250 metres, north of the Bray-Corbie road; and south of the road (where a machine-gun checked progress), 250 metres on a front of 250 metres—which they could have done at night-time without loss . . . The loss of the 31st is given in this account as 188, including twenty-six missing. This fine report apparently brought von Lossberg, in the next day's army order, the Iron Cross (Class 1)."

The Seventeenth remained in the line until the night of 16/17, when it was relieved by the Twentieth Battalion. By this time the gap between the two forward companies had been linked as far as the detached post near B Company's right flank. On the 15th, the enemy had shelled the area heavily at frequent intervals, throughout the day, casualties being eight other ranks killed and five wounded.

Vaux-sur-Somme, in brigade reserve, was the Battalion's destination, and there, in little dug-outs cut in the side of "Nanny Goat Gully," the men sought much-needed rest after the arduous tour. But even this sheltered spot had its disadvantages, for, especially at night, several field-batteries in position nearby were frequently the targets, for high-explosive and gas-shells, which caused much inconvenience and seriously disturbed the men's rest, besides killing one other rank and wounding eleven. At night, parties from each company were detailed for fatigue duties in the front line; therefore, the majority of the Battalion took their sleep during daytime. A stranger strolling down the gully about one hour after breakfast would have been impressed by the display of under-garments placed outside the cubby-holes for sunning and airing, while the owners slumbered. And thereby hangs a story—a story illustrating the consequences of ill-directed zeal. About this time, a universal salvage campaign had been organized, and formations and units were encouraged to compete in the collection of any article, from derelict waggons to broken bully-beef cases. Every battalion had one salvage non-commissioned officer to each company, and it is with one, Lance-Corporal D. Gallway, D Company's representative that this anecdote is concerned. With him the collection of salvage was not merely a duty—it was a positive mania, and many an unfortunate soldier who thoughtlessly had left articles of equipment or clothing lying unguarded, would wake to find them missing. For some time Gallway escaped suspicion, but, alas, Nemesis tracked him down. He had been spotted at his nefarious task. Here, now, was the opportunity to wreak vengeance. Slipping into Gallway's possy during his temporary absence, one of the men purloined his gas-helmet and laid it down temptingly to view in front of another possy, not far away. Ere long it was espied by the ubiquitous salvage-corporal, and whisked away to be added to the ever-mounting dump. The same night gas-shells fell in the gully, whose occupants, had to turn out and don their masks. All except one—Lance-Corporal Gallway, who had salved his own gas-helmet!

The last fortnight of May was spent in routine tours between the front line and reserve positions, without much incident, the records disclosing that, on the 18th, Lieutenant Baldwin of the United States Army left to rejoin his regiment, and that on the 21st, Lieutenant R. E. Masterson was wounded. On the 23rd the Seventeenth relieved the Twentieth Battalion in the sector in front of Heilly, where, the following day, Lieutenant A. T. Doig, a very fine officer, who had been with the Battalion since its inception, receiving his commission on Gallipoli, was killed, while inspecting the barbed wire on his platoon front. By the 29th the Battalion was once more back in reserve in the Vaux-sur-Somme area.

From June 2nd to 16th, the 5th Brigade was billeted near Frechencourt, whence it moved into corps reserve in the Rivery-Camoen area, just east of Amiens. The Seventeenth was allotted bivouacs in the copses in the vicinity of Glisy. In these pleasant surroundings, steps were taken to organize sport and recreation in order to divert the minds of the men from the monotony and strain of their work in the front line. The weather, too, was all that could be desired. Cricket, football and swimming were the most popular pastimes. An inter-company football competition was won by D Company, while a little later a team from the Battalion defeated the representatives of a British unit. An aquatic carnival was also held in the nearby Somme, but, unfortunately, no record has been preserved of the various events, or of the results. One feature of the day was a demonstration swim by the champion swimmer, Lieutenant C. Healy of the Nineteenth Battalion. Humorous relief was forthcoming from a quite-unexpected quarter as the result of the swamping of the pontoon used for starting the races, immersing a number of officers, including Lieutenant Maynard, the starter, who lost his revolver. Everybody enjoyed the officials' discomfiture, and the victims themselves took their unexpected ducking in good part.

Training was not, however, neglected, for soon after arriving at Glisy two miniature rifle-ranges and a hundred-yards range were constructed, in order to carry out musketry and Lewis gun work under Captain Manefield and Lieutenant Massey; the latter trained ninety men as gunners, besides putting through those officers who had had no previous experience in handling that weapon. Gas drill and battalion drill were also part of the daily routine.

While at Glisy awards for gallantry at Morlancourt were promulgated, Private S. Edwards receiving a Bar to the Military

Medal, and Corporal C. G. Williams, Lance-Corporals L. C. Clarke, and G. H. Taylor and Privates A. Makin, W. A. Walsh, A. G. McCaffery, H. G. Murrell, J. T. Gregory, and H. J. Compton, the Military Medal.

The night of June 29/30 found the Seventeenth once more in the line just north of Villers-Bretonneux, remaining there until the night of July 2/3, when it moved back to the Tronville Wood area, several miles to the west, after being relieved by the Twenty-first and Twenty-second Battalions.

The new bivouac area was in every respect as comfortable as the previous one, and all ranks soon settled down in their new "home from home." However, it was not long before they were obliged to modify this estimate, as on the following day an enormous French gun of 13.5-inch calibre, on a railway mounting, with attendant trucks, was brought up to a point close to the bivouac, whence it began to throw shells on a railway junction, eighteen miles distant. This brought prompt retaliation in the form of counter-shelling by German long-range guns and strafing aeroplanes, thus causing no little disturbance of the comfort of the men of the Seventeenth.

In a neighbouring area there was a French formation, included in which were Moroccan troops. These dark-skinned warriors, who occasionally wandered over to the Australians' bivouacs were at first regarded by our men as a novelty, but they were such expert thieves that our men had to hunt them away.

The stay at Tronville Wood was brief, orders being received late in the afternoon of the 4th, for the Seventeenth to relieve the Twenty-second Battalion in brigade support north of Villers-Bretonneux, on the night 6/7. That morning, an attack had been launched by a combined force of Australians and Americans, aided by British tanks and aircraft, on the village of Hamel north-east of the town. The assault which had been planned by Lieutenant-General Monash (who, in May, succeeded General Birdwood in command of the Australian Corps), was entirely successful, the immediate object being to straighten out the line in that locality, thus pushing the enemy further away from Hill 104, and the high ground commanding a view of Amiens. It also served the purpose of disrupting his defences, as well as forming the basis of a full-dress rehearsal for operations on a larger scale. The co-ordination displayed by all the services engaged was perfect, even food, water and ammunition being dropped by parachutes to the battalions on reaching their objectives.

On the night of the 6th, under a bright moon, the Seventeenth began its forward move to the trenches, and all went well until the north-western outskirts of Villers-Bretonneux was reached. Then a German airman, flying low, spotted the column, and proceeded to drop flares. The order was given to lie down, which was prudent, for almost immediately bombs began to fall in the vicinity of the long-drawn-out column, fortunately only wounding two other ranks.

The relief proceeded without further interruption from the enemy, the new position consisting of a series of freshly-dug posts, well to the north-east of the town. These posts, concealed in the crops, which now were about two-feet high, were sited so as to give mutual support in the form of rifle and machine-gun fire. They were not wired, and therefore, the strictest vigilance was called for by the garrisons. In order to guard against surprise, the crops immediately in front of each post were cut down for a score or so of yards.

The wide mantle of growing grain created a new tactical situation, for whereas, a couple of months before, the flat, featureless terrain had been deemed quite unsuitable for "peaceful-penetration" tactics, the cover from view afforded by the growing crops now opened up a wide prospect for the successful employment of these self-same "cutting-out" operations, even during the hours of daylight.

But it fell to the lot of a young sergeant of the Twentieth Battalion, Walter Brown, to discover the possibilities arising from such a state of things, and to demonstrate, in practice, the value of tactics, which, during the ensuing four weeks, were to cause considerable disturbance to the peace of mind of the enemy, and, incidentally, to win additional manoeuvring space for our forces.

On July 5th, Brown was one of an advanced party of his battalion, which was to take over from the Twenty-first Battalion the following day. When the occupants of a nearby enemy-post seemed to be off their guard in the warm morning sunshine, he seized the opportunity alone. Armed only with two Mills bombs he moved quickly across the intervening seventy yards to the German post, and by a magnificent piece of effrontery, succeeded in capturing the whole of the thirteen occupants, and bringing them back to our lines. For this gallant deed, Brown was awarded the Victoria Cross.

Examination of these and other prisoners captured earlier, disclosed that there had been a definite decline in the morale of the Germans in that sector. It was also disclosed that there existed no organized outpost line, and that frequently, groups detailed to man these posts were left without adequate support, and sometimes even without food and water.

Impressed by this information, the corps commander immediately gave orders for the commencement of a series of these "nibbling" tactics along the whole of the Australian sector—tactics, which, ultimately, wrested from the enemy 1,000 yards of territory. Previously it had been anticipated that this gain would require a second Hamel operation to secure.

Battalions of the 7th Brigade on the right of the 5th Brigade initiated a daring succession of these daylight raids; these were followed on the night of the 9th by the Fifth Brigade's two forward battalions, the Eighteenth and the Twentieth, endeavouring to seize a communication trench running at right angles to, and north of the Roman road. The Twentieth on the left were to work down the trench towards the road, while the Eighteenth would advance parallel with the road, and connect with the former battalion. However, the attempt was only partly successful, the battalions failing to make contact owing to the Eighteenth mistaking its objective and occupying a trench 200 yards west of the real one.

Such was the position, when, on the night of the 13th, they were relieved by the Seventeenth and Nineteenth Battalions. The Seventeenth, on the right, was disposed as follows: two companies, D (Mackenzie) and A (Maynard), in front line; B (Finlay) and C (Harnett) in support.

Late in the afternoon of the 15th, verbal orders from Brigade Headquarters were received by Colonel Sadler, that the line was to be advanced and connected with the Nineteenth Battalion on the left; it was to be merely a repetition of the recent attempt by their two sister battalions. This part of the operation was allotted to two platoons of A Company, while south of the road, the two remaining platoons and D Company would send out fighting patrols, and establish a line of posts for the defence of the right flank. At 2 a.m. on the 16th, the two platoons of A Company detailed for the attack, under Lieutenants A. S. West and C. W. Warburton, moved swiftly across the intervening 200 yards, but found that the enemy garrison had departed in haste leaving behind them two dead, a heavy machine-gun, and all their equipment and food. Crossing to the south of the road, the two platoons under Lieutenants S. M. Blackshaw and R. Phelps met strong opposition from machine-gun and shell-fire, the former from their immediate front. But eventually, after subduing these elements, they proceeded to dig-in on the flank of the posts, north of the road. They had evidently inflicted considerable casualties on the enemy. In the meantime, Maynard had requested Captain Finlay to lend him three Lewis guns to cover the ground south of the road, and had established his own headquarters in the post lately vacated by Blackshaw's platoon, and he reported that the Germans could be seen carrying away their wounded.

D Company was also successful; its right platoon, under Lieutenant Willard, rushed a strong enemy post immediately in front with great dash. Guided by Lance Corporal F. Carstens, who had previously located it, Willard and his men got in amongst a most surpised enemy, the young subaltern, little more than a boy, shooting dead one German with his revolver, while five others were disposed of by the rest of the platoon. The other occupants of the post stood not upon the order of their going, leaving one of their number prisoner. The platoon lost Private J. W. F. ("Dusty") Rhoades, killed and Corporal F. L. Johnson, wounded. Johnson, who, in support of his leader, had displayed a fine degree of dash, lay where he fell, undiscovered until day broke, when a search was made for him. He was found lying in the long crops unconscious, but when Willard endeavoured to get the stretcher-bearers to him, they were fired upon from a German post on the platoon's left-front. Several similar attempts were blocked, and it was thought that the wounded man might have to be untended till darkness set in. Then a rattle of musketry from somewhere on Willard's left sent the enemy who were harassing the position, to earth, thus enabling the sorely stricken Johnson to be rescued and carried to the rear.

The left attacking platoon of D Company, Lieutenant V. J. Sullivan's, found no opposition in their path, and when it arrived on what that officer thought to be his objective, he gave orders to dig in. When day broke Sullivan observed only about thirty yards ahead a fairly strongly held enemy post. He had

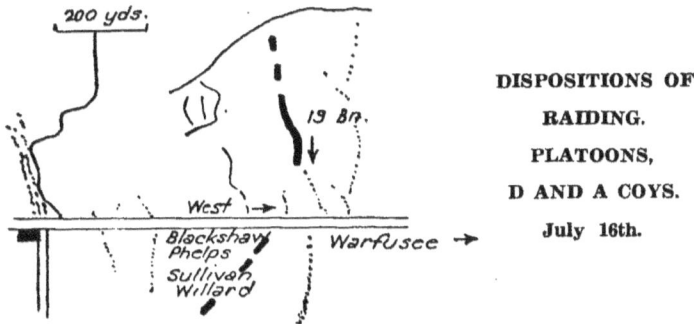

DISPOSITIONS OF RAIDING. PLATOONS, D AND A COYS. July 16th.

over-run his objective, although, apparently, the Germans were unaware of the close proximity of their opponents. But we shall tell the platoon's adventure in Sullivan's own words. It is a story typifying the offensive spirit which inspired the average sub-unit leader, be he subaltern, sergeant, corporal, or, as sometimes was the case, a private soldier. Here is the story, only slightly edited:—

"In the lazy summer days of July, 1918, a pet phrase of those clad with authority was 'peaceful penetration.' The enemy was to be denied any freedom in No Man's Land; every opportunity was to be taken to filch a few yards of ground, with an absolute disregard for the feelings of the company detailed for the unpleasant work.

"One evening, at dusk, a company runner reports to 16 Platoon at a snug post situated on the main road a few hundred yards east of Villers-Bretonneux:—'Platoon commanders will report at Company Headquarters at 22.20 hours.' At the appointed time and rendezous, they are met by the O.C. who apologises for the lack of chairs and other amenities. And then to business. The Battalion is to push forward without delay. The plan is soon expounded, and as neither side holds any regular trench system, very little detail is required. The two companies holding the front line are to go forward and rush the enemy posts.

"The action is timed to start at 02.00 hours the following morning, and the interval is taken up with the issue of instructions by platoon commanders, the packing of the scanty possessions of the men, and the disposal of the spare ammunition and tools to be taken forward. No. 16 is to move forward parallel with road running into the German position, brush aside any opposition and dig in; the platoons on both flanks are to mop up strong points that previously have been indicated. At about 00.30 hours Sergeant Maynard is sent with three men to reconnoitre the route. He returns an hour later to report everything quiet. It is now 02.00 hours and in single file the platoon moves out, eager to get as far ahead as possible before the expected outburst from the flanking platoons begins.

"It is not long before the quiet of the night is broken by bomb explosions, rifle, revolver and Lewis gun fire, mingled with a din of shouting. While the uproar lasts, 16 Platoon hurries forward, until in front can be seen dim forms coming down the road. Our men take cover in the long crops and watch Fritz. He seems puzzled but soon disappears, for the company on the left has started its part of the business. Orders are now given to dig, and while a Lewis gun covers the front, no time is lost in completing the work.

"Four o'clock finds the platoon 'standing-to' in a roughly constructed post concealed by the long crop. The sounds of fighting on both sides have subsided, and the only sign of movement is the stretcher-bearers at work. The objective has been gained, although one platoon of the left company has been held up, and its commander wounded. He has been exchanged by the enemy and allowed to be taken from the field in daylight. Lieutenant Willard has captured the strong post on the right after a short fight.

"Daylight reveals that No. 16 has gone too far forward, and is actually within thirty yards of a barbed-wire screen put up by the enemy—so close, that for safety, it is considered wise to keep quiet and watch for any counter-attack. This inactivity is disastrous to the enemy, who is unaware that a few yards away twenty men lie concealed in the wheat and intently watching his every move. There appear to be about fifteen of them unconcernedly moving about in their post. On our side the men are getting restless. Here is a first-class target; why can't they 'have a go at it'? After some time the commander decides to let them. One burst of rifle and Lewis gun fire from the whole platoon abruptly ends the enemy's walk, and sends every man to earth. (Doubtless it was under cover of this very firing that Willard's men rescued the wounded Johnson).

"Quietness again descends and the platoon commander has just settled himself to discuss a frugal breakfast of tinned peaches and bread brought to him by his batman, Private Angus McDonald, when the word reaches him that a single German has been sighted ahead evidently trying to locate the post. The platoon commander has a look, and spies the enemy. Turning to Lance Corporal W. Hughes, who is standing alongside him, he pulls from his pocket a packet of Capstan cigarettes and says: 'Get that man and these cigarettes are yours.' Hughes's rifle cracks, and the German's cap flies into the air as he falls dead. The prize has been won.

"The morning's work is now complete—the enemy has shown no sign of resentment. The frugal breakfast is then finished, and while a sentry group keeps watch, the rest of the platoon lies down in the friendly cover of the crop and enjoys a well earned sleep.

"And, perhaps, the London papers will say that increased activity is being displayed by the Australians east of Villers-Bretonneux."

Such is the account of the doings of this enterprising band on that particular day. It is a typical daily example of the swift, silent incursions into the enemy's territory, along the whole corps front—incursions designed to foster our morale, wrest the initiative from him, tear chunks out of his morale, and gain more elbow room to deliver a combined powerful blow.

Two incidents arising from the enterprise remain to be told—one salted with grim humour, but ending on a note of tragedy. It will be recalled that A Company's objective was an enemy post a hundred yards or so to the west of, and parallel with, the trench on which the Nineteenth Battalion was to bomb down. However, when dawn came, there was no sign of that unit in the section of the trench about thirty-five yards to the front. This was due to the trench not being continuous, as it appeared to be, in the map. But what our men did see, was a group of Germans, still in occupation. Lieutenant West, a fine athlete, collected four men, amongst them Private Broder (who had won the Military Medal at Passchendaele), and although warned by Corporal H. B. Grant that he would be acting contrary to orders, led his party in a headlong rush towards the German trench, into which they jumped with loud yells. There ensued a fight in which Grant and the remainder of the platoon gave support by rifle fire. Soon, however, West's men could be heard calling for bombs, and Private F. J. Sullivan made an attempt to get some across to them, but the brave fellow fell riddled with bullets.

Eventually, Broder and one of the men got back to our trench, under cover of the platoon's fire, and reported that West had been hit on the head with the butt of a rifle and knocked out. The other two members of the party had evidently been killed.

Simultaneously, with the foregoing incident, a party of Germans had blundered on Lieutenant Blackshaw's post south of the Roman road; they were promptly shot up. They left one of their number wounded, and his loud cries brought two of Blackshaw's stretcher-bearers, one of them Private P. C. Begg, to him. They were about to carry the wounded man into Blackshaw's post when a German stretcher-party approached under cover of a white flag, and claimed their comrade. It appeared that the man had been in the act of throwing a bomb, when a burst of machine-gun fire struck his arm, and in his excitement, he failed to clear the bomb, which duly exploded and inflicted a number of wounds.

An argument ensued between the rival stretcher-bearers, and at last our men agreed to hand over the wounded German— a sergeant, in exchange for Lieutenant West. Over to the German trench went Begg and his mate, carrying their burden, there to be met by an irate officer, who indicated strong disapproval of their action in approaching his position. Furthermore, he declined to ratify the agreement on the question of an exchange. He could not possibly consider handing over an officer in return for one sergeant. It was inequitable. However, Begg and his mate were firm, insisting that the original arrangement must stand, and finally the German consented to the transfer, whereupon our men carried the sorely stricken West back to their lines. The unfortunate lad had received a blow on his skull, which was fractured. He was unconscious. He died the following day. In addition to West, two other ranks were killed, and four wounded.

The closing scene of this dramatic interlude concerns Corporal Grant, now in command of West's platoon post. Grant relates that for about two hours after his officer had been brought back, the situation was quiet; nevertheless a strict look-out was kept. Suddenly his sentries observed movement in the German trench opposite. Quietly, he ordered his men to stand to their arms. Not a minute too soon, for presently an officer sprang on to the parapet waving an automatic pistol. In Grant's post, three rifles cracked, and the German fell back into his trench. He was quickly followed by a second officer who tried to rally his men to go forward, but Grant promptly shot him. The remainder appeared to be disorganized, and moved about in the trench, offering excellent targets for our men,

Grant himself accounting for several Germans who were standing almost shoulder to shoulder. The corporal's vigilance had nipped this counter-attack in the bud, and during the next hour or so, he and his men had the satisfaction of observing about forty enemy wounded being carried to the rear.

On July 18th, the Eighteenth Battalion took over the line, the Seventeenth moving back into support just north of Villers-Bretonneux. Here the Battalion lost a fine young non-commissioned officer, Corporal G. J. Beddows, who was killed by a shell. He was buried by Padre Tugwell.

About this period, the American personnel attached to units of the Australian Corps for training and experience, began to arrive. One American platoon was absorbed into every Australian company, and very quickly accustomed themselves to their new surroundings. They were fine physical specimens, and free and easy in their manner, like our own men, with whom they formed a ready friendship.

From July 23rd to 30th, the Battalion was once again in the front line, being relieved on the latter date by its opposite number, the Eighteenth Battalion.

Additional awards for gallantry displayed at Morlancourt were announced during this period, Captain H. Ronald receiving the Distinguished Service Order; Lieutenants G. Small, C. J. Sams, U. K. Walsh and T. Ridley the Military Cross, and Company Sergeant-Major J. H. Murphy and Lance Corporal C. F. Cracknell the Distinguished Conduct Medal.

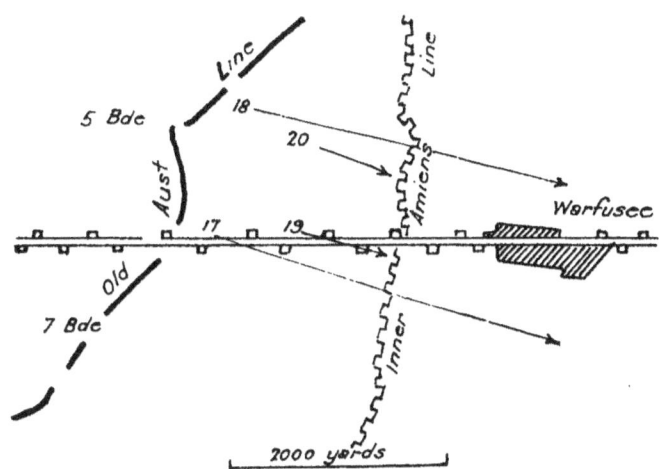

DISPOSITION OF 2ND DIVISION.
On August. 8th

CHAPTER XV.

Position of rival armies at end of July—Foch decides to deliver his supreme counter-stroke—Amiens sector chosen for initial blow—Monash's plans—Seventeenth's objective, Warfusee-Abancourt, August 8th—Operation goes with clock-work precision—Smith of the A.I.F. rides to battle on a tank—Casualties light, many prisoners taken.

AFTER four years of war the Allies and the Germans had found themselves in a position in which neither side could claim a decisive advantage over the other. It now appeared to be a question as to which of the adversaries could sustain the strain on their morale for the longer period. The two powerful blows delivered by the Germans earlier in the year had failed to destroy their opponents, but so far, as in the case of the wearing-down battles of 1916-1917, to what extent the enemy's morale was affected by these failures, there was no reliable indication available to the Allied High Command. In fact, even at the end of July, preparations were being made in Allied countries for a continuation of the war into 1920.

On May 27th, the third and last phase of the great German offensive was launched—against the French in the Champagne sector. This was followed by an attack in the direction of Compiegne. But in each case, after some initial success, the attackers were brought to a standstill. On July 15th, the enemy again struck, this time near Rheims, and here again, although his preliminary attempt was successful, the advance was ultimately held east of the city. Launching a furious counter-attack, the French, on July 18th, threw the Germans back in disorder over the Marne.

The crisis had passed, and Foch, the Generalissimo of the Allied Armies, judged that the time had arrived for the supreme Allied counter-offensive to be delivered—he had been coolly and resolutely planning it for several months. It was now a question as to which part of the front would provide an opening likely to ensure the complete success of the initial operation. Of all the sectors on the Allied front the one in the vicinity of Amiens appeared to be the most promising for that purpose. Here, the Germans, evidently underestimating the recuperative powers of the British Army, had made the mistake of neglecting to improve their defences. Additionally, a successful offensive in this locality would remove the threat to

Amiens, the key strategic centre situated just in rear of the junction of the French and British Armies.

In the middle of July, General Rawlinson, commanding the Fourth Army, had submitted a plan of attack on this self-same sector. This plan was approved by Sir Douglas Haig and, a week later, by General Foch.

At this stage the Fourth Army comprised four Australian divisions, from south of Villers-Bretonneux to the Ancre, and from the latter place northwards to Albert, the three divisions of the III Corps.

Preparations were immediately put in hand for an operation in which surprise was to be the principal factor. Between July 30th and August 8th, a remarkable feat of organization was performed—three cavalry and fourteen infantry divisions, over 3,000 guns and 450 tanks were concentrated east of Amiens without the Germans suspecting their presence. Air support was to be provided by seventeen squadrons of the Royal Air Force.

The initial objective was the seizure of the old Amiens outer defence system several miles east of Villers-Bretonneux. The First French Army on the right of the Fourth Army was placed by Foch under orders of Haig. The date ultimately fixed for the attack was August 8th.

The 12-mile front allotted the Fourth Army was about equally divided between the Canadian Corps (which had been brought down from the north), right; Australian, centre; and III Corps, left. The average advance to the objective — the Amiens outer defence line—was 10,500 yards.

The role of the cavalry was to push through the infantry of the Canadian and Australian Corps, and to take advantage of any opportunity that might present itself to seize and hold an objective until the infantry arrived, after which they could carry out exploitation to the south-east.

In addition to its normal tasks, the air arm was called upon to assist in drowning the noise of tanks when assaulting, providing smoke screens and observing for the artillery.

The artillery would provide the creeping barrage for the advancing infantry, counter-battery work, and the shelling of villages and localities suspected of being used as assembly places for the enemy's reserves.

On the Australian Corps front, that great leader, Lieutenant-General Monash (who had already distinguished himself by the genius of his organising capacity, while commanding the 3rd Division at the battle of Messines), was engaged in perfecting, to the last detail, preparations for the part his corps was called upon to perform.

The corps front extended from the Amiens-Nesle railway on the right, to the Somme. Monash planned that the objective for the first day was to be the old Amiens line 9,000 yards distant. This line could be used in case of counter-attack and also to cover the deployment for further advances. For this purpose he decided to employ four divisions in the actual assault, with one in reserve. The attack would comprise three phases as follows:—

    "A"—Set piece attack with barrage 3,000 yards
    "B"—Open warfare .... 4,500 yards
    "C"—Exploitation .... 1,500 yards

The 2nd and 3rd Divisions were allotted the task of carrying out "A" phase, and the 5th and 4th "B" phase, while the 1st Division was held in reserve. The 14th Brigade (5th Division) and 1st Brigade (1st Division) would complete "C" phase.

The problem of reducing the fatigue factor for the 5th and 4th Divisions was solved by the method of leap-frogging. Thus, prior to the attack, these two divisions would lay up in the area immediately in rear of the starting line. The scheduled time for the completion of "A" phase was 143 minutes, followed by a pause of 100 minutes, to allow time for the advance and deployment of the "B" phase divisions, who would thus be able to rest preparatory to leap-frogging the 2nd and 3rd Divisions into the "B" and "C" phases.

To ensure secrecy, orders were issued that all movements of troops and transports should only take place under cover of darkness, and to police this order No. 3 Australian Flying Squadron was detailed to fly continuously by day over the area.

The barrage for "A" phase was provided by eighteen brigades of field-artillery (six gun batteries), 432 guns in all, in addition to medium and heavy artillery, bringing the total to 680 guns.

"A" phase was defined by a spur running northwards from La Motte, adjoining Warfusee-Abancourt, to the Somme, and in the valley of Cerisy, in front of this spur, large numbers of enemy guns had been located.

The barrage line would be dead straight on the whole of the Corps front, the infantry tape-lines being 200 yards short of the artillery "start line."

By a system of sound and visual spotting, the position of enemy guns was accurately plotted, thereby dispensing with the necessity for each individual gun in its fighting-pit to fire a series of registration rounds on defined reference points in order to rectify any error in line or range of each gun. In its place, a new scientific method known as "calibration" was employed to ascertain and catalogue each gun to go into action, whenever required, without any previous registration whatsoever. These tests were carried out on a special range behind the battle zone. What an economy this measure proved to be

Lieut.-Col. R. M. SADLER, D.S.O., M.C.
C.O. 1918-1919.

GROUP OF SERGEANTS, 1918.

THE OFFICERS — JULY 1918. Colonel Sadler is seventh from the left in the front row.

is shown in the casualty list of the corps on the evening of August 8th.

In addition, 168 tanks, male and female, and sixteen armoured cars would support the attack. The male tank was equipped with both cannon and machine-guns, the female tanks only with machine-guns.

We will now return to the Battalion, which, on August 1st, was in support in the vicinity of Hill 104. All was quiet on the 5th Brigade front. The weather was hot and sultry.

On the morning of the 2nd, members of the Battalion staff were at breakfast in a recess leading from the trench in which Headquarters was situated, when it received a direct hit by a 5.9-inch shell, killing Captain F. G. Barnett, the Adjutant, as well as the officer in command of the company belonging to the American battalion, attached, and seriously wounding Captain L. M. Piggott, the Medical Officer, and several batmen.

At this critical period the loss of these officers was a blow to the Battalion, and all ranks deeply regretted the passing of Barnett, who had been with the Seventeenth for most of his service. To Colonel Sadler, especially, it was a grievous setback to be so suddenly deprived of the services of such a zealous and efficient aide. Barnett was replaced by Lieutenant A. F. Gilbert, Assistant Adjutant, also an original member of the Battalion, who had gained his commission in the field, and Captain A. L. McLean came in as Medical Officer. McLean, like Piggott, had already seen considerable service and possessed high intellectual attainments. The war had interrupted his researches in the field of pathology, which, even then, were beginning to attract notice within the profession. He had accompanied Dr. Mawson on his expedition to the Antarctic a few years before, and wore on his left breast the ribbon of the rare medal awarded for exploration in Polar regions. Fate, however, willed that four years later he should himself fall a victim to the very scourge he had set out to conquer.

On the night of August 3rd, the Seventeenth was relieved by the Twenty-fourth Battalion and moved back into trenches in the vicinity of Blangy-Tronville. Falling rain made the going very difficult.

Sunday, the 4th, was spent in the cleaning of arms, ammunition, adjustment of equipment, and "make and mend" purposes generally. The following day the Battalion embused to attend practices in attacking with tanks, in the vicinity of Vaulx-en-Amienois, returning to bivouac at about 6 p.m. the same day. The bayonet strength at this date was 500.

As yet no information had been given to the troops of the impending operations, although there was a universal feeling that something unusual was afoot. Even commanding officers of units were kept in ignorance of the fact until August 6th, and it was only on the following day they were permitted to take the men into their confidence.

On the 6th, the Seventeenth moved to the Aubigny Switch system, which had been allotted as a staging area. Here Colonel Sadler held a conference with his officers and explained the details of the forthcoming operations. Later, the part they would have to perform, was carefully explained to all ranks.

The 2nd Division was to attack on a two-brigade front, the 7th right and 5th left. There were two objectives—the "Black Line" to the west of Warfusee-Abancourt, and the "Green Line" running through the eastern outskirts of that twin village. The Nineteenth and Twentieth Battalions were allotted the Black Line, and the Seventeenth and Eighteenth Battalions the Green Line. Each battalion would be in two waves. Thus the Seventeenth's dispositions were: B (Finlay) right, and C (Harnett) first wave. A (Maynard) and D (Mackenzie) left second wave.

The brigade frontage would be 1,000 yards, the distance between lines being forty yards, and between waves, 100 yards.

The "Jumping-off Line" marked out in tape would be laid by the engineers, assisted by a party under Lieutenant F. W. Tindale, a considerable distance to the rear of the then front line. After the laying of the tapes was completed, Tindale and four non-commissioned officers would remain, the latter to act as right markers, while the rest of the party would report back to their companies to act as guides.

It will be noted that the jumping-off tapes were to be laid some distance to the rear of the existing front line; therefore, it would be necessary to bring back the units holding that area. So it was arranged that these troops, the 6th Brigade, would withdraw to its allotted concentration area three hours before zero, leaving a screen in the line, which would, in turn, be withdrawn 30 minutes before zero. The Seventeenth would be in position on the Jumping-off Line one hour before zero, which was fixed for 4.20 a.m. on the 8th.

The attack was to be preceded by tanks and would conform to the artillery barrage. On reaching the Black Line, the Seventeenth would pass through the Nineteenth, and on arriving at Warfusee would pass to the right of the village; the Eighteenth taking similar action on the left, less the fourth wave of each of these units, which would mop up the village, assisted by tanks. Immediately the Green Line was captured, the troops would dig in and consolidate the position.

One company (12) tanks, would operate with the 5th Brigade, of which one section (3) tanks, would work with the Seventeenth. These tanks would move through the infantry so as to be 100 yards in front of the Jumping-off Line three minutes after zero. Two tanks "Auld Reekie" and "Leeds" would carry extra tools, grenades, Lewis gun panniers and small-arms ammunition.

The artillery barrage would open 200 yards from the Jumping-off Line, and remain there for three minutes; thence it would creep forward at the rate of 100 yards every two minutes for 200 yards—100 yards every three minutes for 800 yards, and then 100 yards every four minutes to the "Green Protective Barrage Line." The 18-pounder guns would fire three rounds per gun, smoke, on the starting line and three rounds per gun, smoke, on the Green Protective Barrage Line. Barrage maps were made available for each company.

The Battalion would have two machine-guns allotted it, which would move in rear of the third wave. On the capture of the Green Line they would take up suitable positions for defence.

There followed details of arrangement for maintaining communications, such as S.O.S. and Success Signals, flags, ground flares, smoke bombs, tin discs and telephones.

Battle-order dress would be worn, each man carrying 220 rounds of small-arms ammunition, extra rations and two filled water-bottles. In addition, flares and tools would be distributed proportionately throughout the companies. Two officers were detailed for liaison duties with the battalion on either flank; Lieutenants G. Small (right), and E. W. Dark (left).

An unusual feature would be the attachment to each battalion of a German speaker, with two men to assist him. They would be identified by appropriately marked arm-bands.

The final instructions centred on the locations of Battalion Headquarters and Regimental Aid Post during various stages of the attack.

The distance to be covered by the first two waves (Nineteenth and Twentieth) was a little over 2,000 yards, while that of the third and fourth waves (Seventeenth and Eighteenth) was about 4,000 yards, the longest hitherto traversed by the Australian Corps.

In the Aubigny Switch trench the Seventeenth went about its preparation for the "stunt," which all ranks believed to be a "moral certainty"; and there were many glum faces among those officers and men detailed to remain behind as a nucleus for rebuilding the Battalion after the battle. "What had they done to be left out of it? Wasn't it crook?" And foremost among these grumblers were several who had served with the Seventeenth since its inception. They claimed that their long service entitled them to preference to go in with the "mob," apparently failing to realise that that was the main reason for their having received preference in the opposite direction. One sergeant, the holder of the Military Medal, when informed by his company commander that he had been included as one of the nucleus, waylaid in turn each of the other officers of the company to seek their influence on his behalf in an endeavour to get the "Skipper" to reverse his decision. A stretcher-bearer, also with the Military Medal, who a day or so previously had been remanded by the Commanding Officer on a charge of "Absent Without Leave," induced his company commander to allow him "to go in with the boys." The gallant lad lost his arm as the result of the action.

Thus far, preparations for this big-scale attack had gone forward without a hitch, but on the afternoon of the 7th an incident took place that gave much cause for concern. A German shell—apparently fired by chance—fell in the middle of a park of 17 supply tanks concentrated in an orchard on the outskirts of Villers-Bretonneux, and set some of them on fire. Would the enemy suspect anything? There followed a period of suspense, but as he did not follow up with any further shelling it was manifest that he did not think anything unusual was afoot.

As the long twilight of that calm August day closed, the tension was relaxed. Action was now the word. There followed last-minute inspection and checks. Then, at 10.30 p.m. led by its guide, each company moved off silently in single file on the approach march to the Jumping-off Line, and, to quote the words of the Australian Official Historian, "even in this night march the men felt that, whatever might lie in front, all was right behind them." Their confidence had been further strengthened when, during the course of the previous afternoon, a message from their great leader General Monash was read to all ranks:—

For the first time in the history of this Corps all five Australian Divisions will to-morrow engage in the largest and most important battle operation ever untaken by the Corps. They will be supported by an exceptionally powerful artillery, and by tanks and aeroplanes on a scale never previously attempted. The full resources of our sister Dominion, the Canadian Corps, will also operate on our right flank, while two British Divisions will guard our left flank . . .

Because of the completeness of our plans and dispositions, of the magnitude of the operations, of the number of troops employed, and of the depth to which we intend to overrun the enemy's positions, this battle will be one of the most memorable of the war; and there can be no doubt that by capturing our objectives, we shall inflict blows upon the enemy which will make him stagger, and will bring the end appreciably nearer. I entertain no sort of doubt that every Australian soldier will worthily rise to so great an occasion . . . and be animated by no other resolve than a grim determination to see through to a clean finish, whatever his task may be . . . for the sake of Australia, the Empire, and our cause.

I earnestly wish every soldier of the Corps the best of good fortune and a glorious and decisive victory, the story of which will re-echo throughout the world, and will live forever in the history of our homeland.

JOHN MONASH.

While the companies were moving forward, from all directions the clanking of the tanks was heard as the squat steel monsters, with engines throttled, nosed their way forward to their allotted positions. It seemed incredible that the enemy could not hear this, too, despite our low-flying planes patrolling up and down the position. But again nothing happened, and in due course the companies deployed on their right markers. On completion of the manoeuvre the men were ordered to lie down in the warm, dry crops. So far, so good, and all ranks, who prior to moving off, had been given a hot meal (which reflected credit on the Quartermaster, Lieutenant A. J. R. Davison and his staff), now waited contentedly for "the balloon to go up."

On the Australian and Canadian front all was quiet, excepting for the drone of our aeroplanes, which could be plainly seen in the starlight night; but away to the left, in the direction of Morlancourt, on the III Corps front, the intermittent bickering of artillery could be heard.

Towards 4 o'clock, however, a mist began to settle over the flat, open terrain, and as time went on became so dense that it was barely possible to observe human shapes more than a few yards away. This might prove awkward, as the continuation of mist and smoke might easily prove detrimental to our troops in the advance. Before long the fog had obscured even the nearest groups of men from each other's vision. But nothing could be done about it; leaders who possessed compasses would have to shape their course by these and the rest be guided by their own sense of direction after the advance began. By this time 100,000 men and their machines were waiting on their marks filled with a quiet elation and an unerring sense that victory lay before them. Not even the wet blanket of fog was to be allowed to extinguish that spirit.

At 10 minutes past 4, company commanders quietly passed the order: "Stand-to," and presently an equally quiet-voiced runner, looming-up silently out of the mist, would report his platoon "all present and correct." Meanwhile, the tanks had crept forward to their allotted positions in front of the waiting infantry. 4.19—Wristlet watches, previously synchronised, were raised to eye level, while the second hands ticked out that last fateful minute. Twenty seconds to go—10, 5—Zero! and simultaneously the gigantic orchestra of 680 guns crashed into the opening bars of the overture to the first act of the drama of the "Battles of the Hundred Days." (The term is borrowed from the title of Major-General Sir A. Montgomery's book, "The Story of the Fourth Army in the Battles of the Hundred Days, Aug. 8 to Nov. 11, 1918.")

The show was on! Force of habit asserted itself; nearly

every man pulled out a cigarette and lit it. Three minutes wait for the barrage to lift and then forward. Everyone listened intently, expectantly, for the customary retaliatory fire by the enemy's artillery; but none came. And there was a good reason for this—our batteries detailed for the purpose had blotted out his gun positions and deprived him of the wherewithal to reply.

The problem confronting company and platoon commanders was that of keeping control in the almost impenetrable fog. The course lay obliquely across the Roman Road.

Under the circumstances it was impossible to maintain any cohesion, other than in the smallest groups, so section commanders led their men forward by instinct. They came under some stray machine-gun fire, but fortunately having no visible targets, the enemy gunners' efforts were largely futile, and the advance went on slowly and steadily under the creeping barrage. B Company, the right forward company, under Finlay, their dashing young commander, who had won his commission on Gallipoli, kept steadily on and met with little opposition. Arriving at Warfusee, the company, together with elements of others which had lost touch in the mist, kept steadily on to their objective, working round the southern edge of the village. By this time the fog began to lift and this enabled B Company, assisted by tank Number 23, "Buffoon," to capture three 4.2-inch howitzers.

During the advance a fine example of boldness and enterprise was given by one of B Company's young section leaders, Lance-Corporal P. L. Anderson. The fog had begun to lift and revealed a party of about 50 Germans retiring hastily across the company's front, obliquely from the right flank. They had with them three machine-guns. Anderson, who was a footballer and in first-class physical condition, straightway led his section, which was on the left flank, so as to head off the enemy. Outstripping his men, he succeeded in holding up the Germans, who surrendered immediately they observed Anderson's section bearing down on them.

Captain Harnett, in command of C Company, on Finlay's left, lost touch with his sections soon after the advance began. However, with Company Sergeant-Major N. J. Dulhunty and ten men of his Headquarters group, under his personal control, he advanced steadily. When near the enemy outpost-line several machine-gun nests were encountered and dealt with promptly, many of the occupants surrendering to the party. Crossing the Roman road they were overtaken by one of our tanks to which they attached themselves. This tank was dragging behind it a tangled mass of barbed wire, and Harnett relates that he and his men had to keep a wary eye on the monster's movements, and give it a wide berth as it pursued an irregular course, sweeping a wide arc with its improvised wire broom every time it diverged to the right or to left. A little further on, with the assistance of the tank, this group subdued four machine-guns, killing some of the crews and capturing about 20 others. Near the southern outskirts of the village they observed, in a sunken road ahead, a battery of 4.2-inch howitzers which the enemy was attempting to withdraw. They shot the horses and captured the four guns intact, but the crews escaped. Nearing the south-eastern edge of Warfusee a battery of 5.9-inch howitzers was seen to be firing point blank on the 7th Brigade, which was advancing on the right. The enemy gunners had not observed the party, which, led by Harnett, dashed forward on the flank and captured the four guns, together with one officer and 45 gunners. Harnett, who had recently rejoined the Battalion, after a sojourn in Australia, where he had been invalided from Gallipoli, undoubtedly acted with great dash and determination, where hesitation could easily have resulted in disaster for the determined little band. They lost only three men.

Maynard, with A Company, was allotted the task of supporting Finlay, but instead of attempting to follow the oblique course laid down in orders, this sagacious subaltern gave his men instructions to turn hard right as soon as the advance began and make for the Roman road which they crossed, and after deploying to the south, moved on to the objective, keeping the road on their left flank. As the advance continued, the fog began to lift, and showed our troops on the right and left moving forward in good order. The going was easy and the enemy defence seemed to have been demoralised. Approaching Warfusee, Maynard encountered a tank, the commander of which reported that the Germans in the village were putting up no resistance. As Maynard's men enveloped the southern side, five tanks pushed their way through, levelling the buildings that lay in their path. Germans were issuing from cellars and dugouts and surrendering in considerable numbers to the mopping-up waves. In this work Lieutenants Pettit and Willard were prominent, displaying boldness and enterprise. Indeed, so numerous were the prisoners, that it was impossible to provide adequate escorts for them. So they were formed up on the main road in the direction of Villers Bretonneux, and ordered to march. A little to the west of the town, a cage had been established for the reception of prisoners, but so numerous were these that it was not long before there was only standing room in the enclosure, while an ever-increasing number of Germans were congregated outside waiting their turn to be admitted. Maynard himself was wounded early in the advance, but pluckily kept on until the objective was reached. Then he reported for medical aid.

Lieutenant Willard has related a humorous incident in connection with the taking of prisoners. Whilst in the company of Pettit, mopping up Warfusee, their party rounded up 68 Germans who surrendered. Being short of men, Willard detailed only one, Private Murray, to take charge of them and march them to the cage. The column with its lone escort departed, but in about half an hour Murray reported back to Willard. When questioned by that officer as to what he had done with his prisoners, he replied: "Well, sir, we started off well, but I could not catch up with the bastards."

D Company supporting Harnett's advance, like the other companies, was quickly enveloped by the fog and reduced to control of individual sections by their leaders. The advance was comparatively uneventful, one of the main considerations being our own tanks, which nosing in and out of patches of mist might easily mistake friend for foe. Lieutenant V. J. Sullivan, with some men of his platoon encountered Lieutenant F. H. E. Harries and a party of C Company, and the two groups joined forces. Feeling their way forward this small force suddenly heard the clanking of a tank immediately in their rear. Presently the monster loomed up out of the thinning mist, with an object resembling a thick plank of wood sticking upright from the back of its hull. As they and their men made way for the tank Sullivan and Harries shouted: "Don't shoot! We are Australians!" However the tank lumbered forward, ignoring them. As it passed Sullivan, the object on its back resolved itself into a human shape. It was Lieutenant H. J. Smith ("Smith of the A.I.F.") who had elected to adopt this quick and direct means of transit to the objective, leaving the men of his platoon to their own devices. As the tank came abreast of them he bawled a greeting to his two brother-officers, and with arms waving semaphore fashion (a typical mannerism of his) disappeared in a swirl of fog. Wright, his company commander, who had only just missed participation in this operation, had spoken truly when he dubbed Smith "The Unpredictable."

Later Sullivan and Harries joined that happy warrior on the Green Line, and observing a couple of German field-guns a short distance to their front, decided that here lay an opportunity for "Death or Glory." No sooner said than done. Off they went in a concerted rush, but, alas, the gun-pits were untenanted. Glory had eluded their grasp. On the gun-barrels, marked in chalk, were the words: "Captured by the 18th Battalion A.I.F."

Shortly afterwards Smith parted company with Sullivan and Harries, and the latter, collecting a few men in the vicinity, proceeded to examine a line of deep dugouts, nearby. One of these contained a considerable number of the enemy, who, upon seeing Sullivan—he was in the lead—signified their desire to surrender. But after they had reached the surface and had observed how weak, numerically, were their captors, some of them gave indications of becoming recalcitrant. Sullivan, realising how serious this might be for his small band, promptly shot the leading German dead. The remainder, threw down their rifles, and were placed under the escort of Private R. Barrett and immediately marched to the rear.

In Battalion Headquarters, north of Villers-Brettonneux, Colonel Sadler received a message that the Seventeenth was in touch with the enemy on the western edge of Warfusee-Abancourt. He immediately moved forward and on reaching the Green Line, at 7.10 a.m. he found elements of his four companies digging in. After reconnoitring the position, he ordered B and C Companies to consolidate the ground in the vicinity of the objective, with A Company in support at the south-east of the village and D in reserve in a position to the north-east. Battalion Headquarters was established in a quarry a little to the north of D Company's position.

The work of the tanks was excellent and their co-operation, and the skill with which they were handled in the thick fog, was universally praised by our men. It was while he was acting as an infantry observer with one of the fighting tanks, Private G. Johansen of the Seventeenth displayed gallantry. On several occasions he got out of the tank and guided it through the mist, at times under heavy fire from the enemy, to keep in touch with the infantry's progress. On one occasion he and another man killed eight Germans before he was able to return to the tank.

Immediately after the capture of the Green Line, the Regimental Medical Officer, assisted by Padre Tugwell, established his Aid Post in the eastern side of the village, and soon his post was functioning as a small advanced dressing-station, until the arrival, late in the afternoon, of the Field Ambulance detailed for that purpose.

Padre Tugwell's participation in the action created quite a stir in the Chaplains' Department, away back at the Base, and resulted in Colonel Sadler receiving a "Please Explain." It happened thus: A day or two prior to the attack, Padre re-received instructions direct from the Department to report to a certain Base Hospital for the period of operations. He appealed to Colonel Sadler, who upon due consideration ruled the correspondence out of order, as it was addressed direct and not through the proper channels. So Padre participated in the battle, and with his boon companion, McLean, gave splendid service, helping the wounded, and going in amongst the men, issuing cigarettes and exchanging jokes. History does not relate how the Commanding Officer explained away the situation.

The Brigade Roman Catholic Chaplain, Padre Clune, was also to be seen moving about the forward zone, bringing comfort and cheer to all.

And so the curtain fell on the first act in the great drama, which had been uniformily successful on the greater part of the front. Except for a temporary hitch on the III Corps Sector, all objectives set down for the day had been taken. The Seventeenth's casualties were extremely light, four other ranks being killed and Lieutenants Maynard and Sullivan and forty-five other ranks wounded. Unhappily, the four killed (Sergeant L. Maynard, Privates G. A. Campbell, H. Hanson and Lance-Corporal E. Young) were struck by a shell fired, it was thought, from one of our 6-inch batteries.

The number of prisoners captured by the Battalion was well over 200. In addition, three 5.9-inch and several 4.2-inch howitzers, eight "77" field guns, a large dump and a quantity of signal material, were taken.

Throughout the action the artillery barrage was excellent, blanketing the enemy's counter-barrage concentration of field-pieces, and rendering them almost completely ineffective.

The 8th Brigade, 5th Division, which had moved up and rested for 100 minutes in the Cerisy Valley, "moved forward in splendid style," to quote from Colonel Sadler's report, passing through the 5th Brigade on the Green Line and taking their objective.

At noon an order was received from 5th Brigade Headquarters to discontinue consolidation of the Green Line. So the troops took advantage of the occasion to do some salvage work and collect souvenirs. Valuable documents were found in the dug-outs of the 5.9-inch battery, that had been taken by Harnett and his small band.

The weather had remained fine, though cool and cloudy.

Orders had been received by the Seventeenth to stand-by in readiness to move at one hour's notice, but by nightfall it was still at Warfusee-Abancourt, and the tired but contented troops made their way towards the deep, roomy dug-outs, in search of shelter and a good night's rest.

CHAPTER XVI.

Exploiting the initial success—Low state of enemy's morale revealed—Seventeenth again moves forward—Colonel Sadler loses the Battalion—Seventeenth arrives in nick of time—Framerville attacked and captured—Many prisoners and much material taken—To Fouilloy to rest and recuperate.

THE blow dealt the enemy by the British Fourth and the French First Armies on August 8th had been a devastating one. By the end of the day nearly every objective had been taken, while practically the entire German formations opposite the Fourth Army, including reserves and artillery, had been destroyed or captured. On the other hand our losses had been extremely light. The tally of captures was enormous. On the Australian Corps front alone 7,925 prisoners, 173 guns, in addition to scores of trench mortars, and hundreds of machine guns were included in the total. The Corps casualties amounted to about 2,000.

Never before had the Diggers witnessed an operation in which all arms, cavalry, artillery, engineers, infantry, tanks, armoured cars, and air force had participated on such a large scale and had been carried out with such complete success. It was not until they saw the never-ending streams of guns and transport going forward to take up positions in order to support further attacks and to keep the advancing troops supplied with ammunition and food, did they realise the extent to which organization had contributed to the victory—organization, for which the genius of their leader, Monash, was largely responsible.

Not the least important result, however, was the revelation of the extent to which the enemy's morale had been undermined. As already mentioned in the previous chapter, up till then the Germans had succeeded in concealing it from the Allies; indeed, in his foreword to the "Story of the Fourth Army in the Battles of the Hundred Days," Field-Marshal Lord Rawlinson has written: ". . . Preparations were even made in Allied Countries for the provision of men and material to enable the war to be continued, not only through 1919, but into 1920." But this blow had knocked away the props from one of the most important parts of the enemy's defence structure, and had revealed its stark weakness. It was, indeed "Der Schwarze Tag"—"the Black Day" for the Germans.

The morning of August 9th broke fine, with a slight ground-mist. During the previous night a wire was received from 2nd Divisional Headquarters that the 1st and 2nd Divisions would advance on the 9th, the 5th and 6th Brigades to be in position just behind the Blue Line at 11 a.m. Later, this order was countermanded, and as before, the 7th Brigade would attack on the right of the 5th Brigade.

During the morning a number of conflicting messages, regarding the movement, were received by Colonel Sadler from 5th Brigade Headquarters. However, about 10.50, a definite instruction was received that battalion commanders were to assemble at a conference to be held at 11 a.m., to discuss the proposed operations, and that in the meantime the Seventeenth would move immediately to a concentration point just east of Bayonvillers, about two miles south-east from the Battalion's present position.

Colonel Sadler, accompanied by Lieutenant G. R. McPhee, his Intelligence Officer, immediately proceeded to the rendezvous, where they arrived about 11.20, and were joined a little later by the Brigade Commander, the three other battalion commanders and tank officers. General Martin informed them that it had been decided to exploit the enemy's disorganized state, and he then proceeded to issue verbal orders for an attack on the village of Framerville, about two miles east of the old Amiens defence line, which had been the objective for the third phase of the preceding day's attack. The Seventeenth was allotted the major position of the village as its objective, the Twenty-seventh, being on its right and the Eighteenth Battalion on the left. From three to five tanks would support the attack on the village itself. Two Vickers guns would be allotted to the Battalion.

In the meantime, Captain Harnett, the senior officer, acting on instructions received from Colonel Sadler prior to the latter's departure for the conference—to move the Seventeenth up to an appointed rendezvous—a point north of Bayonvillers, and to arrive there at noon, assembled the Battalion and set out for the rendezvous in artillery formation. But there was no sign of the Commanding Officer when the destination was reached. Harnett thereupon gave orders for the companies to have lunch, in anticipation of the early arrival of Colonel Sadler. Sitting or reclining in the tall crops, in the uniformly flat country, the troops were completely hidden from view, even from a short distance. Time passed, the troops had consumed their meal, but still there was no sign of Colonel Sadler. To the north and south as far as the eye could see, there was presented an extraordinary sight, as units advancing in artillery formation moved past on each flank of the Seventeenth, while a glance to the rear showed the supporting battalions also moving up, their echeloned sections presenting a stirring spectacle as they proceeded at a steady pace. It was now about 3.30 p.m. and the necessity for a forward move was definitely indicated; so Harnett, after conferring with his brother company-commanders decided to advance. Just as the Seventeenth was about to move off, Lieutenant J. G. Edmondson, attached to 5th Brigade Headquarters, came up and informed Harnett that Framerville was the objective of the Battalion and that zero was set for 4.30 p.m. The distance to be covered was nearly two miles, which would leave little time for reconnaissance and the issue of detailed orders for the attack. Without further ado, Harnett gave the signal to advance.

Turning again to Colonel Sadler's movements, we find that after the conference of battalion commanders with the Brigadier, the former went forward to the Blue Line, in order to reconnoitre the position and to draw up their operation orders for the assault on the village. Before leaving the conference they were informed by General Martin that messages would be forwarded to battalions to move up to the Blue Line. For some unexplained reason the Seventeenth never received the message, and had it not been for the fortuitous meeting with Edmondson a distinctly awkward situation would have eventuated.

Arriving at the Blue Line and having made his dispositions, Colonel Sadler began to look about for his battalion, which by now should be putting in an appearance. One o'clock, and no sign of it. He began to get anxious; accordingly he dispatched McPhee with instructions to find and guide it on to the sector. In due course McPhee returned and reported that he could find no trace of the Battalion. Thereupon Colonel Sadler decided that the search should be renewed, this time by both McPhee and himself; he was by now thoroughly mystified and anxious. Suddenly, observing, nearby, a German cavalry horse, saddled, but with only one stirrup, and quietly cropping the grass, he had an inspiration. Straightway, he swung himself into the saddle and galloped off in the direction of the previously appointed rendezvous. But there was no sign of the Seventeenth. Deeply concerned, he spurred his charger in the direction of 5th Brigade Headquarters, with the intention of checking the message sent from there.

On the way he encountered Lieutenant Edmondson, who informed him that he himself was proceeding in the direction of the rendezvous, and if he saw the Battalion he would pass the order on to Harnett. In his hurried search the Commanding Officer had missed his troops who were obscured by the long crops, where Edmondson, as already stated, subsequently found them. In the meantime, the Colonel continuing his search, encountered numerous other battalions, and just as he came up to one of these (the Twentieth), his horse foundered, so he borrowed another from that unit. This new mount was already very fatigued, and proved to be of little use, and so its rider was obliged to move at a maddeningly slow pace back to the jumping-off line, where, shortly after his arrival, he was joined by McPhee, who reported that the Seventeenth was moving up in artillery formation, a fine spectacle, indeed.

During the advance it had been subjected to constant attacks by enemy aircraft, but fortunately without any casualties. "Thank God, you've come!" said Colonel Sadler to Harnett. The Battalion had arrived at 4.20 p.m. ten minutes before zero. A hurried conference with company commanders, a brief verbal outline of the plan of attack and the disposition of the four companies, was all that time permitted.

Between the Battalion and the objective, Framerville, the ground sloped very gently upwards, and there was no sign of the enemy infantry. But above, and comparatively low, a series of fierce dog fights between the rival aeroplanes was going on.

While company commanders were conferring with Colonel Sadler, the tanks allotted to the 5th Brigade slid into their positions ready for the start.

The order of companies was as follows: A (Blackshaw) right and D (Mackenzie) left, forward companies; and B (Finlay) and C (Harnett) in rear, deployed in artillery formation down to sections, with a screen of scouts well out in front. There would be no artillery support for the advancing infantry.

A minute before zero, the enemy switched a battery of 4.2-inch howitzers on to the Seventeenth, and some low flying aeroplanes dropped their bombs on the sector. One shell fell amongst C Company's Headquarters group causing several casualties. They included Harnett and Sergeant H. Hodgson, both being wounded, the latter seriously. Hodgson subsequently died, and his passing deprived the Battalion of a fine soldier and good comrade, whose cheerfulness and good humour never failed to inspire those under his command. He had served with the Seventeenth from its inception. Harnett remained long enough with the company to hand over the command to Lieutenant F. H. E. Harries, a capable and level-headed officer, who had proved himself to be most reliable under all circumstances.

The time for the advance was at hand. The forward movements of the tanks was the signal to go. Suddenly the wide flat country-side was alive as the troops rose from their cover in the long crops. There was little artillery fire from the enemy and this was directed against the tanks, which, one after another, were knocked out. But the advance continued steadily at a marching pace. The Germans, however, evidently had no stomach for fight, for, as the Seventeenth approached the outskirts of Framerville, numbers of them fled in the direction of the village, while two officers and 150 other ranks surrendered without firing a shot.

By 5.10 p.m. Framerville was in our hands and the work of consolidation began. The enemy had retired across a re-entrant and took up a position on the opposite ridge about 1,000 yards distant. On observing this, Colonel Sadler immediately recommended to the Brigade Commander, that it would be an advantage to push on while the enemy was still disorganized and secure this ridge. He estimated that in the circumstances this should prove an easy task. Such a move would outflank the enemy at La Flaque, a group of buildings standing between the Roman road and Framerville, which had been holding up the Eighteenth Battalion on the Seventeenth's left flank, inflicting heavy casualties on the former unit. General Martin, however, vetoed the proposal.

In this action, the Battalion's casualties were again light, only two being killed, one of them Private T. Binns, while two officers, Captain E. T. Harnett and Lieutenant E. D. Miller, and 25 other ranks were wounded. During the process of consolidation, Lieutenant T. R. Read and his batman pushed on into the village of Raineville on the forward slope of the re-entrant. Shortly afterwards the batman returned and reported that he had lost sight of Read in the village, but he could not explain what could have happened to that officer. It was subsequently learned from a German deserter that Read had been wounded and taken prisoner, and later it was confirmed that the unfortunate fellow died of his injuries.

Towards the end of the long afternoon the troops were presented with an unusual sight. A British observation balloon unit had followed closely in the wake of the advance, almost to the Blue Line, and regardless of the fact that it was within range of enemy field-guns, the crew had sent their clumsy craft aloft. Unfortunately, however, about 7 o'clock, the pilot of one of our aeroplanes, mistaking it for an enemy balloon, brought it down with a burst of machine-gun fire, much to the regret of the watching troops on the ground, who had been loudly praising the brave crew.

The 2nd Division had completed its task, having taken all its objectives, though not without heavy casualties in the battalions on the right and left of the Seventeenth. The Nineteenth Battalion, in immediate support of the Seventeenth had moved up and commenced to dig in a little to the west of Framerville, but at 9.45 p.m. its commander received instructions from 5th Brigade Headquarters to move back to the Blue Line. The left supporting battalion, the Twentieth was allotted the task of forming a line of posts in order to protect the flank of the Eighteenth on the left of the Roman road, as the 12th Brigade of the 4th Division had not yet come up.

Framerville must have been used as the headquarters of a corps or a division, for the place contained a vast amount of stores and material, ranging from transport waggons to bicycles with iron tyres, fitted to the wheel-rims by series of springs. In the great orchard behind the village were numerous dug-outs and shelters comfortably furnished, probably for use by staff-officers. The orchard was very carefully approached by the company responsible for its capture, and it was during this phase that Lieutenant Smith—he who had ridden the tank, the previous day—was the central figure of a humorous incident.

Smith had observed what he believed to be some field-guns partly hidden in the cluster of trees. Collecting a party of men he moved under the cover of a hedge to a position on the flank and at a signal from their enterprising leader, the group charged with loud yells, only to find on arrival at their objective, that they had captured, not a battery of field-guns, but a group of field-kitchens. That happy warrior, Smith, thereafter, was never allowed by his brother officers, to forget the episode of the "cutting-out of the cookers."

In a nearby building that had been used as a hospital, Captain McLean found a handy corner in which to establish his Aid Post, and was also able to indulge his scientific bent by examining the collection of drugs and medical supplies left behind by the Germans. He succeeded in salving considerable quantities of these, although the building was being shelled by the enemy.

The night passed without any incident, and on the following morning (the 10th), our heavy and medium artillery began shelling. Unfortunately for A and D Companies the gunners had selected the orchard in which our troops were stationed as the target area. For nearly an hour this heavy shelling continued, and only ceased after urgent message to Battalion Headquarters, from Mackenzie, who was in command on the spot, had finally reached Corps. Fortunately only a few casualties, wounded, resulted from this strafing. Among those wounded was Lieutenant A. E. Warner.

Earlier in the morning Captain C. C. Finlay had moved through the western position of Rainecourt, in charge of a strong patrol. During the course of their investigations his men came under fire of the enemy's guns, and were, therefore, obliged to withdraw before their task was fully completed. However, during its search the patrol saw no sign of any Germans.

During the course of the day, orders were received that the 5th Brigade, in conjunction with troops on the left, would advance its line on the night 10/11 to the high ground on the other side of the gully from Framerville. The operation would be carried out by the Nineteenth and Twentieth Battalions. For this purpose the Seventeenth would withdraw its posts to the west of Framerville by 3.30 a.m. on the 11th. Zero was set for 4 a.m. At 5.30 a.m. the Seventeenth's companies would reoccupy the posts.

The attack was completely successful, and by 5 a.m. the Nineteenth, which had passed through the Seventeenth, was well on its objective, having taken some prisoners in the process.

The morning was foggy, which considerably assisted the attacking force and kept down casualties. Parties of the Seventeenth assisted in carrying wounded to the rear and in collecting prisoners. From Raineville, the Nineteenth on the further ridge was being subjected to some desultory fire from a machine-gun. Major Bateman, acting in command of the Nineteenth, who had taken up his Headquarters in Framerville, now requested Mackenzie to send a patrol into Raineville to locate and suppress the nuisance. 2nd-Lieutenant C. R. Nicholson was duly detailed for this duty and lost no time in leading his men into the village. After a close search they located the offending gun, which, together with a crew of eight, they scuppered. In a partly demolished house on the eastern side, the patrol found a German absolutely nude, who was wounded in the arm. He seemed to be quite insane, for when Nicholson and his men came upon him he was executing a wild dance to the accompaniment of bloodcurdling screams. The patrol also took prisoner a German signaller.

At 6 p.m. on the 11th the Battalion received orders to move back after dark to the old Amiens defence line, which was in due course effected without loss. The total casualties for the two days were eighteen other ranks killed and four officers and thirteen other ranks wounded. In addition, one officer, Lieutenant Read, was posted as missing.

This is an interesting extract from Colonel Sadler's report on the operation: "A word must be said in praise of the organization of the General Staff in preparation of the recent operation. From an infantryman's point of view nothing was forgotten, and nothing neglected. The information supplied as to roads, artillery, reserves, etc., were found to be correct in almost every detail.

"The rationing arrangements, too, were good. Great credit is due to the Battalion's Quartermaster, Lieutenant A. J. R. Davison, and to the Battalion Transport for the manner in which food and supplies were brought up to the forward area. The men received their rations, both wet and dry, just as though the situation was normal.

"In conclusion I feel that I must express a deep feeling of admiration of the splendid officers and men under my command. Although tired after a long and active tour in the line northeast of Villers-Bretonneux they went forward to both attacks in the cheeriest of spirits and with a grim determination to thrash the enemy and to uphold the reputation of their Battalion."

One incident in this tour in the line remains to be recorded. On the 10th orders were received for a party under Lieutenant R. R. F. Willard to proceed to Corps Headquarters, where an inspection was to be made by his Majesty the King, who had specially come to France to visit his victorious Armies. However, owing to a delay in the receipt of the instructions, Lieutenant F. W. Tindale was substituted for Willard, who had been awarded the Military Cross for gallantry in the July raid. For the same action Corporal F. L. Johnson received the Military Medal.

August 12th and 13th were quiet, and in their own comparatively comfortable possies the men of the Seventeenth settled down to enjoy a well-earned rest and to sleep. The weather remained fine and hot. The Battalion remained in this position until the 17th, on which date orders were received for the 5th Brigade to proceed to a rear zone for a rest. At 10 p.m. that night, the Seventeenth embused at Bayonvillers and was transported to Fouilloy, two miles north of Villers-Bretonneux. The morale of all ranks was high. On other sectors of the British and French fronts the enemy was being driven back by a series of blows dealt with great precision and power. Through Fouilloy there passed long columns of Germans taken prisoner by the Third Army in the sector on the left of the Fourth Army. To the men of the Seventeenth watching the unusual spectacle with suppressed elation, there came the realisation of the prospect of an early end of the war. At last the Allies were on top. Now was the time "to hop in and get it over."

Whilst the Seventeeth was at Fouilloy, the award of the Distinguished Conduct Medal to Private G. Johansen was announced.

The Battalion's casualties between August 8th and 14th totalled seven officers and 120 other ranks.

CHAPTER XVII.

*Victorious advance of Australian Corps—Haig continues his blows—
2nd Division moves up—5th Brigade Group arrives at west bank of
Somme—Monash orders 5th Brigade to capture Mont St. Quentin—
The approach march—Major L. G. Fussell displays prescience—Mont
St. Quentin assaulted—A "soldier's battle"—Operation a complete
success—High praise for 5th Brigade.*

WHILE the Seventeenth was recuperating in the bright, warm summer days at Fouilloy, many miles behind the battle zone, the victorious advance of the French and British armies continued to develop on an ever-widening front, pinning down a large number of German divisions. Realising that the initiative had passed to his opponents, Ludendorff decided on a "strategic retirement" in the Ypres-Lys area and the shelter of that portion of the Hindenburg Line behind Bapaume, as he did in 1917. But in the repetition of that manoeuvre the enemy was not allowed to withdraw with the same degree of immunity as before. On August 21st, Haig launched the Third Army (Byng) and later the First Army (Horne) on the sectors to the north of the Fourth Army, and by the 30th Bapaume was in our hands, and the formidable Hindenburg Line seriously threatened east of Arras. Another large haul of prisoners, 34,000 men and twenty-seven guns was made, and the old Somme battlefield cleared of thirty-five German divisions. While these operatives further north were in progress, the Fourth Army, conforming with the Third Army's advance, was moving on Peronne nearly twenty miles to the east of Villers-Bretonneux, with the Australian Corps as a spearhead, moving astride the Somme.

At Fouilloy, on August 25th, General Martin held a conference at 5th Brigade Headquarters, at which the four battalion commanders, the officers commanding the 5th Field Company Engineers, 5th Field Ambulance and 5th Trench Mortar Battery, were present. The following information was given to these officers: The 1st Division, advancing south of the Somme, would be relieved by the 5th and 2nd Divisions, while the 3rd Division would remain north of the river. The objectives would be unlimited. The 2nd Division would have the 6th Brigade in line, the 5th Brigade in support, and the 7th Brigade in reserve. In the course of the advance the 5th and 2nd Divisions would come up against the Somme at that part where it flowed across our front in a northerly direction to Peronne, at which place it bent back on a westerly course; therefore, it was the river line south of that historic town, which was allotted to the 5th Division as its immediate objective. Peronne itself would be the objective of the 2nd Division, whose left boundary would be the east-west stretch of the river. General Martin intimated that the advance would not be made in a continuous line, but that the 5th Brigade would act as a "Group" complete with Engineer and Field Ambulance units and probably supported by three brigades of field artillery. It was also thought that an allotment of twelve tanks might be made to the 2nd Division.

On August 26th, at 7 p.m., the Seventeenth embused at Fouilloy, and was transported to a point about a mile and a half to the east of La Motte. From La Motte it marched, via Morcourt, north of the Roman road, to a previously arranged rendezvous at which it arrived at 11 p.m., and settled down for the night. The Battalion strength was twenty-three officers and 362 other ranks. The following day orders were received that the Brigade Group was to keep approximately 3,000 yards in rear of the 6th Brigade. In conformity with this instruction Major L. G. Fussell, who was acting in command while Colonel Sadler was on leave in England, moved the Seventeenth in artillery formation into position, arriving there at 6 p.m. It was while this move was in progress that Lieutenant T. Ridley and eight men were hit by a shell, Ridley, being mortally wounded. He was a typical specimen of the aggressive platoon-leader, and had won his way up from the ranks despite the handicap of lack of education, by sheer force of character, refusal to acknowledge defeat, and by a personality which inspired all those who were brought into contact with him. The Military Cross he had been awarded, together with the Distinguished Conduct Medal and the Russian Order of St. George (4th Class) had been richly merited. His death deprived the Battalion of one of its best platoon-leaders and a stout and trusty comrade.

On the previous day, the British Commander-in-Chief had issued orders which modified the role of the Fourth Army, for the time being, to a steady advance, pressing the enemy closely on all portions of the front, while the Third and First Armies would assume the task of attacking the strong Hindenburg defences.

The 28th found the Seventeenth at Cappy, on the south bank of the Somme, the 6th Brigade, which was in the lead continuing the advance east of Herbecourt. The Eighteenth Battalion was ordered to move along the southern bank of the river to capture the bridgeheads at Feuilleres and Clery. Further orders received on the 29th resulted in the 7th and 5th Brigades taking over from the 6th Brigade, which was to follow closely in rear. The pursuit of the enemy, who was withdrawing across the Somme, would be pressed with vigour. General Monash hoped to be able, not only to clear the retreating Germans quickly from the Somme bridgeheads, but also to throw a couple of Australian brigades across the bridges and seize the high ground, in the centre of which stood Mt. St. Quentin, two miles to the east of Peronne. By thus forcing the enemy from that town and breaking the Somme line south of it, the 5th Division would cross the river six miles south of Peronne, and the 2nd Division immediately south and north of that place, the 7th Brigades objective being the high ground east of Peronne, and that of the 5th Brigade Mont St. Quentin. Peronne itself would be by-passed, and would be mopped up later. During the advance to the river the 5th Brigade would be disposed as follows: Nineteenth and Eighteenth in front line, with Seventeenth and Twentieth Battalions in support.

At 5.15 on the morning of the 29th, the Seventeenth left its position and moved in artillery formation into close support of the Nineteenth Battalion, and by 8.30 a.m. was in touch with that unit south of Meraucourt Wood. During this manoeuvre two battalions of the 7th Brigade passed through the right companies of the Seventeenth, and as the War Diary records, "making a fine spectacle."

The forward movement continued, and a little later the two leading companies of the Battalion ran into a light artillery barrage, but suffered no casualties. Here a fine sight presented itself to our men when a battery of Royal Horse Artillery trotted through into action.

The 5th Brigade was now on the high ground looking down upon the Somme. So far the advance had not met with any opposition. At 11 o'clock the Nineteenth Battalion, which had nearly reached the western bank of the river, ran into heavy machine-gun fire, causing the advance to be slowed up and eventually halted. The Eighteenth, the left forward battalion, worked well round on the Nineteenth's left flank in an endeavour to clear the enemy from a patch of wooded ground and strip of trench on the river bank, where it was canalised, but was also held up. By 5 p.m. no progress had been made, so an order was issued by 5th Brigade for the battalions to remain in their present positions pending an organized attempt to cross the river.

At 11.30 p.m. the four battalion commanders held a conference with Major W. P. McCallum, the young brigade-major of the 5th Brigade, who had brought with him an order that, by 5 a.m. on the 30th, the Nineteenth Battalion, assisted by the 5th Field Company, was to effect a crossing of the Somme, which, except where it was canalised, meandered through broad marshes dotted with tiny islets. It presented a very stiff obstacle to infantry lacking adequate bridging material. The crossing would be made opposite Halle, north of Peronne, and a bridge-head established on the east bank in order to cover the advance of the Seventeenth, which was ordered to be in position by 4.30 a.m. The Eighteenth Battalion on the left would carry out a similar crossing at Ommiecourt in order to protect the advance of the Twentieth Battalion.

But there arose an unforeseen obstacle, for, as the result of a reconnaisance by the engineers, of the river crossings, it was disclosed that, whereas no difficulty was anticipated in bridging the canal, it would be impossible, in the allotted time, to complete the operation of throwing a bridge from bank to bank of the wide, sluggish stream. At 4.40 a.m., therefore, orders for the move were cancelled and others substituted, resulting in the withdrawal of the Seventeenth, Eighteenth and Twentieth Battalions to the western edge of Mereaucourt Wood, leaving the

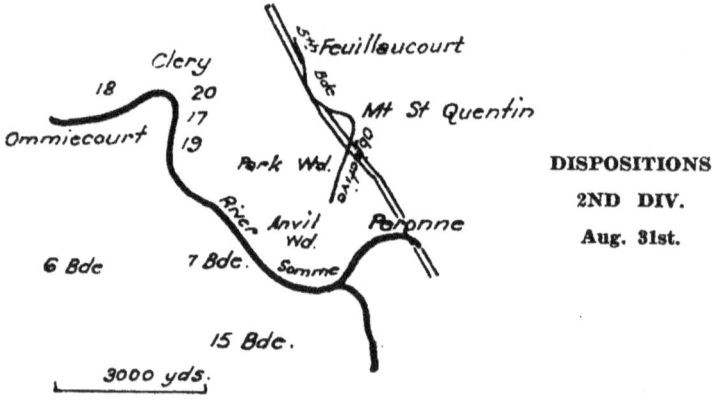

DISPOSITIONS 2ND DIV. Aug. 31st.

Nineteenth Battalion in the vicinity of Ommiecourt to cover the position overlooking the Somme at that point. The withdrawal of the Seventeenth was effected by 7 a.m. on the 30th.

The reason for this change in the plan of attack was the inability of General Monash's Corps, which, by the 29th, had reached the bank of the Somme on the whole front from St. Christ to Clery, to effect a crossing, owing to the enemy blowing up all the causeways over the river, and because of his machine-gun defence, which foiled attempts to establish bridgeheads on the east bank.

Time was vitally important. The enemy had been observed grouping his forces and organizing for a vigorous defence. The hostile shelling increased. A captured enemy order, dated the

29th, made it clear that he had determined to stand on the line of the Somme as far north as Peronne.

General Rawlinson, the Fourth Army Commander, decided to turn the enemy position on the line of the Somme and to seize the high ground north of the Cologne River from Buire Wood to Nurlu. He issued orders for the 111 Corps to attack the position from the west, and for the Australian Corps to force the river in as many places as possible at, and north of, Peronne railway bridge, and then to attack the Buire Wood-Nurlu position from the south-west, working up the three ridges which ran down to the river from Buire Wood.

South of Peronne the Australian Corps was to confine itself to seizing any opportunity of gaining a foothold on the east bank of the river.

As the advance to Buire Wood progressed, the Australian Corps, pivotting on Peronne, was to form a flank south-east along the high ground north of the Cologne River.

The commanding height of Mont St. Quentin was the key to the position, the capture of which would threaten the safety of the whole of the enemy's line. If it could be taken by a sudden rush it would simplify the tasks of the two attacking corps. It was important that the enemy should have no respite for his tired troops to improve this naturally strong position.

Mont St. Quentin itself was not very high, but it commanded a view of the flat country for many miles on all sides. Its slopes were covered with thick belts of barbed wire and scarred with trench systems, affording great possibilities for a strong defence. The ruins of the village situated on the western slope provided facilities for observation and fire.

It was subsequently learned from prisoners that the German High Command had issued instructions that Mont St. Quentin was to be defended at all costs, and to ensure this had entrusted the position to the 2nd Guards Division.

General Monash fully realized the importance of seizing Mont St. Quentin at once. He, therefore, decided that it should be taken from the direction of Clery, and that then Peronne could be captured by an attack from the north-west.

The 2nd Division was allotted the task of capturing Mont St. Quentin, and the 5th Division, less one brigade, Peronne.

The operation was planned to be executed in two phases, the first beginning on August 30th, involved the seizure of Clery by the 5th Brigade moving along the north bank of the river through the area of the 3rd Division; and the second, the assault on Mont St. Quentin and capture of Peronne and the high ground east of that town. The 6th and 7th Brigades would be held in reserve.

At Mereaucourt Wood the 5th Brigade, less the Nineteenth

Battalion, which, as previously stated, was covering the front at Ommiecourt, were given breakfast. At 8 a.m. a conference of battalion commanders was held at 5th Brigade Headquarters, and by 9 a.m. orders were issued for the three battalions to cross the river by the Feuilleres bridge, then, turning east, proceed through Clery, thence carry out the second phase of the operation.

At 10.30 a.m. the approach march began, the Twentieth leading, followed by the Seventeenth and Eighteenth Battalions. Changing front on crossing the river and shaking itself into artillery formation, the Seventeenth moved along the north bank until it reached the western outskirts of Clery, at which point it conformed to the movements of the Twentieth Battalion, which had entered Eleu Alley, part of a system of trenches skirting the north of the village. It was then about 1.45 p.m., and no opposition had been encountered. The first phase of the operation had been successfully accomplished.

Shortly afterwards, the Twentieth Battalion was fired upon from a trench east of Clery, but with the assistance of elements of the Fortieth Battalion, 3rd Division, the trench was cleared and several prisoners taken. The advance continued under a continuous sniping, machine-gun and artillery fire from the high ground to the east, in consequence of which progress was slowed down, and finally halted.

A little later, Major McCallum, the Brigade Major, arrived with orders from General Martin that the attack should begin without delay. At a conference of company commanders of the Seventeenth it was pointed out to him that as the ground to the east of Clery on which the Battalion would have to deploy was being swept by hostile artillery fire, such an operation would be likely to end in disaster. McCallum, himself a first-rate soldier quickly appreciated the situation. Thereupon he intimated that he would return to Brigade Headquarters and suggest to General Martin that he might go up personally and view the position. In due course the Brigadier arrived, and after a close reconnaisance, expressed concurrence with the views of the company commanders. Any further move forward would have to be carried out under cover of darkness.

The Brigadier returned to his Headquarters and shortly afterwards a warning order was received by Major Fussell that the 5th Brigade would probably attack at dawn. Confirmation of this arrived at about midnight.

At 3.30 a.m. on the 31st, Fussell held a conference with his four company-commanders and explained to them that the advance would begin at 5 a.m. against the general objectives Anvil Wood - Mont. St. Quentin and Feuillaucourt. The 3rd Division would attack on the left of the 5th Brigade. The order of the attack by the Brigade would be as follows: The Nine-

Maj. L. G. FUSSELL, M.C.

Pte. W. L. ANDERSON.

Sgt. M. J. McKAY, D.C.M., M.M.   Chaplain F. W. TUGWELL.

Lieut. F. W. TINDALE.   Capt. A. L. McLEAN, M.C., R.M.O.

GROUP OF OFFICERS.
(Back)—Lieutenants R. R. F. Willard, M.C., V. J. Sullivan, M.C., C. W. Warburton, R. E. Massey, M.M.
(Front)—Lieut. C. R. Maynard, Capts. E. T. Harnett, C. C. Finlay.

teenth (after crossing the river, which the engineers had succeeded in bridging at Ommiecourt) would be the right of the attack, with objectives Uber Alles and Gott Mittuns trenches; Seventeenth, Mont St. Quentin, and Twentieth Feuillaucourt, with the Eighteenth Battalion in support. Five artillery brigades would barrage the start line from zero (5 a.m.) for thirty minutes and would then lift to Uber Alles trench, Mont St. Quentin and Feuillaucourt, where it would remain for a further thirty minutes, after which it would lift to the protective line Anvil Wood-St. Quentin Wood. Machine-gun companies would be distributed amongst the attacking battalions, plus two Stokes mortars per battalion. The four companies would attack in line in the following order: A (Allan), C (Small), D (Manefield) and B (Ronald). The Battalion strength, as at this date, was shown as eighteen officers and 357 other ranks.

For the men of the Seventeenth, as with other units of the 5th Brigade, the past three days had been strenuous ones, and now, without an opportunity to snatch even a few hours' sleep, they were about to be launched into an operation which would require all the doggedness and endurance they possessed. As Allan, A Company's commander, afterwards said: "We were all so absolutely done-in that we nearly went to sleep." It was due to the forethought of Major Fussell that the tired men were able to brace themselves to continue the advance.

Perhaps the situation may be best described in this vigorous young officer's own picturesque style: "The War Memorial authorities have many trophies of the campaign, from the 8th August onwards, from Big Berthas downwards, but one that would have taken a prominent place in spite of its diminutive size, would have been the torn piece of an envelope on which was scribbled a few words written in the flickering light of a candle and taken down over one of Lieutenant Ned Raine's (Signalling Officer's) worst phones—the operation order for the attack on Mont St. Quentin.

"The words, some twenty in all, were decipherable to me only, but on being interpreted, meant that the 5th Brigade would attack next morning at 5 a.m., and that the Seventeenth Battalion would make the actual assault on the Mount itself under an artillery barrage at zero, etc., etc.

"The company commanders were called in at once, and while the attack orders were being read, one of these officers fell sound asleep, an incident that gave some indication of the condition of all ranks after their strenuous work of getting thus far; and the main attack yet to take place in a few hours!

"But such a situation had been foreseen, and two young runners had been sent back with a written order to get a 5-gallon jar of rum from Headquarters (anybody's). In the C.O.'s own handwriting, to the order was added the words: 'Do not return to this Battalion without the rum.' Then two more runners were sent back by an alternative route with a similar order.

"To the everlasting glory and fame of the A.S.C., and as a tribute to the devotion of the Battalion runners, each pair of whom came back with 5-gallons.

"It was Capt. Manefield who made the suggestion at the conference that each company commander should lead his company forward from Clery in the first phase of the attack, until spotted by the Hun, when all hands would rush the trenches like bushrangers, in the approved Ned Kelly style.

"The suggestion was contagious and was adopted enthusiastically by everybody present, despite what might appear to be its lack of the slightest resemblance to the tactics as laid down in the 'book of the words.'

"How it suceeded against Princess Elizabeth's Own Prussian Guard, who, unfortunately for them, had just relieved the Landwehr garrison troops about an hour before the attack, is now history."

The welcome issue of rum helped to invigorate the tired troops. Then began the move to the jumping-off position. Time was pressing, and it was realised that it might be difficult to arrive there before zero, as in all probability pockets of enemy resistance would be encountered on the way. Allan's Company, nearest the river, encountered fairly heavy machine-gun and rifle-fire from strong posts on the bank, but with a yell his men charged each in turn, mopping up everything in the way, and the enemy surrendered freely. The prisoners belonged to the Prussian Guard. One man of A Company, Lance-Corporal O. E. Stranlund, single-handed, charged one post over fifty yards of open ground, and although he was shot in the ankles, succeeded in killing the whole of the crew. Sergeant J. T. Rixon, also single handed attacked a machine-gun post, killing three of its occupants and capturing the remainder.

D Company was successful in taking prisoner a number of Germans belonging to the 81st Regiment. The casualties had, so far, been light, but as the Battalion approached the jumping-off line, it was met by heavy machine-gun fire from the right flank, which caused several casualties. Allan was able to observe that this fire came from the direction of Park Wood, some distance away on his right flank, whereupon he wisely decided, there and then, to engage the enemy, and thus protect that flank of the Battalion. He, therefore, arranged with Small, who, with C Company was next in line, to take over A Company's sector in addition to his own.

It was now nearly daylight. Our barrage had commenced, and soon the crest-line of Mont St. Quentin was shrouded in a pall of smoke from the bursting shells. In pursuance of the tactics previously agreed upon, companies went into action adopting a series of rushes and pausing only to fire with their

Lewis guns on targets in the form of groups of the enemy, many of whom elected to stay not upon the order of their going under the swift advance of their opponents. Here was an occasion on which the two great principles of war—Surprise and the Offensive spirit—could be given effect. And the manner in which these principles were applied is now history.

The majority of the enemy, stupefied by the audacious and rapid advance of the Seventeenth, hardly fired a shot, and surrendered. The number of prisoners soon became an embarrassment, as it was impossible to provide a sufficient number of escorts, so they were ordered to make their own way to the rear. We quote Allan's description of this remarkable spectacle: "I saw hundreds of prisoners streaming down in our direction from Mont St. Quentin, and I remember thinking that it reminded me of the mob leaving the Sydney Cricket Ground after a football final. I 'chatted' one of my N.C.O.'s who was moving back with prisoners and told him that we were all wanted forward. He replied: 'Have a heart, Sir! I've got a General here. Take a look at the beautiful spurs he's got. If I don't take him back, some of those blasted base-wallahs will get them.' So I let him go."

The advance proceeded with increasing tempo, and at 7 a.m. Major Fussell sent a message to 5th Brigade Headquarters: "Seventeenth well on objective. Enemy barrage on the western flank slopes of Mont St. Quentin gradually shortening and not very heavy."

As usual, the leaders, company, platoon and section, displayed both dash and courage. Captains Manefield, Ronald and Allan and Lieutenant Small showing a fine example by moving well ahead of their companies and thus inspiring them to greater efforts.

Lieutenant W. L. Flood led his platoon in a most gallant manner, and when at one stage his company was held up by a machine-gun, Flood, regardless of his personal safety, rushed the gun single-handed and killed two of the enemy. His daring action resulted in the capture of the gun and twenty-two prisoners.

Another young subaltern, 2nd-Lieutenant F. W. Croft, also displayed fine leadership and courage, both during the advance and in the process of consolidating the position after the objective had been taken. During the latter phase he clung to a position on the left flank of the company which was in the air, and he and his men beat off several counter-attacks.

Croft was supported by a very courageous and experienced non-commissioned officer, Sergeant M. J. McKay, who with almost reckless disregard for his own safety during the attack, exposed himself so that he was better able to supervise his platoon. During the defence of the captured village McKay again showed his splendid qualities as a fighter and leader. He was one of the original members of the Battalion.

While the remaining three companies of the Seventeenth were assaulting Mont St. Quentin, Allan, with A Company, assisted by Lieutenants R. T. Phelps and W. A. Robertson, moved forward in small groups and cleared Park Wood and Halle. This operation was carried out in the face of determined opposition from enemy machine-guns. Sergeant Rixon was again prominent, and although his group suffered severely, they pushed on until held up by heavy fire from Prague and Florina trenches. From his position Allan could see that the Mount had been taken, so he reorganized his company and withdrew to Galatz Alley in order to form part of a defensive flank.

On the left of the Seventeenth, the advance of the Twentieth had been unchecked, and about 7 a.m. that battalion reported all objectives taken together with 550 prisoners. The Twentieth's casualties had been very light.

On the right the Nineteenth Battalion encountered a fair amount of opposition, but it continued to make good progress and took eight officers and 360 other ranks prisoner, among them being members of the 81st, 259th and Alexander Guard Regiments.

General Martin now ordered the support battalion, the Eighteenth, to move to the northern edge of Park Wood and take up a position on the right flank of the Nineteenth. So far everything had gone well. The 6th Brigade, which was by now on the north bank of the river in the vicinity of Clery, was ordered by General Rosenthal to move up and pass through the 5th, continuing the advance, while the 7th Brigade, south of the river, was to cross immediately the 6th was clear. At the same time the 14th Brigade, 5th Division, was instructed to cross the Somme near Clery and swinging to the right, to move along the river bank and seize the high ground to the east, and thus secure the right flank of the attack north of the river.

On the Mount, the handful of men comprising the 5th Brigade, strung out on an extremely attenuated line, were beginning to feel the enemy reaction. On both flanks and between the widely dispersed posts of the Seventeenth, the Germans began to infiltrate our positions east of the main road through the village. C Company on the right had been subjected to heavy fire from its open flank towards Peronne. The parties of the Seventeenth were mostly invisible to each other, and entirely unsupported, so they fell back across the main road to Elsa trench. Mingled with them were men of the Nineteenth Battalion, which by now had most of its companies in position at right angles to the main road. Small, the gallant young subaltern in command of C Company moved to the left in order to try and gain touch with the Twentieth Battalion, but whilst returning from his mission accompanied by 2nd-Lieutenant J. L.

Richardson, both were killed by a heavy trench-mortar bomb. Small's death was a severe blow and one which the Battalion could ill afford to suffer. He had served with the Seventeenth since its inception, and enjoyed an unusual degree of popularity with all ranks of the unit.

The enemy shelling became more intense, and towards noon, was falling heavily on the Seventeenth and Twentieth, causing many casualties. So General Martin ordered two companies of the Eighteenth to reinforce the left of the Seventeenth. The move was completed just in time, as the enemy, following up his artillery bombardment, launched a heavy counter-attack on the hard-pressed remnants of the Seventeenth, who, however, held its ground, although desperately short of ammunition.

The position of the Twentieth, which was lining the western edge of the main road, had also become precarious, as the 3rd Division had failed to come up on its left. Enfiladed from the direction of Feuillaucourt, Major McDonald withdrew a few hundred yards to the west, the gap between his battalion and the Seventeenth being filled by the two companies of the Eighteenth and some machine-guns.

The position of the 5th Brigade was now a salient, the southern flank of which was held by part of the Eighteenth, with the Nineteenth Battalion; the Seventeenth faced east opposite Mont St. Quentin and part of the Eighteenth, with the Twentieth Battalion continuing the line, as mentioned above.

The 5th Brigade had had a gruelling time, the Seventeenth alone having been subjected to five counter-attacks, which caused it to give ground. But the end of the day found the exhausted remnant still clinging to the western edge of the Mount, while forward of the main position elements of the Seventeenth, Nineteenth and Twentieth still hung on in Elsa trench along the main road, where the Twenty-third Battalion, 6th Brigade, found them as it passed through the next morning to retake Mont St. Quentin, the trench being crowded with their dead.

At about 7.30 p.m. the enemy could be seen mustering in an area south-east of the village, apparently for a counter-attack, but prompt Stokes mortar and artillery fire caused him to disperse. The position remained precarious owing to the numerically weakened and disorganized condition of companies, while the enemy continued a policy of active sniping, making movement of our men extremely difficult. In order to alleviate the position, the Eighteenth Battalion was instructed to work up right and left of the village, but here, also, such strong opposition was encountered that the movement was found to be impracticable.

The four companies remained in their positions during the night August 31st September 1st, during which period ammunition and rations were taken up to them. Extreme care had to be exercised in the guidance of these parties, and it was due mainly to the devotion and sound judgment of the runners detailed for this purpose, that the tasks were successfully accomplished. One such instance of this splendid work by the runners, has been recorded. A young runner, Private W. L. Anderson, who, all day had been carrying messages under heavy fire, volunteered to guide a party carrying rations to C Company. After a slow and tortuous journey through seemingly endless communication trenches, the party reached a point in rear of the Seventeenth's position, when they came under heavy shell-fire. Anderson, realising the position, told the carriers to shelter as best they could, while he went forward alone to locate C Company. He had not proceeded very far before he found Lieutenant Flood and Private D. Cranny. He then returned and guided the carrying party to its destination. Anderson's pluck and tenacity was typical of that displayed by runners and stretcher-bearers. It subsequently brought the lad a well merited Mention in Despatches. His conduct throughout the whole of the operations on the Amiens sector had been of an outstanding character.

The field-artillery barrage was most effective, and a tribute to its good work was paid by Major Fussell, who related the following incident:—"During the afternoon preceding the attack, a Forward Observation Officer came into the village looking for targets and immediately found one, which consisted of what appeared to be a small, shallow trench, recently dug on the forward slopes of the ridge in front overlooking our position.

"The Huns were running, two at a time, over the crest of the ridge into the trench, and when some twenty had reached their objective, this young red-headed subaltern decided to dust them up.

"I was at the 'phone with him and suggested H.E. instead of shrapnel. I facetiously added 'Up 1,000 and twenty minutes left' at his ranging shot, but it wasn't long before white puffs of bursting shrapnel were dotted along that trench with battery-fire.

"I could not resist a bit of a dig at him as he remarked on the good shooting, and offered to bet there were no dead Huns owing to his use of shrapnel.

"Next day I walked over to the trench just to see the effect of the fire and found there twenty-one dead, and very dead at that, and one who would soon be. Let none question the hitting power of those 18-pounders of ours!

"Later I met a company sergeant-major (20th Bn.) coming back, slightly wounded, in carge of about 200 prisoners. I told him to send four of them over to the trench to pick up the only live Hun in it."

The enemy was comparatively quiet during the night, and although exhausted, our troops maintained a vigilant attitude whilst awaiting the eagerly expected relief which they expected the following morning.

And so ended the battle of Mont St. Quentin in which all ranks of the 5th Brigade displayed the greatest valour. Perhaps, no greater praise than that given by General Rawlinson's Chief-of-Staff (Major General Montgomery) could be conferred on the troops who took part in the initial operation. He wrote: "The attack on Mont St. Quentin, with only hastily arranged artillery support and without a creeping barrage, ranks as one of the most notable examples of pluck and enterprise during the war. Confronted with a task of storming a very strong position defended by picked troops, the 5th Brigade comprising only 1,800 fighting troops overcame every difficulty and gained a footing on Mont St. Quentin, which they maintained in spite of the enemy's numerous counter-attacks.

"It was a soldier's battle, throughout which the physique, individuality and bravery of the Australians were very conspicuous. There were only 1,200 men in the leading battalions when they attacked, and it is doubtful if at the end of the day there were more than 600 men covering 4,000 yards. Owing to the intense hostile fire, and with men so widely scattered, control by company officers was well nigh impossible, but the fighting spirit of the men carried them through."

Major Fussell has narrated another incident, which he observed during the course of the battle:—

"The Huns present very few opportunities for one to write up any chivalrous action of theirs, as Fritz is not built that way. But it should be recorded that at the Seventeenth's R.A.P. at Mont St. Quentin, the M.O. of the Prussian Guard Regiment, who was taken prisoner with the other officers, came forward and offered to help Captain McLean, our M.O., who was certainly kept busy enough at the time.

"The Hun doctor worked very hard indeed; knew his job, of course, and when a shell landed nearby knocking two of our men he was first over and out to their assistance.

"He took charge of the hundreds of prisoners who were held handy and sent them off with our wounded—four to each man. He religiously would not look at wounded Huns until every one of our wounded was sent back.

"The only weak part of this show was these two M.O.'s saying good-bye to each other and exchanging compliments in execrable French that would make any batman smile scornfully, but it was quite evident they had acquired a wholesome respect for each other."

The total casualties of the Seventeenth were eight officers and 151 other ranks, or 50 per cent. of the total strength of the Battalion when it entered the battle.

CHAPTER XVIII.

In billets at Frise—Reorganization and training—5th Brigade wins Divisional Championship—Seventeenth again moves forward—Attack on the Beaurevoir Line—Heavy casualties—Lieutenant A.J.R. Davison has a narrow escape.—Vignacourt—Armistice—The Final Halt.

SEPTEMBER 1st found the Seventeenth in Florina, Gottlieb and Ourcq trenches on the western side of Mont St. Quentin, the total strength of the four companies being eight officers and seventy-five other ranks. Practically all the men were accommodated in dugouts which provided comparative comfort. The casualties recorded for the day were Lieutenant E. R. Raine and two other ranks. On the 2nd, Lieutenant R. W. Pettit, F. W. Johns and S. M. Blackshaw, 2nd-Lieutenant W. R. McCourt and eight other ranks arrived from the nucleus battalion. The following day the Seventeenth and Twentieth Battalions were placed under orders to be ready to move at short notice to protect the right flank of the 2nd Division. Later the same day this order was cancelled and instructions issued for the 5th Brigade to withdraw to Frise. A special congratulatory message was also received from the Divisional Commander, Major General Rosenthal. The Army Commander, General Sir Henry Rawlinson later said that the battle of Mont St. Quentin was the finest single feat of the war.

On the 4th the Battalion moved through Clery, crossed the river at Feuilleres and proceeded to Frise, where it went into billets. There it was joined by the nucleus battalion. During the afternoon, which was fine and warm, the men's packs and blankets arrived. The next four days were devoted to resting and refitting; all ranks also indulged in bathing in the river.

Serious training recommenced on the 9th. An instruction was received from 5th Brigade that discipline and saluting were to receive special attention, and in order to better supervise this, company commanders were ordered to march in rear of their companies. Companies were cut down each to two platoons, and all personnel, such as quartermasters, storemen, batmen, runners, transport men and observers that could be spared, were to be returned to their companies.

Special attention was to be given to the turn-out and loading of the Transport Section. Recreational facilities were also catered for and a brigade sports meeting was scheduled for the 18th. Later, the 2nd Division was to hold a similar meeting.

September 11th was spent rehearsing and training for the Divisional parade and sports, and that evening Captain McLean gave a lecture on the Battle of Loos, at which he was present as medical officer of a British battalion. The same day, also, Major Fussell was ordered to proceed to Aldershot to attend a Senior Officers' Course of Instruction. He had fully earned such recognition by the capable manner in which he had handled the Battalion during the recent operation. He carried with him the good wishes of all ranks when he departed for England.

The following day Colonel Sadler returned from United Kingdom leave.

The Brigade sports were held on the afternoon of the 13th, the championship event being won by the Seventeenth by two points, the Twentieth taking second place. The Seventeenth's band provided the music. The pleasant day concluded with a most interesting lecture by Padre Tugwell, on London, where he had worked as a curate in the slums, in the early days of his ministry.

The next day a Brigade inspection was held by Brigadier-General Martin. He declared he was very pleased with the turn-out of the troops, vehicles and animals.

On Sunday, the 15th, a brigade church parade was held during the morning, and in the afternoon, training for the divisional sports to be held at Eclusier on the 16th. The sports meeting was a great success, the 5th Brigade winning the Cup awarded for the highest aggregate in the championship events, which included foot and hurdle races, mounted races, tug-of-war, and a band contest. A feature of the proceedings was a totalisator erected by the 7th Field Company, and it did a roaring business. But as most of the winners were hot favourites, the dividends were not large. One exception was the Mule Race, in which "Toby," belonging to the Eighteenth Battalion, romped home well ahead of the other "donks."

September 24th was a sad day for the 5th Brigade, for then orders were received for the reduction of the strength to three battalions. This was in accordance with the principle laid down earlier by the War Office; the reduction had already been given effect to in several other brigades of the Australian Corps. Wastage of manpower, exceeding replacements, had necessitated the step. The personnel of the unit selected for disbandment, the Nineteenth Battalion, was to be distributed amongst the other three battalions.

General Martin assured the Commanding Officer of this splendid battalion that in the selection of the Nineteenth for that purpose there was no question of efficiency or fighting value involved; nor would it lose its identity, as in future the 5th Training Brigade in England would be known as the Nineteenth Battalion.

However, much to everyone's satisfaction an order was received the following day suspending action for the present, and, as an interim measure, each battalion would be reduced from four to three companies. In the Seventeenth, A Company was broken up to reinforce the remaining three companies. The order was carried out the same afternoon.

On September 27th, the Battalion began to move in the direction of the Bussy area, and on arrival there went into bivouac. The following night it moved to the Longavesnes area. Here Captain H. T. Allan received orders to report to 5th Division Headquarters as Liaison Officer. Speculation was rife amongst the troops as to how soon they would again be in action. The preceding day, an American Corps operating under the orders of General Monash, had launched an attack on the Hindenburg defences, supported by the 3rd and 5th Divisions. The attack was not a complete success, as the Americans, in their eagerness, had neglected to mop-up enemy pockets of resistance and strong points. As a result heavy casualties amongst the supporting Australian Divisions had been inflicted by nests of machine-guns, which had not been cleaned up.

But the Hindenburg Line had been breached, and the gap thus made widened on either flank of the Fourth Army, by the operations of the French on the right, and by the British Third Army on the left. Determined to give the enemy no respite, either to reorganize or carry out an orderly retirement, General Rawlinson gave orders for yet another attack, which was designed to carry his Army over the last organized line in rear of the Hindenburg Defences, and on to the high ground to the east. This defence system comprised two heavily wired lines of trenches, called the Beaurevoir Line. Rawlinson decided to attack on October 3rd.

On the Australian sector of the Fourth Army front, the 5th Brigade relieved the 8th Brigade of the 5th Division, between Joncourt and Mint Copse. The 5th Brigade was ordered to remain under orders of the 5th Division until the command of the Sector had passed to the 2nd Division.

On the night of October 1/2 the Seventeenth moved from Hargicourt and relieved the remnants of the sorely tried Thirtieth and Thirty-second Battalions, at Joncourt. During this move the Seventeenth was subjected to moderately heavy shelling and some bombing by enemy aircraft, which killed two other ranks and wounded Lieutenant F. A. Fitzalan. The relief was completed by 2 a.m. on the 2nd.

No operation was undertaken on the 2nd, which passed without incident. During the afternoon General Martin had held a conference with his four battalion commanders, during

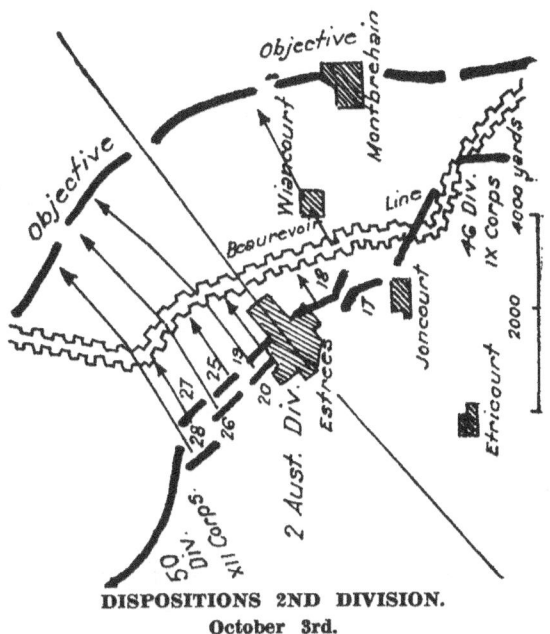

DISPOSITIONS 2ND DIVISION.
October 3rd.

German Field Gun,
captured August 8th.

Capt. A. J. R. DAVISON.

which they discussed the operation set down for the following day.

Just after dark, the enemy laid down a steady bombardment with mustard-gas shells, which lasted, with brief intermissions, throughout the night. In his Headquarters located in an old German dugout, Colonel Sadler issued verbal orders for the attack to his three company commanders. The 2nd Division was to go forward on a two-brigade front, the 5th on the right and the 7th, left, with the 6th in reserve. The 5th Brigade would be formed up to a two-battalion front, the Eighteenth, right, and Nineteenth, left, with the Seventeenth and Twentieth in support.

The objective of the two leading battalions was the Beaurevoir system, and that of the support battalions, the high ground north and east of Wiancourt. The Seventeenth's companies would be disposed in line on a 2,000 yards front, in the following order: D (Mackenzie); right, B (Ronald); centre and C (Wright) left. Four tanks would co-operate on the right sector of the Brigade. The barrage would be laid by five brigades of field-artillery. Zero was fixed for 6.5 a.m. on the 3rd.

During the early hours of the 3rd, the three companies began the approach march to their allotted positions on the jumping-off tape. It was very dark, and the low ground which they had to traverse, was drenched with mustard-gas. The advance was very slow, as the men wearing gas-masks and weighted with extra Lewis gun panniers and belt-boxes containing Vickers gun ammunition, had literally to feel their way forward. They were compelled to lower the eye-pieces of their masks whenever visibility was completely obscured. But all went well, and a little after 5 o'clock, companies were in position on the taped line, the operation being supervised by Colonel Sadler, in person. Here a hitch occurred. It was found that the artillery barrage-tables had not arrived, so Colonel Sadler returned to his Headquarters to try to locate them. Fortunately these had been delivered only a few minutes previously, so once more Sadler, accompanied by Lieutenant W. R. Haigh, his adjutant, made his way back to the companies. It was then 5.45.

At 6.5 a.m. our artillery barrage came down, and was followed by numerous flares that shot up along the enemy's front line immediately in front of the 5th Brigade. For six minutes our field-guns lashed the wire in front of the German trenches with shrapnel. Then they lifted their fire and the infantry began to move forward under its cover. As yet, only one of the tanks had arrived, but by 6.30 the Eighteenth had seized their objective on the right flank and taken a large number of prisoners. On their left flank, however, the battalion was not so successful.

On the right of the Seventeenth, D Company lost its Headquarters group when a shell fell on it, killing everyone except-

Mackenzie. Included amongst the killed were Acting Company-Sergeant Major W. G. Chamberlain and Sergeant E. G. Cowcher, two original members, and Private E. Frost, a lad of 17, who was entering his first action. Pushing through the trench captured by the right company of the Eighteenth, D Company moved down into a shallow valley running south-east, at the end of which stood the village of Wiancourt. Here it came under heavy fire from the village, causing several casualties. But the advance was not delayed. Company Sergeant-Major J. F. Watson (Supernumary) and Sergeant M. J. McKay with a party of men rushed the guns under covering fire of Lewis guns on either flank, and killed the crews. A good haul of prisoners was taken, including an officer of high rank. As there was a dearth of men available for escort duty, these prisoners were formed into batches and ordered to make their way back to our lines under their own officers. D Company's advance was delayed owing to the necessity for mopping-up the village. In this task it was assisted by the single tank, as yet, in action. Leaving Wiancourt, the company moved up the gently rising ground on the farther side, where it came under fire from a section of enemy artillery and some machine-guns about 1,500 yards distant on a ridge. The tank was knocked out, and as there was no sign of troops on either of his flanks (it transpired later that the British troops on the right had swept on over the ridge), Mackenzie paused to reorganize his scattered platoons.

B Company, in the centre, found itself unable to keep pace with D, owing to the oppostion met by the Eighteenth Battalion on that sector. The enemy machine-gun fire was heavy, but, Lance Corporal P. L. Anderson and Privates C. W. Beaumont, C. Bonner and E. S. ("Tich") Gordon, with the aid of riflegrenades, succeeded in silencing a gun immediately in front, thus enabling the company to pass through the Eighteenth, and continue the advance. But this was not effected without casualties, which included Lieutenants R. W. Pettit and T. L. Adam. The remnants moved past the left flank of Wiancourt village, where Captain Ronald was hit, leaving only one officer, Lieutenant G. K. Richmond, on his feet. Arriving at the further slope of the shallow valley Richmond took up a position on the left of D Company. He found that his men were short of ammunition, so he immediately dispatched a runner to Battalion Headquarters to report the situation.

C Company on the left was responsible for a front of about 500 yards. Soon after the advance began, the left leading platoon, under Lieutenant H. J. Smith, which should have kept the Estrees Road as its left guide, suddenly moved half right across the company front, in artillery formation. Wright saw him and his men no more that day. It transpired that Smith's impetuous nature was responsible for this seemingly unaccountable action, for observing the centre company of the Eighteenth

Battalion was meeting stiff opposition, he decided to "hop in" with that unit. Shortly afterwards he was wounded. This was Captain Wright's first set-back. The second check came when, looking across the road on his left, he saw that the Nineteenth and Twentieth Battalions had also been held up by the strong point across the Estrees road. Here, Lieutenant W. A. Robertson was wounded. The enemy wire, which was both high and thick, had not been affected by our artillery bombardment, and his shells and machine-gun fire began to take toll of Wright's company and of the Eighteenth Battalion in front of the wire. Sergeant R. C. White made a gallant but unsuccessful attempt to find a way through the wire. Moving along the Estrees road could be seen some of the tanks arriving late, but just when it was hoped they would be of assistance to C Company, they were knocked out by anti-tank gun fire from the strong point. Realising that it would be impossible to advance without further artillery support, Wright conferred with his remaining subaltern, Harries, and as a result decided to retire to a small stretch of sunken road, a short distance away, and thus give our artillery a chance to shell the wire. Shortly after taking position in the sunken road a British tank officer came up to Wright and offered him the co-operation of his tank which was behind a rise a little to the left rear. However, Wright, realising the futility of any such attempt declined the offer, and decided to await the outcome of his message sent by runner calling for artillery support. But as time went on and no reply was received, Wright decided to proceed in person to Battalion Headquarters and state the position to Colonel Sadler. On arrival there he found that the Commanding Officer had gone forward to view the position for himself, so Wright returned to his Company. Here he found a change for the better had occurred, during his absence his Company, together with elements of the Eighteenth Battalion, were in occupation of the trench from which they had met opposition. The changed circumstances were largely the result of the boldness and leadership of Lieutenant J. Maxwell of the latter battalion who subsequently received the award of the Victoria Cross.

About 500 yards in front of Wright's position the ground began to dip into the shallow valley already described, so he decided to push forward and take up a position overlooking the depression. In the three-feet-high crops the men dug furiously with their entrenching tools, under a scourging machine-gun fire from the opposite ridge, which caused several casualties. To the right rear, some 300 yards distant, was a line of gun-pits from which Wright observed a German officer moving in the direction of his own lines. If he were allowed to get back, he might be able to give his fellows some useful information. Thereupon Harries, with his rifle, brought the German down with one shot.

But the gassing, to which the Battalion had been subjected, was beginning to tell. Men, half-blind, were ordered to the rear, and soon Wright found himself left with only ten men. He could not go forward because he lacked the numbers. But he had several Lewis guns and a quantity of ammunition, so he decided to wait until reinforcements arrived. In the meantime, should the enemy attempt to assemble for a counter attack, he would be in a position to break it up. Across the Estrees road, on the left, several similar parties of Australians could be seen digging in. But, on his right, no sign could be observed of B and D Companies, which, by that time, had reached the foot of the opposite slopes where they waited for ammunition, and for the artillery support they had asked for, to clear the ridge of a couple of field guns and several machine-guns holding up the advance. Colonel Sadler had instructed Company Sergeant-Major E. F. Edwards and a party from Battalion Headquarters to move forward with supplies of ammunition, and about the same time General Martin ordered the right company of the Eighteenth Battalion to move through Wiancourt in support of D and C Companies. It was then about 10 o-clock. The arrival of the Eighteenth's company was timely for the gas was beginning to take effect on the men of the Seventeenth, already sadly reduced by casualties. Mackenzie was compelled to hand over D Company to Lieutenant H. R. Booth and retire. Later, Booth himself was evacuated through the same cause. Meanwhile, Colonel Sadler accompanied by his Intelligence Officer, Lieutenant G. R. McPhee, went forward as far as Wiancourt. What he saw there caused him to be concerned for the safety of his left flank, because of the failure of the Eighteenth Battalion to secure its objectives, the two Beaurevoir lines. He immediately returned to Brigade Headquarters and suggested to General Martin using the right company of the Eighteenth to form a defensive flank on his left. But the Brigadier replied that he did not anticipate any danger from that quarter and had, in fact, ordered the company in question to move up in support of D and B Companies, as already described. Shortly afterwards both Colonel Sadler and Lieutenant E. M. Dark became affected with gas, and were compelled to retire. Already Lieutenants Haigh and McPhee and nearly all Headquarters had been evacuated, gassed. But before leaving for the Regimental Aid Post the Commanding Officer sent for Captain Wright to take over the command. This was at about 2 p.m.

Leaving the small remnant of his Company in charge of a Sergeant (Harries having been evacuated), with orders to report to the nearest post of the Eighteenth Battalion, after darkness fell, Wright proceeded to Battalion Headquarters, and on arrival there was received by Sergeant T. Beer the only one of Headquarters personnel who had not been evacuated. After having heard his story and seeing the blankets over the two entrances to the Headquarters dug-out, Wright concluded that a third opening existed. He found what he suspected—a long horizontal slit at ground level (the pill box had been built as a machine-gun post). Sergeant Beer immediately proceeded to seal it with a long plank and a quantity of earth. He then flapped the blankets, drove out the gas that had caused so many casualties, and thus made the place habitable.

During the night of October 3/4 the 5th Brigade was relieved by the 6th Brigade, the Seventeenth being ordered to withdraw to the vicinity of Joncourt.

The following morning a muster revealed that only five officers and sixty other ranks remained with the Battalion. The casualties had been exceptionally heavy, eighteen officers wounded or gassed, eighteen other ranks killed, eighty-five wounded and 113 gassed. The exceptionally high proportion of gassed cases was no indication of any laxity in the Seventeenth's gas discipline. As related earlier in the chapter, the men had been compelled to wear their gas-masks enduring many hours of bombardment by gas-shells, and then move forward to the jumping-off tape through a poison-laden atmosphere. In the circumstances, it was physically impossible for men, laden with additional material, to refrain from removing the mouthpieces for brief periods, in order to obtain some measure of relief.

The officer casualties included Captain H. T. Allan, Lieutenants C. Blackford, R. E. Masterson, H. R. Booth, 2nd-Lieutenants W. Moore and C. R. Nicholson. Captain Allan had been attached as Liaison Officer to the British brigade on the right. Mention of this brigade recalls Colonel Sadler's tribute to the splendid co-operation of the Sherwood Foresters, the Liaison Officer from which, a rosy cheeked subaltern, showed an utter disregard for his personal safety; subsequently he received a decoration as a result of a recommendation by Colonel Sadler. The latter has also recorded the good work of the elderly men of the British labour battalion operating near the Seventeenth Headquarters. Under heavy shell-fire these old fellows maintained the nearby road in a state of repair.

The Quartermaster, Lieutenant A. J. R. Davison had a narrow escape when riding forward to Battalion Headquarters on his nearly blind, but trusty mare. A shell burst under the faithful beast killing it outright, but Davison was unharmed.

By 7 a.m. on the 4th, the concentration of the Battalion was completed, and by 9 o'clock a hot meal had arrived, after which the men turned into the possies they had built, for a good sleep.

At 2 p.m. a party, with limbers was sent forward under Lieutenant Richmond to search for the bodies of those who were killed, and to salvage Lewis gun material. The party was successful in locating most of the dead, and, in addition, retrieved five Lewis guns and 100 magazines.

The capture of the Beaurevoir Line was the last action fought by the Seventeenth, and it is fitting here to quote from the War Diary of the 5th Brigade, dated October 4th. This records that General Martin saw his four battalion commanders at Brigade Headquarters and told them he had been informed by General Rosenthal, the Divisional Commander, that General Monash was very pleased with the work done.

At 10 p.m. on the 5th, verbal orders were received from 5th Brigade Headquarters for the Seventeenth to hold itself in readiness to proceed to the Hervilly area. The following day the Battalion moved out of Etricourt and proceeded to its destination by march route, arriving there by 12, noon. The men who were very tired after their march, turned in for a sleep. On the 7th the Battalion entrained at Tincourt for the Amiens area and then moved to Vignacourt by a long tiring night march.

On October 10th, the Nineteenth Battalion was disembodied and its A Company, comprising 134 other ranks, together with sixteen officers were transferred to the Seventeenth. The officers were: Captains R. C. A. Anderson, J. S. Douglas, W. L. Trenery, M.C.; Lieutenants G. H. Peden, W. T. Bastin, C. A. Niven, R. I. Lillie, A. J. Charker, W. L. Hall, R. J. Fitzroy, A. C. Bird, A. W. Kirke, M.C.; M. Hayes, W. A. S. Hughes, M.C.; L. W. S. Seaborn, and 2nd-Lieut. L. H. Brand, D.C.M.

The loss of its identity must have been a blow to every member of this fine battalion, and every effort was made by the men of the Seventeenth to welcome to their ranks the Battalion's quota of the wearers of the chocolate and green colour patches, and help them to adjust themselves to their new surroundings.

The remainder of October and the early part of November was spent in training and recreation. At about noon on November 11th, the Battalion was carrying out musketry exercises about three miles away from Vignacourt when Colonel Sadler, who had rejoined only a few days previously, rode up with the information that hostilities had ceased, pending the arrangement of terms for an Armistice. Back in the village the rest of the day was given over to revelry, and many a bottle which had been saved by the good folk of Vignacourt for this occasion, was produced and shared around. Each little dwelling produced a French flag, which was gallantly displayed in celebration.

On the Sunday following the signing of the Armistice a solemn ceremony was held in the village cemetery, where lay the bodies of many Australians who died in field hospitals nearby. The care of the graves was handed over to the schoolchildren of Vignacourt, who had readily accepted the sacred trust. During the afternoon, in the large village church, a Thanksgiving service was held, with the co-operation of the Cure and his choir. The Seventeenth supplied its own organist whose repertoire of appropriate music was limited, but who improvised army songs in so solemn a fashion that they were not recognised by the French people.

The service was taken by the Cure and Padre Tugwell in conjunction, and went off smoothly. Lieutenant C. Robins sang "Land of Hope and Glory" magnificently. It was a most impressive ceremony.

The record of awards granted for the period of the operations which began in August are incomplete. However, amongst those who received decorations were:—Lieutenant-Colonel R. M. Sadler, the Distinguished Service Order; Captain E. T. Manefield, Lieutenants W. L. Flood, F. W. Croft, and 2nd-Lieutenant C. R. Nicholson, the Military Cross; Sergeants M. J. McKay and J. T. Rixon, the Distinguished Conduct Medal; J. Emanuel, Military Medal and Bar; Corporal C. G. Williams and P. J. Broder, Bar to the Military Medal; Sergeant R. C. White, Corporal O. E. Stranlund, Lance-Corporals A. Bartlett and P. L. Anderson and Privates G. Richards and J. H. Wood the Military Medal.

On November 20th the Battalion entrained for Bohain (then the rail-head). Thence, by march route, it proceeded through Valenciennes, Avesnes and Frisches, in wet weather. After staying ten days at Frisches the Seventeenth crossed the Belgian frontier at Sivry and billeted in the village of Silenrieux about seven miles from Charleroi, where the Battalion spent its fourth Christmas in surroundings as cheerless as the preceding three.

Early in January, 1919, orders were received for the Seventeenth to proceed to Montignies-le-Tilleul, a suburb of Charleroi, and shortly after its arrival Colonel Sadler handed over the command to Capt. E. T. Harnett and departed for England.

Late in January orders were received for the Battalion to be broken up into drafts according to length of service, and to proceed to England in readiness for return to Australia. Before long, the Seventeenth was reduced to a bare nucleus, and on April 25th the final draft, under the command of Captain Harnett, entrained at Montignies-le-Tilleul, homeward bound.

This chronicle would not be complete without a reference to the work of the departments that supplied the needs of the Battalion, whether in the thick of battle or in billets. The splendid deeds of the stretcher-bearers already have been recorded in some detail, and have perhaps, overshadowed, the consistent service rendered by the men responsible for the administrative and supply arrangements. Recognition of their good work is to be seen in the awards of Meritorious Service Medals to Company Quarter-Master Sergeant R. C. Austin, Sergeant T. A. H. Breaden (Battalion Orderly-Room Sergeant) Sergeant J. R. Mackie (Transport), Lance-Corporal J. C. Black (Medical Details), and Private W. "Spud" Murphy (Cooking).

Neither should be withheld a tribute to the fine service rendered by the succession of chaplains—Colwell, Fernie, Tugwell and Clune, M.C. (Roman Catholic Chaplain to the 5th Brigade). Their tolerant outlook and sympathetic understanding of the problems confronting the soldier on active service found a ready response from men whose religion expressed itself mainly in terms of staunch loyalty to a mate, and alacrity to "hop in for their cut when the whips were cracking."

The contribution to the spiritual and moral well-being of the Seventeenth by these chaplains, was invaluable.

The Final Halt has been signalled, and the story of the Seventeenth has ended. It is a plain story of plain men drawn from many walks of life and banded together in a fellowship born of mutual hardship and danger—hardship and danger which often tested them to the limits, both of their mental and physical endurance. In situations which might have daunted the stoutest hearts they were sustained by a gay humour and a courage typical of the breed from which they sprung.

There developed a unity of purpose and the team spirit, which the black and green diamond-shaped colour patch symbolised. And from this experience arose a Comradeship which, twenty-seven years after the close of the Great War, remains the most treasured possession in the hearts and minds of the "Boys of the Old Brigade."

THE 17TH BATTALION
(THE NORTH SYDNEY REGIMENT)
AUSTRALIAN MILITARY FORCES

THE volunteer movement in New South Wales began in 1860. In that year there was formed a company of infantry named St. Leonards Rifle Corps. It took its title from the sparsely populated district on the northern side of Sydney Harbour in which it was recruited.

From the date of its formation to the present time, the corps has performed unbroken service, and can therefore claim to be the progenitor of The North Sydney Regiment.

The year 1885 signalised the entry, for the first time, of Australian troops into a theatre of war. News of the disaster which befell General Gordon's ill-starred expedition to Khartoum, and the murder of its gallant leader, deeply stirred the Empire. In the State of New South Wales this feeling found expression in a wave of patriotism culminating in an offer by New South Wales to the Britsh Government to furnish a contingent to join the expedition that Britain was organizing for the reconquest of the Soudan, and to avenge the death of Gordon.

The offer was gladly accepted by the British Government, and on April 3rd, 1885, the contingent, comprising one battery of field artillery, four companies of infantry, and ambulance details, embarked at Circular Quay, Sydney, on the transports "Iberia" and "Australasian."

Included in the contingent was a quota of men from the then North Sydney Company (late St. Leonards Rifle Corps) of the First Regiment of Infantry.

It is recorded that on the day following the call for volunteers to join the contingent, over 200 men of the regiment lodged their applications for enlistment.

So strong was this upsurge of patriotic feeling that organizations and individuals vied with each other to contribute to the Patriotic Fund, which, before long, was swelled by thousands of pounds. A Sydney coachbuilder intimated that his employees were desirous of presenting "a perfectly constructed ambulance car"; and a large number of applications were received from young ladies from all over the colonies "expressing their willingness and desire to accompany the troops on their expedition as ambulance nurses," to quote the "Sydney Morning Herald" of the period. As examples of the generous gifts that were made, a wine merchant presented twenty-five cases of claret for use of the troops; and a company of manufacturers donated fifty cases of American hop-bitters.

The "Londoners Club" appointed a committee "for the express purpose of watching over and assisting the widows and children of those of the volunteers who may be fated not to return."

In due course the contingent disembarked at Suakin, on the Red Sea, and was brigaded with the Guards. The whole force was commanded by General Graham, who decided to march on the wells at Tamai, where Osman Digna was said to be in considerable force.

Graham's force, which numbered 900 bayonets and four guns, included the Australians. It moved out and in due course arrived at Tamai. Osman had decided not to wait, and the affair resolved itself into little more than a skirmish. The Australian casualties were three men wounded, Privates Downey, Harrison and Learoyd.

Shortly afterwards hostilities were concluded, and the New South Wales contingent re-embarked at Suakin for the return journey, arriving at Sydney on June 12th. There had been many cases of sickness, but all ranks had shown a commendable degree of discipline, which evoked the following message from General Graham to the War Office in London: "The Australian Contingent have cheerfully borne their share of hardships and have shown themselves worthy companions."

Every member received the British medal and Khedive's star granted for the campaign.

Thus ended the first venture by Australians, as a body, into the field of warfare. The seeds of a military tradition had been sown; moreover, the experience gained was, doubtless, of inestimable value when, a little more than a decade later, another and much greater event impelled men from every British colony to take up arms on behalf of the Mother Country.

This time the cause of the strife was racial. Following the Boer War of 1881, during which the Britsh forces suffered more than one defeat, the Transvaal, or South African Republic, was accorded a modified independence. From then on it was a common feeling among the Boers that they, and not the Britsh, must be predominant in South Africa. Eventually, on October 9th, 1899, President Kruger, of the Transvaal, sent an ultimatum to the British Government demanding the removal of some troops which had been sent to Cape Colony and Natal as reinforcements and repudiating the British claim to interfere on behalf of the Uitlanders. On October 12th, the united forces of the Transvaal and Orange Free State invaded Natal. The war which followed ended in the final surrender of the Boers in May 1902.

By the year 1899 the military forces of the State of New South Wales had expanded into seven infantry regiments and a national guard battalion, in addition to the cavalry, artillery and engineer arms of the service. The First Regiment comprised ten companies which were located as follows: four companies, Sydney, and one each at North Sydney, Yass, Wagga Wagga, Albury, Young and Hunter's Hill. Its motto was "Primas agat primus."

The commanding officer was Lieutenant-Colonel A. Weeks, and the North Sydney Company (E) was officered by Captain V. Horniman and 1st-Lieutenant H. W. Watts.

There was also a thirty-seven-year-old captain, William Holmes, who commanded D Company, and who, fifteen years later, was to gain a reputation as one of Australia's most distinguished soldiers, first as commander of the Australian naval and military forces which captured New Guinea in 1914; then as commander of the 5th Brigade and later the 4th Division A.I.F., until his death in 1917.

As in the case of the Soudan war, the outbreak of hostilities in 1899 was the signal for a rush of volunteers for active service. Forthwith, the New South Wales Government organized a company of infantry for that purpose.

This was the only Infantry Contingent despatched from New South Wales. It was subsequently mounted and became E Squadron 1st N.S.W. Mounted Rifles. The company was recruited from the First, Second, Third and Fourth Regiments. In addition, three men from the Field Artillery were selected as transport drivers.

We have it, on the authority of the Official Record of the Australian Contingents in the South African War, that the recruits were carefully selected, not only on account of physique, but with regard to good character; and no man was enrolled who had not during the previous year classified in the musketry course as either a marksman or a first-class rifle shot, and was efficient generally. They were required to be between 20 and 40 years of age, preferably single, height 5 feet 7 inches and upwards, chest 35 inches and upwards.

The establishment was one captain, three subalterns, one colour-sergeant, four sergeants, six corporals, two buglers and 108 privates; total 125. E Company of the First Regiment was represented by a goodly quota.

The commander was Captain James Gordon Legge, afterward General Officer Commanding the 2nd Division A.I.F. in 1915-1916. The senior subaltern was W. Holmes, who had dropped a rank for the occasion.

The company embarked on November 3rd, 1899, in the transport "Aberdeen," which had on board the squadron of Mounted

Rifles that was destined to be A Squadron of the N.S.W. Mounted Rifles.

The principal engagements in which the corps took part were with Major-General Clements's column, the relief of Colesburg, and the advance on Bloemfontein, February 3rd to April 2nd, 1900.

After a brief rest it joined General Ian Hamilton's column on April 22nd and fought at Diamond Hill. It also took part in the campaign against De Wet and subsequent operations, culminating in the action at Bothaville, where it captured seven guns.

In this campaign Holmes was promoted to the rank of captain. He was wounded at Diamond Hill, in June, and was subsequently invalided to Australia.

He received a mention in despatches and was awarded the Distinguished Service Order and the Queen's Medal with four clasps.

With the coming of Federation in 1901, responsibility for the defence of Australia passed into the hands of the Commonwealth Government, which in 1909 introduced universal training.

The new system necessitated both a reorganization and a reallotment of unit areas; thus we find that in 1914, from the North Sydney, Mosman and Manly districts, the 18th (North Sydney) Infantry was raised. It comprised headquarters, six companies and one machine-gun section. The 18th was commanded by Lieutenant-Colonel G A. Rourke, and included in the list of subalterns were the names of Blair A. Wark, who won the Victoria Cross in the Great War, while serving with the Thirty-Second Battalion A.I.F., and Harold Woodford Johnson, who served with the Seventeenth Battalion A.I.F. and later became Staff Captain, 5th Brigade. He was awarded the Military Cross.

As battle honours the 18th Infantry was given "Suakin 1885" and "South Africa 1899-1902."

On the outbreak of war in 1914 the great bulk of enlistments were by men who had had a sound basis of training under the compulsory scheme. The Australian Imperial Force owes a great debt to these young citizen soldiers who made a notable contribution to its efficiency.

Early in 1916 the Australian Government decided that the sixty infantry battalions into which the A.I.F. had expanded should have their numerical designations and their traditions vested in corresponding units of the Commonwealth's militia army after the war. Thus, these traditions would be preserved and handed on to the descendants of the units which assisted in the creation of Australia's military name and fame.

The reorganization resulting from this decision found the 2nd Battalion of the 17th Regiment under Major G. F. Diamond,

V.D., with companies at Manly, Mosman and Neutral Bay, and the 5th Battalion 17th Regiment with Lieutenant-Colonel G. A. Rourke, V.D., in command, centred on North Sydney and Artarmon.

Following a decision by the Australian Government to reduce the training period from eight to three years, a further reorganization found the 17th, in 1922, again reduced to a single battalion recruited from North Sydney, Mosman and Manly districts. Major F. A. S. Boyden was the commanding officer.

During 1923 Colours were presented to the Battalion by Major-General Brand, G.O.C. 1st Division. The colour-bearers were Lieutenants C. H. Neville and V. Levitt.

In addition to "Suakin" and "South Africa," the Regimental Colour had emblazoned on its green field the battle honours won by the A.I.F. Battalion, whose traditions the young Battalion was so worthily upholding. They were: "Somme 1916-1918," "Pozieres," "Bapaume 1917," "Bullecourt," "Ypres 1917," "Menin Road," "Amiens," "Mont. St. Quentin," "Hindenburg Line," "Gallipoli 1915."

Brigadier-General E. F. Martin, C.B., C.M.G., D.S.O., V.D., was appointed Honorary Colonel in 1924 and in the same year Lieutenant-Colonel G. F. Murphy, C.M.G., D.S.O., assumed command of the Battalion.

In 1926 the name was changed to the 17th Battalion (The North Sydney Regiment), and the motto "Facta probant" was adopted.

During the period of Colonel Murphy's tenure of the command, the 17th Battalion became affiliated with the East Surrey Regiment (the old 31st and 70th Foot) which was raised in 1702. A strong liaison grew up between the two corps, which persists. Gifts were exchanged between the officers' and sergeants' messes of each Regiment. Part of the mess property of the 17th is a magnificent silver cigarette box and lighter which was presented by the East Surreys, and is used on formal mess nights. The officers of the 17th wear the same pattern of buttons as the East Surrey Regiment, special permission to do so having been granted by the King. The officers of the East Surreys supplied sufficient buttons for an initial issue to their Australian "opposite numbers."

The East Surreys' badge, an eight-pointed star, was also adopted by the 17th Battalion.

In 1931 a new commanding officer, Lieutenant-Colonel W. G. L. Bain, was appointed. Colonel Bain was responsible for promoting an active liaison with the Seventeenth Battalion A.I.F. Association. As a tangible expression of this link, the latter body presented the daughter unit with a trophy for competition between companies. At a later date the officers of the old

TROPHY PRESENTED TO 17TH BATTALION
(The North Sydney Regiment)
BY THE SEVENTEENTH BATTALION ASSOCIATION.

2ND DIVISION MEMORIAL, MONT ST. QUENTIN.   Unveiled by Marshal Foch.

Seventeenth presented the regimental band with aiguilettes, which enhanced their smart turn-out.

Twice annually, on the nearest Sundays to Anzac Day and Armistice Day, representatives of both units have attended special services in St. Thomas's Church, North Sydney, on the north wall of which is placed the wooden cross that marked the resting place of the men of the Seventeenth who fell at Pozieres. Memorial wreaths are placed on the cross.

In 1935 Brigadier-General H. A. Goddard, C.M.G., D.S.O., V.D., was appointed Honorary Colonel of the 17th Battalion (The North Sydney Regiment) in succession to Brigadier-General Martin, and in 1937 Lieutenant-Colonel E. G. Galleghan, E.D., succeeded to the command, vice Lieutenant-Colonel W. G. L. Bain.

On March 6th, 1938, the 17th carried out the ceremony of Trooping the Colour (the Regimental Colour only is trooped by a Line Regiment), on North Sydney Oval, in the presence of Brigadier J. L. Hardie, Commander, 1st Division, the Honorary Colonel, Brigadier-General H. A. Goddard, and a great concourse of people.

Lieutenant T. B. O'Shanesy carried the Colour.

On the outbreak of war in September, 1939, the Battalion was detailed to guard vulnerable points in the fortress area north of Sydney, oil stores and other key points.

The following December, together with the rest of the 9th Brigade, the 17th went into camp at Liverpool for one month.

The Battalion volunteered to transfer in a body as a unit of the 2/A.I.F. that was being raised, but the offer was declined by the authorities. There followed a rush for enlistment individually. About this time (May 1940) additional divisions were being formed for overseas service and one of the new units was to be named 2/17th Battalion. Nine officers and a quota of other ranks of the militia unit were selected to form the nucleus of the new battalion. Colonel Galleghan was appointed to the command of the 2/30 Battalion A.I.F. He took with him seventeen officers of the 17th.

Galleghan showed great gallantry during the Malayan campaign, in which the 8th Division took part. He was subsequently awarded the Distinguished Service Order.

Lieutenant-Colonel C. E. Morgan, M.M., succeeded to the command of the 17th. Under his energetic leadership the battalion reached a high state of efficiency. High hopes were held that it would be transferred to an operational area north of Australia to help stem the threatened Japanese invasion.

All ranks were fighting fit. Marches of twenty-five miles a day across country were commonplace. Extensive training was carried out in the rugged country north-west of Sydney.

An epic of this training was a march of thirty-eight miles in eleven hours, after a week of strenuous manoeuvres. The whole Battalion, including clerks, cooks and motor transport drivers, marched. All ranks carried 100 rounds of ammunition and two grenades, while each section carried its own Bren guns. Twelve men only dropped out through exhaustion and sore feet.

The expectations of fighting as a unit were not to be realised. In October 1942, in common with certain battalions, the 17th was required to supply 600 other ranks as reinforcements to units in the battle area.

The following month the remnants of the Battalion went into camp north-west of Sydney and carried out a modified form of training, mainly in the form of classes for officers and non-commissioned officers.

During this period the Battalion was given the task of fostering 6,000 troops of the 9th Division, which had just returned from its brilliant campaigns in North Africa. Included in this force was the 2/17th Battalion.

The 17th remained in cadre formation until January 1944, when orders were received for its disembodiment, the remaining personnel being drafted as general reinforcements to the A.I.F.

The final act in the life of the 17th Battalion (The North Sydney Regiment) was staged on Sunday, April 24th, 1944, when the ceremony of the laying-up of the colours was carried out at St. Thomas's Church, North Sydney. Included in the congregation of over 1,000 persons were members of the 2/17th and veterans of the Seventeenth Battalion A.I.F. The ceremony was both colourful and impressive, and provided a fitting "curtain" on the life of the Regiment.

It is hoped that, the war ended, the 17th Battalion (The North Sydney Regiment) will be re-formed, and thus be enabled to carry on the glorious traditions of the two service battalions which carried that honoured title.

Nominal Roll

No.	Name.
3	ABBEY, James Edward
3208	ABBOTT, Arthur Roy
158	ABBOTT, Frederick
412	ABBOTT, James Elleby
4351	ABBOTT, Oswald Victor
1340	ABBOTT, Sydney
6762	ABDULLAH, Charles
3810	ABELL, Joseph Frederick
6767	ABERLEY, Alex. L. E.
4651	ABRAHAMS, Clarence N.
6028	ABRAHAMS, Francis Wm.
4051	ACKLAND, Arthur Bell
6030	ACKRALL, William John
7009	ADAIR, James
5536	ADAM, David Ford
Lt.	ADAM, Thomas Laurie
1876	ADAMS, Frank Edward
1126	ADAMS, Lancelot William
4823	ADAMS, Richard Alfred
4353	ADAMS, Sidney Leopold
476	ADAMSON, Cuthbert D.
6026	ADAMSON, Joseph
795	ADAMSON, William
813	ADDISON, Percival Ed.
3451	ADSHEAD, William
4658	AGNEW, Andrew
809	AGNEW, Clement Ogilvie
2270	AGNEW, James Josiah
4653	AHERN, Eugene
Lt.	AITKEN, James
2551	AITKEN, John
1506	AKERMAN, William
2101	AKERS, William
7158	ALCHIN, Herbert
7159	ALCHIN, Horace
1128	ALDWORTH, Arthur
6516	ALEWOOD, Sydney Geo.
6651	ALEXANDER, Bruce P.
7007	ALEXANDER, George
2872	ALEXANDER, Jessel A.
484	ALEXANDER, Robert
812	ALGIE, Arthur
810	ALLAN, Hugh E. U.
Capt.	ALLAN, Herbert T.
6027	ALLAN, John Horseburgh
2326	ALLEN, Alfred Robert
2327	ALLEN, George
1877	ALLEN, George Alfred

No.	Name.
2554	ALLEN, George William
6272	ALLEN, Herbert Fredk.
Lt.	ALLEN, Joshua Henry
Capt.	ALLEN, Leslie St. John
801	ALLEN, Sidney T.
1653	ALLEN, Thomas James
2128	ALLEYN, William
6393	ALLPORT, Joseph C.
6425	ALLUM, William Henry
6899	ALLSEP, Alfred John
2328	AMERY, Pirie
5781	AMY, Arthur F. L.
6763	ANDERSON, Abner
4653	ANDERSON, Albert M.
5939	ANDERSON, Alec L.
153	ANDERSON, Alexander
803	ANDERSON, C. J. S.
5537	ANDERSON, John
4354	ANDERSON, John Alex.
5295	ANDERSON, Lawrence
2773	ANDERSON, Percy A.
4655	ANDERSON, Peter L.
Capt.	ANDERSON, Robert C.
3758	ANDERSON, Wilfred L.
1508	ANDERSON,, William V.
1510	ANDERSON, William G.
428	ANDREW, John
1652	ANDREW, Tasman B.
811	ANDREWS, Albert
3209	ANDREWS, Charles G.
6032	ANDREWS, Edward T.
479	ANDREWS, Harold Dale
807	ANDREWS, Richard S.
157	ANDREWS, Thomas
155	ANNETT, William John
1879	ANSELL, Thomas
486	ANTHONY, Frederick J.
2106	ANTROBUS, William D.
4656	APLIN, Frederick John.
1880	APPEL, Leslie
806	APPLETON, Horace L.
805	APPLETON, Joseph R.
156	ARBUCKLE, James
4052	ARCHER, Aubrey Leslie
5292	ARGALL, Preston E.
6031	ARMITAGE, William D.
6517	ARMOUR, Melville

No.	Name.	No.	Name.
1129	ARMSTRONG, Cecil Roy	497	BALL, Thomas
5173	ARNOLD, Bert	3455	BALMAIN, James
390	ARNOLD, Gerald Tinlin	3454	BALMAIN, Peter
5782	ARNOLD, William C.	5784	BALSTRUP, Gordon H.
7008	ARTHUR, Charles G.	3254	BANBURY, Eddie C.
9672	ARTHY, Clarence H. W.	2918	BANBURY, Gavin Irving
6518	ASH, Ben	2331	BANKS, George W.
4053	ASHBROOKE, George	1060	BANNISTER, James W.
6519	ASHCROFT, George C.	1883	BARATGIN, Richard R.
1507	ASHTON, William G.	5303	BARBER, Andrew M.
480	ASQUITH, Edward H.	a1505	BARBER, Ernest
4054	ATKINS, Clarence H.	6778	BARCLAY, Alexander
4355	ATKINSON, Ernest	b2865	BARDEN, Cecil James
7006	ATKINSON, George H.	420	BARKER, Clive
4657	ATKINSON, Herbert	1503	BARKER, Lambert M.
3751	ATTHILL, Arthur Noel	3469	BARKER, William F. J.
4055	ATTWOOD, John N.	170	BARKS, John Henry
4973	ATTWOOD, Percy	499	BARLING, Frederick S.
15301	AUGHTON, Edward	4358	BARNES, Edward
2912	AUHL, Walter Edward	171	BARNES, Herbert
481	AULD, Alexander	4057	BARNES, Hiram Walter
6161	AUSTEN, Hurben Sydney	824	BARNES, James
5291	AUSTIN, Frederick	3017	BARNES, Leslie Ernest
482	AUSTIN, Ralph Aslin	5311	BARNES, Samuel
802	AUSTIN, Reginald C.	6779	BARNES, Stanley
1652	AUSTIN, Robert G.	Capt.	BARNETT, Frederick G.
808	AYERS, William	1663	BARNIER, James A.
5293	AYLIN, Charles Arthur	500	BARR, James W. J.
5296	AYLING, Albert Edward	3021	BARRELL, George W.
814	BACK, Frank	1130	BARRETT, Richard
a2859	BACKHOUSE, Leslie J.	1519	BARRETT, William
6769	BACON, Frederick W.	1345	BARRIE, Walter James
4056	BADGER, Alfred Reg.	4359	BARRINGHAM, Horace
4659	BAGGETT, Arthur E.	5301	BARRY, John
827	BAGNELL, Roy	2585	BARTLETT, Alfred
1881	BAGULEY, Samual R.	4977	BARTLETT, Bertie C.
2468	BAILEY, Gilbert	1615	BARTLETT, James S.
5783	BAILEY, Harry Curno	4660	BARTLETT, Josepn John
1363	BAILEY, Henry James	834	BARTLETT, Owen J. T.
1882	BAILEY, Neil Roy	2579	BARTLETT, Thomas
159	BAILEY, Thomas Robert	5785	BARTLETT, William
1611	BAILEY, William Elvin	6402	BARTOLO, Charles
4376	BAILLIE, Donald	3477	BARTON, Charles H.
169	BAIN, John	1520	BARTON, David
5453	BAKER, Arthur P. A.	6520	BARWELL, James
1603	BAKER, Charles Robert	1884	BASSETT, Thomas
4976	BAKER, Edwin Charles	a1695	BATMAN, Lionel E.
5307	BAKER, Ernest James	502	BATT, Logan
2330	BAKER, Frederick	1070	BATTEN, Leonard
2469	BAKER, Norman Selwyn	4661	BATTLE, Ernest James
2542	BAKER, Percival George	1513	BATY, Henry S.
2589	BAKER, William Charles	6436	BAUDEN, Walter E.
496	BALDWIN, Archdale J. R.	6034	BAVID, Frederick John
5297	BALDWIN, George E.	1505	BAXTER, Albert E.
4973	BALDWIN, Gerald	159	BAXTER, Robert G.
4974	BALDWIN, Thomas	1131	BAYLISS, Kenneth H.

No.	Name.
1132	BAYLISS, Leslie
1660	BEALE, Cecil Ernest
4058	BEALIN, Francis Mark
1812	BEATON, Arthur T.
2292	BEATTIE, Ernest F.
6273	BEATTIE, James Leslie
2291	BEATTIE, Joseph N.
4662	BEAUMONT, Charles W.
3022	BEAUMONT, Walter H.
1521	BECKE, Samuel
1658	BECKER, Ambrose E.
2567	BECKETT, William A.
3763	BECKHAUS, Andrew B.
4360	BECKINGHAM, Roy
1886	BECKMAN, Victor W.
4060	BEDDOWS, Arthur H.
4061	BEDDOWS, George John
871	BEER, Thomas
6521	BEGER, Cyril John
503	BEGG, James
426	BEGG, Percy Campbell
2465	BEHAGG, Frederick
1636	BEHAN, Maurice James
5538	BEHETS, Arthur L.
4067	BEHRENS, Frederick E.
Lt.-Col.	BEIERS, Harold M.
2595	BEITSCH, John G. W.
1516	BELL, Henry George
2109	BELL, Leonard
817	BELL, Robert
1394	BELL, Scott
4362	BELL, Walter George
2334	BELLEW, Thomas C.
6274	BENFIELD, Joseph P.
1133	BENNETT, George
4363	BENNETT, Harry O.
2568	BENNETT, John
164	BENNETT, John Edward
3770	BENNETT, Norman
402	BENNETT, Percy
1054	BENNETT, Samuel
4377	BENNETT, Walter F.
4978	BENSLEY, Dudley O.
4375	BENSON, Charles Leslie
1515	BENTLEY, Herman F.
3458	BERGHOFER, Victor A.
a1659	BERNARD, Frank
1134	BERNBERG, Roy
3464	BERRY, Albert Charles
6400	BERRY, Charles Joseph
6771	BESHEWATIE, George J.
1616	BETLAND, Ernest
6766	BETTS, Edward
6781	BEVERLEY, Alfred E.
818	BEWLEY, George R.
6275	BICKNELL, William J.

No.	Name.
a2864	BINNS, Thomas
1814	BIRCH, Clyde Mc.
6715	BIRCHALL, Henry
4364	BIRD, Larry
487	BIRD, Leslie James
6037	BISHOP, Benjamin F.
1661	BISHOP, Charles Leslie
5791	BISHOP, Stanley
4667	BISSETT, Colin
488	BLACK, George Scott
5789	BLACK, Hector
1395	BLACK, Jack Colin
a1607	BLACK James
160	BLACK, Sydney George
2591	BLACK, William
1135	BLACKBURN, William H.
6175	BLACKETT, John T.
Lt.	BLACKFORD, Charles
2110	BLACKLER, John Cecil
6044	BLACKMAN, Norman W.
Lt.	BLACKSHAW, Sydney M.
6772	BLACKSTONE, Jack H.
1136	BLACKWOOD, John
775	BLAIKIE, John
4668	BLAIR, Harry
1511	BLAIR, William
2111	BLAKE, Herbert Percy
4374	BLAKE, Lindsay T.
1657	BLAKER, Charles M.
2596	BLANCH, Edward C.
4064	BLANCHARD, Alfred S.
6773	BLANCHE, Laurence
7017	BLAND, William Henry
2336	BLAXLAND, Keith H.
4669	BLENNERHASSETT, Richard Newman
6774	BLISS, Sydney John
1817	BLOOM, Julius Sydney
6385	BLYTH, William
2563	BOARDMAN, Leslie M.
3783	BOESENBERG. Clar. J.
1137	BOLTON, Cecil J. F.
4381	BOLTON. Richard
4671	BOND, William
5539	BONE, George Albert
1138	BONHAM, Percy Alfred
4670	BONNER, Charles W. A.
414	BONNER, John
4981	BOON. Eric David John
2570	BOOTH, Eric Lyster
Lt.	BOOTH, Henry R.
1887	BOOTH, John Henry
1139	BOOTH, Walter
1140	BORTZELL, Samuel
6276	BOSTON, Leslie
1662	BOSWELL, Frederick J.

No.	Name.
1141	BOSWELL, Stephen A.
4675	BOTHAMLEY, Wilf. S.
172	BOTT, Hubert Ebenezer
3470	BOTTCHER, Albert
4673	BOTTLEY, Henry
1665	BOURKE, Francis R.
3778	BOWDEN, Arthur H.
4365	BOWDEN, Edwin F.
4871	BOWEN, Michael
1142	BOWER, Samuel James
5788	BOWLING, Alexander
161	BOWMAKER, John M.
7016	BOWMAN, Arthur P.
6041	BOWMAN, Tom
3452	BOWSHER, William E. A.
1143	BOXALL, Albert Henry
180	BOYD, George
828	BOYD, William Edward
4676	BOYLE, Francis A.
4382	BOYS, James Henry
b2865	BOYTON, Gordon S.
6776	BRABSTON, William
3774	BRADBROOK, Chas. F.
3468	BRADDOCK, Arthur W.
Lt.	BRADFORD, Bert
4677	BRADFORD, Robert B.
5792	BRADFORD, William
1888	BRADLEY, Henry
2112	BRADLEY, Reginald C.
5304	BRADLEY, Robert
3768	BRAGG, Leonard
5786	BRAMALL, Arthur T.
1377	BRANDISH, Edward
6528	BRANDON, Samuel
4832	BRANSON, George
6277	BRASINGTON, Moss V.
6278	BRASINGTON, Wm. J. P.
173	BRATTON, George W.
1628	BRAY, Albert Charles
2580	BRAY, Frank
6035	BRAY, John C.
6780	BRAYE, Arthur
2471	BREADEN, Thomas A. H.
1326	BREADNER, Cecil G.
7170	BREEZE, Ernest G. G.
3767	BREMMER, Colic Mc.
7129	BRENNAN, Edward
5306	BRENNAN, George
489	BRENNAN, Henry
5600	BRENNAN, Hylton
819	BRENNAN, Patrick A.
784	BRENNAN, Thomas T.
4366	BRENOCK, William J.
1144	BRETT, Arthur James
787	BREWER, Edward G.
2113	BREWER, Hector Robert

No.	Name.
789	BREWER, John Henry
1890	BRIANT, Thomas A.
2339	BRIDGE, Benjamin T.
6474	BRIGDEN, Henry C.
1655	BRIGDEN, Stanley S.
3762	BRIGGS, Frank
7172	BRIGGS, Matthew
1145	BRINDLEY, Clive C.
823	BRINKER, Harry
6527	BRISBY, Frank
1146	BRISCOE, Alfred E.
763	BRITT, George T.
4068	BRITTEN, Joseph
6045	BROADBENT, George C.
5681	BRODER, Patrick John
6036	BRODIE, Robert A.
a2867	BROGDEN, William A.
395	BROOKES, Walter
2232	BROOKS, Cyril William
4069	BROOKS, Ernest E. J.
1378	BROOKS, Harold Weston
165	BROOKS, John Alfred
2340	BROOKS, Thomas A.
7015	BROSIE, Cyrus David
Hon. Lt-Col.	BROWN, Arthur B. D.
Lt.	BROWN, Arthur Spencer
491	BROWN, Cecil John
1877	BROWN, Charles Roy
5545	BROWN, Clarence H.
490	BROWN, Claud Charles
394	BROWN, Ernest
Lt.	BROWN, Frank
2466	BROWN, Frederick W.
5300	BROWN, George
4678	BROWN, George C.
3779	BROWN, George R. G.
50834	BROWN, Gordon W.
2/Lt.	BROWN, Harold
4070	BROWN, Harold W.
2341	BROWN, Henry F.
4368	BROWN, Herbert L.
2581	BROWN, James S. D.
6522	BROWN, Jerome S. T.
5302	BROWN, Jesse William
1613	BROWN, John Michael
3456	BROWN, Leslie
3785	BROWN, Oscar W.
6279	BROWN, Rupert
3457	BROWN, Thomas Henry
5310	BROWN, Thomas W.
4683	BROWN, Walter B.
492	BROWN, William
1504	BROWN, William
5544	BROWN, William Henry
163	BROWN, William H. J.

No.	Name.
6040	BROWN, William S.
166	BROWNE, Alfred B.
829	BROWNE, Herbert F. T.
1149	BROWNLOW, Stanley
5299	BRUCE, Allan R. W.
1150	BRUCE, Herbert F.
Maj.	BRUCE, Herbert Leslie
5790	BRUCE, Roderick M. L.
5312	BRUCE, Stanley N.
838	BRUSH, Robert Sydney
2273	BRYANT, Benjamin
821	BRYANT, George
1893	BRYANT, Henry
5787	BRYANT, Walter A. A.
3456	BRYANT, William A.
2285	BRYCE, James Sydney
1512	BUCHANAN, Angus Mc.
4380	BUCHANAN, Charles E.
3773	BUCHANAN, Ernest G.
1894	BUCHANAN, Herbert E.
3760	BUCHANAN, Robert S.
7019	BUCK, Frank E. B.
3782	BUCKINGHAM, George M.
4370	BUCKINGHAM, Rupert G.
2036	BUCKLAND, Frank M.
7014	BUCKLEY, Edward T.
4075	BUCKMAN, Donald
3776	BUCKRIDGE, George W.
2593	BUDD, Arnold
1548	BUERCKNER, George L.
6777	BUFFREY, Leonard J.
Lt.	BUHL, Leo
a2860	BULMER, David
6523	BULMER, Edward W.
a2863	BULMER, Emanuel
822	BUNKER, Albert E.
1151	BURGESS, Ernest H.
748	BURGESS, Francis A.
6280	BURGESS, Frederick G.
6042	BURGESS, Leslie Hope
6473	BURGESS, Walter F.
4565	BURGESS, William
5440	BURGESS-KILOH, Theodore William
1895	BURGIS, John Robert
6043	BURKE, Alexander
4352	BURKE, Edward
5559	BURKE, Leonard V.
6038	BURKE, Thomas
175	BURKE, Thomas Francis
6281	BURKETT, William
1152	BURLEY, Frederick W.
833	BURN, Matthew R.
2914	BURNETT, Gordon J.
2343	BURNS, Francis
6289	BURR, Frederick

No.	Name.
3461	BURRELL, William H. T.
4074	BURT, William Alfred
2344	BURTON, Charles H.
4378	BURTON, Charles J.
5919	BURTON, Charles W.
2345	BURTON, Robert A.
Capt.	BUSBY, Harold Oscar
6033	BUSH, Thomas H. V.
3780	BUTCHER, Percy B.
367	BUTLER, Arthur
7012	BUTLER, Harry W.
1153	BUTLER, Roy
7130	BUTT, Harry
1896	BUTTERWORTH, J. B.
6681	BUTTSWORTH, Wesley.
5793	BYDEN, Harold
1154	BYFORD, John
5305	BYRAM, George W.
5541	BYRNE, David Joseph
b2866	BYRNE, Harold Sydney
7018	BYRNE, Herbert John
3466	BYRON, Edward
3467	BYRON, Thomas John
3792	CABLE, Charles G. C.
Maj.	CADDY, James Pascoe
1897	CAESAR, Cuthbert S.
1679	CAHALAN, Andrew E.
1524	CAHILL, Henry
190	CAHILL, Thomas James
7174	CALDWELL, Allan E.
4076	CALLAN, John N.
5546	CALLAWAY, Henry
6410	CALLOWAY, Herbert F.
5799	CALMAN, Walter L.
6794	CAMBRIDGE, John
1898	CAMBRIDGE, Rich. M. O.
1156	CAMERON, Alexander
a2049	CAMERON, Donald C.
2114	CAMPBELL, Angus
7026	CAMPBELL, Arthur L.
6900	CAMPBELL, Clarence S.
504	CAMPBELL, Claud
1522	CAMPBELL, Colin
5795	CAMPBELL, Edward A.
851	CAMPBELL, George H.
5328	CAMPBELL, Glen Allan
6291	CAMPBELL, Gordon
1159	CAMPBELL, John K.
179	CAMPBELL, Joseph
5685	CAMPBELL, Matthew T.
6895	CAMPBELL, Reginald
6541	CAMPBELL, Robert E.
6292	CAMPOS, Miguel
7023	CAMPTON, John Joseph
2889	CAMROUX, William H.
6048	CANAVAN, Richard

No.	Name.	No.	Name.
6660	CANNON, George H.	3811	CHANDLER, Samuel
6896	CANNON, Michael F.	6407	CHANT, Walter C.
2116	CANSDELL, Dudley S.	5549	CHAPLAIN, Percy C. M.
6427	CANSDELL, William J.	1525	CHAPLIN, George C.
507	CANT, William	5548	CHAPMAN, Alfred E.
3488	CANTELLO, John	1527	CHAPMAN, Morrice
7131	CAPARARO, Oliver C.	1799	CHAPMAN, Robert
982	CAPELL, Thomas Mayo	7133	CHAPMAN, Sidney H.
505	CAPLE, Francis James	7162	CHAPMAN, William J
506	CAREW, Joseph Henry	Lt.	CHAPMAN, William S. B.
547	CAREY, George	406	CHAPPELOW, David
2124	CAREY, George William	6411	CHAPPLE, Willaim E.
7173	CARGILL, Sidney Daniel	855	CHARLES, Frank
1381	CARLOW, Charles	1526	CHARLTON, John Pender
5320	CARLOW, Jack Mervyn	5551	CHARTERS, Alfred
529	CARMICHAEL, Robert D.	Lt.	CHEADLE, Francis B.
6283	CARMICHAEL, Sydney V.	1944	CHESSELLS, George A.
852	CARNEGIE, Thomas L. M.	2121	CHESSOR, William
5797	CARNEY, John T. D. D.	5550	CHEVERTON, Frank W.
2620	CARNLEY, George H.	1901	CHICK, Gordon John
1667	CARR, John Errol	2038	CHILDS, George Henry
7022	CARR, Reginald Francis	1354	CHINCHI, Alfred John
425	CARR, Reighman L. P.	1531	CHISHOLM, Joseph
2118	CARRIGAN, Hilton W.	187	CHISHOLM, Kenneth B.
2119	CARROLL, Cecil W.	7134	CHOPIN, Charles F. G.
5323	CARROLL, Richard J.	510	CHRISTENSEN, Lars P.
4989	CARROLL, William G.	a1519	CHRISTIE, George
5326	CARRUTHERS, Wm. G.	183	CHRISTOPHER, James
1160	CARSTENS, Fred	511	CHURCH, Cyril
2120	CARTER, Arthur W.	a747	CHURCHE, Herbert E.
2347	CARTER, Ernest C. H.	521	CHURCHILL, William J.
6282	CARTER, Joseph E.	519	CHURCHYARD, A. E.
5672	CARTER, Rupert A.	4691	CHURTON, Ernest R.
4676	CARTER, William H.	5334	CLARK, Frederick H.
2877	CASEY, John	a1614	CLARK, Frederick W.
1161	CASEY, Sydney William	2122	CLARK, James
5547	CASHMAN, Francis T.	b2880	CLARKE, Cecil Richard
5688	CASON, William Gatton	2037	CLARKE, Charles
5427	CASSELS, Robert	6053	CLARKE, Harry George
508	CASSIDY, Edward W.	1904	CLARKE, Jack Mortimer
6422	CASSIDY, Thomas E.	1903	CLARKE, Joseph
6543	CASWELL, Henry D. V.	2349	CLARKE, Leo Alexander
6784	CATHELS, James	522	CLARKE, Leslie Charles
4079	CATOR, Ernest	858	CLARKE Noble William
2235	CATTS, Arthur George	5796	CLARKE, William Joseph
509	CAVANAGH, Harry C.	3482	CLAUSEN, Hans Ove C.
1163	CAVANAGH, Horace W.	530	CLAY, George William
853	CHADWICK, Geoffrey	1905	CLEAR, John
1164	CHAFFE, John	5332	CLEARY, Joseph
1899	CHALK, Joseph F.	1629	CLEAVE, Charles Sydney
1362	CHAMBERLAIN, Wm. G.	427	CLEAVES, Arthur Leslie
854	CHAMBERLIN, John	4387	CLEGG, William Roy
3789	CHAMBERS, Alfred H.	3793	CLELAND, Duncan
6286	CHAMBERS, James J.	6775	CLEMENT, David Lionel
Capt.	CHAMBERS, Leslie K.	6050	CLEMENTS, William P.
4385	CHANDLER, Henry A.	520	CLEMSON, George
		182	CLIFFORD, Frederick
		6531	CLIFFORD, William A.

No.	Name.
Lt.	CLIFTON, Harold Ernest
5552	CLINGAN, Ernest E. H.
2894	CLISSOLD, Herbert W.
4086	CLOWES, Joseph
5314	CLUNIE, Thomas
7698	CLUNIES-ROSS, Robert
5318	COBLEY, Albert Edward
7030	COCHRUE, Thomas L.
5316	CODDINGTON, W. C.
5331	COE, John Augustus
856	COGHLAN, Joseph
418	COHEN, Arthur
1165	COHEN, Daniel Joseph
6052	COHEN, Roy Gordon
513	COLBERT, Alfred
5682	COLBRAN, Frank
4990	COLE, Arnold Amos
4398	COLE, Godfrey Laurence
1907	CLUFF, George
533	COLE, Harold William
5794	COLEMAN, Cecil Hall
6185	COLEMAN, Cyril Charles
5793	COLEMAN, Francis G.
3038	COLEMAN, Frank W.
2123	COLEMAN, Frederick R.
7135	COLLIER, William H.
6539	COLLINS, Clyde Reginald
3036	COLLINS, Cyril Boldero
3563	COLLINS, Frederick H.
2124	COLLINS, George E.
1671	COLLINS, Michael J.
2227	COLLINS, Reginald J.
527	COLLINS, Robert Percy
6047	COLLINS, Sydney
2125	COLLINS, Thomas J. J.
5442	COLLINS, William
6046	COLLISON, Frederick S.
1908	COLVIN, John Reginald
4995	COLVIN, Robert
Capt. Chap.	COLWELL, Fred.
3802	COMBELLACK, Josiah
839	COMBS, Victor C. R.
524	COMERFORD, John J.
177	COMMONS, Hugh
185	COMMONS, Hugh
6406	COMPTON, Alfred C.
840	COMPTON, Henry James
5553	CONGLETON, Robert S.
1166	CONLON, James C.
4694	CONLON, Patrick
189	CONNELLY, Joseph
1044	CONNELLY, Thomas J.
1167	CONNOCHIE, William D.
5555	CONNOR, Charles
2350	CONROY, Frederick
4682	CONVOY, Charles Rignold
5330	CONVOY, Harold Collin
5325	CONYNGHAM, Harold
1168	COOK, Albert Victor

No.	Name.
7020	COOK, Arthur Frederick
7029	COOK, Charles
Capt.	COOK, Clement Erwin
843	COOK, George Frederick
7175	COOK, Herbert
4692	COOK, John
4088	COOK, William
6782	COOKE, Arthur William
1169	COOKSON, Frederick
5929	COOLEY, Alfred Oscar
1170	COOM, William Alfred
1171	COOMBES, Francis J.
1669	COOMBES, Matthew J.
188	COOMBES, Robert E.
5333	COOPER, Albert
6409	COOPER, Edward
2602	COOPER, Herbert C.
1530	COOPER, Horace W.
761	COOPER, Samuel
1172	COOTE, William John
6284	COPP, Percy John
6395	COPPIN, Alexander A.
2127	COPPOCK, William J.
3803	CORBETT, Albert E.
1393	CORBETT, Arthur John
1909	CORBETT, George H. S.
4389	CORBETT, Thomas A.
3790	CORBEY, Phillip
4089	CORK, Harry
1910	CORKILL, Arthur Jack
1073	CORLESS, Samuel
2531	CORLETT, Robert D.
842	CORLISS, Albert Michael
4090	CORMACK, Sydney A.
1523	CORNALLY, Henry F. T.
5792	CORNING, Asa
1675	CORNISH, Thomas
1533	CORNWALL, John Henry
6536	CORNWALL, Thomas
4397	CORNWELL, James M.
1672	CORNWELL, Norman
2236	CORRIE, Ernest Walter
1670	CORSELLIS, A. C. L.
2048	CORSIE, Phillip C.
6285	COSGROVE, Thomas
849	COSTELLO, Allan
3787	COSTELLO, Charles A.
1351	COSTELLO, Michael
5798	COTTER, Ambrose L.
6404	COULON, Adolphus J.
3490	COULTER, John Robert
6538	COURTLY, Charles
Lt.	COURTNEY, Frank
6537	COUTURE, William
3800	COVINGTON, David H.
1348	COWAN, Keith Thomas
4695	COWAN, William
1173	COWCHER, Edward G.
844	COWDEN, Alexander

No.	Name	No.	Name
848	COWDERY, Edward D.	4699	CUMMING, David
850	COWLISHAW, John Y.	5317	CUMMING, David
181	COX, Edward Thomas	1171	CUMMING, John
837	COX, Edwin Thomas	7027	CUMMINGS, Charles E.
Lt.	COX, Henry James	6408	CUMMINS, Bertie
4391	COX, William R. V.	1677	CUNLIFFE, Wilfred T.
525	CRACKNELL, Charles F.	4702	CUNNINGHAM, Cecil B.
1911	CRACKNELL, Reg. W.	1528	CUNNINGHAM, E. A.
526	CRADDOCK, Cecil W.	4394	CUNNINGHAM, Innes C.
1050	CRAIG, Charles Harper	404	CUNNINGHAM, John
3564	CRAIG, Francis Lamb	1176	CUNNINGHAM, Thomas
3658	CRAIG, Hugh Normandy	5558	CURRIE, Leslie Thomas
1912	CRAIG, John Henry D.	7028	CURTIN, William James
5327	CRAIG, Joseph Robert	2355	CURTIS, Alfred George
398	CRAIG, Thomas Brown	1395	CURTIS, Charles
1174	CRANE, Richard	2604	CURTIS, Francis
1681	CRANE, William James	432	CURTIS, George Gordon
3484	CRANES, Charles A.	6288	CURZON, Harold
1682	CRANFIELD, John O.	1177	CUSACK, John
1807	CRANNEY, Daniel	6165	CUSTER, Albert James
846	CRAWFORD, Daniel M.	845	CUTHBERTSON, L. G.
1673	CRAWFORD, Spencer	5321	CUTHILL, David
2128	CRAWFORD, Thomas C.	6061	CUTTING, Edwin Percy
5319	CRAWLEY, Alan M.	401	CUTTING, James Walker
2129	CREBERT, Harold C.	5560	DAINES, Harry Charles
6287	CREIGHTON, R. C. J.	4400	DAISLEY, William
4696	CRESSY, Richard Vauv	1915	DALEY, John Percival
6785	CREW, Harold Percival	385	DALGLISH, Robert M.
6783	CREW, Stanley John	1076	DALTON, Richard S.
5686	CREWE, William Randle	6047	DALY, John Hubert
1529	CRISP, John Thomas O.	1178	DALY, Patrick Jerome
368	CROCKER, Frederick E.	1537	DALY, Patrick John
Lt.	CROFT, Frederick W.	1805	DANIEL, Thomas
1913	CROFT, Sydney Roy	1916	DARBY, Frank Anthony
6289	CROOK, Robert James	5698	D'ARCY, Martin John
517	CROOK, William Henry	3496	DARE, Arthur John
3492	CROPP, Herbert	1917	DARK, Douglas Wade
3801	CROSS, Wilfred	Lt.	DARK, Eric Wyndham
2353	CROSS, William	4408	DAVEY, Alfred
408	CROSSKILL, Harold	4401	DAVEY, Arthur
1685	CROTHERS, Warwick E.	2629	DAVIDSON, Alex. H.
857	CROUCH, John Lewis	1181	DAVIDSON, George
4393	CROWE, John Joseph	2039	DAVIES, Alfred Owen
4697	CROWE, William Henry	1536	DAVIES, Arthur
400	CROWLEY, Charles L.	861	DAVIES, Edwin
176	CROWLEY, George	5561	DAVIES, Eric Miller
5512	CROWSON, Arthur	1182	DAVIES, Horace
1525	CROWTHER, Fred. A.	4402	DAVIES, John
7025	CROWTHER, William	1684	DAVIES, Neal
859	CRUICKSHANK, R. S.	3495	DAVIES, Reginald Sydney
5441	CRUMP, Edward	1179	DAVIS, Augustine George
1175	CUDDEFORD, Fred. G.	2296	DAVIS, Cecil Rex
2661	CULLEN, Edgar Richmond	5697	DAVIS, Cyril Hugh
2895	CULLEN, G. W. J.	197	DAVIS, Ernest
3798	CULLEN, Richard	2286	DAVIS, Frederick Leslie
3791	CULLEN, Sidney	6428	DAVIS, George Alfred
532	CULLEN, Thomas Nicoll	4403	DAVIS, John Thomas
2891	CULLEN, William Henry	2135	DAVIS, Joseph Henry
405	CULLINGHAM, Henry	193	DAVIS, Louis Joseph

No.	Name.	No.	Name.
Lt.	DAVIS, Mark	867	DILLON, Edgar W. J.
4388	DAVIS, Sydney	195	DILLON, Francis W.
5054	DAVIS, Thomas Baden	210	DILLON, Joseph Francis
1180	DAVIS, Wilfred	4097	DIRCKS, Charles
5689	DAVIS, William Stanley	872	DIXON, Christopher
Hon. Capt.	DAVISON, A. J. R.	4705	DIXON, David William
5800	DAVISON, Hastings	6429	DIXON, Ernest Sylvester
5802	DAWES, Albert James	3052	DIXON, Frederick W.
384	DAWKINS, Francis R.	202	DIXON, Lancelot Henry
6544	DAWSON, Albert C.	4098	DIXON, Phillip Vernon
2474	DAWSON, Edward	6674	DOBBIE, William James
1634	DAWSON, Eric Athol	3792	DOBINSON, Albert
198	DAWSON, John	377	DODD, Richard
2891	DAWSON, Kenneth Ewen	5804	DODD, William
1184	DAWSON, Rupert Leslie	4100	DOHERTY, Edward
5337	DAWSON, William John	6791	DOHERTY, Harley James
873	DAY, Charles Edward	6412	DOHERTY, Jack Joseph
199	DAY, Edward	4404	DOHERTY, John Thomas
748	DAY, William Joseph	Lt.	DOIG, Allan Terrence
6789	DEACON, John Joseph	2282	DOLAN, Alfred Terrence
7031	DEAN, Charles Frank	1346	DOLAN, John
5810	DEAN, Leonard Stanley	2132	DOLING, Albert Edward
5343	DEAN, Sylvester	6413	DOMINEY, Winston A.
4099	DEARBERG, Fred. W.	7037	DONALD, Joseph Beeston
2475	DEARN, Maurice E.	Lt.	DONALDSON, James C.
5342	DEATH, Albert Thomas	3814	DONEHUE, Robert
3037	DEBELLE, Edward B.	2627	DONKIN, Harold H.
1630	DE CARTERET, G. W.	2180	DONNELL, Edward
1185	DEERING, Eden F. C.	3223	DONNELLY, Roy T.
869	DE-GRUCHY, Ivon Oscar	1055	DONOVAN, James
60	DEIGHTON, Arthur H.	203	DONOVAN, Roger Bede
6790	DELAHUNT, Hubert Y.	536	DOOGAN, Matthew J.
6787	DEL-RIEGO, Francisco	5003	DOOLEY, Thomas V.
4279	DE LUCE, Henry M.	2/Lt.	DOONE, Colin
Lt.	DEMPSEY, Cornelius T.	6792	DORAN, Josiah
5690	DENGATE, Herbert E. H.	3809	DOREY, Charles
201	DEONCK, William	3807	DOREY, Ernest Roy
7032	DERKENNE, Walter G.	2133	DORMER, Frederick H. B.
6645	DERRICK, Frederick T.	5801	DOUBLEDAY, Fred. A.
1919	DEVENISH, Arthur G.	5807	DOUBLEDAY, Sydney N.
3812	DEVINE, Frank	1687	DOUGHERTY, Robert
7033	DEVINE, Thomas Henry	6055	DOUGHTY, William L.
2/Lt.	DEVITT, William George	5565	DOUGLAS, Alroy Clyde
2474	DEWHURST, Royston C.	2879	DOUGLAS, Gordon
6786	DE-WITT, Norbert F. H.	5338	DOUGLAS, Ronald N.
1538	DICK, Arthur Morrison	1800	DOUGLAS, George
5803	DICK, Reginald Charles	Lt.	DOULL, David Farquhar
Lt.	DICKENS, Glen Mervyn	1187	DOW, Arthur
535	DICKER, Walter Charles	2878	DOWLING, Eric M.
6293	DICKERSON, Bertie	1213	DOWLING, Frederick
6296	DICKSON, Clarence Ian	5670	DOWNES, James John
1920	DICKSON, Leslie C.	866	DOWNES, John Joseph
6292	DICKSON, William	5341	DOWNEY, Thomas
194	DIDCOTE, Harry Fifield	191	DOYLE, John Michael
1617	DIDCOTE, William	2136	DOYLE, Joseph
63	DIFFORD, Herbert R.	6547	DOYLE, Raphael C.
7138	DIFFORD, Solomon O.	4101	DOYLE, Robert
5563	DIGGELMAN, Eugene W.	5004	DOYLE, William
7034	DIGGELMAN, John B.	7621	DRAKE, Edward Stanley

No.	Name.	No.	Name.
4406	DRENNAN, Albert E.	2/Lt.	EDWARDS, Ernest F.
6435	DREW, Hardie	1928	EDWARDS, Harry C.
6299	DREW, Thomas William	1927	EDWARDS, John Samuel
4102	DREWERY, John	206	EDWARDS, Roy Henry
862	DRISCOLL, John	1370	EDWARDS, Stanley
3790	DRIVER, Frank	2637	EDWARDS, Walter C.
5340	DRYDEN, George S.	207	EDWARDS, William
6298	DRYSDALE, Bruce M.	1540	EEDY, Ronald Frederick
870	DRYSDALE, George	1541	EGAN, Andrew Frank
4708	DRYSDALE, William J.	369	EGAN, John Raymond
3708	DUBOIS, William George	416	EGGINS, Robert Clive
5005	DUDLEY, Frederick M.	2137	EGOROFF, Alexander
6294	DUDLEY, William Henry	2142	ELDER, Walter Clifford
4397	DUFFY, John Francis	3820	ELDER, William Thomas
6545	DUGAN, Hillary Clifton	541	ELDERSHAW, Athol G.
2134	DUGAN, John Ernest M.	5344	ELLERMAN, John W.
1214	DUGGAN, Patrick Joseph	1606	ELLIOTT, Fred. Elijah
860	DUGGAN, Samuel A.	877	ELLIS, Francis William
1924	DULHUNTY, Norman J.	Lt.	ELLIS, Henry
4407	DUNCAN, Andrew Milne	542	ELLIS, James Albert
1925	DUNCAN, Robert	6162	ELLIS, John Eric
4103	DUNHAM, Lewis	6415	ELLIS, Stanley William
1926	DUNLOP, William D.	2138	ELLIS, William John
1212	DUNN, Andrew George	544	ELLISON, James William
5564	DUNN, Charles William	5811	ELRINGTON, Albert L.
3811	DUNN, Robert George	423	ELSMORE, William E.
864	DUNN, Sidney	1692	EMANUEL, Jack
2359	DUNN, William Payton	7040	EMERSON, Joseph P.
2360	DUNNE, Morton James	6902	EMERY, George Samuel
5007	DUNNETT, Joseph	6012	ENDICOTT, Eli
5443	DUNSHEA, Charles J.	6302	ENGLAND, Francis G.
3498	DUNSTAN, Oswald F.	6187	ENGLAND, Humphrey
1635	DURAND, Alfred	7039	ENTWISTLE, John
5809	DURHAM, Erick A. K.	4105	EPHRAIM, Eric Vivian
1389	DWYER, James	6303	ESCOTT, Amos
1686	DWYER, John Vincent	5568	ESTALL, William
4409	DWYER, Thomas B.	3823	ETHERIDGE, Horace
4709	DWYER, William James	6414	EVANS, Alfred Solomon
3827	DYKES, John Charles	878	EVANS, Arthur Henry
5567	EADES, Edgar Stanley	2638	EVANS, Claude
1327	EALES, Stanley	387	EVANS, Frank
3227	EARL, Harold Arthur	875	EVANS, James Robert
a1957	EARLS, Edward Joseph	3503	EVANS, John Henry
1059	EARNSHAW, Arthur S. E.	3226	EVANS, Lancelot Bertred
874	EAST, Arthur Ernest	797	EVANS, Norman George
4399	EAST, Carleton J. W.	2880	EVANS, Robert Joseph
1392	EAST, Joseph	2538	EVERETT, Charles H.
6795	EASTICK, Claude E.	2642	EWER, Herbert
6557	EASTON, Leonard C.	1190	EWING, Frederick
1691	EASTON, Sydney James	543	EWING, Thomas Alister
6553	EATON, Sidney	1929	FACKERELL, Herbert W.
a1530	ECKFORD, Eric Godfrey	4106	FADDY, Frederick
6555	EDDY, Arthur	3826	FAHEY, John Joseph
21	EDELSTEN, William	1546	FAHEY, Percy Andrew
1188	EDGAR, Robert	3506	FAHEY, William Francis
6300	EDGERTON, Frank J.	3830	FAIRBAIN, W. J. L.
Lt.	EDMONDSON, John G.	410	FAIRLEM, William
876	EDWARD, Victor	2362	FALLON, William Henry
3819	EDWARDS, Alfred H.	1618	FARRELL, Thomas

No.	Name.
1215	FARRIMOND, Harold L.
3505	FARROW, Arthur
2822	FAULKNER, George A.
2643	FAULKNER, W. F. F.
65	FAWCUS, James
Lt.	FAY, James Joseph
3815	FAY, James Sydney
1930	FEGAN, Walter William
1547	FELAN, James Roy
4107	FELL, Leslie William A.
4412	FELTON, Edward S.
419	FENTON, Harold Clifton
1191	FENWICK, James
4713	FERGUSON, Archibald
2648	FERGUSON, Dugald Mc.
6796	FERGUSON, F. J. V.
Chap.	FERNIE, Edward H.
849	FERNON, Cecil Bruce
545	FERRALL, Herbert A.
2298	FERRIS, Ernest Harold
5813	FERRIS, George R.
1931	FIDDLING, John
1693	FIELD, Edgar Alfred
209	FIELD, John Leslie
5822	FIELD, John W. F. E.
6676	FIELD, Stanley Ormond
883	FIELD, Thomas William
552	FILBY, Kenneth
6797	FINDLAY, John
Capt.	FINLAY, Cuthbert Clive
3828	FINLEY, Arthur
6556	FINNERTY, Roger F.
1697	FISCHER, John Emil
2898	FISHER, Alfred
2294	FISHER, Ernest
2478	FISHER, Frank Samuel
548	FISHER, James
5819	FISHER, William Allen
4413	FISK, Gordon
Lt.	FITZALAN, Russel Austin
3829	FITZGERALD, E. F.
879	FITZPATRICK, James
5674	FITZPATRICK, John F.
5570	FLACK, James Alfred
3825	FLACK, Roy Stutchbury
3824	FLACK, William John
2276	FLANAGAN, Stephen M.
880	FLANAGAN, William
3834	FLEMING, Edward S.
2366	FLEMING, Leslie
2480	FLETCHER, James
2481	FLETCHER, Sidney
Lt.	FLOOD, William Leonard
4109	FLOWERS, William
217	FLOYD, Dudley Armand
215	FLUKE, Walter Henry
5571	FLYNN, Charles
6804	FLYNN, Leslie Francis
6803	FLYNN, Michael Joseph

No.	Name.
882	FOGARTY, Edward
5821	FOGGON, Charles
2139	FOLLAN, Arthur
216	FOOT, Alfred
213	FOOTT, John Lumsden
3508	FORD, Burton A. L.
5572	FORD, Leslie
7177	FORD, Leslie Llewellyn
Lt.	FORD, Robert Paul
884	FORD, William Leslie
4408	FORDHAM, Charles Hill
6798	FORDHAM, Victor L.
3512	FORGIE, James
5816	FORREST, James
887	FORSYTH, Harry R.
5817	FOSDICK, Ernest
1072	FOSTER, Daniel Edward
2002	FOSTER, Frederick A.
1216	FOSTER, Harry
4414	FOSTER, Henry Charles
750	FOSTER, Henry George
2651	FOSTER, Stephen
2894	FOSTER, Wallace Henry
1192	FOSTER, William
5346	FOSTER, William
4111	FOSTER, William Henry
5812	FOWLES, Albert James
5815	FOX, Eric
2644	FOX, John Raven
3230	FOXLEY, Fred. T. N.
1694	FOY, Eustace Ernest H.
2466	FOY, Victor John
1544	FRAIL, Herbert Mills
4112	FRAME, Andrew
4719	FRANCE, Joseph D.
4720	FRANCE, Sidney F.
551	FRANCIS, Albert
2367	FRANCIS, George E.
5012	FRANCIS, John Patrick
1065	FRANCIS, John William
885	FRANKLIN, John
5013	FRANKLIN, Thomas W.
424	FRASER, Allan William
3511	FRASER, Thomas M.
1933	FRASER, William Ross
5814	FREARSON, Norman
1052	FREEBAIRN, Andrew
1193	FREEMAN, George S.
7043	FREEMAN, George S.
5820	FREEMANTLE, Fred.
5691	FREESTONE, Herbert J.
7060	FRENCH, George
2140	FRENCH, John Rose
6057	FROST, Eric
5823	FROST, George F. P.
1696	FROY, Joseph Patrick
2238	FRY, Robert Leslie
5573	FULLALOVE, W. A. V.
6304	FULLAM, Francis Myles

No.	Name
6467	FULLARD, Henry
214	FULLER, Charles Upton
5818	FULTHORP, John
212	FULTHORPE, Ralph R.
3832	FULTON, David
3827	FULTON, Thomas
6431	FUNNELL, Frederick J.
3805	FUNNELL, William A.
7178	FURGERSON, John J.
2479	FURNESS, F. R. C.
210	FURNESS, Norman
Mjr.	FUSSELL, Leslie George
4416	FUTCHER, William L.
6652	GAAL, James Victor M.
5351	GABBE, Ernest Charles
5824	GADD, Frederick
6186	GAFFNEY, Richard
2141	GAHAN, Norbert
6800	GALE, Blair Crawford L.
1195	GALLAFENT, Albert E.
3557	GALLAGHER, Hugh
4113	GALLAGHER, T. J. E.
433	GALLIENNE, Stanley C.
1800	GALLOGLY, George H.
5355	GALLOWAY, J. G. N.
554	GALLOWAY, John
4417	GALLWAY, David
a1537	GALVIN, Patrick
3844	GANE, Harold William
2882	GANNON, Frederick
896	GANNON, George N.
4722	GANNON, John Henry
5574	GANT, John Samuel
3840	GARDINER, Alex. M.
3842	GARDINER, Leslie James
4588	GARDINER, Samuel M.
229	GARDINER, Sydney
3518	GARLAND, Arthur G.
434	GARLICK, Thomas N.
5015	GARNER, Robert G.
5350	GARRARD, Herbert
225	GARRETT, William
1554	GARSTANG, Leo. F.
8426	GATES, Ernest John
1811	GAVEL, William Peters
220	GAVIN, Charles
5348	GAVIN, Harold Percival
2906	GAYLARD, Henry C.
4428	GEARY, Thomas Edward
2485	GEDDES, Robert Roy
2156	GELL, Charles F. K.
1934	GENTIL, Blake
1550	GEORGE, Andrew
1935	GEORGE, Clifford H. D.
2483	GEORGE, Francis H.
4724	GEORGE, Louis F.
7046	GEORGE, William L.
890	GERAGHTY, David
1196	GERHARD, Henry G.

No.	Name
5451	GERMAN, Jethro
4725	GERRITSEN, Johanes W.
4726	GIBB, Hugh
1730	GIBBONS, Michael P.
862	GIBBS, Aladdin
895	GIBBS, Leslie
555	GIBSON, Alfred Louis
2141	GIBSON, Archibald K.
.727	GIBSON, Arthur
562	GIBSON, Kenneth Roy
6561	GIBSON, Oswald George
4418	GIBSON, Percy Clive
5827	GIBSON, Robert
218	GIBSON, William John
Lt.	GILBERT, Arthur F.
222	GILBERT, Francis J.
2540	GILBERT, William John
4117	GILCHRIST, Alexander
5576	GILES, Joseph
1700	GILL, Albert Ernest
6307	GILLESPIE, William
b2663	GILLETT, Charles L.
370	GILLETT, Dudley
6166	GILLIES, John Grant
4419	GILLIES, Kenneth J.
6310	GILLIES, William J. T.
7047	GILLIGAN, James W.
3232	GILLIGAN, Patrick L.
2371	GILMOUR, Harry
2623	GILMOUR, Robert B.
447	GIMBERT, Henry J. H.
3514	GIVNEY, Llewellyn W.
1219	GLANVILLE, Thomas P.
4172	GLASSCOCK, Herbert G.
4420	GLASSFORD, E. J. C.
5825	GLASSON, Alfred Henry
6063	GLAZIER, Charles F.
2873	GLEESON, Stephen F.
6062	GLEESON, Thomas J.
1349	GLEN, Wilfred James
2656	GLENDAY, James
765	GLOVER, Leonard
766	GLOVER, William R.
446	GOAD, Reginald Bateman
5347	GOBERT, Charles Alfred
4278	GOCHER, Charles T.
5575	GODDARD, Harold W.
T/Brig. Gen.	GODDARD, H. A.
5018	GODDARD, Trevor F.
891	GODDING, Fines Henry
1937	GODFREY, Cyril Gilbert
1075	GODFREY, Edward A.
2372	GOING, Alban Hedley
6903	GOLDBY, William H.
557	GOLDING, Sidney
5578	GOLDRICK, Keven D'A.
2/Lt.	GOMBERT, France
892	GOOD, Andrew George
1220	GOODA, Alfred Charles

No.	Name
565	GOODE, Arthur W. N.
5349	GOODGER, Bernard L.
5571	GOODMAN, Augustus F.
2373	GOODMAN, Claude W.
1197	GOODMAN, Jordan
4729	GOODMAN, Sydney
3520	GOODMAN, William John
1808	GOODWIN, Arthur
7045	GOODWIN, Roland Egbert
3841	GOODWORTH, Frank Val
5829	GOOSE, Leslie
897	GORDON, Arthur Stanley
999	GORDON, Ernest Silvester
227	GORDON, John
900	GORDON, Leslie Andrew
6915	GORHAM, Reginald L.
4119	GOSLING, Fred.
5021	GOULD, Arthur
1066	GOULD, John William
4730	GOULDEN, Arthur
6812	GOWER, Edward Arthur
5022	GRACE, William Herbert
5352	GRAHAM, George
2374	GRAHAM, James Alex.
6064	GRAHAM, Joseph
5938	GRAHAM, Matthew John
2895	GRAHAM, Samuel John
5354	GRAHAM, Theo.
899	GRAHAM, Thomas
1938	GRAHAM, William
4120	GRAINGER, Herbert W.
894	GRANGE, Frank Gordon
5826	GRANGE, Samuel Walter
559	GRANT, Allan
4733	GRANT, Douglas Kinnear
6305	GRANT, Henry Bradford
6802	GRASNICK, George A.
800	GRAVENOR, George L.
1556	GRAVES, Frederick
3846	GRAY, Cyril Tudor
1557	GRAY, Edward
4121	GRAY, George David
1696	GRAY, Samuel Harford
6061	GRAY, Tom
2375	GRAY, Victor Herbert
4122	GREAYER, Joseph
4734	GREBER, Arthur P. V.
5828	GREEN, Albert Henry
6311	GREEN, Ernest R.
2658	GREEN, James
893	GREEN, James Stephen
223	GREEN, John Henry
6309	GREEN, John Frederick
3836	GREEN, Sydney Clarence
560	GREEN, William
6805	GREENAWAY, B. M.
415	GREENBERG, Joseph S.
898	GREENLAND, Alfred
4429	GREENSLADE, Harold

No.	Name
85	GREENWOOD, Joseph
6306	GREER, Albert John
5577	GREGORY, Joseph T.
228	GREIG, John James
5830	GREVILLE, Roderic H.
1698	GREY, Vivian Frank
1939	GRIEVE, Alexander J. T.
2376	GRIFFIN, Michael J.
4732	GRIFFIN, William
3835	GRIFFITHS, Harry H.
2898	GRIFFITHS, Henry G.
415	GRIFFITHS, Jack
Capt.	GRIFFITHS, Llewellyn
3516	GRIFFITHS, R. C. E.
1198	GRIFFITHS, Robert H.
1199	GRIFFITHS, William H.
260	GRIMES, John
2378	GRIMSON, George S.
4174	GRINDLEY, David
1342	GRIX, Alfred
4431	GROOM, Arthur
4124	GROOM, Edgar
221	GROOME, Frank
4426	GROSSLER, Herbert
2911	GUMBRILL, Ernest A.
6799	GUNNELL, Graham B.
5579	GURTON, Benjamin J.
2379	GUTHRIE, George
Capt.	GUYMER, Ernest Albert
1704	HACKETT, Percival B.
1705	HACKETT, Richard B.
2142	HACKETT, Roy
7140	HADDOW, William
7050	HADLEY, Harry G. W.
1709	HADLOW, Arthur Henry
6807	HAGEN, Bernard A.
Lt.	HAIGH, William Richard
6808	HAIN, William James
3529	HALE, Arthur
Capt.	HALE, Rupert Edward
6924	HALES, Henry
1222	HALL, Cecil Claude
1396	HALL, Edwin Lewis
4735	HALL, John Patrick
568	HALL, Roy Thomas
371	HALL, Tom
903	HALLETT, Percy
6070	HALPIN, William Martin
Lt.	HAM, William Joseph
236	HAMILTON, Alex. Hugh
6069	HAMILTON, Henry E.
1329	HAMILTON, Max
1701	HAMILTON, Peter
5834	HAMILTON, T. A. B.
2143	HAMMELL, William John
1940	HAMMERTON, Arthur E.
4125	HAMMOND, Gilbert
901	HAMMOND, William
2295	HAMPTON, Duncan B.

No.	Name.	No.	Name.
5589	HANDS, Claude Beswick	5702	HARVEY, Edward P.
4739	HANLEY, Nicholas	a2913	HARVEY, Richard E.
4126	HANLON, William Henry	5360	HARWOOD, Frederick J.
1734	HANN, Douglas Paul	372	HASSALL, Frank M.
574	HANNA, Hugh	1806	HATCHER, Cecil Stewart
Lt.	HANNAFORD, Charles R.	4447	HATHAWAY, George
1200	HANNAN, Robert Ernest	2390	HATTLEY, George
5027	HANNAN, Stephen James	4443	HATTON, William George
2240	HANNAY, Thomas A.	3252	HAVENSTEIN, C. F.
4441	HANSEN, Alexander F.	5450	HAWKER, Eric A. E.
6068	HANSEN, Carl	3845	HAWKINS, Edward J.
6810	HANSEN, Louis Julius	458	HAWSON, William Cowell
3087	HANSON, George Edward	578	HAY, Kenneth Arthur
6820	HANSON, Hugo	1202	HAYDON, Thomas James
6320	HANWRIGHT, James	1944	HAYE, Stanley
238	HARDING, Ernest W.	234	HAYES, Arthur James
4442	HARDISTY, Jack	1058	HAYES, Harry O. S.
2144	HARDY, Frederick J.	3074	HAYES, Matthew
3849	HARDY, Leslie Charles	6315	HAYES, Michael
2381	HARDY, Lloyd Davenport	911	HAYES, Patrick Joseph
2647	HARDY, Reginald	4444	HAYLAN, Thomas
6819	HARE, Ernest	5583	HAYWARD, Ernest
902	HARGRAVES, Colin	3850	HEAD, Allen Robert
237	HARGREAVES, Bert	5839	HEALEY, Alfred Edward
5359	HARMAN, John	4741	HEALEY, Thomas Dillon
239	HARMAN, William Henry	1328	HEALY, William Patrick
Capt.	HARNETT, Edward T.	3531	HEAP, Frederick W. C.
1344	HARPER, Adrian Charles	572	HEAP, George
3075	HARPER, Alfred	2903	HEAPS, John
1942	HARPER, Joseph	2391	HEARD, Oliver Holmes
1943	HARPER, Mark	7051	HEARN, William
575	HARPER, Peter Hubert	1945	HEARNE, Felix
1223	HARPLEY, Ernest Alex.	753	HEATH, Thomas
Lt.	HARRIES, Frederick H. E.	1390	HEATH, Volataire Robert
2146	HARRINGTON, M. J.	233	HEATHCOTE, Herbert
4129	HARRIS, Arthur Edward	1203	HEDDLE, Reynolds J.
7142	HARRIS, Charles P.	1225	HEFFERNAN, Eneas P.
3537	HARRIS, Herbert W.	2923	HEFFERNAN, Patrick F.
Lt.	HARRIS, John	5835	HEHIR, William
6073	HARRIS, Joseph Ernest	1204	HELSON, Ernest George
7180	HARRIS, Robert	4445	HELY, Carlyle Edward
1042	HARRIS, Thomas	Lt.	HEMBROW, Bertie Hay
5580	HARRIS, William James	579	HEMINGWAY, Cecil T.
5831	HARRISON, Charles J.	1619	HEMMY, Frederick N.
6317	HARRISON, David	3852	HEMSLEY, Robert Henry
3533	HARRISON, Joseph C.	1690	HENDERSON, Albert E.
2241	HARRISON, Joseph Henry	915	HENDERSON, Alfred T.
6814	HARRISON, Richard W.	2541	HENDERSON, James F.
6164	HART, Ernest	2907	HENDERSON, John D.
1201	HART, Frederick	232	HENDERSON, Joseph G.
1224	HART, Frederick	5030	HENDERSON, Leslie G.
1227	HART, Harry Julian	4446	HENDERSON, Mat. M.
6416	HARTIGAN, George L.	4432	HENDERSON, Oliver R.
576	HARTLE, Frederick W.	913	HENDLEY, Eugene
2386	HARTLEY, William	5117	HENDLEY, Sidney C.
3527	HARTLEY, William Allan	4132	HENDRY, Crawford
2387	HARVEY, Alfred	1947	HENNESSY, John
577	HARVEY, Arthur	5579	HENNESSEY, Patrick J.
5840	HARVEY, Edward	571	HENNINGHAM, H. W.

No.	Name.
4743	HEPBURN, Varie
6067	HEPWORTH, George W.
1948	HERBERT, George
3082	HERBERT, Robert J.
453	HERD, Thomas
1706	HERMAN, Harold Ellis
5361	HERNE, Charles Parnell
1708	HEUSTON, Arthur Noel
2486	HEWATT, Albert Ernest
1566	HEWSON, Allen
4133	HEYDON, Arthur R.
4134	HIAM, Charles Edward
5832	HIBEL, Joseph Hunter
6815	HICKEY, Phillip
569	HICKLING, George W.
777	HICKS, Wilfred Augustus
904	HICKSON, Percy Gordon
3086	HIGGINS, Arnold Leopold
6065	HIGGINS, Arthur
2874	HIGGINS, Aubrey Henry
912	HIGGINS, Harry
5582	HIGGINS, Joseph Samuel
2392	HIGGINS, Leslie Vincent
908	HIGGS, Henry Rudolph
3251	HIGGS, Kenneth
916	HIGH, George
6066	HIGLEY, Harold Ernest
1949	HILDER, Leslie Howard
6312	HILDER, William F.
3247	HILL, Arthur James
393	HILL, Charles Rowland
1206	HILL, John James
397	HILL, John Rowland
882	HILL, Harry
5831	HILL, Kenneth Charles
2524	HILLEARD, Edward
6904	HILLS, William Blair
6657	HILTON, Alexander
4135	HINCKS, Bertie
242	HINDER, William L.
5584	HINES, David George
1207	HINES, Phillip Edward
6072	HINKS, Charles Edward
907	HINTON, William Frank
1208	HOARE, Reginald R.
241	HOBAN, William Joseph
580	HOBBA, Jack
581	HOBSON, James
7055	HODGE, Bertram
1547	HODGE, William
3847	HODGE, William
754	HODGETTS, Stewart H.
4434	HODGSON, Ernest W.
906	HODGSON, Henry
1620	HODSON, Henry James
2149	HOFF, Harry
1733	HOGAN, Michael A.
6818	HOGAN, Patrick
1950	HOGBIN, Alfred William

No.	Name
582	HOLDEN, Fred.
6570	HOLDEN, Norman P.
5838	HOLDORF, Lewis W.
2042	HOLFORD, Frederick
2043	HOLGATE, Frederick J.
2150	HOLLAND, Collin S.
1703	HOLLAND, Hector G.
7052	HOLLAND, Joseph
2546	HOLLIDAY, Charles R. G.
2395	HOLLINGUM, Tom S.
5356	HOLLOWAY, David
573	HOLM, Robert James
1710	HOLMAN, Thomas
Mjr.	HOLMES, Basil
3525	HOLMES, Ernest C.
6816	HOLMES, Kenneth Milton
4436	HOLMES, Robert C.
7143	HOLT, Cecil Victor S.
6813	HOLTSBAUM, William U.
5032	HOMER, James William
778	HOOD, Andrew Thomas
3528	HOOD, George Edward C
1209	HOOD, William Robin
2283	HOOKER, Allan
1562	HOOLER, James
1951	HOOPER, Richard James
2666	HOOPER, William J. P.
2/Lt.	HOPKINS, Vernon N.
2152	HOPPER, Edward Henry
1707	HORSFIELD, Percy
3701	HORSLEY, George J. C.
4136	HORSLEY, Stanley John
5837	HOSKINS, William
6313	HOSKINS, William T. V.
230	HOUGH, James
4438	HOUSTON, Archibald W.
2/Lt.	HOUSTON, Colin
566	HOUSTON, Robert
1210	HOUSTON, Thomas
3091	HOWARD, Albert Edward
1952	HOWARD, Albert F.
3532	HOWARD, James John
905	HOWARD, John
7053	HOWARTH, Wesley V.
3094	HOWE, Henry F. P.
5358	HOWES, Edward A. F.
4138	HOWES, William Henry
5836	HUBBARD, Edward W.
3816	HUBBARD, John G. I.
6573	HUCKER, Bertie James
767	HUDSON, James
917	HUDSON, Stanley Claude
909	HUGHES, Alfred Edward
1211	HUGHES, Edward
1702	HUGHES, Frank C.
2008	HUGHES, Walter
411	HUGO, James Ernest
2397	HUISH, Alfred Henry
7048	HULBERT, Vivian V.

No.	Name.
5585	HULM, Burgess
5586	HULM, Walter
919	HUME, Walter Douglas
910	HUMPHREYS, Thomas O.
6817	HUMPHREYS, H. C.
2482	HUMPHRIES, W. J.
1226	HUNDT, Frank
2875	HUNT, Alfred Stanley
3530	HUNT, Charles Edward
2672	HUNT, George B. F.
5357	HUNT, Reginald Alfred
6075	HUNT, Walter Lindsay
2487	HUNTER, Bertie James
4140	HUNTER, James Harold
6076	HUNTER, Joseph James
6071	HUNTINGDON, Lorne T.
5587	HUNTLEY, Charles E.
6319	HUNTLEY, Daniel
240	HUNTLEY, William Edgar
7054	HUTCHINS, Joseph
768	HUTTON, Edward
2679	HUTTON, Francis Percy
4141	HUTTON, John Thomas
1813	HYDE, Ambrose John
5833	HYDE, John
1358	HYLAND, Henry Walter
3540	IKIN, Arthur
739	IKIN, Edward
4450	INGHAM, Francis
5591	INGRAM, Percy Charles
6130	INSKIP, Guy
2686	IONN, Frank
2398	IRELAND, Reginald P.
50892	IRVINE, George Ashfield
2399	IRVING, Samuel George
7058	IRVING, Thomas
1350	IRWIN, John
2659	IRWIN, John Bead S.
3853	IRWIN, Samuel Herbert
Lt.	ISON, Alfred Harold
7063	JACKA, Cyril Knight
4460	JACKA, John Victor
1213	JACKEL, Frederick L.
6575	JACKSON, Albert James
3857	JACKSON, Christopher J.
6822	JACKSON, Claude
3861	JACKSON, Henry B. B.
6077	JACKSON, Herbert E.
a1616	JACKSON, James
1571	JACKSON, James McD.
5593	JACKSON, John P.
1384	JACKSON, Richard A.
1214	JACKSON, Robert
1621	JACKSON, Thomas
588	JACKSON, William
5592	JACKSON, William E.
a1708	JACOBSON, Frederick M.
7144	JAMES, Cubitt W. A.
929	JAMES, George

No.	Name.
4451	JAMES, Henry
7060	JAMES, Thomas Stanley
1612	JAMES, William
1374	JAMES, William Royal
5841	JAMIESON, James M.
247	JANES, Charles Henry
914	JARMAN, Henry
4453	JARRATT, Joseph E.
587	JARVIS, Osmond R.
5038	JARVIS, Victor Hylton
924	JEBB, John James
5362	JEFFCOAT, Harry
4143	JEFFCOTT, William F.
1382	JEFFERSON, Frederick
1570	JEFFREY, Sydney
2400	JEFFREY, William K.
5364	JEFFRIES, Sydney A.
5673	JELBART, Harold T.
7145	JENKINS, Edward J.
585	JENKINS, Thomas W. D.
930	JENNINGS, George
2242	JENNINGS, William J.
7061	JENSEN, Wilhelm A.
4455	JENSON, Rasmus W.
5123	JEREMY, Albert T.
5692	JESPERSON, Edward W.
2401	JEWETT, Joseph A.
4751	JOHANSON, Gus
Lt.	JOHNS, Frederick W.
923	JOHNS, Roy Clive
6433	JOHNS, William Stanley
1954	JOHNSON, Alfred
6434	JOHNSON, Alick O. E.
4144	JOHNSON, Edward E.
4456	JOHNSON, Eric Lionel
2402	JOHNSON, Ernest E.
6080	JOHNSON, Ernest F.
5594	JOHNSON, Ernest M.
a1707	JOHNSON, Frank L.
3084	JOHNSON, Frank M.
1711	JOHNSON, George B. F.
1391	JOHNSON, Harold M.
T/Major	JOHNSON, Harold W.
3255	JOHNSON, Harry
245	JOHNSON, James E.
928	JOHNSON, Leonard
1217	JOHNSON, Robert S. A.
586	JOHNSON, Roy Douglas
1216	JOHNSON, Thomas W.
7062	JOHNSON, Vivian A.
1334	JOHNSON, William
1218	JOHNSTON, Benjamin D.
Capt.	JOHNSTON, Cyril G.
3856	JOHNSTON, Henry J.
1955	JOHNSTON, Joseph
3854	JOHNSTON, Lorenzo
1219	JOHNSTON, Robert J.
Hon./Capt.	JOHNSTON, W. R.
4461	JOHNSTONE, Alex. S.

No.	Name.	No.	Name.
4752	JOHNSTONE, David	2404	KELSO, Edwin Milne
1568	JOHNSTONE, Herbert M.	1718	KELSO, John Alfred
2532	JOINER, John M.	1719	KELSO, Henry Albert
7146	JOLIFFE, Cromwell	595	KELSO, Hilton
591	JOLLY, Robert	6825	KEMISTER, Thomas H.
2155	JONES, Alfred	1957	KEMP, Lloyd Bilby
6079	JONES, Arthur	2405	KEMP, Frederick H.
3549	JONES, Benjamin	1576	KEMP, Joseph
2688	JONES, Charles F. C.	600	KEMP, Leslie Smith
4749	JONES, David	2157	KEMSLEY, Edward B.
2244	JONES, Edward	6084	KENDALL, Harold R.
1712	JONES, Herbert	5595	KENDALL, Henry A.
927	JONES, Horace Roy	6081	KENNEDY, Albert
931	JONES, Hugh Edward	a209	KENNEDY, Aubrey
4748	JONES, James	6328	KENNEDY, Charles P.
2689	JONES, Leslie Noel	596	KENNEDY, Malcolm W.
6179	JONES, Richard	6831	KENNELLY, Herbert C.
6323	JONES, Richard	3553	KENNY, Alfred William
7057	JONES, Sidney Benjamin	6905	KENNY, Frank
1569	JONES, Sydney William	1222	KENNY, Jack Arthur C.
248	JONES, Thomas	252	KENT, Charles
5586	JONES, William Sidney	3864	KENT, Ernest Gordon
926	JONES, William Walter	1958	KENTWELL, Isaac M.
5363	JONES, Wynn	1577	KENWAY, Douglas D.
1220	JOSEPH, Francis	4755	KENYON, John Charles
6399	JOSEPH, Frank Rintel	1953	KEOWN, Sidney John
922	JOWSEY, William G.	1715	KERL, William Winn
1221	JUDD, Sidney	1959	KERNICK, Harry
2156	JUDE, Charles Henry	599	KERR, Andrew
6830	JUPP, George Joseph	4147	KERR, Edward
2403	JUSTICE, Charles	1716	KERR, William Henry
5844	KABLE, Cyril	1960	KERRY, Charles John
5042	KABLE, Herbert	2158	KESHAN, Norman Daniel
5847	KANE, Henry	1961	KESSON, William
2300	KANNAR, John Joseph	5947	KEYS, John
589	KATER, John Stanley	1575	KIBBLE, James Forby
249	KAVANAGH, Joseph	251	KIDD, Ernest
132	KAY, Cecil James	1717	KIERNAN, Frank L.
3862	KAYE, Clarence Oswald	6579	KILFOYLE, Thomas J.
250	KEARNEY, John William	937	KILGOUR, Robert J.
6824	KEENS, Charles Henry	4462	KILKELLY, John Cecil
381	KEEP, James Wortley	1233	KILLIBY, Thomas W. W.
1573	KELLAND, Herbert G.	2863	KILLIGREW, Septimus B.
6577	KELLEHER, Michael	1962	KILLOH, George
590	KELLY, Alfred William	7065	KILMINSTER, Alan H.
5367	KELLY, Cyrus	6823	KINCHINGTON, V.
2929	KELLY, Herbert Albert	5845	KING, Francis Henry
6325	KELLY, James	597	KING, George
1736	KELLY, James Lawrence	2406	KING, George Joseph
769	KELLY, James William	1361	KING, Robert
1622	KELLY, John	5365	KING, Roy Silvester
1231	KELLY, Laurence John	6828	KING, Sydney George
1956	KELLY, Leslie John	5842	KING, Thomas Patrick
1232	KELLY, Thomas	1818	KING, William Wesley
3103	KELLY, Thomas Albert	749	KINSELLA, Alfred E.
6083	KELLY, Vincent Roy	933	KINSELLA, Henry
6324	KELLY, Walter George	1224	KIRBY, Henry
Lt.	KELSALL, C. P.	2700	KIRBY, Richard Leslie
6326	KELSEY, Charles G.	5848	KIRBY, William

No.	Name.	No.	Name.
Capt.	KIRKE, Errol Wharton	6089	LAWSON, Harold C.
934	KIRKPATRICK, George	4149	LAWSON, James
1226	KIRKPATRICK, James	602	LAWSON, James Albert
2049	KIRKPATRICK, Rupert	265	LAWTON, William P.
1376	KIRLEY, Walter Edward	7181	LAYCOCK, Frederick
1574	KIRWAN, Walter E.	1718	LAYTON, Charles G.
5846	KITT, Robert Henry	3419	LEA, Harry Noel
7066	KNEESHAW, Wilfred O'N.	1229	LEA, Thomas William
5308	KNIGHT, George	7068	LEACH, Ormuz Kintore
2159	KNIGHT, Louis Henry	3006	LEAHY, Leslie Joseph
2698	KNIGHT, Thomas R.	4764	LEATHER, Peter L.
753	KNIGHT, William A.	3867	LEAY, James
3552	KNIGHT, William G.	5850	LEBRESE, Patrick Ebor
2922	KNOX, Herbert Hugh	1974	LECKIE, Robert Andrew
253	KNOX, Joseph Edward	4767	LEDWIDGE, Albert G.
4760	KNUST, Oswald Percy	1582	LEDWITH, John Patrick
4759	KNUST, Sydney Arthur	6090	LEE, Alfred John
598	KORFF, Earlston W.	6088	LEE, Henry Joseph
1234	KOSTBAR, Ernest	5853	LEE, William James
5843	KOWALD, Edward V.	2710	LEECH, Andrew John
935	KRANTZ, Albert	3547	LEEK, Cyril Robert
1227	KRUSS, August	740	LEEKS, George
4761	KULLERHEIN, Jacob	743	LEER, Norman Leslie
2160	KUMSAY, Cecil George	1725	LEES, Samuel E. G.
5596	KYLE, William Henry	255	LEESE, Arthur Jackson
2933	LACEY, Harold Neil	5854	LEETE, Arthur
6086	LACEY, Louis	257	LEGGE, Arthur Monday
2407	LADIGAN, Alfred	741	LEIGH, Robert
254	LAING, James	1721	LENEHAN, Anthony
747	LAMBERT, Edward	3855	LENEHAN, Arthur M.
261	LAMBERT, Robert	12	LENNON, James Francis
5849	LAMMI, Hyalmar Anton	6833	LENNON, John
2703	LAMOND, George Henry	2536	LENNY, Harold Edward
5371	LAMPRELL, Samuel	4423	LESLIE, James Gordon
2051	LANCE, Linden John	5372	LESTER, Arthur George
1048	LANE, Harry	1723	LESTER, Robert
Lt.	LANE, Henry Edward	a1724	LE SUEUR, Stanley C.
2868	LANE, William	1230	LETTON, Kenneth Smith
941	LANG, John Joseph J.	4766	LEVINGE, Charles H.
6835	LANG, Robert Edward	2707	LEVINSOHN, Harold A.
1720	LANG, William	1726	LEVY, Godfrey
5855	LANKFORD, Thomas P.	2161	LEWIS, Alma Claude R.
2931	LANSDOWN, Alfred G.	6581	LEWIS, Bernard
2491	LARCOMBE, Randell R.	5852	LEWIS, Caleb Lloyd
1802	LARDNER, James Bert	6583	LEWIS, George William
940	LARKIN, Thomas P.	7148	LEWIS, James Ray
770	LARSEN, Charles P. J.	6331	LEWIS, Joseph James
1724	LAST, Albert George	5599	LEWIS, Joseph Phillip
5370	LATHAM, Henry	742	LEWIS, Kenneth George
6631	LAUGHTON, J. G. St. L.	908	LEWIS, Philip John
258	LAUGHTON, Joseph M.	6582	LEWIS, Reuben
1580	LAW, Horace Henry	3851	LEWIS, Stanley George
1238	LAWLER, Edwin	1810	LEWIS, William Henry
608	LAWLER, Timothy	259	LEWIS, William Robert
4465	LAWLESS, John William	7171	LEY, Emile
4463	LAWLESS, William	1723	LIDDELL, Edward James
1963	LAWRENCE, David	264	LIDDY, Edward
3545	LAWRENSON, H. B. L.	1367	LILLIS, Leo
2719	LAWSON, Andrew John	6087	LILLYMAN, Percival J.

No.	Name.	No.	Name.
2163	LINDSAY, Irvine A.	5876	MADDIGGAN, Harold J.
7069	LISTER, Sidney Harold	957	MADDOCKS, Charles F.
4151	LISTON, James	6430	MAGEE, Thomas James
Lt.	LITTLE, Reginald Phelps	619	MAGILL, George Scott
4152	LITTLE, Robert Hugh	4484	MAGRATH, Victor A.
3107	LIVERMORE, Tom D.	1590	MAGUIRE, Cyril James
4153	LIVINGSTONE, John	4470	MAGUIRE, Edward
4478	LIVINGSTONE, V. E. R.	6183	MAGUIRE, Edward J. F.
609	LLOYD, Clyde Allan	1333	MAGUIRE, Eric Lindsay
Lt.	LLOYD, Leonard	3579	MAGUIRE, John G. O.
606	LLOYD, Robert	3585	MAGUIRE, Samuel F. D.
1732	LLEWELYN, Llewelyn H.	620	MAHANAY, Percy
719	LOCK, Henry Peter	5930	MAHER, John Albert
6834	LOCK, Kingsley	270	MAHER, Linus Edward
1613	LOCKE, Arthur Edward	1246	MAHER, Michael
6333	LOCKE, Charles	5053	MAHON, Matthew Henry
Lt.	LOCKWOOD, Frederick R.	6585	MAHONEY, Alfred
1240	LOCKWOOD, John M.	2413	MAHONY, Cornelius J.
5851	LOCKYER, Henry E. W.	1964	MAILEY, Henry Charles
5368	LOCKYER, William H.	Lt.	MAILLER, Frederick A.
3546	LODWICK, Robert Cool	6296	MAIN, Hugh
263	LOGAN, James	5862	MAIN, John
1727	LOHMER, Frank Hood	6103	MAKIN, Arthur
4261	LONG, Frank William	3884	MALKIN, William
4466	LONG, Richard Thomas	4471	MALLIN, Henry
Capt.	LONSDALE, Frank L.	1233	MALONE, Thomas
2165	LORIMER, Alexander	4773	MALONEY, Claude A.
5856	LOVE, John Orr	1965	MALONEY, Henry
5704	LOVE, Victor John	5382	MALTBY, George
754	LOVE, William	1739	MALTHOUSE, F. J.
2409	LOVE, William John	Capt.	MANEFIELD, Ernest T.
3868	LOVEGROVE, Edward	2166	MANION, Michael
6332	LOVERIDGE, Arthur N.	2717	MANN, Arthur Campbell
3544	LOWDEN, O'Dwyer	3897	MANN, Guy Edward
604	LOWE, Albert Leslie	1966	MANNING, Henry C.
270	LOWE, George Stephen	1240	MANNING, William J.
4155	LOWRIE, Ernest	762	MANSELL, Charles
5369	LOWRIE, James Purves	1967	MANSELL, Thomas A.
2/Lt.	LOWTHER, Eric Lionel	3889	MANSFIELD, Alfred B.
Maj.	LUCAS, Cecil Rodwell	950	MANSFIELD, Arthur
1366	LUFFMAN, Bertrand E.	6112	MANSFIELD, David F.
2411	LUMB, Thomas Ezra	6684	MANSFIELD, S. G. G.
2412	LUSTENBERGER, F.	2033	MANSFIELD, William
6914	LUSTY, Walter	6588	MANSON, Eli Frederick
262	LYALL, Alexander	5873	MANSON, John
6091	LYNCH, Albert Victor	4472	MANSON, Robert J.
7070	LYNCH, Denis	6092	MANSON, William
1231	LYNCH, Edward Stephen	3877	MANSTED, Joseph
1232	LYNCH, George	6106	MAPLE, Herbert G.
477	LYNE, Clive Kennedy	5055	MARA, George Joseph
Lt.	LYONS, John Maher	2935	MARCH, Osmond H.
4468	LYONS, Raymond	6649	MARCHANT, Noel
1801	LYONS, Thomas Henry	1235	MARKHAM, William P.
a1173	LYTHGOE, Joseph	3561	MARKS, Luckett
429	MABBOTT, George J.	3564	MARKS, Norman E. F.
290	MACK, William	5384	MARLAN, Ernest William
782	MACKIE, John Reid	2414	MARMON, Charles G. E.
6661	MACKIE, Robert H. H.	4473	MARNEY, Albert Edward
7073	MACKRELL, George	966	MARR, Henry

No.	Name
4156	MARR, Thomas Bede
2167	MARRION, Thomas
3859	MARROTT, William J.
2044	MARSDEN, James
6432	MARSH, Digby
6334	MARSHALL, Andrew
2168	MARSHALL, Cyril John
3882	MARSHALL, Edward Roy
5864	MARSHALL, Frederick
3326	MARSHALL, Herbert J.
6648	MARSHALL, John E.
6848	MARSHALL, John W.
4474	MARSHALL, Lawrence
4157	MARSHALL, William
7165	MARSHALL, William G.
623	MARTIN, Albert Roy
4772	MARTIN, Alfred
622	MARTIN, Archibald
283	MARTIN, Cecil Sydney
T/Brig.-Gen.	MARTIN, E. F.
960	MARTIN, Edwin John
5870	MARTIN, Ernest
4771	MARTIN, Ernest Victor
4475	MARTIN, Frederick
1740	MARTIN, George
4158	MARTIN, Gilbert S.
5865	MARTIN, Harold
6094	MARTIN, Herbert M.
6336	MARTIN, John
1239	MARTIN, John Cecil
4159	MARTIN, Joseph Henry
3886	MARTIN, Roy Mathieson
1238	MARTIN, Selby John
275	MARTIN, Sydney Frank
269	MARTIN, Thomas E.
Lt.	MARTYN, Cecil John
5860	MARTYN, Harry A.
5364	MARTYN, Leslie David
5850	MASKIELL, Charles A.
416	MASKIELL, William W.
7074	MASON, Alfred Ernest
5056	MASON, Cecil George
5869	MASON, Frank
952	MASON, Frederick G.
1672	MASON, James
1236	MASON, Richard
7183	MASON, William
2492	MASON, William Henry
Lt.	MASSEY, Roland Edward
5606	MASSINGHAM, H. C.
496	MASTERS, George S.
1237	MASTERS, Walter H.
Lt.	MASTERSON, Reginald E.
958	MASTERTON, John
5380	MATHERS, George
5061	MATHERSON, Hugo J.
1243	MATHEWS, Arthur J.
Lt.	MATHEWS, Herbert G.
3885	MATHIESON, John
267	MATTERSON, Patrick
2415	MATTHEWMAN, L. H.
Maj.	MAUGHAN, John M.
7075	MAUNSELL, Robert
Lt.	MAWDESLEY, James E.
1968	MAXWELL, Herbert
945	MAY, Frank
2171	MAY, Frederick William
6838	MAY, George
1234	MAY, Gordon James
5604	MAYBERRY, Robert A.
1608	MAYBURY, Valentine J.
Lt.	MAYNARD, Charles R.
6102	MAYNARD, George
285	MAYNARD, Henry
1242	MAYNARD, Leopold
6396	MAYNARD, Norman C.
3317	MAZE, Henry J. R. H.
5064	MAZOUDIER, F. A.
1737	MEAD, Sydney
5373	MEADOWCROFT, C. H.
478	MEALING, Albert E.
4774	MEANEY, Wilfred W.
5857	MEANEY, William G.
953	MEDLEY, Robert Dunn
954	MEDLEY, William T.
1585	MEEHAN, Arthur James
1728	MEEHAN, John Thomas
4161	MEEHAN, William James
423	MEEK, John George
7077	MEILANDT, Fred.
5449	MELLER, Wallace R.
4162	MELROSE, Bernard
5375	MELVILLE, David M.
1742	MELVILLE, William
Lt.	MENDELSOHN, Berrol
1244	MERCER, Harry A.
5871	METHVEN, Stuartson C.
2013	MEWBURN, Albert G. E.
a1571	MEYER, Oswald William
3562	MEYN, Roy Harold
6340	MIATT, Frederick James
6839	MICHELL, Frederick R.
5866	MIDDLETON, James D.
Maj.	MIDDLETON, Sydney A.
266	MILES, Phillip Charles K.
86	MILES, William James
Lt.	MILLAR, James Alex.
1247	MILLAR, John Struthers
286	MILLARD, William H.
636	MILLER, Amos
964	MILLER, Charles Henry
3131	MILLER, David
Lt.	MILLER, Eric Duncan
943	MILLER, Gordon H.
4779	MILLER, John Edward
6109	MILLER, Joseph Charles
3580	MILLER, Victor
1970	MILLER, Walter James
5603	MILLER, William

No.	Name.
2172	MILLER, William Arthur
624	MILLER, William H.
5703	MILLIGAN, Eric
a1301	MILLINGTON, F. E.
1969	MILLS, Jack Leslie
5605	MILNE, James
4780	MILNER, Reginald
6417	MILLS, George G. R.
6418	MILTHORPE, George R.
2173	MILTHORPE, John L.
625	MINES, Frederick C.
6093	MINSHALL, Richard
1586	MINTORN, Norman F.
3898	MITCHELL, Aubrey E.
6101	MITCHELL, Ernest J.
6338	MITCHELL, Gilderoy L.
5374	MITCHELL, Herbert L.
963	MITCHELL, John L.
6840	MITCHELL, K. St. C.
273	MITCHELL, Ralph L.
6342	MITCHELL, William
4777	MITTEN, Horace Edgar
a281	MOCK, Lawson Richard
2732	MOFFAT, Richard
4164	MOFFATT, John
626	MOFFATT, Roy Wallace
2443	MOLLISON, John Bruce
2174	MOLONY, Francis W.
2175	MOLONY, Harold Armour
4476	MONAGHAN, Edward J.
6335	MONKS, Eric Wilfred D.
4477	MONTAGUE, Charles L.
4478	MONTAGUE, Harold L.
1249	MONTGOMERY, H. E.
1813	MONTGOMERY, Robert
2181	MOODY, James
1977	MOON, Norman Ernest
4165	MOORE, Albert Henry
5872	MOORE, Arthur E.
4479	MOORE, Edward
2734	MOORE, Frederick
2178	MOORE, John Augustus
5867	MOORE, John Thomas
3874	MOORE, Joseph Aloysius
5377	MOORE, Leonard S.
1749	MOORE, Percy Albert
6841	MOORE, Richard Zadock
1540	MOORE, Samuel Lowe
1803	MOORE, Sydney Roy
5383	MOORE, Thomas
4167	MOORE, Vivian
Lt.	MOORE, Watler
6602	MOORE, William Ronald
1250	MORAN, Edward
5376	MORAN, James Joseph
1245	MORAN, John
627	MORE, Angus Stuart
3873	MORE, Harry
3888	MORE, Robert Edward

No.	Name.
634	MORELAND, Richard
617	MORGAN, Reginald
6920	MORGAN, Richard Henry
1587	MORGAN, William G.
4168	MORIARTY, J. F. J.
1751	MORLEY, Thomas Wilson
628	MORREN, Fred. William
1251	MORRIS, Arthur Noel
Lt.	MORRIS, David
5378	MORRIS, Edward James
3887	MORRIS, George A.
3879	MORRIS, James Cullen
6842	MORRIS, James Joseph
281	MORRIS, John
7081	MORRIS, Percy Earl
1738	MORRISBY, Risby C.
2858	MORRISBY, Rokeby E.
289	MORRISON, Alexander
779	MORRISON, Alex. D.
5874	MORRISON, James McR.
629	MORTON, Frank Clive
7168	MOSES, Jack
4169	MOSMAN, Irvine B.
7082	MOSSFIELD, John W.
6843	MOTT, Harold Angus
Capt.	MOULSDALE, Fred. W.
4783	MOULT, Charles
630	MOUNTFORD, Ernest A.
791	MUDDLE, Harry
5607	MULHOLLAND, W. R.
7084	MULLENS, Terence M.
2417	MULLIGAN, Alfred G.
3268	MULLIGAN, Bernard
2224	MULLIGAN, Michael J.
959	MULLINS, Michael
5381	MULLINS, Robert James
2955	MULLINS, William
2179	MUNRO, Andrew
2180	MUNRO, Clarence C.
282	MUNTON, Thomas
4483	MURDOCH, James C.
944	MURDOCH, William H.
5379	MURDOCH, William R.
3140	MURNANE, Thomas M.
6111	MURPHY, Charles E.
6098	MURPHY, Francis
Capt.	MURPHY, Francis J. P.
1063	MURPHY, James
Lt.	MURPHY, Joseph Henry
280	MURPHY, Thomas
1594	MURPHY, Thomas
6594	MURPHY, Thomas J.
949	MURPHY, William
5701	MURRAY, Alfred
7087	MURRAY, Andrew
837	MURRAY, Donald
6660	MURRAY, Edward Cecil
1750	MURRAY, Frank A. R.
7085	MURRAY, Frederick J.

No.	Name.	No.	Name.
1623	MURRAY, George Gilbert	1388	MACDONALD, William J.
2493	MURRAY, Harry	4488	McDONELL, Charles J.
6108	MURRAY, James Francis	5683	McDONNELL, Horace H.
5875	MURRAY, John	967	McDONNELL, William J.
6837	MURRAY, Oswald R.	1978	MacDONOGH, Oliver
1624	MURRAY, Reginald E.	6167	McDOUGALL, Angus J.
6096	MURRAY, Robert	5877	McDOUGALL, John
5671	MURRAY, Stanley	2/Lt.	McDOWELL, Alexander R.
5324	MURRAY-COWPER, N. D.	6846	McDOWELL, Hughey
6341	MURRELL, Henry G.	4489	McDOWELL, James
1735	MUTCH, James	1259	McEACHARN, W. A.
4171	MYERS, Fred.	1056	McENALLY, John
2861	McANALLEY, Henry J.	4494	McETEE, Frank
1583	McARTHUR, George	253	McEWAN, William
6836	MACAULAY, Martin R.	1593	McFADDEN, Edward
4486	McAULIFFE, Joseph	Lt.	McFADDEN, Robert
Lt.	McBRIDE, Charles A.	6659	McFADYEN, Arthur J.
962	McBRIDE, Charles Joseph	5611	McFADYEN, Donald
3880	McCAFFREY, Andrew J.	1255	MACFARLANE, Alex.
6592	McCALL, John Campbell	375	MACFARLANE, M. R.
2182	MacCALLUM, Alexander	6678	McFARLANE, Vernon B.
7167	McCALLUM, Leslie	835	McGARVA, Matthew
Lt.	McCARTER, Victor	1261	McGAUGHEY, John W.
4789	McCARTHY, Harold E.	4798	McGAULLEY, Francis R.
378	McCARTHY, Herbert	6346	McGINLEY, John Henry
1256	McCARTHY, John Joseph	374	McGINTY, Frederick J.
610	McCARTHY, John T.	2418	McGLASHAN, Arthur W.
288	McCARTHY, Stephen	4490	McGOULRICK, Joseph F.
1974	McCARTHY, Thomas	3893	McGOVERN, Roy S.
4790	McCARTHY, Thomas J.	965	McGOWAN, Patrick
6845	McCARTIN, John K.	274	McGRATH, John Francis
968	McCARTNEY, Francis	615	McGRATH, John Joseph
4173	McCARTNEY, Russell W.	5868	McGRATH, Michael E.
1591	McCLEER, John Edward	948	MACGREGOR, Daniel
63	McCLINTOCK, G. T.	1743	McGRIGOR, William L.
Lt.	McCLURE, James Howe	6105	McGUINNESS, John H.
6350	McCLYMONT, Arthur J.	4491	McGUINNESS, William J.
6343	McCONACHIE, James	6344	McGUIRE, Mervyn R.
1975	McCORD, Thomas Harold	1258	MACGUIRE, William
1252	McCORD, William	279	McHENRY, Albert
Lt.	McCOURT, William R.	3878	McILWAIN, Eric H.
1976	McCOY, Thomas Norman	6589	McILWRAITH, George
1977	McCOY, Wilfred Stanley	434	McINERNEY, Daniel C.
Lt.	McCULLOCH, Edward H.	4796	McINNES, Alexander J.
955	McCULLOCH, William L.	1979	McINNES, John Robert
5861	McCURLEY, Leslie James	5613	McINNES, William Angus
2859	McDERMID, Hume D.	5388	MACINTOSH, Alexander
Lt.	McDIARMID, John James	956	McINTOSH, Charles
1592	McDONALD, Alfred	771	McINTOSH, George
5612	McDONALD, Allan C.	612	McINTOSH, Robert Henry
7078	McDONALD, Angus	1980	McINTYRE, Sylvester R.
1748	McDONALD, David	271	McINTYRE, William F.
618	McDONALD, Donald	616	McKAY, Alexander C.
276	McDONALD, Finlay	295	McKAY, Alfred H. B.
942	McDONALD, Hugh	2419	McKAY, Andrew Raymond
611	McDONALD, John E.	2543	McKAY, Daniel
6349	McDONALD, John G.	1387	McKAY, George C. C.
277	McDONALD, Murdoch	781	McKAY, Magnus James
946	MACDONALD, John A.	6601	McKAY, William Angus

No.	Name.	No.	Name.
1260	McKECHNIE, Angus D.	1383	NAISH, Ernest
5386	McKEE, Osmund Charles	Lt.	NALDER, Gordon F.
1981	McKENZIE, Andrew J.	2251	NANCARROW, R. W.
6100	McKENZIE, George A.	2252	NANCARROW, Roland V.
1564	McKENZIE, Howard D.	5389	NAPIER, Robert Kenneth
1338	McKENZIE, Hugh	4495	NAUGHTON, Ernest C.
7076	MACKENZIE, John F. N.	2741	NAYLOR, Charles John
Capt.	MACKENZIE, Keith W.	973	NEAL, George Douglas
2545	McKENZIE, Kenneth G.	4496	NEAVE, Edward L.
Lt.	MACKENZIE, L. G.	3900	NEGUS, Walter Allan
1816	McKENZIE, Robert B.	638	NELSON, Edward John
1982	McKENZIE, Sydney Roy	1265	NESBITT, James Alfred
1821	McKENZIE, William A.	2/Lt.	NEVEN, Edward Denis
3575	McKINLAY, Clarence A.	640	NEVEN, James
3115	McKINLAY, William	1264	NEVILLE, Curtis
3569	McKINLEY, Ronald John	748	NEVILLE, Harold
6104	McKINNIREY, Lawrence	Lt.	NEW, Ernest Crego
2247	McLAREN, Alexander M.	5619	NEWELL, Kenneth G. T.
2727	McLAREN, Benjamin H.	4802	NEWELL, William F.
5387	McLAUGHLAN, James R.	5163	NEWEY, Walter Roy
4179	McLEAN, Charles A.	a1577	NEWMAN, Henry John
942	MACLEAN, Harry	1074	NEWMAN, Joseph Lewis
2266	McLEAN, Martin	b2962	NEWMAN, Martin
4492	McLEAN, Reginald D. J.	2762	NEWMAN, William Allen
268	McLEAN, Roderick C.	5616	NEWNS, John Frederick
4869	McLEAN, Thomas A.	298	NEWSTEAD, Arthur J.
1063	McLEAN, William B.	969	NEWTON, James Edward
1369	McLEAY, Arthur Roy	5879	NEWTON, Rupert H. D.
613	McLEAY, Donald A.	1815	NICHOLAS, William O.
6158	McLEOD, Donald Bennett	1595	NICHOLS, Neville
1254	McLEOD, Warwick J.	Lt.	NICHOLSON, Charles R.
1745	McMAHON, John Joseph	4181	NICHOLSON, James
284	McMAHON, Michael Peter	7088	NICHOLSON, Scott L. O.
780	McMANUS, Michael J.	1266	NICOLL, Charles R.
2184	McMASTER, H. W. V.	4182	NIDDRIE, Albert
Maj.	McMASTER, Robert M.	4183	NIDDRIE, Reginald John
6927	McMILES, Robert	4184	NIDDRIE, William
6596	McMILLAN, Francis A.	6351	NIES, Theodore Marshall
5609	McMULKIN, Leslie James	3901	NIGHTINGALE, Roy
5385	McMURTRIE, John J.	1343	NIMMO, Sylvester James
2730	McNAIR, Livingstone F.	5617	NIX, Rupert Henry
294	McNAIR, William	6210	NIXON, Arthur
6847	McNAMARA, Henry R.	5865	NIXON, Walter
614	McNAMARA, Robert M.	4185	NOAH, Henry Lionel
3120	McNAMARA, William A.	1040	NOBLE, Andrew
2420	McNAUGHTON, George	1267	NOBLE, Henry William
272	McNEALLY, John Horace	5390	NOBLE, Robert Henry
6345	McNULTY, Albert E.	2185	NOKE, John Stanley
383	McPAUL, Harry D. B.	1372	NOLAN, William Michael
Lt.	McPHEE, George Roy	1596	NOON, James Thomas
4493	McPHERSON, Edgar W.	1753	NOONAN, John
746	McPHERSON, John	6113	NORMAN, Hugh
1752	MacPHERSON, John E.	5882	NORMAN, Sydney C.
1368	McPHILLIMY, Norman R.	2502	NORQUAY, William
5858	McQUARRIE, John	4186	NORRIS, Dennis William
2500	McTAGUE, Bernard M.	4187	NORRIS, Francis Roland
1057	McVICAR, Hugh Graham	2/Lt.	NORRIS, George William
6114	NAGLE, Norman Clifford	6352	NORTH, Garnett R.
637	NAGLE, William J.	a2956	NORTHEY, Richard

No.	Name	No.	Name
5880	NUGENT, Francis John	6181	OSMOND, William
389	NUGENT, Frank Leslie	652	O'TOOLE, James P.
5881	NUMMELIN, Karl W.	1986	OUTRAM, Samuel
Lt.	NUNN, John Reginald	50923	OVERTON, John W.
65	NUNNS, William Thomas	378	OWEN, James
297	NYMAN, Abraham	4192	OWEN, Peter
3596	OAKEY, Sidney	3644	OWEN, Philip Ernest
5391	OAKMAN, R. M. T.	5127	PAGE, Francis Allan
7090	OBERG, Edwin Thomas	2254	PAGE, Frederick G.
2187	O'BRIEN, Arthur	6850	PAGE, George Thomas
7091	O'BRIEN, Charles	303	PAGE, Stanley
2188	O'BRIEN, Daniel A.	302	PAGE, Stephen
7092	O'BRIEN, Denis	744	PALLISTER, George R.
5693	O'BRIEN, Luke	1045	PALMER, Arthur J.
974	O'BRIEN, Robert John	7153	PALMER, Eric Gouley
300	O'BYRNE, Thomas P.	6122	PALMER, Ernest
6115	OCKENDEN, C. R.	3601	PALMER, Reginald
980	O'CONNELL, David F.	Lt.	PALMER, W. H. B.
646	O'CONNOR, Leo. F.	656	PAPPS, Cyril
647	O'CONNOR, Peter R.	6213	PAPPS, Stanley Graham
975	O'CONNOR, Roderick	2757	PARDEY, Frederick R.
6606	O'CONNOR, Thomas A.	1761	PARDEY, Harold
1215	O'CONNOR, Thomas W.	2537	PARIS, Henry Hyden
3593	O'DONOVAN, Thomas	6121	PARKER, Ebb Richard
4189	O'DRISCOLL, Peter	3755	PARKER, Frederick H.
4193	OFFORD, Albert E.	1987	PARKER, Herbert B.
1269	OGILVIE, Charles W.	5937	PARKER, Herbert L.
1371	OGILVIE, John Lyall	5706	PARKES, Herbert L.
Lt.	O'GRADY, Walter J. S.	657	PARKES, Roy Horace
5612	O'HANLON, James A.	2045	PARKINS, Reginald T.
1614	O'HARA, Daniel	3905	PARKINSON, Louis J.
299	O'HARA, Hamilton H.	6120	PARR, William
5883	O'HARAN, Patrick	379	PARRY, Jack Percival
6855	O'HEHIR, John	4194	PARRY, John
979	O'KEEFE, Edward J.	305	PARSONS, Charles E.
3594	O'KEEFE, Patrick A.	4195	PARSONS, John Edward
5621	OLDHAM, Herbert	3151	PATERSON, Allan
650	O'LEARY, John George	665	PATERSON, James
6878	O'LEARY, William L.	1270	PATTERSON, Harry
2966	OLIVER, James Inglis	983	PATTERSON, Malcolm
4190	OLLIVER, Oswald T.	2509	PATTERSON, Thomas E.
4191	OLSEN, Alfred	1271	PAUL, Hugh Lindsay
7093	OLSEN, James Galbert	1625	PAYNE, Harry
2455	OLSEN, Norman Peter	6857	PAYNE, William
841	O'MEARA, Matthew J.	4196	PEACE, Walter
654	O'NEIL, Henry	6125	PEACHMAN, William E.
4499	O'NEILL, Edwin John	b1582	PEACOCK, Norman
6603	O'NEILL, Eugene L.	1347	PEARCE, Charles
1051	O'NEILL, Francis P.	309	PEARCE, Frank
3595	O'NEILL, Henry E.	4198	PEARCE, William H. L.
297	O'NEILL, John	1272	PEARS, Arthur
1984	O'NEILL, John Thomas	661	PEARSON, Harold John
2190	ONIONS, George A.	660	PEARSON, Henry B.
1985	ORMAN, William G. H.	6124	PEARSON, Leslie B.
976	ORRELL, Joseph R.	5392	PEARSON, Thomas H.
5620	O'SHANNASSY, D. E.	304	PEAT, Henry
4500	O'SHANNESSY, Patrick	1991	PEATE, William
977	O'SHEA, William	662	PEATFIELD, Ernest G.
5622	OSMAN, William Sydney	4502	PEATY, Wilfred Le G.

No.	Name.	No.	Name.
2427	PECK, John	6354	POOLE, William
1578	PEGRUM, William H.	6609	POPE, William Fred
4199	PELLING, William	1992	PORTEOUS, Neville L.
6597	PENDERGAST, Leslie	5886	PORTER, John Stevens
313	PENDLETON, Alfred	312	POST, Joseph
Lt.	PENFOLD, Herbert W.	4811	POTTER, Alfred W.
2506	PENKETH, Percy J.	1993	POTTER, Arthur G.
1988	PENMAN, John	1994	POTTER, Miles
4356	PENNANT, Thomas H.	2760	POTTS, Donald McI.
6119	PENNY, Charles E.	981	POULTON, Derrick E.
5073	PEPPER, Raymond L.	1631	POULTON, Francis E.
6610	PERIGO, Norman D.	3600	POWELL, Aubrey G.
4503	PERKINS, Edward C.	1995	POWELL, Eric Gordon
b2971	PERKINS, William H.	4508	POWER, John Francis
663	PERKS, Frederick W.	5074	POWER, Terence
a2966	PERRY, George F.	5394	POWER, Thomas
a2961	PETERS, Charles E. D.	6208	PREDDY, Edward C.
7096	PETERS, Harry Miner	3321	PRESS, Charles Edmund
6612	PETERSEN, Chris. L.	306	PRICE, John Elias
Lt.	PETTIT, Rodney W.	4202	PRICE, John Smith
36651	PHELPS, Kenneth	4814	PRICE, Patrick Cyril
Lt.	PHELPS, Reginald T.	2431	PRITCHARD, Henry A.
396	PHILIP, George A.	2046	PRITCHARD, Joseph R.
6858	PHILLIPS, Arthur H.	1273	PRITCHARD, Reuben F.
2192	PHILLIPS, Charles	3659	PRITZLER, W. S. B.
2/Lt.	PHILLIPS, Charles H.	307	PROCTOR, W. W. G.
4504	PHILLIPS, Daniel	985	PROSPER, S. J. J.
6849	PHILLIPS, Laurie A.	1274	PRYKE, Thomas Joseph
1989	PHILLIPS, Leslie C.	5445	PRYSE, L. N. S. W.
2193	PHILLIPS, Thomas	Lt.	PULLING, Guy Harris
2430	PHILLIPS, William G.	6118	PURCELL, Robert H.
6683	PICKERING, George G.	7154	PURVIS, John Turnbull
6662	PIDDINGTON, George B.	Lt./Col.	PYE, Cecil Robert A.
666	PIDDINGTON, H. R. M.	Lt.	PYE, Raymond Elton
6123	PIERCE, Herbert E.	1990	PYKE, George Alfred
6117	PIERPONT, Henry J.	6353	PYKETT, Frederick
308	PIGGOTT, Percy	2279	QUARTLY, Walter R.
6375	PIGGOTT, Ronald T.	1996	QUILTY, Maurice
421	PIKE, Idris Charles	5397	QUINN, Henry John
5393	PILGRIM, William D.	5387	QUINN, James Arthur
3599	PILKINGTON, Walter	6355	QUINNELL, Bertie E.
1820	PINCHAM, Claude V.	6860	RABE, Robert James
2288	PINCOTT, William John	Lt.	RABEY, Walter October
642	PINSON, William John	315	RACE, George James
5885	PIPER, Charles E.	318	RADFORD, Cyril Ray.
5395	PITT, Alfred Joseph	6377	RADFORD, Edward J.
4201	PLATT, Reginald Theo.	4817	RADLEY, Harry
5933	PLEASANTS, Jack	Capt.	RAE, Douglas Frank
1991	PLUMB, Reg. W. A.	Lt.	RAE, Frederick George
2815	PLUMMER, Elver G.	Lt.	RAINE, Edmund Ralston
1356	PLUNKETT, Fred. W.	3162	RAINE, Thomas F.
5616	POCKNALL, Ben. J.	6169	RAIT, Samuel Fry
3602	POINER, Herbert Alex.	1276	RAITT, John William
1626	POLLOCK, Alexander	6861	RALPHS, Eric Clyde
3904	POMERY, Victoria	6922	RAMAGE, Vivian Rule
2255	POOLE, Frederick A.	Lt.	RAMSAY, Harrie S.
1757	POOLE, Frederick W.	3652	RAMSAY, Robert
4505	POOLE, James Joseph	5891	RAMSEY, Frederick T.
4506	POOLE, John Thomas		

No.	Name.	No.	Name.
2194	RAND, Frank William	2436	RIGLEY, Lancelot J.
2766	RANDLE, Frank	6170	RILEY, George Thomas
4511	RANKIN, Arthur	3910	RINGROSE, Joseph M.
4512	RASHLEIGH, Arthur C.	5890	RIORDAN, William W.
2768	RATCLIFFE, Edmond	669	RITCHIE, Horace
2196	RATH, Harry Henry	1999	RIVERS, Charles W.
a1712	RATH, John Patrick	3155	RIXON, James Thomas
2195	RATH, William Henry	3917	ROACH, Timothy M.
2/Lt.	RAVELL, Walter Henry	4515	ROBB, Thomas
5402	RAWSON, Geoffrey	3166	ROBERTS, Alfred G.
Lt.	READ, Ernest Archibald	1285	ROBERTS, David
1997	READ, Frederick E.	4517	ROBERTS, Edward P. K.
Lt.	READ, Tom Rowles	7155	ROBERTS, John
6133	READFORD, Walter A.	4823	ROBERTS, Joseph A.
5625	REECE, Harold	3913	ROBERTS, Thomas
2432	REED, Alfred A. B.	1763	ROBERTS, Thomas H.
1615	REED, Thomas	2199	ROBERTS, Trent
1064	REES, John	1337	ROBERTS, William A.
1102	REES, Thomas B.	2257	ROBERTSON, David
5632	REES, Thomas James	5887	ROBERTSON, Henry
991	REES, Victor John	314	ROBERTSON, Herb. W.
3918	REEVE, John	3288	ROBERTSON, John G.
6132	REGAN, Reginald J.	6908	ROBERTSON, John S.
3912	REGLIN, Norman S.	376	ROBERTSON, John T.
2433	REID, Charles Porteous	6188	ROBERTSON, Leslie
50934	REID, George Alex.	7120	ROBERTSON, Thomas D.
3286	REID, Mersey Albert	2000	ROBERTSON, W. R.
1278	REILLY, Felix	Lt.	ROBERTSON, W. A.
4219	RENNARD, Jesse	Lt.	ROBINS, Charles
788	RENTELL, Harry E.	4516	ROBINS, Roy Reginald
6916	RESTELL, G. H. E.	3915	ROBINS, William John
6617	REYNOLDS, Albert G.	6139	ROBINSON, Frank Bede
b2722	REYNOLDS, Clarence E.	6394	ROBINSON, Frank Bede
6134	REYNOLDS, William E.	7099	ROBINSON, Harold E.
4220	REYNOLDS, William H.	5399	ROBINSON, Laidley C.
6650	RHODES, John W. F.	5400	ROBINSON, Robert H.
3916	RHODIN, William H.	5634	ROBINSON, Vivian D.
1765	RICE, Percy Albert	6615	ROBINSON, William
691	RICHARDS, George	6863	ROBINSON, William E.
Capt.	RICHARDS, George J.	5889	ROBSON, George H.
4513	RICHARDS, Henry	5624	ROBSON, Oscar Lester
2197	RICHARDSON, James	2200	ROCHE, Cyril John
2/Lt.	RICHARDSON, John L.	316	ROCHFORD, William D.
5684	RICHARDSON, Leslie N.	1335	ROCKLIFF, Herbert
Lt.	RICHARDSON, Stan. R.	2272	ROCKS, Leslie
3609	RICHARDSON, Thomas	2271	ROCKS, Patrick Bede
2198	RICHARDSON, W. J.	2/Lt.	RODDIS, George E.
1627	RICHES, Herbert	28976	RODERICK, Thomas J.
Lt.	RICHMOND, George K.	2001	RODGERS, Anthony T.
2435	RIDDICK, Frederick T.	675	ROE, William
1762	RIDDINGTON, Sydney J.	7098	ROFFEY, William A.
6160	RIDDLE, Alfred Frank	2050	ROGERS, Hurtle
a4593	RIDGE, George Henry	7097	ROGERS, Joseph James
1232	RIDLEY, Henry Hope	670	ROGERS, Reginald R.
319	RIDLEY, Simon	1364	ROGERS-HARRISON Harry Roy
Lt.	RIDLEY, Thomas		
1277	RIGBY, James Matthew	5629	ROGERSON, James
1684	RIGG, William Leslie	5630	ROGERSON, John

No.	Name.	No.	Name.
6852	ROLES, George	Capt.	SALIER, Horace James
6127	ROLFE, Clarence Rolber	2004	SALISBURY, George R.
5313	ROLLAN, Alexander B.	6142	SALISBURY, Lance J.
3907	ROLLINSON, Arthur A.	676	SAM, Henry Herbert
6357	ROMEY, Cecil	1776	SAMPSON, David
Capt.	RONALD, Harry	Lt.	SAMS, Charles James
4822	ROOSE, Hugh Francis	4214	SAMUEL, Alexander D.
6358	ROPER, George	5895	SANDERS, William R.
320	ROPER, Norman H.	2005	SANDERSON, Norman R.
5625	ROSE, William Arthur	4230	SANDON, Leslie J.
Lt.	ROSS, Allan Clunies	Lt.	SANDS, Cleve Chisholm
5628	ROSS, Donald	689	SARGENT, Arthur H.
2201	ROSS, James	678	SAULT, David James
2438	ROSS, James Delprado	6909	SAUNDERCOCK, A. R.
6356	ROSS, John Walter	6627	SAUNDERS, Abe
2845	ROSS, Maurice Joseph	a2990	SAUNDERS, Daniel G.
Lt.	ROSS, Robert Murray	2979	SAUNDERS, Edward T.
1766	ROSS, Theodore	679	SAUNDERS, Frederick J.
671	ROUT, Leslie Hopkins	1005	SAUNDERS, Harry A.
5083	ROWAN, John Thomas	5412	SAVAGE, Alfred C.
1284	ROWE, Walter	5418	SAVAGE, Henry
6359	ROWE, William	1373	SAVILLE, Alfred D.
5626	ROWELL, Maurice E.	5932	SAW, John
4518	ROY, Thomas Albert	6135	SAWLE, Francis T.
994	ROYAL, Sidney	1289	SAWYER, Leonard Lynn
1287	ROYALL, Reginald H.	2261	SAYERS, Alfred John
1764	ROYAN, George Alex.	4216	SCANLAN, James
6853	ROYDE, Benjamin T.	328	SCHWEITZER, Stan. G.
2284	ROYDS, Leonard	2782	SCHWONBERG, C. G.
5455	ROZEA, Alan Broadley	5636	SCOTT, Alexander
1288	RUBIE, Phillip J. H.	4232	SCOTT, Cuthbert H.
1281	RUDD, Norman Henry	6366	SCOTT, Ernest
5401	RUDDER, Reginald B.	319	SCOTT, James
2439	RUDKIN, William Henry	6146	SCOTT, Norman
5627	RUELLE, James	7101	SCOTT, Robert
2002	RUSHWORTH, Henry	7103	SCOTT, Robert Bruce
6126	RUSSELL, Claude C.	5413	SCOTT, Thomas
2003	RUSSELL, Forbes	4217	SCULLIN, Thomas E.
6130	RUSSELL, Robert	6864	SCURR, Rupert George
7100	RUSSELL, Stanley G.	6174	SEABROOK, George R.
3164	RUST, James	6147	SEABROOK, Theo. Leslie
4519	RUTHERFORD, H. B.	2/Lt.	SEABROOK, William K.
409	RYAN, Albert Edward	333	SEAEGG, Augustus
674	RYAN, Arthur Joseph	6159	SEALEY, Herbert C.
992	RYAN, James	5086	SEARCH, William A.
1633	RYAN, James	2442	SEATON, Ernest
990	RYAN, John	1293	SEE, William Samuel
2979	RYAN, Michael Thomas	6398	SELLS, Frederick R.
3165	RYAN, Philip	2514	SELMES, Walter James
3914	RYAN, Roger Patrick	1657	SELWAY, Arthur
2/Lt.	RYAN, Thomas Lloyd	1295	SENDALL, F. W. A. S.
4520	RYDQUIST, Sydney C.	6419	SERGEANT, Arthur J.
790	SABEY, John Warrick	996	SEWARD, Gilbert
7110	SADLER, Philip Alfred	5896	SEWARD, James W.
Lt:/Co.	SADLER, Rupert M.	1771	SEWELL, Claude J.
2205	SADLER, William	2006	SEYMOUR, Alex. A. W.
4824	SAGAR, James	3939	SEYMOUR, Charles A.
327	SAINES, Robert	5699	SEYMOUR, George

No.	Name.	No.	Name.
6630	SEYMOUR, Harry T.	2026	SKERRITT, Alwyn J.
783	SEYMOUR, Rupert L.	4221	SKINNER, Alfred James
995	SHAKESPEARE, J. C.	3909	SKINNER, Charles
3615	SHANAHAN, John J.	4222	SKINNER, Ellis Gabriel
1290	SHARKEY, Edward B.	2837	SLADE, Alfred Fitzroy
2513	SHARMAN, Mark	3032	SLATER, Ernest
2511	SHARP, Ernest	4223	SLATER, William
333	SHARP, William	2053	SLATTERY, A. J.
1296	SHARPLEY, Gilbert A.	5415	SLINGSBY, Dudley C.
Lt.	SHAW, Harry Edmund	2304	SLOAN, William
3892	SHAW, Thomas William	6666	SLOMAN, Ronald U.
5898	SHAW, Victor Charles	Lt.	SMALL, George
337	SHAW, William	5638	SMART, Alfred James
331	SHEA, Henry Lionel	6885	SMITH, Albert Arthur
2739	SHEA, Harold W. G. T. J.	1777	SMITH, Alberto Edward
6361	SHEAHAN, John	6137	SMITH, Albert George
5404	SHEAHAN, William F. P.	6370	SMITH, Albert Wallace
Lt.	SHEDDEN, Rubert E.	6926	SMITH, Alfred
3930	SHEEHAN, John	3182	SMITH, Cecil Bowden
1277	SHEEN, Albert	3937	SMITH, Clarence Sidney
2512	SHEFFIELD, Leslie A.	6363	SMITH, Claude Lester
5631	SHEIL, William Alex.	4527	SMITH, Claude William
2206	SHELLEY, Charles	Maj.	SMITH, Clive Nigel
5705	SHEPHERD, James E.	1599	SMITH, Crief Clive
2007	SHEPHERD, Leslie A.	6362	SMITH, Ernest J. J.
4218	SHEPHERD, Walter J.	3627	SMITH, Frank E.
Capt.	SHEPPARD, W. H. S.	1582	SMITH, Frederick
2737	SHERIDAN, John W.	Lt.	SMITH, Frederick W. D.
6687	SHERROTT, Joseph W.	326	SMITH, George
Lt.	SHIELD, Richard V.	2448	SMITH, George Alex.
7105	SHIELDS, Archibald H.	2449	SMITH, George Fred.
2835	SHIPLEY, Glen Stanton	4225	SMITH, George Henry
6148	SHOESMITH, William	3931	SMITH, George Oscar
Maj.	SHORT, George Robert	Lt.	SMITH, Harold Jackson
7106	SHORT, Ronald B. N.	6176	SMITH, Henry
1297	SHORTHOUSE, Ralph	5417	SMITH, Henry Forbes
1385	SHUCK, George Henry	4275	SMITH, Henry John
7102	SHUMACK, Henry	1632	SMITH, Horace Victor
5892	SHUTE, Arnold	4575	SMITH, Jack
2207	SIEVERS, Henry	1062	SMITH, James
6667	SILLAR, Ralph S. B.	6368	SMITH, James
2008	SIMONS, George R.	6420	SMITH, Jackson
1007	SIMONS, Stafford	3168	SMITH, John Clarence
3624	SIMPSON, George	4530	SMITH, Peter
680	SIMPSON, Neville Wynn	1774	SMITH, Richard George
4219	SIMPSON, Norman M.	3903	SMITH, Richard Patrick
2047	SIMPSON, Peter	2259	SMITH, Robert George
3927	SIMPSON, Ralph Eric	2216	SMITH, Robert John
2444	SIMS, Frederick G.	3938	SMITH, Robert Septimus
3928	SIMS, William Edwin	3628	SMITH, Sidney
2445	SINCLAIR, Alex. Aikeman	338	SMITH, Sydney Augustus
4543	SINCLAIR, Alfred Joseph	4544	SMITH, Thomas Bertie
1778	SINCLAIR, Ronald	684	SMITH, Thomas Edgely
1767	SISSONS, George F. D.	6865	SMITH, Thomas Oswald
1071	SIVIL, Charles Richard	1399	SMITH, Walter John
5416	SKEEN, Alfred	2534	SMITH, William
5641	SKELLY, Bernard J.	4834	SMITH, William A. C.
4829	SKELSEY, Leslie	4531	SMITH, William Eric

No.	Name.
6866	SMITH, William John
998	SMITH, William M.
3621	SMITHERS, James E.
4227	SMYTH, Cecil Hilton
4228	SMYTH, Walter
Hon. Major	SMYTHE, E. V.
293	SNELL, Henry Irvine
5885	SNELL, Walter Alex.
2530	SNOWDON, Fred. L.
1004	SOLOMON, Percy M.
335	SOMERFORD, W. A.
1294	SOMERSET, Henry C. F
1386	SOMERVILLE, John Ted
755	SOMMERVILLE, T. J.
2834	SOUTHGATE, V. C.
4229	SOUTHWELL, William
6138	SPENCE, Ernest
6910	SPENCE, Norman H.
1598	SPENCER, Frederick
4584	SPENCER, Harold V.
5457	SPENCER, John
889	SPICER, Albert Victor
5637	SPICER, Sydney
Capt.	SPIER, Reginald Vincent
1360	SPIERS, Edmund
1001	SPILLANE, Thomas F.
325	SPINDLER, Ernest F.
6381	SPRING, Gerald Arthur
2208	SPRING, Henry Keith
4230	SPRINGFORD, William
2535	SPROULE, Reg. G. J.
2992	SPURR, Herbert Hector
685	SPURWAY, Roy W.
433	STACE, Thomas
6398	STACK, Edward Michael
3620	STACKPOOL, John
6628	STALDER, Daniel John
324	STAMP, Crichton A.
4533	STANFORD, Arthur J.
5406	STANFORD, William
1299	STANLEY, Frederick R.
1300	STANSBURY, Arthur R.
36	STANT, Richard
1770	STANTON, Leslie F.
4830	STAPLETON, Edward
3623	STAPLETON, William J.
a671	STARR, Bertie George
1291	STARR, William Gordon
5897	STARR, William Henry
a1601	ST. CLAIR, William G.
7109	STEDMAN, Stanley
2783	STEEL, Arthur Leonard
6867	STEELE, Arthur James
5893	STEELE, George Alex.
435	STEELE, Harry
6141	STEELE, John
5894	STEELE, Percy Sidney
2771	STEPHEN, Cecil M.

No.	Name.
3936	STEPHEN, Hibiscus
690	STEPHENSON, Albert
332	STEPHENSON, Frederick
6367	STEPHENSON, Harold
1278	STERLAND, Stanley J.
7108	STERLING, William L.
4535	STEVENS, Edward H.
334	STEVENS, Reginald C.
686	STEVESON, Robert C.
4231	STEWART, Albert J.
3622	STEWART, Alfred R. M.
773	STEWART, Charles E.
1292	STEWART, George S.
997	STEWART, Gilbert
330	STEWART, John
5409	STEWART, Joseph C.
6663	STEWART, Wilfred J.
2044	STIFF, Alexander A. C.
6679	STILLER, Norman A.
761	STILLMAN, Hugh S.
6626	STINSON, James Edward
6624	STINSON, Thomas M.
2012	STIRLING, Neville Roy
2013	STIRTON, Kenneth A.
6632	STOAKES, Arthur Ernest
6665	STOCKHAM, Charles N.
6371	STOCKS, Ernest Joseph
4536	STONE, Charles
5640	STONE, Frederick
4576	STONE, George C. D.
1600	STONE, Hugh Dalrymple
4537	STONE, Joseph Phineas
2775	STONE, Reginald Albert
2450	STONER, William
4232	STORR, Alfred
1375	STOW, Eric Edward
323	STRACHAN, Walter R.
4233	STRAFFORD, Robert W.
4234	STRAHAN, David
1000	STRAHAN, John
5411	STRANLUND, Olaf Ernest
5408	STREET, Harry M.
1303	STUART, Arthur
4538	STUART, Edward G.
1304	STUBBINGS, John J.
6139	STUBBS, Malcolm F.
4539	STUBBS, Robert E.
5407	STUNTZ, John
1006	STUTTER, George
6172	STYLES, Robert
1352	STYNES, Edgar D.
329	SULLIVAN, Arthur G.
4235	SULLIVAN, Francis J.
3906	SULLIVAN, Francis J.
5899	SULLIVAN, James
6881	SULLIVAN, John
4236	SULLIVAN, Martin
Lt.	SULLIVAN, Victor J.

No.	Name.
4540	SUTCLIFFE, Frederick
5405	SUTER, Henry
687	SUTTON, Charles
4836	SUTTON, Harry
3925	SUTTON, John
6369	SUTTON, Joseph George
6140	SUTTON, Thomas A. J.
4541	SWAIN, John Alex.
ə1776	SWAN, Arthur
4238	SWAN, Norman Cedric
4239	SWANBURY, Joseph J.
2209	SWANKIE, John
2210	SWANSON, Donald
5639	SWEETNAM, Hector C.
4542	SWITHENBANK, J. F.
6641	SYKES, Robert L.
2287	SYMONS, Frank R.
388	SYMONS, James Edwin
2800	TACON, Ivan George
4545	TAIT, Alfred Alexander
417	TAIT, Andrew Scott
774	TAIT, Robert
3189	TALBOT, James Gavin
5905	TALBOT, John William
757	TALBOT, Nelson
1341	TALBOT, Sidney
1782	TANNER, George
6378	TANNER, James
Lt.	TAPLIN, Archibald S.
2015	TARGETT, Henry
5646	TAYLOR, Albert G. V.
4277	TAYLOR, Alexander J.
6686	TAYLOR, Arthur V.
5644	TAYLOR, Charles
4547	TAYLOR, Charles F.
1053	TAYLOR, Edgar James E.
4840	TAYLOR, Edward
Lt.	TAYLOR, Edwin David
1601	TAYLOR, George Henry
343	TAYLOR, Harold Parker
340	TAYLOR, Harry
751	TAYLOR, Henry Gordon
2211	TAYLOR, James Herman
382	TAYLOR, James Horace
Lt.	TAYLOR, John Peebles
3630	TAYLOR, Richard H.
7113	TAYLOR, Robert
3933	TAYLOR, Thomas Henry
2790	TAYLOR, Thomas S.
5645	TAYLOR, Walter Edwin
6149	TAYLOR, William B.
1019	TAYLOUR, Angus E.
3944	TEAGUE, Hugh Charles
4548	TEEBOON, Frederick H.
5092	TEMPLEMAN, Wilfred P.
4549	THEOBOLD, William
6923	THICKINS, William H.
1009	THOMAS, Alfred

No.	Name.
6379	THOMAS, Alfred
2988	THOMAS, Charles Victor
2016	THOMAS, Frederick M.
1015	THOMAS, George Albert
6374	THOMAS, Ralph W. H.
4244	THOMAS, Robert Ernest
594	THOMPSON, Albert E.
2000	THOMPSON, Albert E.
6421	THOMPSON, Alexander
6375	THOMPSON, Alex. F.
694	THOMPSON, Claude E.
5900	THOMPSON, George
1306	THOMPSON, George H.
6376	THOMPSON, George W.
1338	THOMPSON, H. C. V.
1787	THOMPSON, James
2509	THOMPSON, James H.
5448	THOMPSON, John Webb
6869	THOMPSON, Karl P.
1309	THOMPSON, Leslie S.
6380	THOMPSON, Martin
4537	THOMPSON, Percy
1011	THOMPSON, Robert H. S.
4551	THOMPSON, Spencer H.
776	THOMPSON, Victor G.
1602	THOMPSON, Vivian
6150	THOMSON, Albert R. B.
5454	THOMSON, James
5906	THOMSON, John
1049	THOMSON, Percy Elliott
5908	THOMSON, Walter A. H.
4552	THORNBOROUGH, H. G.
341	THORNE, Percy Edwin
4553	THORNTON, Norman F.
2274	THOROGOOD, George E.
696	THORPE, Arthur
5420	THORPE, Donald
399	THRELFALL, Thomas M.
5903	THRUPP, Chelmsford K.
5907	THRUPP, Harry B.
1012	THURGAR, Reginald A.
4245	THURSTON, James
286	THWAITE, Oliver R.
1786	TIBBEY, George Basil
1785	TIDMARSH, Ernest J.
2826	TIERNEY, John
1017	TIERNEY, John Joseph
5421	TIFFEN, Robert C.
6633	TILLEY, Edwin Ernest
Lt.	TIMS, Charles
Lt.	TINDALE, Frederick W.
703	TINDALL, Albert E.
1013	TINGLE, Arthur
2018	TITTERTON, Herb. C.
3635	TOBIN, Bob Bishop
2453	TOBIN, Thomas Joseph
1310	TOMLINSON, George

No.	Name.	No.	Name.
6373	TONNETT, Louis T. A.	2034	URQUHART, Leslie E.
5648	TOOGOOD, Alfred R.	5656	VALLANCE, Reginald G.
Lt.	TOOHEY, John Thomas	5911	VANDYK, Jack
4843	TOOLEY, Arthur Wilfred	763	VAN DYK, Johan
346	TORPY, Patrick Edward	6638	VAN HEMELRYCK, F.
4246	TOWERS, Charles B.	403	VANSTONE, John
2824	TOWNS, David	710	VAUGHAN, Charles T.
5096	TOWNSEND, Bennett	3637	VAUGHAN, Gregory
342	TOWNSEND, Cecil	1313	VAUGHAN, Owen
2793	TOWNSEND, William H.	5655	VEITCH, Raymond C. J.
6870	TOWNSEND, William T.	711	VENN, Frederick G.
380	TOWNSHEND, Walter M.	347	VERRALL, Sydney
5649	TRANTER, Harold	2/Lt.	VERRILLS, Ernest James
Lt./Col.	TRAVERS, R. J. A.	785	VEYSEY, David Thomas
6911	TRAYNOR, Peter	712	VICARY, Richard
2218	TRAYNOR, Timothy	413	VINCENT, William C.
756	TRELEVAN, Richard	709	VINE, Frederick James
1339	TREMAIN, William C.	1314	VINE, Walter
5904	TRENBERTH, John E.	713	VIRGOE, Percy Charles
697	TRENOUTH, G. G. R.	1315	VITNELL, Ernest E.
698	TRENOUTH, Sidney J.	1020	VOUSDEN, Charles F.
2454	TRIMBLE, Thomas	6382	VOVIL, Edward John
6377	TRIPCONY, William J.	3948	WADDINGTON, Stanley
1010	TROTT, William T.	5436	WADDUPS, Walter
1018	TROTTER, Ernest Weir	729	WADE, Wesley George
5423	TROUP, Charles Ferriss	6883	WADHAM, William V.
5422	TROUP, John William	1397	WAGHORNE, Charles D.
699	TROWBRIDGE, Albert J.	1795	WAGNER, George
7157	TROY, Dumphy Gordon	6389	WAKEHAM, Richard H.
3940	TRUELAND, John Miller	4250	WALDER, William
1008	TUBB, James Ernest	1791	WALDRON, Thomas F.
4248	TUCKER, Arthur R. F.	354	WALKER, Archibald G.
1784	TUDOR, Sydney Ernest	2022	WALKER, David Henry
Chap.	TUGWELL, F. W.	6642	WALKER, Edward A.
1311	TULLY, Cyril George	2281	WALKER, Henry Arthur
4847	TULLY, Robert Herald	759	WALKER, Herbert A.
3449	TURK, Herbert	357	WALKER, Horatio E.
2226	TURNER, Albert	5100	WALKER, James
700	TURNER, Edward	6643	WALKER, John
5653	TURNER, George Gilbert	7117	WALKER, Thomas John
701	TURNER, Stanley	1023	WALKER, William
5901	TURNER, Sydney Alfred	5101	WALLACE, Alva
341	TURTON, John Fred. A.	5102	WALLACE, John F.
2227	TUXWORTH, Frank V.	2/Lt.	WALLACE, Thomas A.
6872	TWEDDLE, William	4251	WALLACE, Thomas Roy
6634	TWEEDIE, David E.	2219	WALSH, Albert John
2020	TYLER, Henry	2023	WALSH, Charles Henry
1379	TYRRELL, Stanley W.	3945	WALSH, Francis James
5936	TYSON, Walter	352	WALSH, James
5426	UDEN, Edgard Harold	5678	WALSH, John William
3194	UEBEL, Charles Alex.	3955	WALSH, Leo. Darcy
7115	UHR, Harold Ray Devlin	Lt.	WALSH, Ulrick Kerwick
4059	ULM, Adrian	1041	WALSH, William Alex.
7156	UNDERWOOD, Charles A.	1355	WALSHE, Eric Dalrymple
1289	UNDERWOOD, Joseph	6386	WALTERS, Frederick W.
5666	UNSWORTH, James	50983	WALTERS, Harry D.
1312	UPTON, Frederick H.	1037	WALTON, Wellington T.
2021	URQUHART, Edward	5940	WANKLYN, John C.

No.	Name.
5438	WANLESS, Stephen
Lt.	WARBURTON, Carl W.
1021	WARD, Arthur Matthew
2820	WARD, Henry
6391	WARD, Joseph Philip
2673	WARD, Reginald Harry
3950	WARDROP, Percy C.
2455	WAREHAM, Albert L.
b2992	WARK, William John A.
5427	WARLAND, Kenneth
1039	WARN, Richard Leslie
Lt.	WARNER, Alfred E.
2801	WARREN, George E.
3960	WARREN, Harold Victor
3946	WARREN, Robert Henry
6387	WARRY, Walter H.
3949	WASHINGTON, H. A.
4252	WASSON, Arthur
2289	WATERS, Alfred
5667	WATERS, Harold P.
5433	WATERS, John William
4253	WATERWORTH, John
714	WATKINS, Albert H.
351	WATKINS, Ernest
1318	WATKINS, Errol Sydney
715	WATKINS, John Edward
4254	WATKINS, Raymond W.
752	WATSON, Arthur Gordon
2024	WATSON, George V. E.
2816	WATSON, George W. R.
3306	WATSON, James
1317	WATSON, James Fletcher
4256	WATSON, John
3643	WATSON, John Alec
716	WATSON, Joseph William
5897	WATSON, Leslie Ernest
2995	WATSON, Prosper V.
717	WATSON, Robert Fletcher
2004	WATSON, Spencer
4557	WATSON, Thomas D.
3684	WATSON, Walter
2456	WATSON, William Dunn
1789	WATSON, William Henry
4558	WATSON, William Lyall
6898	WATT, Leslie Fyvie
6178	WATT, Walter
4258	WATTERSON, John A.
4559	WATTS, Arthur Graham
3639	WATTS, Horace Cecil
3647	WAUGH, Charles G.
407	WAUGH, William Edgar
5915	WAY, Cecil
6873	WAY, Morton
6432	WEATHERALL, A. G.
1800	WEATHERLAKE, L. G.
1035	WEBB, Francis G. L.
358	WEBB, Frederick Albert
7118	WEBB, Ronald

No.	Name.
6890	WEBB, Sidney Frank
4560	WEBER, Charles Henry
2265	WEBSTER, Frederick O.
2539	WELCH, James Fred.
2458	WELCH, John
5665	WELLER, Edward
3645	WELLER, Walter
353	WELLS, Clifford E. A.
1319	WELLS, John
786	WELSH, George
6156	WELTCH, Clarence H.
718	WENHAM, William
4561	WESLEY, Samuel
Lt.	WEST, Albert Smethurst
737	WEST, Arthur Lionel
7119	WEST, Frederick
738	WEST, Norman Charles
6669	WEST, Robert V.
6639	WEST, Thomas
1794	WESTERN, Charles L.
1796	WESTON, Harold Ernest
6177	WESTON, Joshua B.
4852	WESTON, Reginald Roy
3957	WESTON, William H.
2459	WHALEN, Hugh
1067	WHALEY, Leo. William
4855	WHARTON, Harry Oscar
5428	WHEAT, Leslie
3640	WHEATLEY, Alfred J.
5447	WHEATLEY, Robert
1038	WHEELER, Francis H. C.
2293	WHELAN, Claude J.
7120	WHELDON, Thomas Luke
723	WHETTAM, Henry E. E.
5664	WHILES, William
5439	WHISKER, Alexander N.
5917	WHITAKER, James
6668	WHITE, Charles
5107	WHITE, Charles Edwin
2544	WHITE, Clifford Harold
392	WHITE, Donald Hugh
5661	WHITE, Edwin
2522	WHITE, Frederick
1028	WHITE, George Harold
2025	WHITE, George Henry
5437	WHITE, Hubert E. N.
1321	WHITE, Joseph John
6889	WHITE, Rex William D.
3646	WHITE, Ronald Currie
6875	WHITE, Sydney John
3947	WHITEHEAD, G. C. L.
2027	WHITEHURST, Darcy C.
3198	WHITELAW, Arthur W.
5927	WHITELEY, Alex. T.
5926	WHITELEY, Charles H.
5928	WHITELEY, Richard J.
6152	WHITEMAN, Thomas G.
483	WHITESIDE, Robert

No.	Name.
349	WHITFIELD, Clifford
2026	WHITFIELD, Edwin
5923	WHITICKER, James F. F.
1357	WHITLOCK, William A.
2028	WHITTAKER, George
6390	WHITTAKER, William J.
b3001	WHITTING, Frank
3956	WHYTE, Alexander
1104	WIELAND, Harry
5090	WIGGETT, Prince Victor
5910	WIGGINS, William N.
1034	WIGNALL, Thomas
836	WILCOCKSON, Joseph D.
2519	WILDE, George James
6154	WILKINS, Max. Le Coef
5914	WILKINSON, Henry C.
3652	WILKINSON, R. F. C.
2029	WILKINSON, Thomas C.
Lt.	WILLARD, Rupert R. F.
6641	WILLARD, Stacey E.
5618	WILLIAMS, Albert E.
5912	WILLIAMS, Albert E.
4259	WILLIAMS, Arthur
6876	WILLIAMS, Arthur
5435	WILLIAMS, Basil
Lt.	WILLIAMS, Bernard S.
722	WILLIAMS, Charles G.
2810	WILLIAMS, Charles R.
5920	WILLIAMS, Charles S.
5666	WILLIAMS, David
6912	WILLIAMS, Ernest
6204	WILLIAMS, Francis E.
6877	WILLIAMS, Frank L.
7121	WILLIAMS, Frederick O.
4856	WILLIAMS, Henry C.
2507	WILLIAMS, Horace H.
4260	WILLIAMS, John
5432	WILLIAMS, John
4564	WILLIAMS, John D. C.
4573	WILLIAMS, John Lloyd
5431	WILLIAMS, Norman
7122	WILLIAMS, Robert H.
1792	WILLIAMS, Robert R.
1026	WILLIAMS, Rupert
2035	WILLIAMS, Russell E.
348	WILLIAMS, Thomas
726	WILLIAMS, Thomas H. J.
3195	WILLIAMS, Walter Ernest
1033	WILLIAMS, Walter R.
5906	WILLIAMS, Wm. A. S.
5696	WILLIAMSON, A. W.
2460	WILLIAMSON, Fred. A.
366	WILLIAMSON, Frederick
7125	WILLIAMSON, Kyle
6153	WILLIAMSON, Leslie E.
1025	WILLIAMSON, Leslie J.
730	WILLICK, Bertie Clyde
5108	WILLIS, Horace Russell

No.	Name.
6161	WILLIS, Stanley Dean
4868	WILLS, Albert S. D.
724	WILLSON, Osborne A.
2031	WILSON, Alexander
5916	WILSON, Alfred L.
4566	WILSON, Alfred Reginald
5694	WILSON, Charles E.
4571	WILSON, Frederick
2809	WILSON, George Cecil
4263	WILSON, George W.
5109	WILSON, Henry
1798	WILSON, Herbert John
4858	WILSON, James
1797	WILSON, James Arthur
5659	WILSON, James William
2032	WILSON, John
2819	WILSON, John
361	WILSON, Kenneth Bertie
1322	WILSON, Richard
1022	WILSON, Robert James
4567	WILSON, Thomas
1024	WILSON, William
6385	WILSON, William
2223	WILSON, William James
1320	WINCH, James Hanson
5913	WINDSOR, Leslie James
5657	WINGFIELD, Bernard C.
5660	WINTERBOTTOM, A. H.
6879	WINTON, Arthur Stanley
1032	WISHART, James Leslie
1793	WITT, Arthur
6157	WITT, Ernest Harold
4265	WITT, James Kenneth
350	WOLFE, Arthur Richard
4568	WOMSLEY, William O.
5430	WONG, Richard Wesley
1323	WOOD, Harold Laxton
2278	WOOD, Hubert John
1380	WOOD, James Gerard
2462	WOOD, Norman
2811	WOOD, Robert
4569	WOOD, Robert
4862	WOOD, Roy Rhodes
1030	WOOD, Thomas
1324	WOOD, William Basil
1353	WOODBURY, Robert
5112	WOODHOUSE, Edward E.
3649	WOODHOUSE, Harold
732	WOODROW, Reginald J.
2828	WOODS, Frederick
733	WOODS, George
3923	WOODS, John
7169	WOODS, William
359	WOODWARD, Herbert
734	WOOF, Robert
735	WOOLAND, Arthur J.
4266	WOOLDRIDGE, F. C.
6182	WOOLFE, Neil Edmund

No.	Name.	No.	Name.
2/Lt.	WOOLLEY, Charles R.	2203	WRIGHT, John Talbot
4267	WORSNIP, James	1027	WRIGLEY, Edwin Robert
6155	WORTH, Hector Clayton	728	WYATT, Percival
2224	WORTHINGTON, H. J.	5918	WYLIE, James Lindsay
2297	WORTHINGTON, N. J.	4270	YATES, Alfred Ernest
1029	WORTHINGTON, R. C.	364	YATES, Peter
Lt.	WORTHINGTON, R. C.	2225	YEEND, Norman Hector
4570	WOTTON, John Malcolm	4574	YEO, Herbert Jackson
5663	WRAY, Frederick	363	YEOMANS, Bertram W.
3690	WREN, James	6392	YEOMANS, Frederick
5921	WRENNALL, Harry	1325	YORK, Frank William
4268	WRIGHT, Alfred Alan	2/Lt.	YOUNG, Alexander S.
356	WRIGHT, Edgar Sydney	6913	YOUNG, Ernest
736	WRIGHT, Edwin Victor	2226	YOUNG, George Gray
3202	WRIGHT, Eric John J.	1610	YOUNG, John
6388	WRIGHT, Henry	794	YOUNG, John Muir
Capt.	WRIGHT, John Lawrence	1042	YOUNG, William John

LIST OF MEMBERS OF THE 17th BATTALION WHO SERVED UNDER AN ASSUMED NAME

●

3810 ABELL, Joseph Fred.	Served as	DEARIE, Frederick J.
1657 BLAKER, Charles Major	,, ,,	BAKER, Charles
6385 BLYTH, William	,, ,,	WILSON, William
1613 BROWN, John Michael	,, ,,	BROWN, John Mitchell
5544 BROWN, William Henry	,, ,,	BROWN, Henry
7019 BUCK, Frank Ernest B.	,, ,,	BUCK, Ernest Frank
1548 BUERCKNER, George L.	,, ,,	JAMES, George Leslie
4352 BURKE, Edward	,, ,,	ALLAN, John
507 CANT, William	,, ,,	CARSON, William
547 CAREY, George	,, ,,	FIELD George
2235 CATTS, Arthur George	,, ,,	CARTER, Arthur George
1354 CHINCHI, Alfred John	,, ,,	FURLESS, Alfred John
5054 DAVIS, Thomas Baden	,, ,,	MANLY, Thomas
727 GIBSON, Arthur	,, ,,	WOOD, Charles
4172 GLASSCOCK, Herbert G.	,, ,,	MYERS, William Henry
260 GRIMES, John	,, ,,	LYONS, John
777 HICKS, Wilfred Augustus	,, ,,	FRASER, Wilfred A.
1953 KEOWN, Sidney John	,, ,,	JOHNS, Sidney
4423 LESLIE, James Gordon	,, ,,	GORDON, James
620 MAHANAY, Percy	,, ,,	MAHADY, Percy
1540 MOORE, Samuel Lowe	,, ,,	GIBSON, George
5683 McDONNELL, Horace H.	,, ,,	DUNCAN, Ronald Angus
965 McGOWAN, Patrick	,, ,,	McGOWEN, John
2545 McKENZIE, Kenneth G.	,, ,,	CAMPBELL, John
1215 O'CONNOR, Thomas W.	,, ,,	JACKSON, Thomas
396 PHILIP, George Alison	,, ,,	ALISON, Philip George
2044 STIFF, Alexander A. C.	,, ,,	MAISDEN, James
6923 THICKINS, William H.	,, ,,	BELL, Richard
6883 WADHAM, William Victor	,, ,,	SINCLAIR, Victor
2203 WRIGHT, John Talbot	,, ,,	RUSSELL, Jack

Honour Roll of the Dead

K.I.A.—Killed in Action.
D.O.W.—Died of Wounds.
D.O.D.—Died of Disease.
C.N.S.—Cause Not Stated.
D.O.I.—Died of Illness.
D.O.INJ.—Died of Injury.
† Soldier's Grave Not Known.

Reg. No.	Name.	Cause of Death.	Place of Death.	Date.
3208	Abbott, A. R.	D.O.W.	France	6/9/1918
412	Abbott, J. E.	K.I.A.	Gallipoli	27/8/1915
6028	Abrahams, F. W.	K.I.A.	France	31/8/1918
6030	Ackrall, W. J.	K.I.A.	France	18/4/1918
5536	Adam, D. F.	K.I.A.	Belgium	9/10/1917
3451	Adshead, W.†	K.I.A.	France	2/8/1916
2101	Akers, W.†	K.I.A.	France	26/7/1916
4352	Burke, E.	K.I.A.	Belgium	9/10/1917
801	Allen, S. T.	K.I.A.	Gallipoli	7/12/1915
6393	Allport, J. C.	D.O.W.	France	27/10/1917
2328	Amery, P.	D.O.W.	England	20/8/1918
6763	Anderson, A.	D.O.W.	France	18/10/1918
5939	Anderson, A. L.	K.I.A.	Belgium	20/9/1917
803	Anderson, C. J. S.	D.O.D.	France	29/11/1918
5295	Anderson, L.	K.I.A.	Belgium	20/9/1917
2773	Anderson, P. A.	K.I.A.	France	18/4/1918
428	Andrew, J.	D.O.W.	Gallipoli	9/11/1915
3209	Andrews, C. G.†	K.I.A.	France	4/8/1916
6032	Andrews, E. T.	K.I.A.	Belgium	20/9/1917
486	Anthony, F. J.†	K.I.A.	France	28/7/1916
2106	Antrobus, W. D.†	K.I.A.	France	26/7/1916
4656	Aplin, F. J.	K.I.A.	France	8/11/1916
5292	Argall, P. E.	K.I.A.	Belgium	20/9/1917
4055	Attwood, J.N.†	K.I.A.	France	3/5/1917
4659	Baggett, A. E.†	K.I.A.	France	3/5/1917
5783	Bailey, H. C.	D.O.W.	France	4/10/1918
1611	Bailey, W. E. T.	D.O.W.	France	10/5/1917
6034	Baird, F. J.	C.N.S.	Germany	15/10/1918
2469	Baker, N. S.	D.O.W.	France	29/7/1916
2589	Baker, W. C.†	K.I.A.	France	26/7/1916
5784	Balstrup, G.H.	D.O.W.	Belgium	22/9/1917
3469	Barker, W. F. J.	K.I.A.	France	27/7/1916
499	Barling, F. S.	K.I.A.	Gallipoli	13/10/1915
4057	Barnes, H. W.	D.O.W.	France	6/3/1917
5311	Barnes, S.†	K.I.A.	France	15/4/1917
Capt.	Barnett, F. G.	K.I.A.	France	2/8/1918
2585	Bartlett, A. "M.M."	K.I.A.	France	31/8/1918
4977	Bartlett, B. C.	K.I.A.	Belgium	9/10/1917
1615b	Bartlett, J. S.†	K.I.A.	France	3/5/1917
834	Bartlett, O.J.T.	D.O.W.	France	15/10/1917

Reg. No.	Name.	Cause of Death.	Place of Death.	Date.
5785	Bartlett, W.	K.I.A.	Belgium	20/9/1917
1884	Bassett, T.†	K.I.A.	France	3/5/1917
6436	Bawden, W. E.	K.I.A.	France	15/5/1918
3022	Beaumont, W. H.†	K.I.A.	France	3/5/1917
4360	Beckingham, R.	K.I.A.	Belgium	20/9/1917
4060	Beddows, A. H.†	K.I.A.	France	3/5/1917
4061	Beddows, G. J.	K.I.A.	France	18/7/1918
817	Bell, R.†	K.I.A.	France	26/7/1916
164	Bennett, J. E., "M.M."	K.I.A.	France	26/7/1916
3770	Bennett, N.†	K.I.A.	France	3/5/1917
402	Bennett, P.	D.O.W.	England	7/8/1916
1659a	Bernard, F.	K.I.A.	France	2/3/1917
6771	Beshewatie, G. J.	K.I.A.	France	16/4/1918
1616	Betland, E.	D.O.W.	France	15/5/1917
6766	Betts, E.	D.O.W.	France	14/10/1918
2864	Binns, T.	D.O.W.	France	9/8/1918
5791	Bishop, S.	D.O.W.	Belgium	27/9/1917
488	Black, G. S.	K.I.A.	France	28/2/1917
5789	Black, H.†	K.I.A.	France	3/5/1917
2591	Black, W.†	K.I.A.	France	3/5/1917
2110	Blackler, J. C.	K.I.A.	France	13/6/1916
4668	Blair, H.	K.I.A.	France	10/1/1918
2111	Blake, H. P.	D.O.W.	France	29/10/1917
2596	Blanch, E. C.	K.I.A.	France	13/6/1916
6773	Blanche, L.	K.I.A.	France	31/8/1918
1817	Bloom, J. S.	K.I.A.	Gallipoli	5/11/1915
3783	Boesenberg, C. J.	D.O.W.	Belgium	20/9/1917
1138	Bonham, P. A.†	K.I.A.	France	15/4/1917
1139	Booth, W.	K.I.A.	France	18/4/1918
1141	Boswell, S. A.	D.O.W.	Alexandria	31/1/1917
3470	Bottcher, A.	K.I.A.	Belgium	20/9/1917
1665	Bourke, F. R.†	K.I.A.	France	3/5/1917
161	Bowmaker, J. M.	D.O.W.	H.S. "Aquitania"	22/9/1915
7016	Bowman, A. P.†	K.I.A.	France	31/8/1918
1143	Boxall, A. H.	D.O.W.	France	9/11/1916
828	Boyd, W. E.	K.I.A.	France	9/4/1918
4676	Boyle, F. A.	D.O.W.	England	31/12/1916
2865b	Boyton, G. S.†	K.I.A.	France	3/5/1917
4677	Bradford, R. B.	K.I.A.	Belgium	9/10/1917
5304	Bradley, R.	K.I.A.	France	19/5/1918
5786	Bramall, A. T.	K.I.A.	Belgium	20/9/1917
6528	Brandon, S.	K.I.A.	France	14/5/1918
1628	Bray, A. C.†	D.O.W.	France	31/12/1916
1326	..Breadner, C. G.	D.O.D.	France	19/4/1916
	Breen, D.	D.O.D.	Gladesville, N.S.W.	17/8/1915
7129	Brennan, E.	K.I.A.	France	14/5/1918
1655	Brigden, S. S.	D.O.W.	Belgium	22/9/1917
3762	Briggs, F.†	K.I.A.	France	3/5/1917
1146	Briscoe, A. E.	D.O.D.	Egypt	24/12/1915
2232	Brooks, C. W.	D.O.W.	France	17/8/1916
7015	Brosie, C. D.	D.O.W.	France	22/5/1918
1877	Brown, C. R.	K.I.A.	France	15/4/1917
394	Brown, E.†	K.I.A.	France	2/8/1916
5544	Brown, H. (stated to be W. H.)	K.I.A.	France	2/3/1917
4070	Brown H. W. "M.M."	D.O.W.	France	2/6/1918
3456	Brown, L.	K.I.A.	Belgium	20/9/1917
3457	Brown, T. H.	D.O.W.	France	3/5/1917

Reg. No.	Name.	Cause of Death.	Place of Death.	Date.
6040	Brown, W. S.†	K.I.A.	France	3/5/1917
166	Browne, A. B.	K.I.A.	Gallipoli	27/8/1915
5790	Bruce, R. M. L.†	D.O.W.	France	13/4/1918
1893	Bryant, H.	K.I.A.	France	27/7/1916
2285	Bryce, J. S.†	K.I.A.	France	15/4/1917
7019	Buck, F. E.	D.O.D.	England	16/5/1919
3776	Buckridge, G. W.	K.I.A.	France	15/4/1917
1895	Burgis, J. R.	D.O.W.	France	30/7/1916
6038	Burke, T.†	K.I.A.	France	3/5/1917
6281	Burkett, W.	K.I.A.	Belgium	20/9/1917
2914	Burnett, G. J.	K.I.A.	France	31/1/1918
6681	Buttsworth, W.	K.I.A.	Belgium	9/10/1917
5541	Byrne, D. J.	D.O.W.	France	8/5/1917
7018	Byrne, H. J.	D.O.W.	France	19/7/1918
1679	Cahalan, A. E.†	K.I.A.	France	25/8/1916
1524	Cahill, H.	D.O.W.	France	29/7/1916
504	Campbell, C.	D.O.W.	Egypt	17/11/1915
6900	Campbell, C. S.	K.I.A.	France	20/7/1918
5328	Campbell, G. A.†	K.I.A.	France	8/8/1918
851	Campbell, G. H.	D.O.W.	France	18/4/1917
3488	Cantello, J.	D.O.D.	France	19/5/1916
5320	Carlow, J. M.	K.I.A.	Belgium	20/9/1917
1667	Carr, J. E.†	K.I.A.	France	25/7/1916
4989	Carroll, W. G.†	K.I.A.	France	3/5/1917
507	Carson, W.	K.I.A.	France	3/5/1917
2235	Carter, A. G. (stated to be Catts, A. G.)	D.O.W.	France	30/7/1916
2347	Carter, E. C. H.	K.I.A.	France	3/10/1918
6282	Carter, J. E.	K.I.A.	Belgium	9/10/1917
6543	Caswell, H. D. V.	K.I.A.	Belgium	9/10/1917
1362	Chamberlain, W. G.	K.I.A.	France	3/10/1918
Capt.	Chambers, L. K.	K.I.A.	France	29/7/1916
1525	Chaplin, G. C.	K.I.A.	Gallipoli	27/8/1915
1527	Chapman, M.	K.I.A.	Gallipoli	27/8/1915
1799	Chapman, R.†	K.I.A.	France	4/2/1917
7162	Chapman, W. J.†	K.I.A.	France	15/5/1918
855	Charles, F.	K.I.A.	Gallipoli	3/11/1915
2221	Chessor, W.	D.O.D.	H.M.A.T. Argyllshire	13/10/1915
1901	Chick, G. J.† "M.M."	K.I.A.	France	3/5/1917
2038	Childs, G. H. "D.C.M."	K.I.A.	France	3/5/1917
	Chisholm, O. H.	D.O.D.	Sydney, N.S.W.	23/3/1915
7134	Chopin, C. F. G.	D.O.W.	France	3/10/1918
183	Christopher, J.	K.I.A.	Gallipoli	27/8/1915
4691	Churton, E. R.	K.I.A.	Belgium	20/9/1917
2122	Clark, J.	D.O.W.	France	14/11/1916
1903	Clarke, J.	K.I.A.	France	6/6/1916
1904	Clarke, J. M.	D.O.W.	France	29/7/1916
1629	Cleave, C. S.	D.O.W.	Belgium	6/11/1917
4387	Clegg, W. R.	D.O.D.	France	4/2/1917
2894	Clissold, H. W.	D.O.W.	Belgium	5/11/1917
7698	Clunies-Ross, R.	K.I.A.	France	3/10/1918
6185	Coleman, C. C.	K.I.A.	France	4/10/1917
	Coleman, T. H.	D.O.D.	Sydney, N.S.W.	22/3/1915
177	Commons, H.†	K.I.A.	France	3/5/1917
5555	Connor, C.†	K.I.A.	France	3/5/1917
2350	Conroy, F.	D.O.W.	France	3/12/1917
843	Cook, G. F.	K.I.A.	France	23/4/1916
1170	Coom, W. A.	D.O.W.	France	21/4/1917

Reg. No.	Name.	Cause of Death.	Place of Death.	Date.
1171	Coombes, F. J.	K.I.A.	France	31/8/1918
2127	Coppock, W. J.†	K.I.A.	France	15/4/1917
4090	Cormack, S. A.	K.I.A.	France	2/3/1917
1523	Cornally, H. F. T.	D.O.W.	France	16/5/1918
5792	Corning A.	K.I.A.	Belgium	20/9/1917
4397	Cornwell, J. M.	K.I.A.	France	8/11/1916
2236	Corrie, E. W.	K.I.A.	Belgium	9/10/1917
6285	Cosgrove, T.	K.I.A.	France	9/10/1917
6404	Coulon, A. J.	K.I.A.	France	9/8/1918
3490	Coulter, J. R.	K.I.A.	Belgium	23/9/1916
1173	Cowcher, E. G., "M.M."	K.I.A.	France	3/10/1918
181	Cox, E. T.†	K.I.A.	France	3/5/1917
3564a	Craig, F. L.†	K.I.A.	France	13/5/1918
1912	Craig, J. H. D.	D.O.W.	England	17/11/1918
846	Crawford, D. M.	K.I.A.	France	14/5/1918
5319	Crawley, A. M.	K.I.A.	Belgium	9/10/1917
2129	Crebert, H. C.	K.I.A.	France	26/8/1916
6287	Creighton, R. C. J.	K.I.A.	France	12/5/1918
5686	Crewe, W. R.	K.I.A.	France	3/5/1917
368	Crocker, F. E.	K.I.A.	France	3/5/1917
2353	Cross, W.	D.O.D.	France	15/4/1918
857	Crouch, J. L.	D.O.D. H.M.A.T."Aquitania"		20/10/1915
4697	Crowe, W. H.	D.O.W.	France	19/4/1918
859	Cruickshank, R. S.	D.O.W.	France	10/11/1916
1175	Cuddeford, F. G.	D.O.W.	Gallipoli	16/9/1915
4699	Cumming, D.	K.I.A.	France	8/11/1916
4394	Cunningham, I. C.	K.I.A.	Belgium	9/10/1917
7028	Curtin, W. J.	K.I.A.	France	15/5/1918
4400	Daisley, W.	K.I.A.	France	31/8/1918
1915	Daley, J. P.†	K.I.A.	France	4/2/1917
1178	Daly, P. J.	K.I.A.	Belgium	9/10/1917
3496	Dare, A. J.	K.I.A.	France	26/7/1916
4401	Davey, A.	K.I.A.	Belgium	9/10/1917
861	Davies, E.	D.O. Inj. (Accident)	Egypt	30/6/1915
1182	Davies, H.	K.I.A.	France	29/3/1918
3495	Davies, R. S., "D.C.M."	K.I.A.	France	3/10/1918
1180	Davis, W. "D.C.M." "M.M."	D.O.D.	Persia	7/7/1918
5689	Davis, W. S.†	K.I.A.	France	4/2/1917
384	Dawkins, F. R.	K.I.A.	France	1/8/1916
1634	Dawson, E. A.	D.O.W.	France	10/8/1918
2474	Dawson, E. H.†	K.I.A.	France	3/5/1917
6789	Deacon, J. J.	K.I.A.	France	16/5/1918
5810	Dean, L. S.†	K.I.A.	France	3/5/1917
3810	Dearie, F. J.† "M.M."	K.I.A.	France	3/5/1917
1919	Devenish, A. G.	K.I.A.	France	29/7/1916
2/Lt.	Devitt, W. G.	K.I.A.	France	9/11/1916
Lieut.	Dickens, G. M.	K.I.A.	Belgium	9/10/1917
6293	Dickerson, B.	K.I.A.	Belgium	9/10/1917
194	Didcote, H. F. F.	K.I.A.	France	12/1/1918
1617	Didcote, W. B.	K.I.A.	Gallipoli	27/8/1915
7138	Difford, S. O.†	K.I.A.	France	15/5/1918
195	Dillon, F. W.	K.I.A.	Gallipoli	28/8/1915
872	Dixon, C.†	K.I.A.	France	15/4/1917
4705	Dixon, D. W.	K.I.A.	France	8/8/1918
5804	Dodd, W.	K.I.A.	Belgium	9/10/1917
6791	Doherty, H. J.	K.I.A.	France	31/8/1918

Reg. No.	Name.	Cause of Death.	Place of Death.	Date.
Lieut.	Doig, A. T., "M.C."	D.O.I.	Germany	27/6/1918
7037	Donald, J. B.	D.O.W.	France	24/5/1918
2627	Donkin, H. H.†	K.I.A.	France	26/7/1916
1055	Donovan, J.	D.O.W.	Gallipoli	26/8/1915
6792	Doran, J.	K.I.A.	France	20/7/1918
5801	Doubleday, F. A.	K.I.A.	Belgium	9/10/1917
2879	Douglas, G.†	K.I.A.	France	15/4/1917
5338	Douglas, R. N.†	K.I.A.	France	15/4/1917
1800	Douglass, G.	K.I.A.	Belgium	20/9/1917
2878	Dowling, E. M.	D.O.W.	France	20/6/1916
191	Doyle, J. M.	D.O.D.	England	5/3/1916
6435	Drew, H.	K.I.A.	Belgium	20/9/1917
5340	Dryden, G. S. "M.M."	D.O.W.	France	10/8/1918
2134	Dugan, J. E. M.	D.O.W.	Belgium	31/3/1918
1924	Dulhunty, N. J.	K.I.A.	France	31/3/1918
1528	Duncan, A.	K.I.A.	Gallipoli	24/9/1915
4103	Dunham, L.†	D.O.I.	France	13/8/1917
864	Dunn, S.	K.I.A.	France	18/7/1918
2359	Dunn, W. P.†	K.I.A.	France	3/5/1917
5007	Dunnett, J.	D.O.I.	France	8/8/1917
21	Edelston, W.†	K.I.A.	France	21/11/1916
2637	Edwards, W. C.†	K.I.A.	France	12/5/1918
369	Egan, J. R.	D.O.W.	H.S. "Salta" at sea	4/9/1915
1606	Elliott, F. E.†	K.I.A.	France	26/7/1916
Lieut.	Ellis, H.	D.O.W.	France	16/4/1917
6415	Ellis, S. W.†	K.I.A.	France	21/8/1918
544	Ellison, J. W.	K.I.A.	France	9/6/1916
5811	Elrington, A. L.	D.O.W.	France	16/4/1917
1190	Ewing, F.	D.O.W.	Gallipoli	11/11/1915
3506	Fahey, W. F.†	K.I.A.	France	26/7/1916
410	Fairlem, W. G.	K.I.A.	France	18/7/1918
2362	Fallon, W. H.†	K.I.A.	France	5/8/1916
1547	Felan, J. R.	K.I.A.	France	27/7/1916
1191	Fenwick, J.	D.O.W.	France	16/4/1917
1931	Fiddling, J.	K.I.A.	France	6/6/1916
209	Field, J. L.	K.I.A.	France	26/7/1916
3828	Finley, A.†	K.I.A.	France	28/7/1916
4413	Fisk, G.	K.I.A.	France	12/4/1918
5674	Fitzpatrick, J. F.	K.I.A.	Belgium	20/9/1917
5570	Flack, J. A.†	K.I.A.	France	3/5/1917
3834	Fleming, E. S.	K.I.A.	Belgium	9/10/1917
5571	Flynn, C.	K.I.A.	Belgium	20/9/1917
882	Fogarty, E.	K.I.A.	Gallipoli	3/11/1915
5817	Fosdick, E.	K.I.A.	Belgium	9/10/1917
2002	Foster, F. A.†	K.I.A.	France	15/4/1917
4414	Foster, H. C.	D.O.W.	France	16/4/1917
5346	Foster, W.†	K.I.A.	France	15/4/1917
4719	France, J. D.	K.I.A.	Belgium	20/9/1917
4920	France, S. F.	K.I.A.	Belgium	20/9/1917
1065	Francis, J. W.	K.I.A.	France	7/11/1917
777	Fraser, W. A.	K.I.A.	France	26/7/1916
2140	French, J. R.	K.I.A.	France	31/8/1918
6057	Frost, E.†	K.I.A.	France	3/10/1918
2238	Fry, R. L. "M.M."	D.O.W.	France	3/8/1916
5573	Fullalove, W. A. V.	K.I.A.	Belgium	20/9/1917
6304	Fullam, F. M.†	K.I.A.	France	14/5/1918
6467	Fullard, H.	D.O.I.	France	5/11/1918
214	Fuller, C. U.	D.O.W.	Gallipoli	30/8/1915

Reg. No.	Name.	Cause of Death.	Place of Death.	Date.
1354	Furless, A. J.	K.I.A.	Gallipoli	1/9/1915
2479	Furness, F. R. C.	K.I.A.	Belgium	20/9/1917
6800	Gale, B. C. L.	K.I.A.	France	14/7/1918
1800	Gallogly, G. H.	K.I.A.	France	15/4/1917
554	Gallaway, J. G.	D.O.D.	H.S. "Gascon," at sea	4/10/1915
3844	Gane, H. W.†	K.I.A.	France	11/5/1918
896	Gannon, G. N.†	K.I.A.	France	26/7/1916
4722	Gannon, J. H.	K.I.A.	Belgium	20/9/1917
5574	Gant, J. S., "M.M."	D.O.I.	France	19/11/1918
229	Gardiner, S.	D.O.D.	England	27/12/1916
7179	Gardner, F. L.	D.O.D.	England	7/3/1918
220	Gavin, C.	K.I.A.	Gallipoli	27/8/1915
5348	Gavin, H. P.	K.I.A.	France	3/10/1918
2906	Gaylard, H. C.	D.O.D.	Germany	17/9/1918
6564	Geary, M.P.	D.O.D.	England	1/5/1917
2485	Geddes, R. R.†	K.I.A.	France	15/5/1918
2483	George, F. H.	K.I.A.	France	14/5/1918
4725	Gerritsen, J. W.	K.I.A.	France	3/10/1918
4726	Gibb, H.	K.I.A.	Belgium	20/9/1917
5827	Gibson, R.	K.I.A.	France	31/8/1918
6166	Gillies, J. G.†	K.I.A.	France	15/4/1917
3232	Gilligan, P. L.†	K.I.A.	France	3/5/1917
4420	Glassford, E. J. C.	K.I.A.	France	26/9/1916
446	Goad, R. B.	D.O.W.	France	6/4/1918
1075	Godfrey, E. A.†	K.I.A.	France	15/4/1917
2/Lt.	Gombert, F.	K.I.A.	Gallipoli	28/8/1915
1220	Gooda, A. C.†	K.I.A.	France	3/5/1917
4729	Goodman, S.†	K.I.A.	France	15/4/1917
3520	Goodman, W. J.	D.O.W.	France	4/3/1917
4423	Gordon, J.	K.I.A.	Belgium	9/10/1917
4119	Gosling, F.	K.I.A.	France	2/8/1918
2895a	Graham, S. J.†	K.I.A.	France	3/5/1917
894	Grange, F. G. "M.M."	K.I.A.	Belgium	9/10/1917
5826	Grange, S. W.†	C.N.S.	Germany	10/5/1917
2375	Gray, V. H.	K.I.A.	France	3/10/1918
4122	Greayer, J.	D.O.D.	England	7/5/1917
6311	Green, E. R.	K.I.A.	Belgium	9/10/1917
893	Green, J. S.	D.O.Inj.	Sydney	7/9/1918
4429	Greenslade, H.	D.O.I.	England	20/3/1917
3835	Griffiths, H. H.	K.I.A.	France	27/7/1916
221	Groome, F.	D.O.W.	Egypt	6/10/1915
2379	Guthrie, G.†	K.I.A.	France	26/7/1916
1705	Hackett, R. B.	D.O.W.	France	1/3/1917
Lieut.	Haigh, W. R. "M.C."	D.O.D.	England	26/11/1918
371	Hall, T.	K.I.A.	Gallipoli	27/8/1915
903	Hallett, P.	K.I.A.	France	13/5/1916
5834	Hamilton, T. A. B.†	K.I.A.	France	3/5/1917
2295	Hampton, D. B.†	K.I.A.	France	27/7/1916
Lieut.	Hannaford, C. R.	K.I.A.	Belgium	20/9/1917
2240	Hannay, T. A.†	K.I.A.	France	15/4/1917
3087	Hanson, G. E.	K.I.A.	France	28/7/1916
6820	Hanson, H.†	K.I.A.	France	8/8/1918
238	Harding, E. W.†	K.I.A.	France	3/5/1917
4442	Hardisty, J.	K.I.A.	Belgium	9/10/1917
237	Hargreaves, B.†	K.I.A.	France	26/7/1916
239	Harman, W. H.	D.O.D.	Egypt	11/1/1916
1942	Harper, J.	K.I.A.	France	26/7/1916
2146	Harrington, M. J.	K.I.A.	France	26/7/1916

Reg. No.	Name.	Cause of Death.	Place of Death.	Date.
4129	Harris, A. E.	K.I.A.	France	17/2/1917
6073	Harris, J. E.	K.I.A.	Belgium	20/9/1917
	Harris, W. J.	D.O.D.	Liverpool, N.S.W.	27/9/1915
5580	Harris, W. J.	K.I.A.	Belgium	20/9/1917
6317	Harrison, D.	K.I.A.	France	3/10/1918
3533	Harrison, J. C.†	K.I.A.	France	2/8/1916
6164	Hart, E.†	K.I.A.	France	15/4/1917
1224	Hart, F.	K.I.A.	France	20/9/1917
2386	Hartley, W.	Accid. Killed	Belgium	6/11/1916
	Harvey, A. A.	D.O.D.	Sydney	21/8/1915
372	Hassall, F. M.	K.I.A.	France	6/6/1916
4443	Hatton, W. G.	K.I.A.	France	1/7/1918
911	Hayes, P. J.†	K.I.A.	France	26/7/1916
3583	Hayward, E.	D.O.W.	France	15/3/1917
5835	Hehir, W.	K.I.A.	Belgium	9/10/1917
4445	Hely, C. E.	K.I.A.	France	31/8/1918
3852	Hemsley, R. H.	D.O.W.	Belgium	12/10/1917
1690	Henderson, A. E.	D.O.W.	Gallipoli	29/11/1915
4132	Hendry, C.†	K.I.A.	France	15/4/1917
1706	Herman, H. E.	D.O.W.	H.S. "Samali," at sea	20/11/1915
6065	Higgins, A.	K.I.A.	Belgium	20/9/1917
397	Hill, J. R.†	K.I.A.	France	26/7/1916
5831	Hill, K. C.	K.I.A.	Belgium	9/10/1917
241	Hoban, W. J.	K.I.A.	France	13/5/1918
581	Hobson, J.†	K.I.A.	France	28/7/1916
1547	Hodge, W.†	K.I.A.	France	27/7/1916
906	Hodgson, H.	D.O.W.	France	9/8/1918
2149	Hoff, H.†	K.I.A.	France	26/7/1916
582	Holden, F.	K.I.A.	Belgium	9/10/1917
2374	Holdsworth, H. V.	K.I.A.	France	28/7/1916
1703	Holland, H. G.†	K.I.A.	France	5/2/1917
778	Hood, A. T.	D.O.C.	France	30/4/1918
1209	Hood, W. R.	K.I.A.	Belgium	9/10/1917
2283	Hooker, A.	D.O.D.	France	29/11/1918
2/Lt.	Hopkins, V. N.	D.O.W.	Belgium	21/9/1917
2152	Hopper, E. H.	K.I.A.	Belgium	20/9/1917
230	Hough, J.	K.I.A.	Gallipoli	27/8/1915
2/Lt.	Houston, C.†	K.I.A.	France	3/5/1917
1952	Howard, A. F.	K.I.A.	Belgium	20/9/1917
4138	Howes, W. H.	K.I.A.	Belgium	9/10/1917
6573	Hucker, B. J.	K.I.A.	France	31/8/1918
767	Hudson, J.	K.I.A.	Gallipoli	28/8/1915
917	Hudson, S. C.	D.O.D.	Gibraltar	23/10/1915
2397	Huish, A. H.	K.I.A.	France	9/5/1918
7048	Hulbert, V. V.†	K.I.A.	France	13/5/1918
5586	Hulm, W.	D.O.W.	France	1/3/1917
919	Hume, W. D., "M.M."	D.O.W.	France	16/5/1918
910	Humphreys, T. O.	D.O.W.	Gallipoli	25/9/1915
2482	Humphries, W. J.	K.I.A.	France	3/10/1918
2672	Hunt, G. B. F.	K.I.A.	France	2/8/1916
2487	Hunter, B. J.	K.I.A.	Belgium	9/10/1917
5587	Huntley, C. E.†	K.I.A.	France	3/5/1917
7054	Hutchins, J.	D.O.W.	France	2/9/1918
6130	Inskip, G.†	K.I.A.	France	15/4/1917
5593	Jackson, J. P.†	K.I.A.	France	15/4/1917
1215	Jackson, T.	K.I.A.	Belgium	20/9/1917
1374	James, W. R.	K.I.A.	Gallipoli	1/10/1915

Reg. No.	Name.	Cause of Death.	Place of Death.	Date.
5841	Jamieson, J. M.	D.O.W.	France	19/4/1917
5038	Jarvis, V. H.	K.I.A.	France	15/5/1918
585	Jenkins, T. W. D.	K.I.A.	France	10/6/1916
4455	Jenson, R. W.†	K.I.A.	France	3/5/1917
5692	Jesperson, E. W.†	K.I.A.	France	15/4/1917
6080	Johnson, E. F.	K.I.A.	Belgium	9/10/1917
5594	Johnson, E. M.	D.O.W.	Belgium	5/11/1917
1711	Johnson, G. B. F.	K.I.A.	Gallipoli	1/11/1915
1391	Johnson, H. M.	K.I.A.	France	2/11/1917
1217	Johnson, R. S. A.	K.I.A.	France	27/7/1916
2532	Joiner, J. M.†	K.I.A.	France	26/7/1916
591	Jolly, R.	K.I.A.	France	3/5/1917
1229a	Jones, S. T.	D.O.W.	France	31/7/1918
1228	Jones, W.†	K.I.A.	France	15/4/1917
5363	Jones, W.	K.I.A.	France	3/5/1917
2920	Jorden, L.	K.I.A.	Belgium	20/9/1917
922	Jowsey, W. G.†	K.I.A.	France	28/7/1916
2156	Jude, C. H.†	K.I.A.	France	26/8/1916
2403	Justice, C.	D.O.D.	France	11/4/1917
5042	Kable, H.	K.I.A.	France	14/3/1917
249	Kavanagh, J.	K.I.A.	Gallipoli	27/8/1915
590	Kelly, A. W.	D.O.W.	France	17/8/1918
5367	Kelly, C.	K.I.A.	Belgium	9/10/1917
2929b	Kelly, H. A.†	K.I.A.	France	5/5/1917
1622	Kelly, J.	D.O.W.	France	6/5/1917
1232	Kelly, T.	K.I.A.	France	16/4/1917
6324	Kelly, W. G.	K.I.A.	Belgium	20/9/1917
1718	Kelso, J. A.	K.I.A.	Belgium	20/9/1917
2405	Kemp, F. H.	K.I.A.	France	3/5/1917
600	Kemp, L. S.	K.I.A.	France	26/8/1916
6081	Kennedy, A.	D.O.W.	France	5/11/1917
596	Kennedy, M. W.	K.I.A.	Belgium	9/10/1917
4286	Kenney, A. B.	K.I.A.	France	7/8/1917
3553	Kenny, A. W.†	K.I.A.	France	15/4/1917
1961	Kesson, W.†	K.I.A.	France	26/7/1916
251	Kidd, E.	K.I.A.	Gallipoli	27/8/1915
2863	Killigrew, S. B.†	K.I.A.	France	2/8/1916
7065	Kilminster, A. H.†	K.I.A.	France	3/10/1918
373	King, C. W.	K.I.A.	Gallipoli	27/8/1915
1361	King, R.	D.O.W.	France	27/7/1916
6828	King, S. G.	K.I.A.	France	3/10/1918
5842	King, T. P.	K.I.A.	France	15/4/1917
5848	Kirby, W.	K.I.A.	France	31/8/1918
934	Kirkpatrick, G., "M.M."	K.I.A.	France	15/4/1917
3552	Knight, W. G.†	K.I.A.	France	14/5/1918
598	Korff, E. W.†	K.I.A.	France	30/7/1916
5596	Kyle, W. H.	D.O.W.	France	2/5/1917
254	Laing, J.	D.O.W.	H.S. "Maheno." at sea	30/8/1915
941	Lang, J. J. J.†	K.I.A.	France	15/4/1917
2491	Larcombe, R. R.	K.I.A.	Belgium	9/10/1917
5370	Latham, H.	K.I.A.	Belgium	20/9/1917
6631	Laughton, J. G. St. L.	K.I.A.	Belgium	6/11/1917
608	Lawler, T.	D.O.W.	Germany	2/3/1917
2719	Lawson, A. J.	K.I.A.	Belgium	9/10/1917
1718	Layton, C. G.	K.I.A.	France	23/4/1916
3419a	Lea, H. N.	D.O.W.	France	14/10/1917
7068	Leach, O. K.†	K.I.A.	France	31/8/1918

Reg. No.	Name.	Cause of Death.	Place of Death.	Date.
3867	Leay, J.	D.O.W.	France	17/8/1918
1974	Leckie, R. A.	K.I.A.	France	6/11/1917
6330	Legrey, R. H.	D.O.D.	S. Africa	16/12/1916
1721	Lenehan, A.	D.O.W.	France	2/3/1917
12	Lennon, J. F.	D.O.W.	France	26/5/1918
7069	Lister, S. H.	K.I.A.	France	14/5/1918
4152	Little, R. H.†	K.I.A.	France	3/5/1917
4153	Livingstone, J.†	K.I.A.	France	31/8/1918
1240a	Lockwood, J. M.	K.I.A.	Belgium	20/9/1917
263	Logan, J.	K.I.A.	Gallipoli	27/8/1915
4466	Long, R. T.	D.O.W.	France	8/8/1918
Capt.	Lonsdale, F. L.	D.O.W.	Malta	28/9/1915
5369	Lowrie, J. P.	K.I.A.	Belgium	9/10/1917
2/Lt.	Lowther, E. L.†	K.I.A.	France	27/7/1916
1366	Luffman, B. E. (stated to be Grimes, J.)	D.O.W.	Gallipoli	27/8/1915
260	Lyons, J.	K.I.A.	Gallipoli	27/8/1915
Lieut.	Lyons, J. M., "M.C.," "M.M.," "M.S.M."	K.I.A.	Belgium	9/10/1917
1801	Lyons, T. H.	D.O.W.	Gallipoli	3/10/1915
1173a	Lythgoe, J.†	K.I.A.	France	14/5/1918
290	Mack, W.	D.O.W.	Belgium	17/10/1917
5876	Maddigan, H. J.	D.O.W.	France	14/5/1918
957	Maddocks, C. F.	D.O.D.	Egypt	11/12/1915
1246	Maher, M.	D.O.W.	Gallipoli	30/11/1915
2413	Mahony, C. J.	K.I.A.	Belgium	9/10/1917
1964	Mailey, H. C.	K.I.A.	Belgium	26/9/1916
6296	Main, H.†	K.I.A.	France	3/10/1918
4773	Maloney, C. A.	K.I.A.	Belgium	9/10/1917
5382	Maltby, G.†	K.I.A.	France	3/5/1917
1739	Malthouse, F. J.	K.I.A.	Belgium	10/1/1918
2717	Mann, A. C.	D.O.W.	France	4/8/1916
1240	Manning, W. J.	D.O.D.	"Themistocles" at sea	2/6/1915
6112	Mansfield, D. F.	D.O.W.	Belgium	10/10/1917
5873	Manson, J.	K.I.A.	France	3/5/1917
6092	Manson, W.	K.I.A.	Belgium	9/10/1917
5055	Mara, G. J.	D.O.D.	France	26/11/1918
2167	Marrion, T. (stated to be Stiff, A. A. C.)	K.I.A.	France	26/7/1916
2044	Marsden, J.	K.I.A.	Belgium	9/10/1917
6848	Marshall, J. W.	K.I.A.	France	3/10/1918
4157	Marshall, W.	K.I.A.	Belgium	9/10/1917
4159	Martin, J. H.	K.I.A.	France	3/5/1917
269	Martin, T. E.	D.O.W.	Mudros	21/8/1915
1968	Maxwell, H.	K.I.A.	Belgium	9/10/1917
945	May, F.	K.I.A.	France	15/4/1917
5604	Mayberry, R. A.	K.I.A.	France	3/10/1918
6102	Maynard, G.	K.I.A.	Belgium	9/10/1917
1242	Maynard, L.	K.I.A.	France	8/8/1918
6396	Maynard, N.C.	K.I.A.	France	15/5/1918
1728	Meehan, J. T.,† "M.M."	K.I.A.	France	21/11/1916
5449	Meller, W. R.	K.I.A.	Belgium	20/9/1917
5375	Melville, D. M.†	K.I.A.	France	15/4/1917
2013	Mewburn, A. G. E.	K.I.A.	France	5/11/1917
1247	Millar, J. S.	K.I.A.	France	23/4/1916
943	Miller, G. H.†	K.I.A.	France	2/8/1916
6109	Miller, J. C.	D.O.W.	France	26/4/1918
2172	Miller, W. A.†	K.I.A.	France	3/1/1917

Reg. No.	Name.	Cause of Death.	Place of Death.	Date.
624	Miller, W. H.	K.I.A.	Gallipoli	6/9/1915
6417	Mills, G. G. R. (stated to be Robinson W. R.)	D.O.W.	France	16/4/1918
4780	Milner, R.	K.I.A.	France	15/4/1917
2173	Milthorpe, J. L.	K.I.A.	Belgium	20/9/1917
625	Mines, F. C.	K.I.A.	Belgium	20/9/1917
1586	Mintarn, N. F.	D.O.D.	Cairo	30/6/1915
6338	Mitchell, G. L.	K.I.A.	Belgium	20/9/1917
963	Mitchell, J. L., "M.M."	K.I.A.	France	26/6/1916
6342	Mitchell, W.	K.I.A.	Belgium	20/9/1917
4777	Mitten, H. E.	D.O.W.	France	29/5/1917
2732	Moffat, R.	K.I.A.	Belgium	5/11/1917
2174	Molony, F. W.†	K.I.A.	France	15/4/1917
2175	Molony, H. A.	K.I.A.	Belgium	9/19/1917
1249	Montgomery, H. E.	D.O.W.	Egypt	8/9/1915
5867	Moore, J. T.†	K.I.A.	France	15/4/1917
1749	Moore, P. A.	K.I.A.	France	26/7/1916
1803	Moore, S. R.	D.O.W.	France	4/5/1917
5383	Moore, T.†	K.I.A.	France	3/5/1917
4167	Moore, V.	D.O.W.	France	23/4/1917
5376	Moran, J. J.†	K.I.A.	France	3/5/1917
1587	Morgan, W. G.†	K.I.A.	France	15/4/1917
4168	Moriarty, J. F. J.	K.I.A.	France	30/8/1918
628	Morren, F. W.	K.I.A.	Gallipoli	27/8/1915
281	Morris, J.	D.O.W.	Cairo	31/8/1915
5607	Mulholland, W. R.	K.I.A.	Belgium	20/9/1917
2180	Munro, C. C.	D.O.W.	France	10/6/1916
282	Munton, T.	K.I.A.	Gallipoli	27/8/1915
5379	Murdoch, W. R.†	K.I.A.	France	3/5/1917
T/Mjr.	Murphy, F. J. P.	D.O.D.	Mudros	11/1/1916
6594	Murphy, T. J.	D.O.W.	France	6/9/1918
1623	Murray, G. G.	D.O.W.	Belgium	9/10/1917
5875	Murray, J.†	K.I.A.	France	15/4/1917
4486	McAuliffee, J.†	K.I.A.	France	3/5/1917
962	McBride, C. J.	D.O.W.	France	2/8/1916
3880	McCaffrey, A. J. "M.M."	K.I.A.	France	27/5/1918
288	McCarthy, S.	K.I.A.	Gallipoli	27/8/1915
6350	McClymont, A. J.	K.I.A.	Belgium	20/9/1917
1975	McCord, T. H.	D.O.W.	Belgium	22/9/1917
955	McCulloch, W. L.†	K.I.A.	France	26/7/1916
2859	McDermid, H. D.	K.I.A.	France	3/5/1917
Lieut.	McDiarmid, J. J.†	K.I.A.	France	3/5/1917
276	McDonald, F., "M.M."	K.I.A.	Belgium	20/9/1917
946	MacDonald, J. A.	K.I.A.	Gallipoli	29/8/1915
277	McDonald, M.	K.I.A.	Belgium	9/10/1917
4488	McDonell, C. J.	D.O.W.	France	13/10/1917
1978	MacDonogh, O.	K.I.A.	Belgium	20/9/1917
2/Lt.	McDowell, A. R.	K.I.A.	Belgium	9/10/1917
1056	McEnally, J.	D.O.W.	Gallipoli	24/8/1915
1253	McEwan	D.O.W.	France	1/8/1916
6346	McGinley, J. H.	K.I.A.	Belgium	20/9/1917
2418	McGlashan, A. W.,"M.M."	K.I.A.	Belgium	26/8/1916
4491	McGuinness, W. J.	D.O.W.	Belgium	6/5/1917
6589	McIlwraith, G.	D.O.W.	Belgium	7/7/1918
5613	McInnes, W. A.	K.I.A.	Belgium	9/10/1917
771	McIntosh, G.	D.O.W.	France	27/8/1916
616	McKay, A. C.	D.O.D.	Gallipoli	17/11/1915
1564	McKenzie, H. D.†	K.I.A.	France	26/7/1916

Reg. No.	Name.	Cause of Death.	Place of Death.	Date.
4492	McLean, R. D. J.	K.I.A.	France	15/4/1917
4869	McLean, T. A.	K.I.A.	France	8/8/1918
613	McLeay, D. A.	K.I.A.	Gallipoli	1/11/1915
1254	McLeod, W. J.†	K.I.A.	France	27/7/1916
284	McMahon, M. P.†	K.I.A.	France	26/7/1916
5385	McMurtrie, J. J.	K.I.A.	France	3/2/1917
294	McNair, W.	K.I.A.	Gallipoli	27/8/1915
614	McNamara, R. M.	D.O.W.	France	5/6/1916
2420a	McNaughton, G.	D.O.W.	H.M.A.T. "Carisbrooke Castle"	9/10/1918
383	McPaul, H. D. B.	K.I.A.	France	11/8/1918
746	MacPherson, J.	D.O.W.	France	8/5/1917
5858	McQuarrie, J.	K.I.A.	France	15/4/1917
1615	McTague, E.	K.I.A.	Gallipoli	4/9/1915
1383	Naish, E.	K.I.A.	Gallipoli	4/10/1915
Lieut.	Nalder, G. F.†	K.I.A.	France	3/5/1917
5389	Napier, R. K.	D.O.W.	France	2/3/1917
973	Neal, G. D.	K.I.A.	Belgium	20/9/1917
3900	Negus, W. A.†	K.I.A.	France	26/7/1916
Lieut.	New, E. C.	K.I.A.	Belgium	9/10/1917
2962	Newman, M.	D.O.W.	France	14/5/1917
2762	Newman, W. A.	D.O.W.	Belgium	5/5/1917
5879	Newton, R. H. D.	D.O.D.	France	25/10/1918
7088	Nicholson, S. L. O.	D.O.W.	France	27/5/1918
1343	Nimmo, S. J., "M.M."	K.I.A.	Belgium	9/10/1917
4185	Noah, H. L.†	K.I.A.	France	20/11/1916
2502	Norquay, W.	K.I.A.	France	9/5/1918
5880	Nugent, F. J.	D.O.W.	France	24/5/1917
Lieut.	Nunn, J. R.	D.O.I.	Randwick	9/4/1917
3596	Oakley, S., "M.M."	K.I.A.	Belgium	20/9/1917
5391	Oakman, R. M. T.	K.I.A.	France	3/5/1917
7090	O'Berg, E. T.	K.I.A.	France	14/5/1918
2188	O'Brien, D. A.	K.I.A.	Belgium	20/9/1917
300	O'Byrne, T. P.	K.I.A.	Gallipoli	27/8/1915
980	O'Connell, D. F.	D.O.W.	France	27/7/1916
975	O'Connor, R.†	K.I.A.	France	15/4/1917
1614	O'Hara, D.	D.O.W.	France	2/8/1916
3594	O'Keefe, P. A.	K.I.A.	France	26/7/1916
4190	Olliver, O. T.	K.I.A.	Belgium	20/9/1917
4499	O'Neill, E. J.	K.I.A.	Belgium	9/10/1917
1051	O'Neill, F. P.	D.O.W.	England	18/8/1916
1984	O'Neill, J. T.	K.I.A.	France	6/11/1916
	Osborne, H.	D.O.D.	Liverpool, N.S.W.	20/5/1915
4500	O'Shannassy, P.	K.I.A.	Belgium	26/9/1916
652	O'Toole, J.P.†	K.I.A.	France	26/7/1916
1986	Outram, S.	K.I.A.	France	5/8/1916
378	Owen, J.	D.O.W.	France	14/4/1916
303	Page, S.	K.I.A.	Gallipoli	30/11/1915
3597	Palmer, C. L.	K.I.A.	Belgium	9/10/1917
3601	Palmer, R.	D.O.W.	France	4/6/1918
5937	Parker, H. L.†	K.I.A.	France	15/4/1917
5706	Parkes, H. L.	K.I.A.	France	3/10/1918
305	Parsons, C. E.	K.I.A.	France	23/8/1916
1625	Payne, H.	D.O.W.	France	15/4/1916
6125	Peachman, W. E.	K.I.A.	France	15/4/1917
4198	Pearce, W. H. L.	K.I.A.	France	31/8/1918
1272	Pears, A.	D.O.D.	Egypt	29/9/1915

Reg. No.	Name.	Cause of Death.	Place of Death.	Date.
660	Pearson, H. B.	D.O.W.	France	4/9/1918
6124	Pearson, L. B.	D.O.I.	H.M.A.T. "Miltiades," Sierre Leone	18/5/1917
5392	Pearson, T. H.	K.I.A.	Belgium	20/9/1917
304	Peat, H.	K.I.A.	France	27/7/1916
2506	Penketh, P. J.	D.O.W.	England	29/4/1918
6119	Penny, C. E.†	K.I.A.	France	15/4/1917
4503	Perkins, E. C.	K.I.A.	France	8/11/1916
2971b	Perkins, W. H.†	K.I.A.	France	15/4/1917
5885	Piper, C. E.†	K.I.A.	France	3/5/1917
2760	Potts, D.McI.	K.I.A.	France	13/6/1916
5074	Power, T.	K.I.A.	Belgium	9/10/1917
5394	Power, T.	K.I.A.	France	30/8/1918
1273	Pritchard, R. F.	D.O.W.	Belgium	16/11/1917
307	Procter, W. W.	K.I.A.	Gallipoli	27/8/1915
6118	Purcell, R. H.	Drowned at sea	H.M.A.T. "Warilda"	3/8/1918
7154	Purvis, J. T.†	K.I.A.	France	12/5/1918
Lieut.	Pye, R. E.	K.I.A.	France	17/5/1916
5397	Quinn, H. J.†	K.I.A.	France	15/4/1917
6377	Radford, E. J.	D.O.D.	France	8/12/1918
5891	Ramsey, F. T.†	K.I/.A.	France	3/5/1917
3162	Raine, I. F.	D.O.D.	Waverley, N.S.W.	30/3/1919
6169	Rait, S. F.†	K.I.A.	France	3/5/1917
Lieut	Read, T. R.	K.I.A.	France	9/8/1918
991	Rees, V. J.	K.I.A.	France	26/7/1916
6132	Regan, R. J.†	K.I.A.	France	3/5/1917
3912	Reglin, N.S.	D.O.W.	England	31/8/1916
3286	Reid, M. A.	K.I.A.	France	28/7/1916
1278	Reilly, F.	K.I.A.	France	3/5/1917
6916	Restell, G. H. E.	K.I.A.	France	14/5/1918
6134	Reynolds, W. E.	D.O.W.	France	31/8/1918
6650	Rhoades, J. W. F.	K.I.A.	France	16/7/1918
2/Lt.	Richardson, J. L.	K.I.A.	France	31/8/1918
1232	Ridley, H. H.†	K.I.A.	France	15/4/1917
Lieut.	Ridley, T. "M.C.," "D.C.M."	D.O.W.	France	10/9/1918
6170	Riley, G. T.†	K.I.A.	France	15/4/1917
3910	Ringrose, J. M.†	K.I.A.	France	26/7/1916
1285	Roberts, D., "M.M."	K.I.A.	France	9/8/1918
376	Robertson, J. T.	D.O.W.	H.S. "Maheno," at sea	30/8/1915
6188	Robertson, L.	K.I.A.	France	3/10/1918
3915	Robins, W. J.	D.O.W.	France	25/8/1916
5400	Robinson, R. H.	K.I.A.	France	31/8/1918
5889	Robson, G. H.†	K.I.A.	France	3/5/1917
2200	Roche, C. J.	D.O.W.	France	3/3/1917
1335	Rockliff, H.†	K.I.A.	France	27/7/1916
2001	Rodgers, A. T.	K.I.A.	Belgium	20/9/1917
7097	Rogers, J. J.	D.O.W.	France	30/6/1918
5630	Rogerson, J.	K.I.A.	Belgium	9/10/1917
2845	Ross, M. J.†	K.I.A.	France	2/8/1916
6359	Rowe, W.	K.I.A.	Belgium	20/9/1917
5401	Rudder, R.B.†	K.I.A.	France	3/5/1917
2439	Rudkin, W. H.†	K.I.A.	France	3/5/1917
5627	Ruelle, J.†	K.I.A.	France	15/4/1917
4519	Rutherford, H. B.	D.O.W.	France	16/5/1918
409	Ryan, A. E.†	K.I.A.	France	3/5/1917
992	Ryan, J.	K.I.A.	France	24/8/1916
2/Lt.	Ryan, T. L., "M.M."	K.I.A.	Belgium	20/9/1917

Reg. No.	Name.	Cause of Death.	Place of Death.	Date.
4214	Samuel, A. D.	K.I.A.	France	3/5/1917
689	Sargeant, A. H.	D.O.W.	France	3/2/1917
678	Sault, D. J.†	K.I.A.	France	4/8/1916
6909	Saundercock, A. R.	K.I.A.	France	8/8/1918
328	Schweitzer, S. G.	K.I.A.	Gallipoli	27/8/1915
2782	Schwonberg, C. G.	K.I.A.	Belgium	9/10/1917
6146	Scott, N.	D.O.W.	France	3/5/1917
5413	Scott, T.	K.I.A.	Belgium	20/9/1917
4217	Scullin, T. E.	K.I.A.	France	19/7/1918
6174	Seabrook, G. R.	K.I.A.	Belgium	20/9/1917
6147	Seabrook, T. L.	K.I.A.	Belgium	20/9/1917
2/Lt.	Seabrook, W. K.	D.O.W.	Belgium	21/9/1917
2442	Seaton, E.†	K.I.A.	France	26/7/1916
6419	Sergeant, A. J.	K.I.A.	Belgium	20/9/1917
2006	Seymour, A. A. W.	K.I.A.	France	13/6/1916
3615	Shanahan, J. J.	D.O.D.	France	10/6/1917
2739a	Shea, H. W. G. T. J.	D.O.W.	France	16/4/1917
3930	Sheehan, J.,† "M.M."	K.I.A.	France	3/5/1917
2512	Sheffield, L. A.	K.I.A.	France	26/7/1916
7105	Shields, A. H.	K.I.A.	France	8/8/1918
1007	Simons, S.	K.I.A.	Gallipoli	5/11/1915
4219	Simpson, N. M.†	D.O.W.	France	1/3/1917
680	Simpson, N. W.	D.O.W.	France	29/7/1916
5416	Skeen, A.	K.I.A.	France	31/8/1918
3032	Slater, E.	D.O.W.	France	14/5/1918
2305	Sloan, W.	D.O.W.	France	4/10/1918
Lieut.	Small, G., "M.C."	K.I.A.	France	31/8/1918
5638	Smart, A. J.†	K.I.A.	France	3/5/1917
6363	Smith, C. L.	K.I.A.	Belgium	9/10/1917
2448	Smith, G. A.†	K.I.A.	France	26/7/1916
1062	Smith, J.	K.I.A.	Belgium	20/9/1917
6420	Smith, J.	K.I.A.	Belguim	20/9/1917
3628	Smith, S.†	K.I.A.	France	2/8/1916
2534	Smith, W.	K.I.A.	Belgium	20/9/1917
4834	Smith, W. A. C.	K.I.A.	Belgium	20/9/1917
4531	Smith, W. E.†	K.I.A.	France	9/8/1918
6866	Smith, W.J.	K.I.A.	France	31/8/1918
3621	Smithers, J. E.	K.I.A.	France	2/3/1917
4584	Spencer, H. V.	D.O.W.	France	30/12/1917
5457	Spencer, J.	K.I.A.	Belgium	20/9/1917
1001	Spillane, T. F.	K.I.A.	France	27/2/1917
2208	Spring, H. K.†	K.I.A.	France	15/4/1917
2992	Spurr, H. H.	D.O.W.	France	15/5/1918
433	Stace, T.	K.I.A.	Galipoli	27/8/1915
5406	Stanford, W.†	D.O.W.	France	13/3/1917
4830	Stapleton, E.	K.I.A.	France	14/5/1918
3623	Stapleton, W. J.	K.I.A.	France	6/6/1916
2783	Steel, A. L.	K.I.A.	France	11/8/1918
6867	Steele, A. J.	K.I.A.	France	8/8/1918
690	Stephenson, A.	D.O.W.	France	2/6/1918
	Stevens, F.	C.N.S.	Redfern, N.S.W.	27/11/1915
4231	Stewart, A. J.	K.I.A.	Belgium	20/9/1917
3622	Stewart, A. R. M.	K.I.A.	Belgium	20/9/1917
330	Stewart, J.	K.I.A.	Gallipoli	27/8/1915
5409	Stewart, J. C., "M.M."	K.I.A.	France	31/8/1918
6632	Stoakes, A. E.†	K.I.A.	France	16/4/1918
4536	Stone, C.	D.O.W.	France	2/11/1918
4537	Stone, J. P.	K.I.A.	Belgium	20/9/1917

Reg. No.	Name.	Cause of Death.	Place of Death.	Date.
2450	Stoner, W.†	K.I.A.	France	23/8/1916
5407	Stuntz J.†	K.I.A.	France	3/5/1917
1006	Stutter, G.	D.O.W.	France	6/8/1916
3906	Sullivan, F. J.	K.I.A.	France	16/7/1918
4236	Sullivan, M.†	K.I.A.	France	3/5/1917
4540	Sutcliffe, F.	K.I.A.	France	3/10/1918
4541	Swain, J. A.	K.I.A.	France	14/3/1917
6641a	Sykes, R. L.	K.I.A.	France	9/8/1918
2287	Symons, F. R.†	K.I.A.	France	15/4/1917
774	Tait, R.	K.I.A.	France	3/8/1916
Lieut.	Taplin, A. S.	K.I.A.	France	3/5/1917
1601	Taylor, G. H., "M.M."	D.O.W.	France	1/6/1918
	Taylor, J. F. R.	C.N.S.	Five Dock, N.S.W.	10/2/1918
3933	Taylor, T. H.†	K.I.A.	France	3/5/1917
2790	Taylor, T. S.	K.I.A.	France	26/7/1916
6379	Thomas, A. "M.M."†	K.I.A.	France	31/8/1918
2988b	Thomas, C. V.†	K.I.A.	France	15/4/1917
2016	Thomas, F. M.	K.I.A.	France	27/2/1917
1015	Thomas, G.A.	K.I.A.	Belgium	20/9/1917
4244	Thomas, R. E.	K.I.A.	France	13/5/1918
6421	Thompson, A.	K.I.A.	Belgium	20/9/1917
6375	Thompson, A. F.	K.I.A.	Belgium	20/9/1917
6376	Thompson, G. W.	K.I.A.	Belgium	9/10/1917
5448	Thompson, J. W.†	K.I.A.	France	15/4/1917
1309	Thompson, L. S.	K.I.A.	France	13/6/1916
6150	Thomson, A. R. B.	K.I.A.	Belgium	20/9/1917
2274	Thorogood, G. E.	K.I.A.	France	14/5/1918
696	Thorpe, A.	K.I.A.	Belgium	25/9/1916
1785	Tidmarsh, E. J., "D.C.M."	D.O.D.	France	10/11/1918
1310	Tomlinson, G.	K.I.A.	Gallipoli	25/8/1915
346	Torpy, P. E.	D.O.W.	France	9/10/1918
2824	Towns, D.	K.I.A.	Belgium	20/9/1917
5096	Townsend, B.†	K.I.A.	France	3/5/1917
342	Townsend, C.	K.I.A.	Gallipoli	27/8/1915
5649	Tranter, H.	K.I.A.	France	3/5/1917
1339	Tremain, W. C.†	K.I.A.	France	3/10/1918
6377	Tripcony, W.J.	D.O.W.	France	8/8/1918
3940	Trueland, J. M.	K.I.A.	France	8/11/1916
1784	Tudor, S. E.	D.O.W.	France	30/7/1916
700	Turner, E.	K.I.A.	Belgium	9/10/1917
2021	Urquhart, E.	D.O.D.	England	4/1/1917
5656	Vallance, R. G.	K.I.A.	Belgium	20/9/1917
710	Vaughan, C. T.†	K.I.A.	France	14/5/1918
2/Lt.	Verrills, E. J.	K.I.A.	Belgium	9/10/1917
6382	Vovil, E. J.	K.I.A.	Belgium	20/9/1917
729	Wade, W. G.	D.O.W.	France	3/8/1916
4250	Walder, W.	D.O.D.	Scotland	6/10/1918
759	Walker, H. A.	K.I.A.	France	6/6/1916
4251	Wallace, T. R.	K.I.A.	France	8/11/1916
3955	Walsh, L. D.	D.O.W.	England	3/8/1916
2673	Ward, R. H.	K.I.A.	France	2/3/1917
5427	Warland, K.	K.I.A.	France	31/8/1918
	Warren, J.	D.O.D.	Liverpool, N.S.W.	26/10/1915
5667	Waters, H. P.	K.I.A.	France	3/5/1917
1318	Watkins, E. S.	K.I.A.	France	15/4/1917
716	Watson, J. W.	D.O.W.	Belgium	21/9/1917
2995	Watson, P. V.	K.I.A.	France	9/5/1918

Reg. No.	Name.	Cause of Death.	Place of Death.	Date.
2456	Watson, W. D.	D.O.W.	France	4/5/1916
4558	Watson, W. L.	K.I.A.	Belgium	9/10/1917
3647	Waugh, C. G.†	K.I.A.	France	24/8/1916
353	Wells, C. E. A.	K.I.A.	Gallipoli	11/12/1915
Lieut.	West, A. S.	D.O.W.	France	17/7/1918
1794	Western, C. L.†	K.I.A.	France	7/11/1916
1038	Wheeler, F. H. C.	K.I.A.	Belgium	9/10/1917
5439	Whisker, A. N.†	K.I.A.	France	3/5/1917
5917	Whitaker, J.†	K.I.A.	France	3/5/1917
668	White, C.	K.I.A.	France	3/10/1918
392	White, D. H.	K.I.A.	France	6/11/1916
5928	Whiteley, R. J.†	K.I.A.	France	3/5/1917
2026	Whitfield, E.	K.I.A.	France	2/8/1916
6390	Whittaker, W. J.†	K.I.A.	France	31/8/1918
3956	Whyte, A.	K.I.A.	Belgium	9/10/1917
2519	Wilde, G. J.	K.I.A.	Belgium	20/9/1917
3652	Wilkinson, R. F. C.	K.I.A.	France	9/5/1918
5666	Williams, D.†	K.I.A.	France	3/5/1917
6877	Williams, F. L.†	K.I.A.	France	15/5/1918
4573	Williams, J. L.	D.O.W.	France	25/8/1916
5431	Williams, N.†	K.I.A.	France	3/5/1917
348	Williams, T.	D.O.W.	H.T. "Oxfordshire"	4/12/1915
726	Williams, T. H. J.	D.O.D.	England	8/3/1917
730	Willick, B. C.	K.I.A.	Gallipoli	28/8/1915
6161	Willis, S. D.	K.I.A.	France	9/8/1918
2031	Wilson, A.†	K.I.A.	France	26/7/1916
1798	Wilson, H. J.	D.O.W.	France	26/7/1916
4858	Wilson, J.	D.O.W.	France	12/11/1916
5659	Wilson, J. W.	K.I.A.	France	14/5/1918
1322	Wilson, R.	K.I.A.	France	31/8/1918
4567	Wilson, T.	K.I.A.	Belgium	20/9/1917
6385	Wilson, W. (True Name Blyth, W.)	K.I.A.	Belgium	9/10/1917
1320	Winch, J. H.	D.O.D.	Egypt	1/11/1915
5913	Windsor, L. J.	K.I.A.	France	3/5/1917
1793	Witt, A.	D.O.D.	Mudros	22/9/1915
4568	Womsley, W. O.	K.I.A.	Belgium	9/10/1917
5430	Wong, R. W.	K.I.A.	France	2/3/1917
1030	Wood, T.	K.I.A.	Gallipoli	21/9/1915
5112	Woodhouse, E. E.	K.I.A.	France	31/8/1918
6182	Woolfe, N. E.†	K.I.A.	France	3/5/1917
4267	Worsnip, J.†	K.I.A.	France	3/5/1917
6155	Worth, H. C.†	K.I.A.	France	3/5/1917
2224	Worthington, H. J.†	K.I.A.	France	15/4/1917
1029	Worthington, R. C., "M.M."	K.I.A.	Belgium	9/10/1917
5663	Wray, F.	D.O.W.	France	27/2/1917
6388	Wright, H.	D.O.W.	France	7/9/1918
1027	Wrigley, E. R.	K.I.A.	Belgium	20/9/1917
728	Wyatt, P.	K.I.A.	France	3/5/1917
5918	Wylie, J. L.†	K.I.A.	France	15/4/1917
4270	Yates, A. E.	C.N.S.	Germany	17/4/1917
4574	Yeo, H. J.	K.I.A.	Belgium	9/10/1917
363	Yeomans, B. W.	K.I.A.	Gallipoli	27/8/1915
1325	York, F. W.	D.O.W.	France	23/11/1916
2/Lt.	Young, A. S.	D.O.W.	France	2/3/1917
6913	Young, E.†	K.I.A.	France	8/8/1918
6880	Young, H. B.	D.O.D.	England	8/1/1918

HONOURS & AWARDS

No. or Rank.	Name.	V.C.	C.B.	C.M.G.	D.S.O.	Bar to D.S.O.	O.B.E.	M.C.	Bar to M.C.	D.C.M.	M.M.	Bar to M.M.	M.S.M.	M.I.D.	Congratulatory or Complimentary.	Croix de Guerre.	Decoration Militaire.
158	Abbott, F.										1						
2872	Alexander, J. A.												1	1			
Capt.	Allen, H. T.																
Capt.	Allen, L. St. J.							1			1			1			
4655	Anderson, P. L.							1									
3758	Anderson, W. L.																
806	Appleton, H. L.										1				1		
802	Austin, R. C.										1						
1882	Bailey, N. B.										1			2			
3454	Balmain, P.																
4358	Barnes, E.										1						
Capt.	Barnett, F. G.																
1663	Barnier, J. A.										1						
1130	Barrett, R.										1						
1519	Barrett, W.										1						
2585	Bartlett, A.																
104	Bennett, J. E.				1												
4364	Bird, L.																
4675	Bothamley, W. S.										1						
Lieut.	Bradford, B.												1				
2471	Breaden, T. A. H.							1									
787	Brewer, E. G.										1						
5681	Broder, P. J.										1						
2867	Brogden, W. A.												1	1			
4070	Brown, C. C.										1						
490	Brown, H. W.							1			1						
3461	Burrell, W. H. T.										1						

359

No. or Rank.	Name.	V.C.	C.B.	C.M.G.	D.S.O.	Bar to D.S.O.	O.B.E.	M.C.	Bar to M.C.	D.C.M.	M.M.	Bar to M.M.	M.S.M.	M.I.D.	Congratulatory or Complimentary.	Croix de Guerre.	Decoration Militaire.
4378	Burton, C. J.																
1897	Cambridge, R. M. G.										—						
0784	Cathels, J.										—						
3759	Chambers, A. H.										—						
4385	Chandler, H. A.										—						
1001	Chick, G. J.										—						
2088	Childs, G. H.						—					—					
522	Clarke, L. C.										—						
Lieut.	Clifton, H. E.										—						
7185	Collier, W. H.										—						
840	Compton, H. J.										—						
4889	Corbett, T. A.										—			—			
1173	Cowcher, E. G.										—						
325	Cracknell, C. F.										—						
1673	Crawford, S.							—									
Lieut.	Croft, F. W.							—		—							
Lieut.	Dark, E. W.																
2629	Davidson, A. H.									—							
1181	Davidson, G.																
1150	Davis, W.																
100	Day, E.																
3810	Dearie, F. J.																
201	Deorek, W.									—				—			
3812	Devine, F.																
104	Didcote, H. F.									—							
Lieut.	Doig, A. T.							—		—				—			
2132	Doling, A. E.																
5340	Dryden, G. S.									—							
1059a	Earnshaw, A. S.																
1370	Edwards, S.																
1052	Emanuel, J.																

No. or Rank	Name	V.C.	C.B.	C.M.G.	D.S.O.	Bar to D.S.O.	O.B.E.	M.C.	Bar to M.C.	D.C.M.	M.M.	Bar to M.M.	M.S.M.	M.I.D.	Congratulatory or Complimentary	Croix de Guerre	Decoration Militaire
3503	Evans, J. H.									1	1						
1546	Fahey, P. A.							1							1		
Lieut.	Fay, J. J.													1			
552	Filby, K.										1						
Capt.	Finlay, C. C.							1						1			
3829	Fitzgerald, E. F.							1			1				1		
Lieut.	Fitzroy, R. J.																
Lieut.	Flood, W. L.										1			1			
2044	Fox, J. R.							1									
5012	Francis, J. P.														1		
2288	Fry, R. L.										1						
5818	Fulthorpe, J.													2			
Major	Fussell, L. G.										1						
5574	Gant, J. S.										1						
1780	Gibbons, M. P.										1						
562	Gibson, L. R.										1					1F	
2374	Graham, J. A.										1						
894	Grange, F. G.										1						
223	Green, J. H.									1	1						
6805	Greenaway, B. M.							1									
5577	Gregory, J. T.																
1342	Grix, A.										1						
Lieut.	Haigh, W. R.																
236	Hamilton, A. H.										1						
2144	Hardy, F. J.									1				1			
Capt.	Harnett, E. T.							1									
1700	Hayes, M.										1						
5381	Hennessey, B.																
882	Herne, C. P.										1						
Lieut.	Hill, H.																
Major	Holmes, B.						1							1			

No. or Rank	Name	V.C.	C.B.	C.M.G.	D.S.O.	Bar to D.S.O.	O.B.E.	M.C.	Bar to M.C.	D.C.M.	M.M.	Bar to M.M.	M.S.M.	M.I.D.	Congratulatory or Complimentary	Croix de Guerre	Decoration Militaire
919	Hume, W. D.	1															
588	Jackson, W. K.										1						
2400	Jeffrey, G.										1						
4751	Johanson, F. L.									1							
1707	Johnston, O. G.										1						
Capt. 1231a	Johnston, L. J.										1			1			
4755	Kelly, J. C.										1						
2401	Kenyon, G. J.										1						
934	King, J.										1						
1226	Kirkpatrick, G.										1						
2698	Kirkpatrick, J.										1						
4465	Knight, T. R.										1	1					
Lieut.	Lawless, J. W.													2			
03832	Little, R. P.																
Lieut.	Loveridge, A. N.										1						
Capt.	Lyons, J. M.										1	1	1				
782	Mackenzie, K. W.							1									
3930	Mackie, J. R.										1		1				
6108	Maher, J. A.							1									
Capt.	Makin, A.							1	1								
3889	Mansfield, E. T.										1						
2044	Mansfield, A. B.																
	Marsden, J.							1									
T/Brig.-Gen.	Martin, E. F.		1	1	1									6	1		
1239	Martin, J. C.													1			
298	Massey, R. E.										1						
Lieut.	Mathews, H. G.				1												
Major 1728	Maughan, J. T.										1						
964	Meehan, J. T.																
	Miller, C. H.										1						

362

No. or Rank	Name	V.C.	C.B.	C.M.G.	D.S.O.	Bar to D.S.O.	O.B.E.	M.C.	Bar to M.C.	D.C.M.	M.M.	Bar to M.M.	M.S.M.	M.I.D.	Congratulatory or Complimentary	Croix de Guerre	Decoration Militaire
6418	Milthorpe, G. R.										1						
903	Mitchell, J. L.										1						
626	Moffatt, R. W.										1						
5476	Morris, E. J.										1	1	1				
4483	Murdoch, J. C.																
799	Murphy, J. H.																
949	Murphy, W.																
6108	Murray, J. F.																
6841	Murrell, H. G.								1		1	1		1			
3890	McCaffrey, A. J.										1						
772	McCarter, V.										1	1					
1591	McClear, J. E.										1						
1592	McDonald, A.																
276	McDonald, F.									1	1						
2418	McGlashen, A. W.										1	1					
4796	McInnes, A. J.										1						
781	McKay, M. J.									1	1	1					
1504	McKenzie, H. D.											1					
1982	McKenzie, S. R.																
Capt.	McLean, A. L. (A.A.M.C. attached)							1						1	1		
Major	McMaster, R. M. (A.A.M.C. attached)				1												
Lieut.	McPhee, G. R.																
1074	Newman, J. L.										1				1		
Lieut.	Nicholson, C. R.																
1343	Nimmo, S. J.										1			1			
5617	Nix, R. H.										1						
3596	Oakley, S.										1						
647	O'Connor, P. R.										1						
1269	Ogilvie, C. W.										1						
8855	O'Hehir, J.										1						

363

No.	Rank	Name	V.C.	C.B.	C.M.G.	D.S.O.	Bar to D.S.O.	O.B.E.	M.C.	Bar to M.C.	D.C.M.	M.M.	Bar to M.M.	M.S.M.	M.I.D.	Congratulatory or Complimentary	Croix de Guerre	Decoration Militaire
979		O'Keefe, E. J.													—			
2455		Olsen, N. P.							—									
691		Pearson, H. J.							—			—						
5073	Lieut.	Pepper, R. L.										—						
	Lieut.	Pettit, R. W.							—									
	Lt.-Col.	Pye, C. R. A.																
1760		Raber, W. O.										—						
1276		Raitt, J. W.									—	—						
2196		Rath, H. H.																
1064		Rees, J.																
691		Richards, G.				—						—						
†Lieut.		Ridley, T.				—			—						2			
2436		Rigley, L. J.							—						—			
3155		Rixon, J. T.										—						
1283		Roberts, D.										—						
1763		Roberts, T. H.										—						
Capt.		Ronald, H.																
2204		Ryan, T. L.										—						
Lt.-Col.		Sadler, R. M.																
Lieut.		Sams, C. J.																
6306		Scott, E.																1B
319		Scott, J.				—			—		—	—			—	—		
171		Sewell, C. J.																
2513	Lieut.	Sharman, M.																
	Lieut.	Shaw, H. E.										—						
3630		Sheehan, J.																
Lieut.		Shield, R. V.																
1385		Shuck, G. H.																
3509		Skinner, C.													—			
Lieut.		Small, G.										—						
Lieut.		Smith, F. W. D.							—			—						
Capt.		Spier, R. V.																

† Medal of St. George, 4th Class, Russia ... 1

No. or Rank	Name	V.C.	C.B.	C.M.G.	D.S.O.	Bar to D.S.O.	O.B.E.	M.C.	Bar to M.C.	D.C.M.	M.M.	Bar to M.M.	M.S.M.	M.I.D.	Congratulatory or Complimentary	Croix de Guerre	Decoration Militaire
657a	Starr, B. G.										1						
5400	Stewart, J. C.										1						
6624	Stinson, T. M.									1							
5411	Stranlund, O. E.										1						
1305	Sullivan, V. J.															1F	
2015	Targett, H.										1						
1091	Taylor, G. H.										1						
6379	Thomas, A.							1									
4551	Thompson, S. H.													3	2		
1785	Tidmarsh, E. J.										1						
Lieut.	Tindale, F. W.															1B	
Lt.-Col.	Travers, R. J. A.																1
Lieut.	Walsh, U. K.							1						1			
1041	Walsh, W. A.										1						
1780	Watson, W. H.							1									
5664	Whites, W.										1						
3646	White, R. C.										1						
Lieut.	Willard, R. R. F.																
722	Williams, C. G.															1B	
4571	Wilson, F.										1						
2278	Wood, H. J.										1						
1324	Wood, W. B.															1R	
1029	Worthington, R. C.							1									
Capt.	Wright, J. L.													1			
1610	Young, J.										1						
794	Young, J. M.										1						
	Total	1	1	1	8	1		32	1	18	128	10	8	44	10	5	1

Supplementary List

This List Represents Decorations Awarded Subsequent to Service in the 17th Battalion.

Rank.	Name.	V.C.	C.B.	C.M.G.	D.S.O.	Bar to D.S.O.	O.B.E.	M.C.	Bar to M.C.	D.C.M.	M.M.	Bar to M.M.	M.S.M.	M.I.D.	Congratulatory or Complimentary.	Croix de Guerre.	Decoration Militaire.
Lt.-Col.	Beiers, H. M., originally 17th Bn., transferred to 19th Bn., decorations with 19th Bn.	—	—	—	—	—	—	1	—	—	—	—	—	2	—	—	—
4063	Bisgrove, R. C., 10th Rfts. 17th Bn., did not join unit (attached depot in U.K.)	—	—	—	—	—	—	—	—	—	—	—	1	—	—	—	—
Hon. Lt.-Col.	Brown, A. B. D., originally 17th Bn., transferred to Aust. Provost Corps. Decorations with Provost Corps	—	—	—	1	—	—	—	—	—	—	—	—	2	—	1F	—
Major	Bruce, H. L., originally 17th Bn., transferred to 18th Bn. Decorations with 18th Bn.	—	—	—	—	—	—	1	—	—	—	—	—	—	1	—	—
T/Brig.-Gen.	Goddard, H. A., originally 17th Bn., transferred to 35th Bn. Decorations with 35th Bn.	—	—	1	1	—	—	—	—	—	—	—	—	3	—	1B	—
Major	Johnson, H. W., originally 17th Bn., transferred to 5th Inf. Bde. H.Q., then 3rd Div. H.Q. Decorations with 5th Inf. Bde. H.Q.	—	—	—	—	—	—	1	—	—	—	—	—	2	—	1F	—

Rank.	Name.	V.C.	C.B.	C.M.G.	D.S.O.	Bar to D.S.O.	O.B.E.	M.C.	Bar to M.C.	D.C.M.	M.M.	Bar to M.M.	M.S.M.	M.I.D.	Congratulatory or Complimentary.	Croix de Guerre.	Decoration Militaire.
Major	Middleton, S. A., originally 19th Bn., transferred to 17th Bn., then to 18th Bn. Decorations with 18th Bn.	—	—	—	1	—	1	—	—	—	—	—	—	1	—	—	—
Hon. Major	Smythe, E. V., originally 17th Bn., transferred to 24th Bn. Decorations with 24th Bn.	—	—	—	—	—	1	1	1	—	—	—	—	—	—	—	—
		—	—	1	3	1	1	4	1	—	—	—	1	10	1	3	—

APPENDICES

—◆—

The Battalion's Victoria Cross Winner

(Extract from London Gazette—9th September, 1916.)

WILLIAM JACKSON, No. 588, Pte. 17th Battalion, Australian Infantry, for most conspicuous bravery.

On his return from a successful raid, several members of the raiding party were seriously wounded, in No Man's Land, by shell-fire.

Pte. Jackson got back safely, and after handing over a prisoner, whom he had brought in, immediately went out again under heavy shell-fire and assisted in bringing in a wounded man.

He then went out again, and with a sergeant was bringing in another wounded man when his arm was blown off by a shell, and the sergeant was rendered unconscious. He then returned to our trenches and obtained assistance and went out again to look for two wounded comrades. He set a splendid example of pluck and determination. His work has always been marked by the greatest coolness and bravery.

Table of Rates of Pay

Soudan Campaign, Boer War and Great War 1914-1918.

Rank.	Soudan. Per annum.	Boer War. Per diem.	Boer War. Field allce.	Great War. Per diem.	Great War. Field allce.
		£ s. d.	s. d.	£ s. d.	s. d.
Colonel	—	2 10 0	12 0	2 5 0	7 6
Lieut.-Colonel .	£600/£650	1 5 0	4 0	1 17 6	7 6
Major	£500	1 3 0	4 0	1 10 0	5 0
Captain	£400	1 1 0	3 0	1 2 6	3 6
Lieutenant ..	£325/£355	15 0	2 6	17 6	3 6
2nd-Lieutenant	—	15 0	2 6	17 6	3 6
	Per diem. s. d.				
R.S.M.	9 6	9 0	—	14 0	—
R.Q.M.S.	8 9	8 6	—	14 0	—
C.S.M.	—	8 0	—	12 0	—
C.Q.M.S.	—	—	—	11 6	—
Sergeant	7 6	7 0	—	10 6	—
Corporal	6 6	6 0	—	10 0	—
Bombardier ..	6 0	—	—	—	—
Private	5 0	5 0	—	6 0	—

The Commander of the Australian Corps (1914-18) received £2,000 per annum, plus 17/6 per diem field allowance.

Major-Generals received £1,200 per annum, plus 12/6 per diem field allowance.

Brigadier-Generals received £2/5/- per diem, plus 7/6 per diem field allowance.

The Commandant of the Soudan Expedition received £1,250 per annum.

Establishments

The authorised establishments of battalions of the 5th, 6th and 7th Brigades in 1915 were as follows:

	Officers.	O.R.'s
Battalion Headquarters:		
Lieut.-Col., Major, Adjutant, Q.M., Trans. Off., Sig. Off.	6	
Warrant Off. (R.S.M.), R.Q.M.S., Ord.-Rm. Clerk, Sgt. Bugler, Sgt. Cook, Trans. Sgt., Sgt. Shoemaker, 11 Drivers		18
Machine-Gun Section:		
Subaltern	1	
Other Ranks		34
Signalling Section:		
Subaltern	1	
Other Ranks		25
Four Companies:		
Majors or Captains 8, Subalterns 16	24	
Other Ranks		888
Details		29
(Attached Medical Officer, 1)		
TOTAL	32	994

Vehicles.—9 bicycles, 1 maltese cart, 2 water carts, 9 limbered waggons, 1 cooks' waggon. Total, 22.

Horses.—15 riding, 39 draught, 18 pack. Total, 72.

"From Quinn's Post"

One of the prize-winning poems published in the Anzac Book.

> Celestial star that crossed my path,
> Leaving fair visions in my soul,
> Oh! why did you e'er leave your realm
> And break my heart? With mournful dole
> Now restless night doth me pursue
> And fiends do tempt my soul to hell.
> Ah! gentle maid, if you but knew
> My inner shrine, and it could tell
> My hidden love, as deep, as true,
> As gentle as sweet birds at play;
> Drift back, bright star, and comfort me
> In this unending dreary day.
> —V. N. HOPKINS,
> 17th Bn. A.I.F.

Rations, Scale of

109. The scale of rations on disembarkation after leaving Egypt will be: 1¼ lb. fresh meat or 1 lb. (nominal) preserved meat; 1¼ lb. bread or 1 lb. biscuit or 1 lb. flour; 4 ozs. bacon, 3 ozs. cheese, 2 ozs. peas or beans or dried potatoes, 5/8 oz. tea, 4 ozs. jam, 3 ozs. sugar, ½ oz. salt, 1/20 oz. mustard, 1/36 oz. pepper, 1/10 gill lime juice.

Tobacco not exceeding 2 ozs. per week for those who smoke.

Fresh vegetables whenever obtainable will be issued at the rate of ½ lb. per ration, and when these are supplied peas, beans, or dried potatoes will not be required.

Lime juice will be issued at the rate of 4 issues per week. These issues will be made even when there is a daily issue of fresh vegetables.

The attention of commanding officers is specially drawn to the undermentioned scale of equivalents which will obtain when available: Rice 4 ozs., jam 4 ozs., golden syrup 4 ozs., cheese 3 ozs., preserved meat 6 ozs., fresh meat 10 ozs., dried fruits 4 ozs. (all equivalents of one another.)

Condensed milk: 1 tin equals 8 rations cheese, but condensed milk will not be issued as an equivalent for anything else.

All units will draw the equivalent of rice for half the meat ration on the days on which preserved meat is drawn.

Lord Kitchener's Message to Australian and New Zealand Corps, 25-11-15

●

"His Majesty commanded Lord Kitchener to express his high appreciation of the gallant and unflinching conduct of our men through fighting which has been as hard as any yet seen during the war, and His Majesty wishes to express his complete confidence in the determination and fighting qualities of our men to assist in carrying this war to an entirely successful termination.

"Lord Kitchener has ordered me to express to all the very great pleasure it gave him to have the opportunity, which he considers a privilege, of visiting Anzac, to see for himself some of the wonderfully good work which had been accomplished. Lord Kitchener much regretted that time did not permit of his seeing the whole Corps, but he was pleased to see a considerable proportion of officers and men, and to find all in such good heart and so confidently imbued with that grand spirit which has carried them through all their trials and many dangerous feats of arms: a spirit which he is quite confident they will maintain to the end, until they have taken their full share in completely overthrowing our enemies.

"Boys, we may well be proud to receive such messages and it is up to all of us to live up to them and prove their trust."

W. R. BIRDWOOD.

Apportionment of Seventeenth Battalion on Gallipoli

Garrison.	Officers.	Other Ranks.
C.O., Adjutant	2	
O.C. Garrison Troops	1	
O/cs Firing Line	3	
No. 1 Subsection	1	52
„ 2 „	1	32
„ 3 „	1	44
„ 4 „	1	32
„ 5 „	1	38
„ 6 „	1	20
Bomb-throwers		24
Local Reserves	1	72
Permanent Fatigues		32
Army Medical Corps	1	3
Stretcher-bearers		9
Pioneers		5
Bomb Section (Mortars)		9
Signalling Section	1	11
	15	**383**
Reserve.		
Engineers Fatigue		60
Quartermaster	1	6
Machine-Gun Section	1	34
Balance Reserve	9	247
	26	**730**
Outside Personnel: Bomb Section 18, 19, 20		11
Machine-Guns	1	21

Menu of a Dinner held at Lumbres, 9-2-18

●

12/5/15   4/2/18

17TH BATTALION
A.I.F.

— France —

OFFICERS' DINNER

held at

LUMBRES

on the Ninth February 1918, to commemorate the completion of the Thousand Days Active Service of the Battalion.

— TOASTS —

The King
The Battalion.
Absent Comrades.

——— o ———

Present.—Lieut-Col. E. F. Martin, C.M.G., D.S.O.; **Major** L. G. Fussell, M.C.; Captains E. T. Harnett, H. W. Johnson M.C., E. T. Manefield, R. Hale, H. Ronald, C. C. Finlay, F. W. Moulsdale; Lieutenants J. L. Richardson, A. T. Doig M.C., L. Adam, F. W. Tindale, R. A. Fitzalan, A J. R. Davison, H. J. Smith, F. Courtney, R. P. Little M.M., R. E. Masterson, A. F. Gilbert, T. Ridley D.C.M.

Only the first five were officers of the Seventeenth as at 12/5/15. Hale left Australia as Staff Captain, 5th Brigade. He was only a brief period with the Battalion.

"NUTTY"

●

(A Tribute to a "Bon Cheval.")
By Private J. Hutton.

"Nutty" was a golden chestnut gelding, 17 hands 1 inch in height, and possessing three white socks and a white blaze. On parade he presented a dignified appearance. He was a credit to the "Fussellier Guards" (B Company).

Nutty was a "dinkum" Anzac insomuch that he left Australia early in 1915. Whilst in Egypt he not only won races on the desert, but took part in the "Battle of the Wozzir."

In France he was one of the most distinguished horses, and to his credit, or discredit, he quickly got to know every estaminet and wet canteen in the areas in which the Battalion was billeted. Despite his massive build he was very docile, and was much sought after by unaccomplished horsemen.

In action, he was brave. The "Old Bloke" was with us in every forward area. He was wounded at Bullecourt and shell-shocked on Westhoek Ridge. I have heard it said that if it wasn't for Nutty the Battalion would have perished in the winter of 1916. But that is another story, with a "kick" in it.

I was his groom, and the comradeship that existed between us was well-nigh unbelievable. His happy disposition won him popularity with the troops, and even after many years he remains in their minds, one of the identities of the Seventeenth.

On December 13th, 1918, at the village of Friches, near Mons, I said good-bye to my old pal. I was returning to Australia. I had often prayed for that day, but now I found it hard to leave.

But I had to go, and with a tear in my eye I kissed my noble friend good-bye. Together we had followed the Battalion "O'er moor and fen," for nearly three years.

In many ways he was almost human, and among all the four-footed friends who served us so faithfully and well, he was without a peer.

> Good hunting, Nutty! May the skies be clear and
> the grass lush, old Trooper, wherever
> the fields you graze.

Commemorative Scroll Awarded by H.M. King George V to the Next-of-Kin of the Fallen

•

Surmounted by the Royal Coat of Arms, it reads:
HE WHOM THIS SCROLL COMMEMORATES WAS NUMBERED AMONG THOSE WHO, AT THE CALL OF KING AND COUNTRY, LEFT ALL THAT WAS DEAR TO THEM, ENDURED HARDNESS, FACED DANGER, AND FINALLY PASSED OUT OF THE SIGHT OF MEN BY THE PATH OF DUTY AND SELF-SACRIFICE, GIVING UP THEIR OWN LIVES THAT OTHERS MIGHT LIVE IN FREEDOM.

LET THOSE WHO COME AFTER
SEE TO IT THAT HIS NAME
BE NOT FORGOTTEN.

www.ingramcontent.com/pod-product-compliance
Lightning Source LLC
Chambersburg PA
CBHW021829220426
43663CB00005B/181